HISTORY OF THE WO

I. Katsukawa Shunsho (1726–92): Scene from a Play. Japanese colour woodcut. (British Museum, London)

HISTORY OF THE WORLD'S ART

BY HERMANN LEICHT

*

WITH 5 PLATES IN COLOUR
301 ONE-COLOUR HALF-TONES
AND
186 ILLUSTRATIONS IN TEXT

SPRING BOOKS
LONDON

Originally published in German under the title
KUNSTGESCHICHTE DER WELT
English translation by Bernard Miall

This impression 1963

Published by
SPRING BOOKS
WESTBOOK HOUSE • FULHAM BROADWAY • LONDON
Printed in Czechoslovakia
T 1073

Contents

I. *The Art of the Ice Age* 7
II. *Europe's Ascent Toward Civilization* 21
III. *Africa* 34
IV. *Australia and Oceania* 48
V. *Amerindian Art* 55
VI. *The Ancient Art of the Near East* 75
VII. *India* 87
VIII. *China* 102
IX. *Japan* 119
X. *Egypt* 125
XI. *Greece* 137
XII. *Hellenistic Art* 155
XIII. *The Roman Empire* 162
XIV. *Early Christian Art* 176
XV. *Byzantine Art* 184
XVI. *Russia* 188
XVII. *The Art of Islam* 197
XVIII. *Romanesque Art* 209
XIX. *Gothic Art* 222
XX. *The Renaissance in Italy* 233
XXI. *The Renaissance Era in the North* 250
XXII. *The Age of the Baroque and Rococo* 260
XXIII. *The Classical Tradition* 275
XXIV. *From Classicism to Impressionism* 289
XXV. *From Impressionism to Expressionism* 302
XXVI. *Art Today* 311
List of Plates 317
Index 331

Chapter I

THE ART OF THE ICE AGE

*

IT WAS perhaps 20,000 years before the birth of Christ that the first drawings, paintings and carvings in the world were produced. In the caves which were then the homes of man many manifestations of art have been found, of which the finest and most finished are the wonderful rock-paintings of the Ice Age. Many of these shine from the rock walls to this very day, still fresh and vivid. Yellow ochre, black oxide of manganese, red oxide of iron and white chalk were the pigments, which, with animal fat as a medium, were to last for thousands of years. Vessels have been found in which the colours were still intact.

Prehistoric research has made great advances during the last few decades, and no lover of the fine arts should disregard its findings; for the historical significance of the most ancient survivals is great. They constitute, both in their cultural aspect and in the field of artistic research, the bridge between the natural and the moral sciences. Fascinating though it is to add a few thousand years to the already known periods of history, it is no less interesting, from the material already at our disposal, to achieve some insight into the future; for the art of many primitive peoples, such as the Eskimo, is even to this day in many respects on a level with the art of the Ice Age.

In surveying the art of all times and peoples it is therefore well worth our while to look back at this period. Towards the end of the so-called Tertiary Period—the third, or ligniferous, age of the Earth—the torrid climate which had until then prevailed began to cool. In winter the mountain glaciers extended farther and farther, and in summer they did not recede as far as they advanced. It grew cooler and cooler. In the course of some thousands of years a great part of Europe, Asia and America disappeared under the ice, probably as the result of a cyclical movement of the earth's axis. In consequence, there was a slow and fundamental transformation of all living things. The tropical flora anf fauna, which had hitherto flourished, began to die out and make way for other species. The geological strata tell us how the age of the mammalia ended in cold and starvation. Out of the struggle with this world the ancestor of modern man was born.

Even during the third inter-glacial period, the outlines of Europe, and the scenes that constituted the background of the earliest manifestations of art, were very different from what they are today. Great areas which now lie under the Atlantic were then *terra firma*; the North Sea was only a river; so was the Irish Sea. Over all these northern land-surfaces lay a great sheet of ice, such as today covers the interior of Greenland. The Mediterranean, on the other hand, was a low-lying country, with two inland seas, and a cool but temperate climate, while the Sahara, today a desert, was luxuriantly fertile. Between the icefields of the North, which extended far into Asia, and those of the Alps, lay a rough steppe country, whose fauna included even the hippopotamus and the elephant, until the climate grew cooler, when the woolly mammoth, the rhinoceros, and the reindeer remained, as well as the aurochs and the bison, while the vegetation assumed an Arctic character.

This was the Europe of the Heidelberg Man and the Neanderthal Man, as they are called from the places where their remains were found. The Heidelberg Man lived in the penultimate interglacial period, and was still closely akin to the animal. Neanderthal Man already possessed a fairly large brain, though its stratifications were shallow. He walked with a stooping gait, and could not completely erect his head; his thumb—so important in the development of any sort of technical dexterity—was not so mobile and serviceable as the human thumb. The severity of the approaching fourth, and most extreme, glacial period seems to have gradually exterminated the Neanderthaler, after he had wandered about the world three or four times as long as the present species. He had learned to daub his body with ochre; he had a special way of burying his dead, with various funerary articles; and he possessed simple picks, scrapers, and axes, but none of the more delicate instruments necessary for the execution of works of art. So, as far as he is concerned, no traces have been discovered of anything which could be described, in the strict sense, as art.

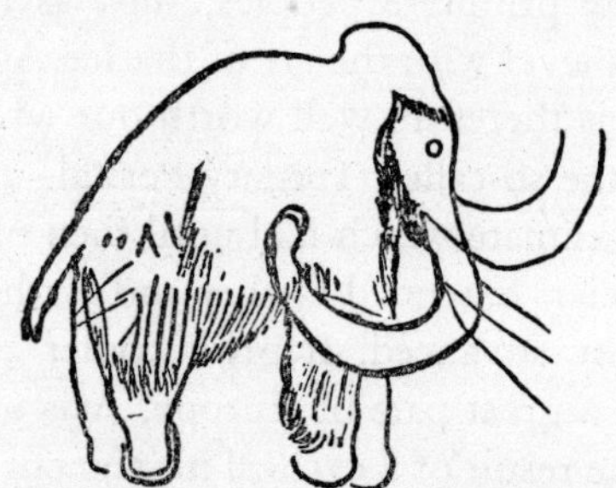

Left: Mammoth—Cave-drawing from Font-de-Gaume
Right: One of more than forty figures of horses in the cave of Les Combarelles
(Capitan, Breuil and Peyrony)

If we wish to penetrate still further into the prehistory of anthropoid creatures, in order to find the beginnings of art—to the Pekin man, for example, or to the so-called protoman of Trinil, in Java—we can easily go back another 200,000 years, or even 500,000; for the experts in this field have very large ideas, and are open to argument. But not every hewn stone, not every piece of scratched horn or antler, can appeal to us as a work of art simply because it was elaborated by the hands of a creature resembling man. We shall find it most natural to begin the history of the species with *homo sapiens*. There is considerable evidence that he came to Europe from Southern Asia, North Africa, and the regions which today lie under the Mediterranean, some 20,000 to 25,000 years ago, when the Fourth Ice Age was about to merge into a warmer epoch. We do not know—we can only guess—how and where, and through what ages, he reached the stage at which one finds him on his first appearance.

At all events, this first actual human being, the gifted creator of the paintings and other artistic productions of the Ice Age, was already very like the modern European, who is his direct descendant. He appeared simultaneously in several races, no more homogenous then than they are today, but all differing very definitely from the Neanderthal Man. They chose to live in the Franco-Cantabrian region to the north and the south of the Pyrenees—a district rich in caves, which offered natural dwelling-houses and hiding-places. Since the winters were still long and inclement, and the summers, though warm, were very short, at first they made only brief hunting expeditions northwards, to the edge of the ice. They lived entirely by hunting, tracking the mammoth, the aurochs, the bison, the reindeer and the wild horse—whose flesh they preferred to any. Near Solutré an open camping-ground has been discovered where, as far as we know, they may have held their assemblies for centuries, and there the bones of some 100,000 horses and many other animals were found. Presumably they used to hunt the little bearded horse of that period, and knew much about its habits; but it is not very probable that they had already domesticated the horse, though lines such as one sees in the illustration on page 8 are sometimes interpreted as depicting bridles or halters. Actually they represent lassoes, which formed part of the hunter's equipment in those times, and which could be made of considerable length without a join, simply by stretching a hide over a round stone, and cutting long strips with a stone knife, working spirally from the centre outwards.

As the climate grew warmer, the time came when groups of these hunter-folk began to stay in the north all the year round, though for a long while the connection with the south would have been maintained. The culture of the age was homogeneous, and its efforts were directed toward gathering and consuming the necessities of life, not toward the production of material goods. That there was already such a high level of artistic creation is extraordinary, and points to the existence, in that early phase of evolution, of the first intellectual aristocracy. For the men, the day's work was hunting; the women and children gathered roots, berries, and snails. No pottery was made, and there was no agriculture. Since metals were not yet known, and since—besides bone and wood—only stone was used to make tools and weapons, the whole of this first cultural stage of humanity is called the Old Stone or Palaeolithic Age, to distinguish it from the later, more advanced, but still non-metallic, stage of culture and artistic achievement which we shall presently describe—the Late Stone or Neolithic Age.

The Palaeolithic Age

The Palaeolithic Age is divided into various periods, according to the forms of implements found in the best-known of the French sources, and elsewhere in Europe; these may be briefly summarized as follows:

The *Early Old Stone Age*, the Old Palaeolithic or Protolithic Age. Its oldest form is the Chellian, so-called after the stage of culture revealed by the implements found at Chelles, near Meaux, on the Marne. Then follows the Acheulian, from St Acheul, Somme, which more or less corresponds with the stage of the implements found at Markkleeberg, near Leipzig, Hundisburg, near Neuhaldensleben, and Weimar. The latest period of the Old Stone Age is known as the Mousterian, from Le Moustier in Dordogne; it comprises the culture of Neanderthal Man, whose widest distribution must be assumed to have occurred somewhere about 50,000 years ago. The relics found in Central Europe—at Neanderthal, near Düsseldorf, and at Sirgestein in Württemberg—possibly originated from about this period.

During the *Later Stone Age*—the Upper Palaeolithic, Neo-Palaeolithic, Mesolithic, or Miolithic Age—appear the first examples of the art and culture of *homo sapiens*. The first epoch of culture is known as the Aurignacian, from Aurignac, Haute Garonne, and is dated 30,000—10,000 B. C.; this applies also to the relics found at Willendorf in Austria. Then comes the Solutrean epoch, called after Solutré, Saône et Loire, about 15,000 B. C., which resembles the Předmostí epoch, in North Moravia, and which was followed, between 15,000 and 8,000 B. C., by the Magdalenian epoch, so called after La Madeleine in Dordogne, to which the epoch of Thayngen, near Schaffhausen, in Switzerland, is most nearly related. By about 8,000 B. C. the greater part of Europe was free of ice, while the actual end of the Ice Age has been placed about 4,000 B. C.

Franco-Cantabrian Culture

Present-day knowledge of the culture of the European Ice Age is derived from relics found in more than 500 different places. They consist principally of weapons and implements, but in some 200 of these places works of art have also been discovered. Some of them contain as many as 300 paintings, sculptures, drawings, and ornaments, and altogether we have thousands of pictures dating from the Palaeolithic Age, representing, in many different ways, a very large number of animals and human beings. We are surprisingly well-informed about the life of this period, since often, together with works of art, we find their actual originals, of which the most varied relics are preserved in the geological strata.

Dancers, maskers, and men disguised as animals, as well as the earliest religious cults, dating from more than 10,000 years ago, are as clear to us as are the people and manners of yesterday. More and more caves are being opened, which have been concealed from intervening ages by fallen debris and obstructed entrances. Today this past is revived in graphic reality: in the crevices of the rocks the flint knife is often found; on the ground lie the tools of the artist or artificer; and footprints in the hardened clay preserve the dance-steps of the first Europeans.

If the top strata are carefully removed from the moist subsoil we come upon the skeletons of men and animals, of cave-bears and little Ice Age snakes. But in the background the images of the prehistoric world loom upon the walls—sculptured representations of the bison, male and female—at the moment of union, revealing the magic of procreation.

Picture of a hunt, full of rapid action. Wrapped in the hide of a bison, a man is hunting or bewitching the game. The Trois-Fréres cavern. (Bégouen and Breuil)

Then, as today, human thought was centred on birth and death, as the eternal milestones of life. Even in the Ice Age the mysteries were already foreshadowed which later inspired the art of the Egyptians, the Greeks, the Romans, and the Christians, and which will continue to obsess mankind so long as this world exists.

In these drawings and paintings, animals are seen with the keen eye of a hunting people; one can usually recognize without difficulty their species, age, and sex. We find them incised on stone, ivory, and bone, on tools and household implements, as well as on objects which serve no useful purpose, so that we cannot say whether they are amulets, or magical symbols employed by the hunter, or works of art inspired by pure love of form.

At last we come to the coloured paintings mentioned at the beginning of this chapter, and the artists' colouring materials. Fine white chalk, yellow ochre, brown and red hematite, as well as black oxide of manganese, crushed and mixed with fat, were often used, applied like oil paint to the roof and walls of the caves. Often these pictures are small and inconspicuous, but they frequently cover an area of several square yards. The best wall-paintings are found in the deservedly famous caves of Altamira, Combarelles, Font-de-Gaume, La Mouthe, Marsoulas, Niaux, and Pair-non-pair.

The first of these caves to be discovered, long before its importance was realized, was the cavern of Altamira, on the Bay of Biscay, in northern Spain. It is in a limestone hill, perforated by many underground water-courses. Surrounded by other caves which have fallen in, it is more than 300 yards long and consists of three successive caverns, the last being shaped like the nave of a church—a natural meeting place and place of worship.

The strata containing relics of cultural interest are more than forty inches deep; they date from the Solutrean and Magdalenian epochs, and in the order in which they lie they make an important and easily legible contribution to the history of primitive art. The earliest pictures are simply outline drawings, made with a flint stylus, or drawn in colour. These are followed by more carefully executed drawings, and by silhouettes, black and red, in which, by a skilful distribution of darker and lighter tones, the bodies of the animals often stand out in plastic relief.

After a period when incised drawing reached its highest point, in the careful detail of its impressive and well-balanced masterpieces, the technique began to degenerate and to produce only small and simply incised drawings. But polychromatic painting, which had begun in a very modest way, now predominated. At first only such portions of the animals as horns, manes, eyes and hooves were drawn in black, their bodies being painted brown or red. Then these colours were used for the outlines as well, which were filled in with a combination of yellow, red and black, with the important places boldly emphasized by incising the outlines. The result was a naturalistic art, and it was thousands of years before a similar art was again produced. Part of the roof of the first hall, a surface of rock nearly fifty feet long, is covered with more than twenty-five polychromatic paintings and some black outline drawings of animals of all kinds, horses, boars and stags standing, or rolling over and rising to their feet again, in the wild fantasy of a hunter's dream. Men, too, are represented, but with far less vigour than the animals. Of this something more will be said in the final survey of Franco-Cantabrian art.

Finally, in the strata of the Altamira cavern, we come to another period, when, though the execution becomes less vigorous, something new appears: outlines of human hands, with comb-like and other similar markings, as we see them in Fig. 1a on the bodies of animals, and red zig-zag bands of parallel stripes. The symbol makes its first appearance in art.

The caves of Combarelles, near Tarjac, in Dordogne, and the grotto of La Mouthe, in the same neighbourhood, are very similar in appearance to the cave of Altamira, and in both the paintings begin at some distance from the entrance, while Pair-non-pair, near Marcampes, in Charente, does not run back very far. In the pictures of bison in the cave of Marsoulas, Haute Garonne, the body is often stippled in red, while the facial surfaces are black. A grazing horse (incised) has symbolic stripes on its body, and in certain grimacing human heads we can recognize masks or disguises, as in the scene represented on page 11. According to modern scholars such paintings represent scenes in which a hunter is putting a spell upon the animals, but the older school points to the fact that the hunter of those days could stalk his game more successfully if disguised, a method employed to this day among primitive peoples.

The cavern of Font-de-Gaume also revealed various peculiar chamfered symbols which for a long while were regarded as outline drawings of prehistoric houses, from which conclusions might be drawn as to the culture of the period. But discovery of the actual originals led to a quite different and surprising conclusion. The drawings here shown, from the same cave, are particularly interesting. One might take one to be a head, showing only the upper part of the face and starting eyes. Actually, it is nothing more than the plan of a pitfall, such as the hunters of those days made at river-bends for the trapping of big game, especially the mammoth, which could hardly be killed by any other means. This interpretation applies also to the drawing below, which comes from Font-de-Gaume too. It is the same with the'houses', which are merely the fall-traps[1] then often used as they are today by the Indians of North America.

Leaping Deer. Incised drawing, on slate 2 $^2/_3$ in. length. Saint-Marcel, Southern France. (Capitan, Breuil and Peyrony)

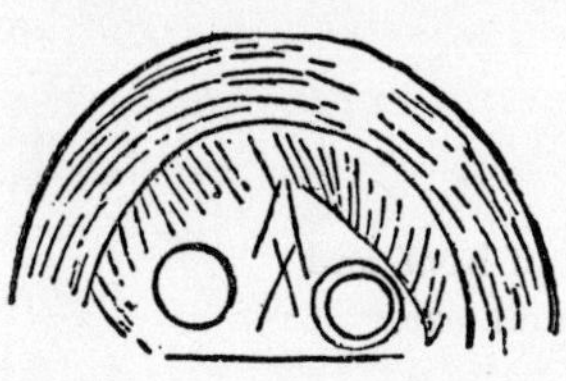

Drawing in the cave of Font-de-Gaume

These examples show us how careful we must be to avoid over-hasty conclusions when interpreting symbols of the art of an epoch of which no written traditions exist. They show us, too, the importance, if we are to understand the artistic expression of an epoch, of exact knowledge of its cultural basis.

There is no doubt that many other markings (cf. Fig. 1a) do actually constitute the earliest symbolic expressions; such, for example, are the arrows and bloodstains on horses and other animals in the cave of Niaux, near Tarascon, which contains many such figures. These hunter's marks may very often have been used as magical formulae; on the other hand, they may have had nothing but a practical purpose, as being the only means by which the hunter of those days could record his feats and declare his right to the prey.

As well as curves and straight lines, circles and spirals are found, but they are sparingly applied as ornamentation, which is, however, seldom undertaken for its own sake. Such motives are usually imitated from Nature, as in the figure on page 14:

[1] Hauser, Kiebebusch, Krause and Lips.

for practically all Franco-Cantabrian art, in every stage, was in close touch with reality, borrowing its motives from natural objects.

The drawings and paintings of this epoch are so numerous, that one can classify them, not only according to the different strata in the individual caves, but also according to general stylistic epochs: an early period, which includes the first Magdalenian and the Aurignacian epochs; a middle period, corresponding with the middle Magdalenian epoch; and a late period, towards the close of this epoch.

Plant tendrils and spiral ornaments on Ice Age articles of bone and antler, from Aruy, Basses Pyrenees. One-third natural size. Piette collection, Saint-Germain Museum

In the first phase, as in all early art, linear motives predominate; the eye follows the defining outline, and in this way seeks to comprehend the image.

The art of the middle Magdalenian epoch, the culminating period, is more plastic, and gradually becomes purely pictorial. Light now helps to model the animal's bodies; the places where the light falls stand out, while the dark places are lost in shadow. Hence the outlines are less distinct; they are faint and broken, and begin to disappear. The separateness of the parts is much less obvious, but instead the whole gains in plastic unity. The eye, now that its attention is divided among the inner portions of the drawing, seeks to comprehend it as a whole, while the details seem of importance only in relation to the whole. Limbs, eyes, ears and horns are no longer exactly defined, but merge into the whole composition. The figures gain in depth, relief, and vitality. To this epoch belong the pictures of animals gazing backwards; these are few in number, but astonishing in their artistic perfection (Fig. 1b). The turn of the head and the execution of the profile are the most surprising of all the achievements of this earliest phase of human art, when we consider its great antiquity, and remember what a long distance art had to travel, many thousands of years later, before pictures in perspective of any great expressiveness and vitality again became possible. Finally, at the close of the Magdalenian epoch, the artist returned to the flat image. The outline, leading the eye along it, was again predominant; bodies began to lose weight and depth, and to merge into one plane. Here we see a great natural process at work for the first time, in the caverns of the Ice Age; art progressing from the linear to the plastic, and then reverting to the linear, a path which it was to trace again and again.

At the same time, we must not give more praise to this prehistoric art than it deserves. One peculiarity can only be regarded as a weakness—its incoherence; the individual figures are mostly juxtaposed without rhyme or reason. The eye of the hunter, the keen observer, can see and retain the images of the animals as they are, but he hardly ever depicts them in any coherent order. Where this cohesion nevertheless does exist, it is mastered only with difficulty.

The minor works of art—small carvings and the like (Figs. 2a and 2b) are decidedly inferior to the paintings and drawings. Like the wall-paintings in the caverns, these articles were probably produced in the place where they were found. Yet it is by no means always the case that the wall-paintings and the numerous little portable works of art are found in the same caves. As places where these small objects have been found, Langerie-Basse, near Tayac, La Madeleine, near Tursac, Cro Magnon, Les Eyzies, and Gorge d'Enfer, with other caves and rock-shelters in Dordogne, call for special mention. Nevertheless, there is a connection between the

The 'Venus of Willendorf'.
Palaeolithic female figure; limestone, with traces of red colouring.
Found at Willendorf, near Krems, on the Danube. Natural History Museum, Vienna

two, and undoubtedly the same hands that were responsible for the carvings, bas-reliefs, paintings, and drawings in the caverns, often adorned with drawings the innumerable little portable objects—made of slate, or mammoth ivory, or the tusks of other animals, or the antlers of reindeer or stags—and gave plastic form to pieces of easily worked stone. Even the clay from the caves was used, and figures made of it were sometimes decorated with drawings or incised patterns. Favourable circumstances have preserved some surprising specimens of this perishable material in the grotto of Tuc d'Audoubert, near Montesquieu-Avantès, in Arriège.

On the whole, the plastic art of this epoch gives more prominence to human beings than do the wall-paintings, and in the naked female figures of Mentone and Brassempouy (Fig. 2a) and the so-called Venus of Willendorf this art forms a bridge between France and Lower Austria, and between Lower Austria and Předmostí in Moravia.

Besides limestone, soapstone and ivory were used for these sculptures, which were sometimes painted red. They have been found in places far from one another, extending northwards from France into Belgium.

In addition to the obese female figures which seem to have been the ideal of that epoch, just as even now they would be that of many Southerners, there are some, but fewer, male figures; altogether one is amazed by the genius of this Palaeolithic art, which covers a quite definite area of Europe, its centres being the North Spanish coastal and mountainous region of Cantabria, and the South of France.

Nevertheless, its influence extends as far as Southern England, Holland, Belgium, Western and Southern Germany, Switzerland, Austria, Moravia, Hungary, and such parts of Russia and Siberia as were then free of ice.

Capsian Art

In addition to the Franco-Cantabrian culture, there was in the Ice Age a second regional culture, the Capsian, which can at once be distinguished from the other by its different implements. The older Capsian culture, contemporary with the Aurignacian, produced swords and various kinds of scraper, but nearly all the chisels were of triangular section, and bow drills did not exist. In this first stage a certain kinship to the Aurignacian culture is still perceptible, and may perhaps be attributed to a common African root. The later Capsian culture developed forms quite unlike those of the contemporary Solutrean and Magdalenian cultures, with a noticeable tendency to produce smaller and smaller implements, including tiny knives, and also triangular and trapezoid flakes, which were used mainly as arrowheads.

No less conspicuous is the difference in the art of this epoch, examples of which have been discovered in some fifty places in Spain alone, mostly on the east coast, but a few in the south. Among the more notable are Alpeca and Minateda in the province of Albacete, Cogul in Lerida, the Valltorta Gorge in Castellon, and the

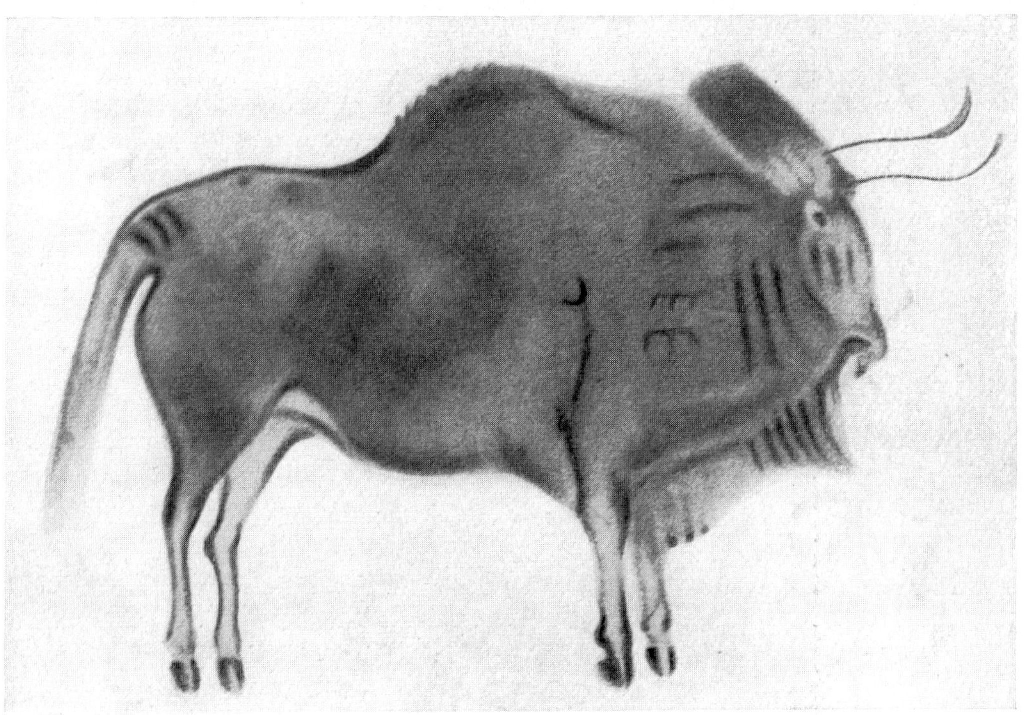

b a

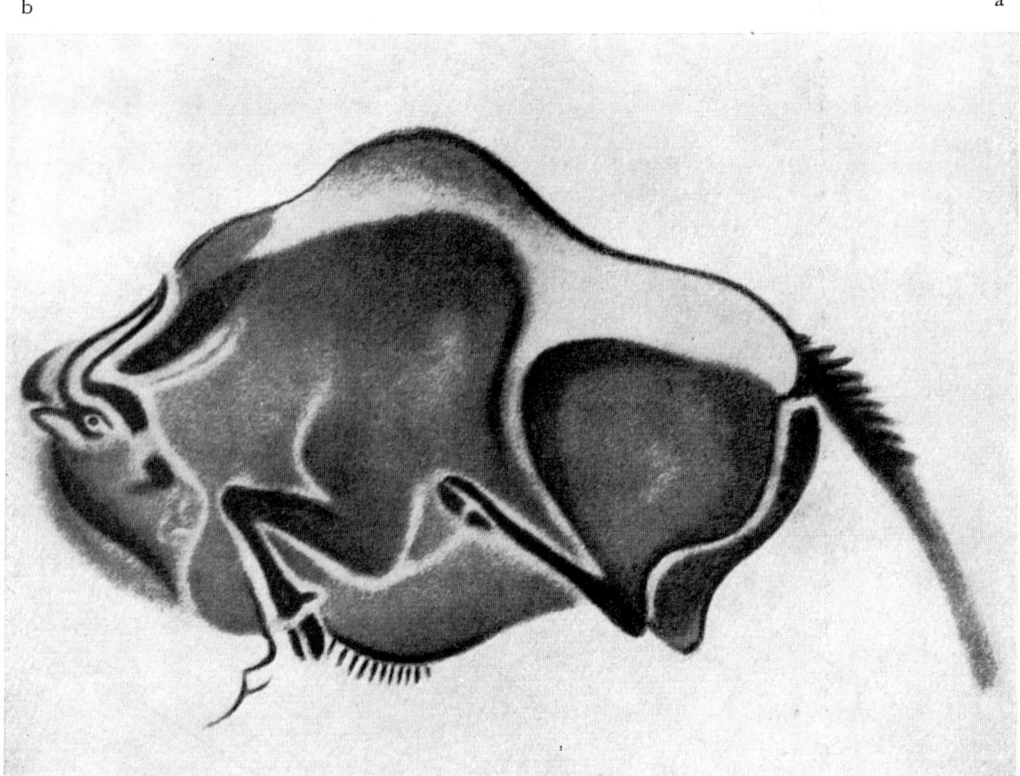

1. (A and B) Polychrome Wall-paintings of the Ice-Age in the Caves of Altamira, Northern Spain.
A Bison, standing; a Bison, lying down and looking round.
Width of pictures, 50 in. and 62 in. respectively.

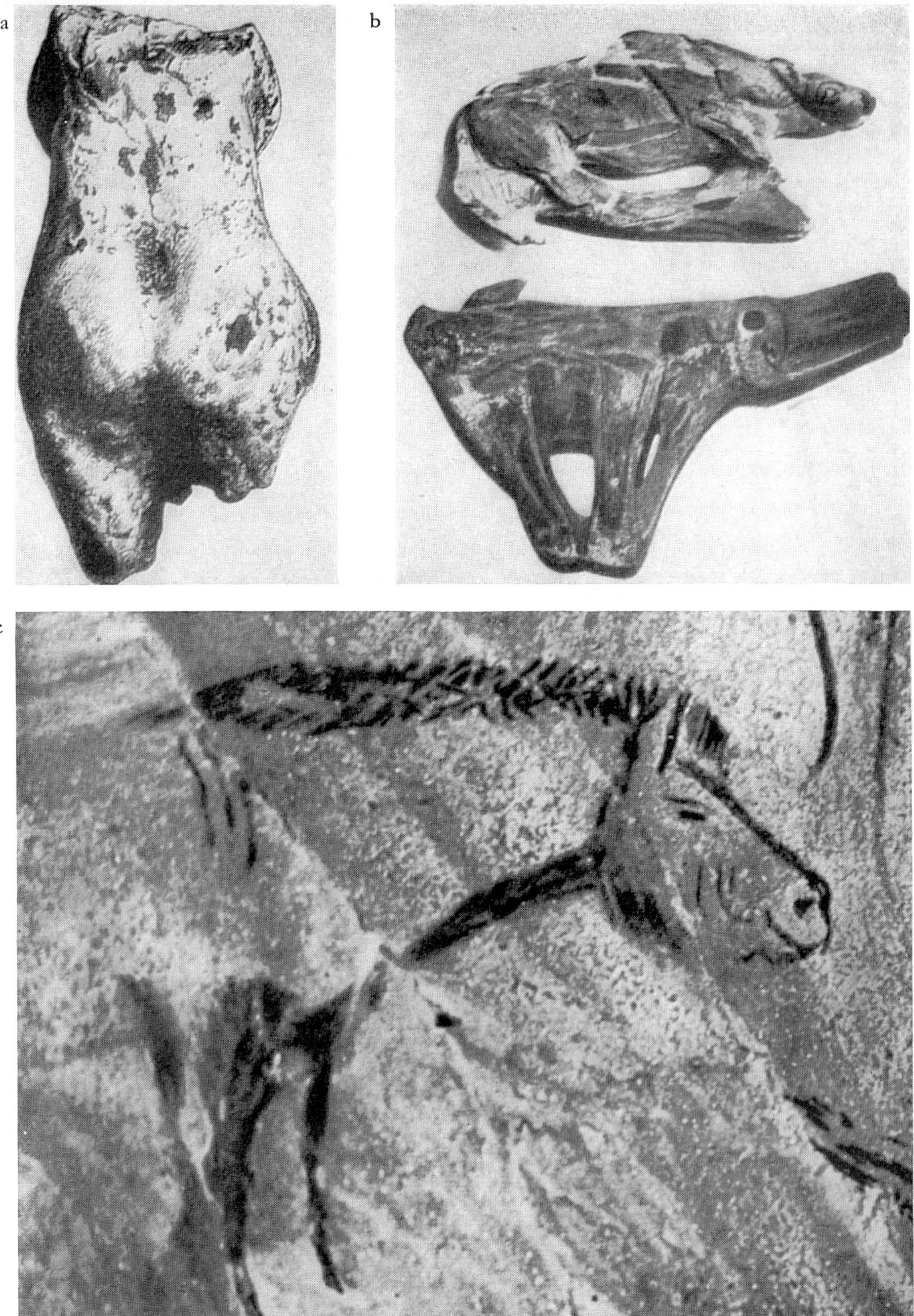

2. (A) Ivory torso of a female figure from the Pope's Cave, Brassempouy, France. Height, 4 in. (Saint-Cric Collection). – (B) Carved bone implements from Southern France, probably used for spear-throwing, as they have hooked projection especially adapted to that purpose—in the Hyaena under the hind legs, and in the Mammoth (lower figure) at the end of th back, while the head could be used as hand-grip. Length of the Hyaena, from La Madeleine, 9½ in. Length of the Mammoth from Bruniquel, 5 in. (British Museum). (C) Wild Horse. Wall-painting in black pigment in the Cave of Niaux near Tarascon Width, about 40 in.

more recently discovered Tormon in Teruel. Since in many of these places there are hundreds of wall-paintings, there can be no doubt as to the nature of this art. The most striking thing about these paintings is that they are no longer confined to the walls of caves, but, in the milder climate of more southern latitudes, they are found also in the open, on rocks and cliffs, standing out like silhouettes, painted mainly in red, but also in black (pages 19, 20). If we look for anything resembling them we shall find it not in Europe, but farther south, in what is now Africa, which could then be reached without crossing the sea. For in the older Palaeolithic epoch, at all events, there was still a terrestrial bridge between the two continents. For this reason Capitan and Morgan gave the name of Capsian to this culture, from the 'finds' at El Gafs, or Gafsa, the ancient Capsa, in Tunis.

This ancient culture reached a more highly developed stage than the Franco-Cantabrian, and extended from central and southern Spain to the Atlas mountains, and the whole of the North African littoral, and even as far as Upper Egypt, where rock-paintings of the same kind, in red and black, have been found.

In Capsian art the animals are often accompanied by human beings, and above all by hunters. The bow was used by hunters at a very early period; from Africa it

Left: Archers, from Alpera. Right: Female figures, from Cogul
(Breuil and Cabré)

was introduced, by way of the Franco-Cantabrian culture of Solutré, to the Central European world, though there it long remained an alien object, since bows and arrows are the typical weapons of a densely wooded area. In North Africa and Spain at this time, unlike the ice-covered Northern Europe, an excessively rainy climate prevailed, much cooler than it is today. Thick forests developed, where the bow was the hunter's natural weapon, but the mainly treeless region of Central Europe hardly favoured its use. The various forms of bow which we see in the accompanying illustration, and in many other paintings, led scholars for a long while to doubt their great antiquity, because the bow with the double curve wrongly regarded as having been built up—and for technical reasons this composite form must have been the result of a long period of evolution; but apparently the weapons depicted were ordinary, though particularly flexible bows, almost the same height as a man.

Although hunting was these peoples' principal occupation, other scenes are represented, though less frequently; one, for example, shows honey being collected (below); others show women in strange bell-shaped skirts (page 17 on the right), with garments on the upper part of the body which often leave the breasts uncovered. Moreover, dog-like animals, still very rare in Franco-Cantabrian art, appear more often in Capsian art, and it almost seems as though the artists of that epoch had already to distinguish between two races of hunters.

Even if we knew nothing else about the culture of this period, the development of these Spanish and North African rock-paintings would tell us, clearly and emphatically, that here, in the Old Stone Age, the transition to something completely new was approaching.

The charmingly naturalistic vigour of these pictures became gradually more stylized. Even in the Ice Age, on European and African soil, this was already happening and was to repeat itself, much later, in the dissolution of the primitive art of classical antiquity: the slow ossification which was to culminate, thousands of years later, in the art of Byzantium. Here one sees it for the first time, as the result of a shift in attitude towards life, which went hand in hand with economic change. it is not accidental that most of these rock-paintings are found in the open. On the warmer soil of Spain and North Africa it was not so much a new style that was announcing itself, as the end of the Ice Age.

Woman gathering honey. Rock painting, Eastern Spain. (Mariscal)

The Mesolithic Epoch

From time to time, a rhinoceros or an elk still appears in the pictures, but the reindeer and the mammoth disappear. Those who produced this art were still a hunting people, but they stood at a parting of the ways. They still wore nothing but animal skins, but personal adornment became more and more the fashion, and many ornaments have been preserved. Animal heads, or complete animal figures, were often worn as amulets. These are found in Central Europe, in the transitional art whose various styles will at least be briefly mentioned by name in the following pages; an art which survived into the forest period that followed the Ice Age—a period known as the Middle Stone Age, or Mesolithic epoch, which lasted in Europe from about 8000 to 2000 B. C.

A mingling of the two cultures was soon in process; the North European form of the Capsian culture being known as the Tardenoisian; this spread throughout Western and Central Europe, from Northern Spain to Ireland and Scotland, and to Poland and Southern Russia, blending to some extent in Southern Germany with the so-called Azilian culture, until it finally merged into the approaching New Stone Age.

Kneeling archer. Cueva Saltadora, Valltorta Gorge (Obermaier and Wernert)

Franco-Cantabrian art became less and less vigorous. Men of the Capsian culture penetrated Central Europe; from Italy came the so-called Campignian culture, and a Nordic culture, based on the use of bone implements, reached Europe from the East. All these cultures made themselves felt, sweeping away the last remnants of the Magdalenian culture, and allowing only a humble existence to a mixed form of the Azilian culture.

Hunter with short breeches
Cueva del Secans, Teruel

At the same time this tendency was opposed by the weaker influence of the Franco-Cantabrian culture. The caves of La Pileta, in the province of Malaga, discovered in 1912, contain paintings which are unmistakably in the Franco-Cantabrian style, and the paintings in the caves of Los Casares, in the province of Guadalajara, first discovered in 1934, confirm this judgment.

It is difficult to measure the duration of the great change that was now occurring in centuries, or even in thousands of years; but we may safely assume that during the last period of Capsian art these people were beginning to cultivate the soil and were becoming acquainted with the potter's art, which may have reached them from Africa.

Transition from one age to another, historically speaking, is always accompanied by a transformation in artistic style. At the close of an expiring epoch we find, in the Spanish drawings, such highly stylized figures of human beings as are shown in the accompanying illustration, which belong to the Capsian school. The curved lines of many of the heads remind one of African, Mediterranean and Mesopotamian art in their novel way of drawing, which no longer copies nature.

Stylization of the human figure in later rock paintings of Eastern Spain and Andalusia. (Breuil)

Peoples who had hitherto lived parasitically, merely as consumers, imitating Nature in their art, now turned to new, creative activities, at first only in order to obtain the necessities of physical life, but later on to satisfy the needs of the spirit. Another age was about to dawn. Europe had begun the ascent toward civilization.

Running Hunter with Bow and Arrows.
Cueva de los Caballos, Valltorta Gorge.
(Obermaier)

Chapter II

EUROPE'S ASCENT TOWARD CIVILIZATION

*

THE last, great retreat of the ice, and the consequent change of climate and the conditions of life, was an event of enormous importance.

Northern Europe, which had hitherto only been sparsely covered with dwarf birches and conifers, now developed enormous areas of unbroken forest, and man found himself living in a green world instead of among ice and snow. Ages passed before he began systematically to sow and cultivate the cereals which he may perhaps have seen growing on the borders of his camping-grounds, though it is certain that this great change took place during the enormous space of time which included the Middle Stone Age.

The huge animals of the Ice Age had disappeared; man began to set plants in the soil; he learnt to sow seeds, and the age of agriculture, of tillage, began. Culture, in its primary sense, implied the cultivation and improvement of the soil, with all that this involved; but it gradually acquired as well a higher meaning. the development and ennoblement of the whole of human effort.

While the hunter and the fisher confined themselves to catching and eating whatever came their way, the husbandman began to mould his environment; he became a builder, building at first a home for himself, no longer being satisfied with what Nature offered him. Soon he began also to erect the first stone monuments and earthen sepulchres, the menhirs, dolmens, cairns, and barrows, which are not peculiar to the Nordic groups of the Stone Age, but extend along the whole of the Atlantic coast, through Southern France and Portugal, to North Africa, Palestine and Asia Minor, and so on towards India. Their point of origin lies in the Danish islands, especially Zealand, where the number of prehistoric stone monuments is said to exceed 3,000. They are scattered along the whole of the eastern coast of Jutland, and occur in Germany and Sweden, where there are dolmens in Schoonen, Halland, and Bohuslän. Together with the stone circles and dolmens in the British Isles, they constitute the first evidences of a prehistoric architecture.

Naturalism and Stylization

If we consider the art of the Neolithic Age and compare it with that of the early

Magdalenian epoch in the Palaeolithic Age, we shall see what a long way humanity had advanced. The fundamental character of the new agricultural world was its stability, permanence, and immutability. The freedom and independence of Palaeolithic drawing was gradually replaced by rigid stylization. In the Croizard monument (page 24) the human being no longer appears as something unique and individual, but as a rigidly determined symbol in a spatial world. The depth which one misses in this monument is lacking also in the idols which were occasionally produced. These, too, have become flat, and unlike humanity; but timeless, like the menhirs, which were set in the landscape, stiff and erect, as milestones of eternity, the ancestors of the obelisks. With superhuman force they were piled up in the open, often reaching a height of sixty feet and more, and there, in Brittany, they remain to this day. In Southern France and England, again, there are enormous stone circles, the finest of which, at Stonehenge (Fig. 3a), surrounds the sanctuary like a wall built by giants; outside this lies the first circle of stones, with a diameter of 100 feet. Thirty great monoliths, some thirteen feet in height, connected by lintels, formed an outer circle round a sanctuary which lay open to the sky, serving, in all probability, a cult of the dead. A second, concentric circle lies within the first, and within this, as the central point, stands the altar-stone. This is a profoundly religious art, based on eternal, rather than on human, transistory values.

In much the same way, no doubt, the agricultural people of Egypt, in the early stages of their civilization, conceived the pyramid, a structure having nothing to do with Nature, but which, in its rigid and definite form, entirely out of scale with humanity, uprears itself into eternity as a monstrous triangle. Even in the Bronze Age the triangle, appearing together with the circle and the spiral, on the stone tombs of the North (Figs. 3c and 4c), still exerted its appeal as an absolute form.

Thus, the change in the manner of life and ways of thought which occurred in the Neolithic Age, was expressed by a complete abandonment of naturalism and an increasing concentration on rigidly stylized forms. Capsian art, though it sprang from a somewhat higher stage of culture, was still, in its style and subject-matter, the art of hunter-folk; in rhythm and movement it conscientiously and lovingly reproduced all the details of its subject, and although the artists of eastern Spain discarded colour, and often contented themselves with outline drawings, yet their intention was still that of the masters of the Franco-Cantabrian style. In the art of the Ice Ages, all forms of expression, whether we consider the movements of the animals, or the representation in paintings or sculptures of human forms and attitudes, come from the same mentality. The quite admirable representation of the shooting of cave-bears in the sculptures of Montespan, and the hieroglyphic arrow on the walls of the Niaux cavern, are merely different expressions of the same magical conception of life.

But now we see the beginning of another way of thinking, in which things themselves become the subject of belief. The animal picture disappeared, not because the animals disappeared, for being domesticated they were even more closely related to man than before, but because there was now no need for the hunter's magic. The new attitude no longer required the presence of figures whose likeness to the originals promised the realization of ardent desire. The world of magic perished with the world of the hunter; yet belief in magic, remaining a profound human need, assumed another form; its symbols now stood not for concrete things but for ideas. This typifies the great cleavage which had occurred in human thought; the division of the world into material and spiritual. A sedentary population felt more in the power of Nature than the roving hunter: for its harvests it needed and hoped for the operation of powers which were beyond human comprehension and immune to human influence. Life, at first, became not simpler, but more difficult, harder, and less independent. This explains why, at first, there was an unmistakable enfeeblement and decline of art.

In connection with this new art, one must not forget to make certain necessary assumptions. Intense and constant attention had trained the eyes of the men of the Ice Age to the sharpest objective perception of things, which the sure hand of the hunter was peculiarly fitted to reproduce; now, along with the great material progress of human culture—the change to a sedentary form of life—other hands took over much of the artistic production of the race.

Among these agricultural peoples, women played a new role, and when purely geometrical ornament was involved, it was certainly more in accordance with the orderly spirit of a woman potter. Ornament becomes showier, and more variously coloured, and at the same time less creative, and confined within narrower limits; but on the other hand it is pleasant, easily remembered, and graceful; in a certain sense, it is the impact on art of the feminine character, to whose conservativeness it is well adapted.

After all, the most faithful portrayal of a real object is a simplification. The gifted animal draughtsmen of the Old Stone Age contrived, by various means, perhaps by indicating the eyes, horns or hair, or by the mere reproduction of the general outline, to evolve numerous abbreviations, which they used, individually, in many ways, either as proprietary markings, or informative symbols, or for other purposes. Such signs were often drawn in almost hieroglyphic forms, but they always seem fortuitous in their lack of arrangement; they are never ornamental, never aligned in rhythmical or symmetrical order.

The Neolithic Age

While in the previous pages we have tried to make clear the essential features of the first great change of style which occurred in Europe, it must be kept in mind that during the long period covered by the Middle Stone Age, new peoples were thrusting toward Europe from Asia. Eventually the cultural stage was reached which we call the Neolithic, or Later Stone Age.

To this age we attribute agriculture, pottery, and the use of polished stone axes, but not, as yet, any knowledge of metals: we must therefore try to understand the word 'age' as meaning a condition of affairs and not as a fixed period of time. The Stone Age of Europe, for example, was by no means contemporaneous with the Stone Age in America, and whereas in Mesopotamia the potter's wheel was invented about 3300 B. C. writing first practised about 3500 B. C., and bronze used in the fifth millennium B. C., the latest researches date the beginning of the European Stone Age about 2000 B. C. It reached its culmination during the following 400 years.

When using the terms 'the Earlier Stone Age' and 'the Later Stone Age' we must not overlook the fact that the difference between these two stages of art and culture was much greater than that between—say—the Neolithic Age and the following epochs of metal-working, where the changes were less far-reaching than those which followed the introduction of agriculture. Hence they did not influence the art of the age so profoundly. One may very often be in doubt as to whether an object should be attributed to the late Stone Age or the early Bronze Age; or whether it dates from the late Bronze Age or the early Iron Age.

During the long Mesolithic epoch the potter's art was used only in a very primitive way, but in the Neolithic Age it was practised more and more frequently; it is of the greatest importance for the classification of styles, because of all arts it most willingly obeys the creative imagination, and the imperishable fired clay, unlike the scanty remnants of woodwork or textiles, affords reliable and continuous evidence of stylistic evolution. If we consider the shapes of the innumerable vessels found in graves and the sites of settlements, we see at first an extremely simple, sometimes clumsy, but absolutely pure ornamentation, which makes it possible to distinguish individual schools of art, often sharply separated from one another, but sometimes inextricably blended. The most obvious differences are between the cultures of the purely agricultural peoples and of those who were still living more or less as hunters.

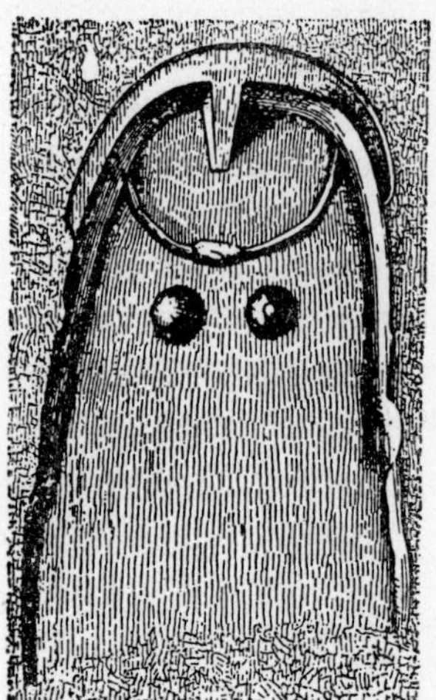

Neolithie stylized female figure from the chalk caves in the Petit-Morin Valley, Marne

In the north-east of Europe conditions of life still resembled those of the Ice Age. Into Finland, Livonia and Russia, and even Siberia, a Scandinavian culture spread with its Arctic rock-paintings. The pottery characteristic of this culture is known as *comb pottery,* the typical form of vessel being a simple beaker of coarse clay mixed with small granules of stone, having a conical base and surrounded with decorative bands of lines, dots, and impressions of the teeth of combs. The dwellings of their makers have been discovered; they were cone-shaped huts, whose simple wooden framework was probably covered with hides; inside was a hearth, surrounded with stones.

a

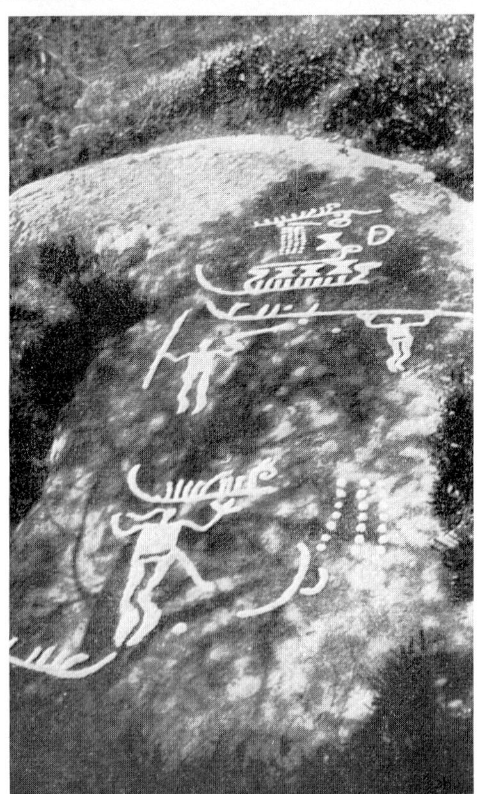

b

c

3. (A) Stonehenge: the most impressive prehistoric monument of northern Europe. (B) Human figures with ships and weapons; also footprints. Rock-drawings of the Bronze Age, near Riksö, in Sweden. (C) Incised images on a stone kist discovered in 1748 at Kivik, in the parish of Mellby, Sweden. The floor of the kist, which points to north and south, and which is 12 ft. 10 in. long, 2 ft. 11 in. wide and 3 ft. 11 in. high, consists of stamped earth; the walls and the cover are stone slabs. Of the two slabs shown, the farther bears symbolic wheels, above which are crescent-shaped ships with spirals. The nearer slab shows four figures marching in front of a chariot, on which the driver is standing; in the middle is a fish-symbol, and horses; below, on the left, a dancer, and behind him four seal-like, stylized figures. All these figures and symbols relate to death and the underworld. About one-tenth natural size. Cf. also the illustration on page 27.

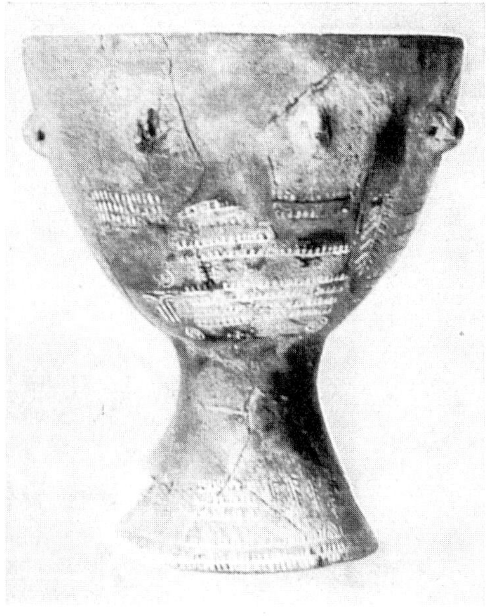

a

b

c

d

4. Vessels and cultic objects from the New Stone Age to the Iron Age.
(A) Neolithic pottery from the Nordic cultural area. Found in 1886, in a stone kist, with remains of the skeleton of a child, at Hornsömmern, Saxony. Symbols and markings deeply indented and filled in with white; very simple technique. Height, 10 in. The absence of a cover and the perforated lugs suggest—as in the case of other 'finds'—that the vessel was a drum, but it may be related to the pedestals and mushroom vessels of the Mediterranean culture. (Halle Museum).
(B) Urn of the Iron Age, with face and flattened cap-like cover. Found at Tlukom in Posen. Height, 7½ in. (Museum für Vor- und Frühgeschichte, Berlin).
(C) Vessel of beaten gold, with neck made separately and soldered on. Found at Werder, on the Havel, Brandenburg. Height, 4 in. (Museum für Vor- und Frühgeschichte, Berlin).
(D) Cultic plaque of the Bronze Age, from the Caucasus. Diameter, 5½ in. (Metropolitan Museum, New York).

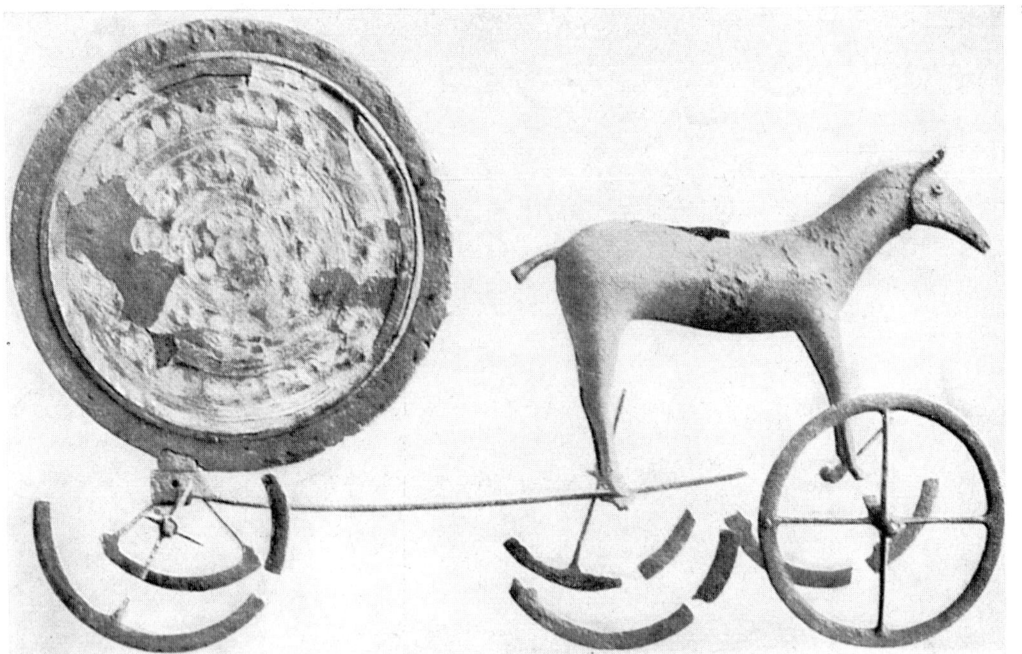

a

b

5. (A) Ceremonial model of a chariot, from the older Nordic Bronze Age, found at Trundholm, Denmark. The bronze disc, overlaid with gold, weighs 3½ lb. The ornaments, concentric circles and spirals, are engraved on both sides; the gold plating on one side repeats this decoration, which occurs also on the head, neck and chest of the horse. The pupils of the eyes are set in resin; apparently a bunch of hair was stuck into the sheath which forms the stump of the tail. Both horse and disc are hollow; the latter was cast in two halves, held together by a ring running round the edges. Length, 23½ in. 1400—1200 B.C. (National Museum Copenhagen).

(B) Bronze chariot of the early Iron Age (Hallstatt epoch) from Strettweg in Styria. In the centre, a female figure, lifting a sacrifial vessel, surrounded by four riders with spear and shield; before them are figures bearing antlers, signifying the sacrifice of a stag. Probably made in a Central Italian workshop after a Cyprian model. The chariot, to judge by the articles found with it, was buried in the fifth century B.C., but may date from the seventh century. Height 11½ in. (Landesmuseum, Graz)

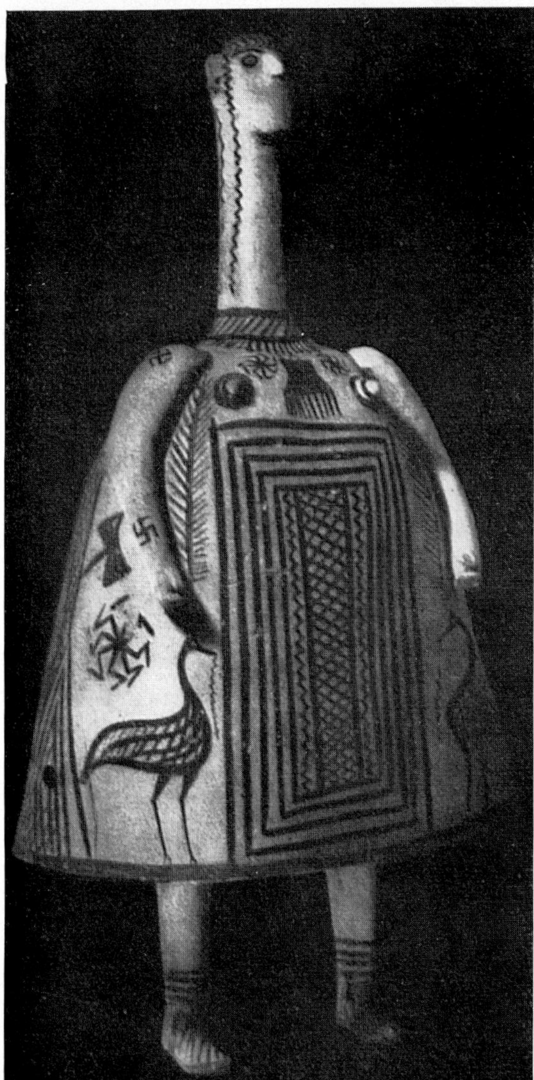

a

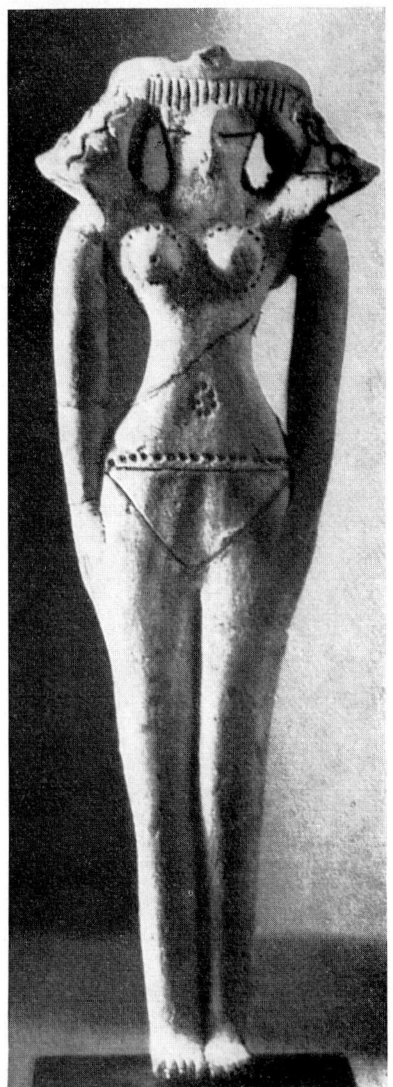

b

c

6. (A) Female idol with bell-shaped dress and movable legs. Cf. text p. 40 and p. 139. Archaic earthenware from Boeotia. Height, 15½ in. (Louvre).
(B) Earthenware statuette of pre-Hellenic age. Oriental influence. Probably from Mycenae. Height, 6½ in. (Louvre).
(C) Reclining Stag. Shield-ornament of beaten gold, found in the Kuban district. Length, 21½in. Scythian art of the seventh—sixth century B.C. (Kostromskaya Stanitsa).

On this northernmost culture is superimposed another, the Megalithic culture, so called after the stone monuments which it created, the 'giants' graves' or barrows and dolmens. We can divide the makers of Megalithic pottery, in spite of its many forms, into two branches: a Scandinavian and a North German. Neither was capable of a free and creative art; their decorations were confined to unpainted ornamentation, either punctured or impressed.

Another art is that of the Lacustrine culture of the West, which is fairly well known, since the water of the lakes has preserved many relics. The pile-dwellings, mainly in Switzerland and southern Germany, and the articles discovered on their sites, are of great interest to the cultural historian, though the Lacustrine art is very simple. The predominant form of pottery is a plain, wide-mouthed, tulip-shaped beaker, though these 'Michelsberger ceramics', as they are called, found also in England and south-western France, include various other forms too.

Ribbon pottery, the fourth great ceramic group, extends over the south and centre of Germany, and through southern Poland and the Ukraine, as far as the Dnieper; following the diluvial deposits westward, it reaches the Rhine valley, South Belgium and Holland, and in the Balkans is found as far afield as Bulgaria and Macedonia. Its simple decorative motives are spirals and wavy lines; but the farther eastwards the more frequently are the vessels accompanied by female images, whose whole character betrays the fact that this art originated in Asia.

String pottery and *bell-flower pottery,* of which more than 4,000 examples have been found, are generally distinguished as the fifth and sixth main groups of ceramics. Their exact delimination may well be left to the experts, who are by no means in agreement. The *string pottery* occurs almost everywhere, and the *bell-flower pottery* undoubtedly originated in Spain, whence it crossed the Rhone and the Rhine on its way to Hungary. This fact alone shows that even during the Neolithic Age there were great movements of populations, by which Europe was acquiring its diversity of character.

The Bronze Age

The Bronze Age, which followed the Neolithic Age, and which in Northern Europe is considered to be from about 1600 to 800 B. C., was also a time of unrest; but now the movement encroached upon the South. About 1200 B. C. occurred the great upheavals of the Mediterranean basin due to the migration of the Dorians to Greece, the conquest of Troy, the devastation of Crete, and the threatened invasion of Egypt by the maritime peoples. Almost at the same time the Iberians began to spread through Spain, and not very much later the Etruscans, coming from Asia Minor, landed in Italy. In the North all was quiet for a long time, until the great folk-migration which was to bring about the dissolution of the greatest State of the Western world—the Roman Empire.

The introduction of bronze heralded the advent of the classic stage of the second development in the world's art, with its combination of the decorative and the functional. This is partly due to the nature of the material. Unlike the stone of the earlier period and the iron of the later period, bronze was, like gold, a material attractive to the creative imagination, being at the same time decorative and easily worked.

It is often difficult to determine where the entirely functional form leaves off and where decorative refinement of functional form begins. The swords and daggers of the Bronze Age, with their richly ornamented hilts; the brooches, made in two portions, with their spiral shelds or hasps; the pendant jars cf thin cast bronze; the great bronze horns or Lurs; these are all fashioned with a refined sense of form and with a frugal expenditure of the precious metal. The heads of the rivets, for example, which serve to fasten the blade to the hilt (Fig. 7b), have of course a practical purpose, but their unnecessary multiplication into a whole row of beads is a surrender to the decorative impulse.

In view of the preponderant artistic importance of bronze in this period this is not the place—since here we are concerned rather with a grasp of essentials than with a complete exposition of the historical material—for any lengthy consideration of the wooden utensils, textiles and ceramics. Ceramics were, in the Stone Age, the basis of decorative art. This function is now usurped by bronze, and metal accordingly takes over the old form of the beaker (Fig. 4c). The reverse influence may also be noted; there are earthenware vessels of the Central European Bronze Age which are among the finest creations of the prehistoric potters, and which, with their sharp corners and thin sides, and the metallic lustre ot their colouring—due to graphite—have developed an orthodox metallic style, to some extent in imitation of the precious gold and copper vessels imported from the South.

If the Bronze Age takes its name from the easily-worked metal, it is remarkable that this is most predominant in the North, where it almost entirely ousted pottery, and was used in a great variety of forms; for it was precisely in the North that no copper was found. There must, therefore, have been a trade which bartered copper and bronze for amber, the gold of the North.

The importance of prehistoric trade is too easily forgotten, or is held to be impossible, by an age which prides itself on its all-embracing means of transport by railway and steamship and aeroplane. The false notion follows that the ancient cultures were self-sufficient, although modern research is constantly refuting any such idea. Many things appear inexplicable only because one overlooks the possibilities of traffic between races, which was actively carried on, even in the earliest ages.

From many different discoveries we can today determine, to some extent, the ancient trade routes of the Bronze Age. Most of these followed the great rivers, but there were also cross-connections. The principal highway was the Danube, and many discoveries have been made on both sides of the Elbe. In the Alps of Salzburg and Tyrol many old mineworkings have been preserved, from which large amounts of metal were sent to the North: much earlier, it came from Spain and Cyprus, while the oldest bronze of which we have knowledge came from Mesopotamia, where there was a thriving metallurgical industry as early as the fifth and fourth millennia B.C. About the turn of the third millennium it reached Cyprus. So at one time bronze came from the East, by way of Troy, Cyprus, the Danube valley, and the Elbe—a route which can be traced to this day by scroll-headed, paddle-headed and ball-headed bronze pins. The bronzes coming from Spain are known by the sword-stick and triangular daggers, new forms without precedent in Central Europe, where the two-handed sword with round or oval pommel was a recent development from the imported long dagger and short sword.

Cf. Fig. 3c: Sketch of a further slab of the kist at Kivik.
TOP LEFT: Probably the ritual of fire-making.
RIGHT: Men with old Germanic wind instruments — Lurs.
BELOW: Figures drawn up in front of a cultic vessel, and scenes before some place of worship.

But in the North, rock-painting still survived, and its finest examples in Sweden (Figs. 3b and 3c) can be distinguished from those of the Ice Age only by the complete stylization of hieroglyphic signs, which take the place of complete representations; as, for example, the frequently occurring footprints, shown in Fig. 3b as dots, which are merely the symbol of the presence of divinities. We shall find these again in the earliest Buddhist art. Often, too, we see weapons in these Swedish paintings, by which we can date the pictures, since in most cases the form of sword portrayed can be clearly recognized. These rock-paintings were continued into the Iron Age, and in them the Gods are often distinguished by a symbol painted upon their bodies. That of the God of Death was perhaps the circle, a symbol which may still survive today in the form of the funeral wreath. Such Bronze Age rock-paintings are found not only in Sweden, but also in Siberia, Spain and Italy.

While in the Germanic regions rock-paintings were predominant, in the East (Fig. 7a) there was a wealth of earthenware statuettes, sculptures, reliefs, and other forms of art. Among the objects found in the Germanic regions the ceremonial model chariot of Trundholm (Fig. 5a) is particularly interesting. It is usually described as a chariot of the Sun, yet it bears lunar numbers, and since the disc is overlaid with gold on one side only, the other side is evidently to be regarded as the dark moon. Prehistoric religion was pre-eminently under the influence of the Moon, and Odin's Ring or Donar's Wheel, with its four spokes (Fig. 3c) signifies the four phases of the moon and the four quarters of the heavens. No other star or planet is quartered in this way, and none is so closely connected with the night, and therefore with the cult of the dead. To the prehistoric peoples the moon was of importance also as a measure of time, so that all cultic ceremonies were held at night.

The bronze car of Strettweg (Fig. 5b) takes us into the Iron Age, and tells us of the spread of the practice of sacrificing deer, especially in the regions settled by Celts. At the same time we see signs of the later sun-worship, of a mythology which has not even to this day entirely died out, and which had its origin in the pagan Sun-Deer. This sun-deer was conceived as bearing a radiant and peculiarly splendid pair of antlers, rising into the heavens, as the old Nordic poems tell us. In its artistic expression, it is instructive to follow the way in which it gradually evolved, symbolically, from simple figures with uplifted hands (as in the accompanying illustration), the next stage being the pair of antlers, and the last, the crown.

Bronze figure from Kiev

The Iron Age

For prehistoric man the use of iron was as far from causing any fundamental change in the form of life as was the previous introduction of bronze. Iron was then smelted from the so-called bog ore, and the objects made of it were worked with the hammer in the same way as bronze. Cast iron was a much later invention. Other factors were of greater importance than the use of the new metal, for there was a transference of power in the prehistoric cultures. In the first half of the Iron Age it was the Illyrian peoples who reached their culminating point, while in the second half the Celts became predominant in Northern Europe, thereby pushing back both the Illyrian and the Germanic elements. At this period Germanic art seems to have undergone an almost complete eclipse; bronze articles are very rare, gold is no longer found, and the earthenware vessels have no special individuality; it is possible that alien forms were adopted.

No general date can be fixed at which the Iron Age can be said to have begun: while bronze was still predominant in many regions, in others the new metal was employed as well. In the region of the eastern Alps iron was first used about 1000 B.C., but in Central Europe if often made its first appearance between 700 and 500 B.C.

In the first half of the first millennium B.C. Hallstatt, in the Salzkammergut, Upper

Austria, was predominant. Here more than one thousand graves have been opened, which reveal a strongly characterized and accomplished art and culture, and for this reason the period is known as the Hallstatt epoch. Not only did the territory of the Hallstatt people include many Bronze Age mines, but its salt deposits attracted traders from Italy, Greece, and the land of the Scythians, so that all kinds of works of art found their way to this region.

Warrior's tombstone of the first Iron Age. About 1/20 natural size.
Villa Franca, in the Val di Magra, Liguria

Part of a bronze bucket or situla of the Hallstatt epoch
(Laibach)

The ceremonial model of a chariot already described (Fig. 5b) is a product of the Hallstatt culture; it shows very plainly that something new and strange was entering into the geometrical peasant art of Northern Europe, namely, the desire to return to the portrayal of human and animal shapes. An Iron Age menhir (page 29) shows instead of the complete stylization of earlier figures (page 24), the beginning of a return to naturalism. At this time the North began to produce urns with human faces (Fig. 4b) or made in the form of houses (below); in this way human life again became an artistic motive. A new kind of modelling and sculpture appeared, more decorative in conception, spreading not only throughout Europe, but over the steppes, and across the Urals, even to China. The region of the Black Sea and the Caucasus was the point of origin of this art.

Urns in the form of Bronze Age Houses
(North Germany)

1. Polleben, Mansfeld Lake District 2. Halberstadt, Hanover
3. Tochheim, on the Elbe 4. Aschersleben, near Magdeburg

Gold Ornament from Hallstatt. First Iron Age.

In the second half of the millennium the Celtic area becomes prominent. We are now already in an epoch contemporaneous with the ripest age of Greece, while in the Roman world laws were beginning to be codified, and the juridical foundations of the Roman State were being laid. It was not long before war broke out between the Romans and the Gauls; and from this point the art of the whole of Europe moves more and more into the light of history.

The second half of the pre-Roman Iron Age is commonly called the La Tène epoch, from the many discoveries at La Tène, near Marin, on the Lake of Neuenburg. It comprises a period whose beginning is placed about the year 500 B.C. but of which all the principal 'finds' date from about 400 B.C. The term is applied also to the objects found throughout the whole of Southern Germany, while farther to the north one speaks of a pre-Roman Iron Age, from which there is a transition to the art of the Age of Migrations, to which we shall return in Chapter XVIII.

Ægean Art

The most perfect works of art which prehistoric Europe has to show are found along the shores and upon the islands of the Ægean Sea. What the Homeric poems tell us of the gleaming, many-pillared palaces of prehistoric antiquity, of the skilful metal-work, the statues and paintings, received complete confirmation in the excavations at the end of the nineteenth and the beginning ot the twentieth century. These revealed the wonders of Crete and of the Greek mainland at Tiryns and Mycenae. This great art, which was distributed over the islands of Thera, Amorgos, Rhodes, Melos and Cyprus, was essentially of the Bronze Age in its greatest period, and unlike the art of the Greek Iron Age, which followed it, it knew only bronze tools and weapons. Iron finger-rings did not appear until its later years.

The Lion Gate, themain entrance to the citadel of Mycenae. (Breasted)

The greatest step forward from the Neolithic Age was the advance in the art of architecture. Soon after the beginning of the second millennium B.C., in place of the old round huts and four-square houses, there appeared those palaces which in Crete, at Knossos and Phaistos, lay spread out in Paradisical heedlessness, without fortifications or protecting walls, while those on the mainland, like the citadel of Mycenae, or that of Tiryns, lay hidden behind mighty walls, or stood on rocky promontories.

The Lion Gate at Mycenae (above) with its heavy lintel, reminds one almost of Stonehenge. But the lions guarding it, like the well-designed palace itself, suggest a high civilization, which had evolved a political life in the extreme south ot the continent, and which culminated before that of the rest of Europe had begun.

The beginnings of Ægean art go back to the third millennium B.C. A people which as yet had no knowledge of the potter's wheel hollowed out of blocks of marble to make round vessels and shallow bowls. Pots and jugs were made of clay, on which patterns were scratched or were painted with dull colours. Soon, however, the hands which covered these vessels with ever-recurring spirals were no longer content with such work, and ventured upon the portrayal of the human figure. At first their efforts resulted in simple, doll-like figures, many of which were found on the islands and the mainland (Fig. 6a and 6b), until new immigrants from the South brought with them the potter's wheel, and therewith the end of the Stone Age.

The so-called 'island art' was replaced by a new period, whose twofold character is rightly described as Creto-Mycenaean. An early period, ending about 1800 B.C., a culminating period, which lasted until 1500 B.C., and a late period, which continued for three centuries longer, can be clearly distinguished. This Minoan culture, which takes its name from Minos, the legendary Cretan king, was the product of an ancient Mediterranean race, the Achaeans of the Homeric epoch. They passed through the Greek peninsula in a first great migration, settling down in permanent strongholds. During the first half of the second millennium B.C. they evolved the Mycenaean culture, as a splendid prelude to the ancient culture of Greece. This would have been impossible without the heritage of Asia and Africa, which, thanks to their geographical position, were able to emerge from the want and misery of the Ice Age thousands of years before Europe, and to advance from the culture of the hunter and the nomad to the culture of the husbandman, and so to the civilization of the city, and the richer and freer development of life which this afforded. In the cities and farm-houses a new relation to Nature was again achieved, and on seals found in Crete we see the first portrayals of the European landscape (below).

The Creto-Mycenaean artists saw Nature with open eyes, and were never weary of representing her splendours. They evolved a technique which employed a wide range of colours; this gave their works an elegance which raises them far above the level of all other relics of prehistoric Europe.

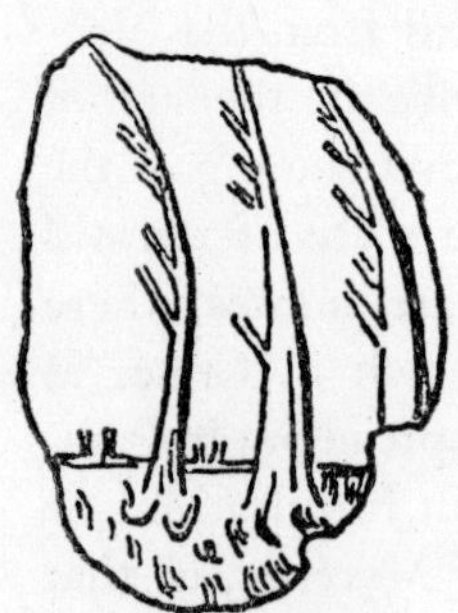

Cretan Seal (Annual of British School at Athens)

Theirs was a 'luxury art', produced for a court which for centuries had so trained its senses that only the most refined and sublimated art could satisfy them. The passion for Nature drove these people out across the sea, and Ægean art reached its height when it devoted itself entirely to the wonders of the deep from which it had emerged. The Ægean artist liked best of all to take his motives from the depths of the sea; seaweeds and rocky reefs, starfish, squid, with numberless fish and sea-shells, were, for the Cretan artists, the familiar forms of a world which only the islander knew. The life hidden in the sea was the favourite theme of all Cretan art; here it was most truly itself, while in its representations of the animal world (Fig. 8c) it was more inclined to follow Oriental models.

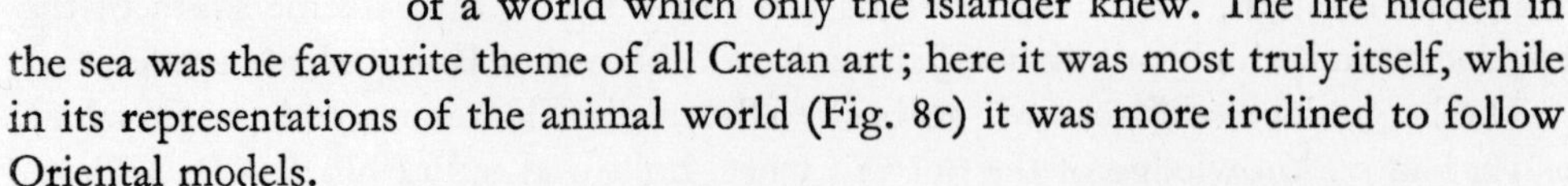

The Cretan 'palace style', as it evolved, increase in brilliance and luxuriance. The walls were covered with marble and bronze, or were radiant with glowing colours. Delicately built women and slender youths (Fig. 8b) were painted on the walls, with an assured sense of style and a refined feeling for decorative effect. The men are often depicted with costly, inlaid weapons, and the women in gorgeous dresses, which effectively stress the contrast between the long robe and the uncovered breasts (Fig. 8a). Little statuettes in faience, exquisitely carved figurines of ivory,

7. (A) Earthenware figure from a grave of the Bronze Age, at Alicevac in the neighbourhood of Kostoc in Yugoslavia. White inlaid ornamentation. Height of figure, $13^{1}/_{4}$ in. (National Museum, Belgrade).
(B) Sword-hilts of the Bronze Age, about half natural size. 900—750 B.C.—Left: Antennae sword from Schussenried, near Waldsee, Würtemberg. Total length, 23½ in. (Altertümersammlung, Stuttgart). Right: Sword with kidney-shaped pommel from Neiderfinow, province of Brandenburg. Total length, 26½ in. (Museum für Vor- und Frühgeschichte, Berlin).
(C) Husbandman ploughing. Red-painted archaic earthenware from Boeotia. Height, $4^{5}/_{8}$ in. (Louvre).

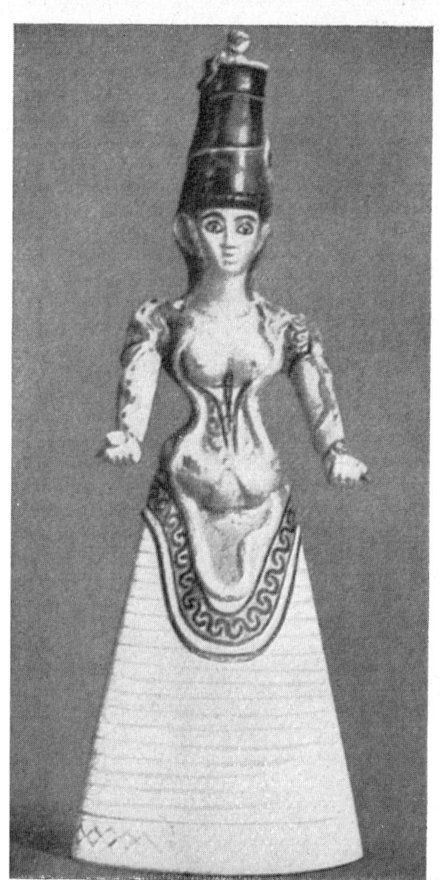

a

b

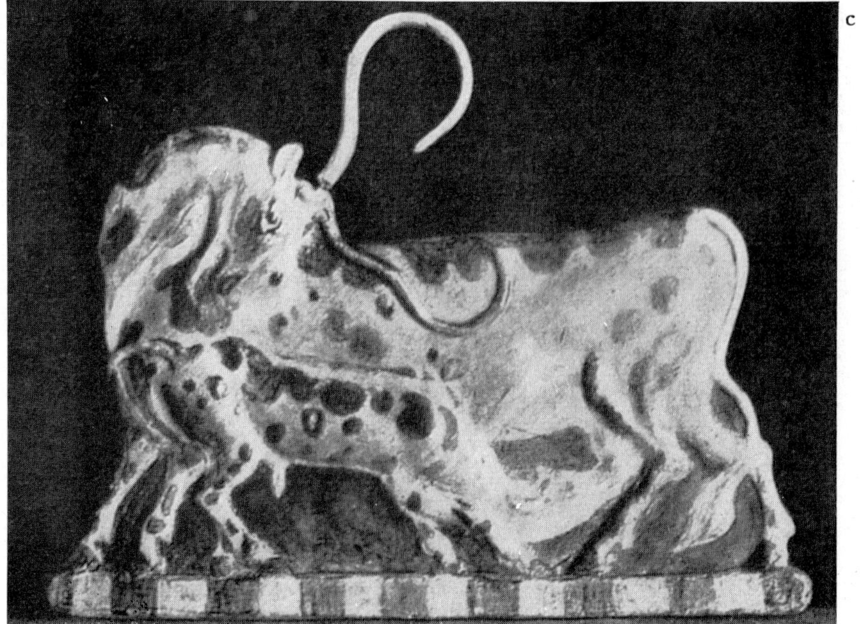

c

8. Works of art from the Palace of Knossos, Crete. Cf. text, p. 32.
(A) So-called Serpent Priestess. Faience of the early stage of Creto-Mycenaean culture (1800—1600 B.C.)
(B) Stucco relief on painted background. Height, 7 ft. 3 in. Best period (1550—1400 B.C.).
(C) Goat with kid. Faience relief of early period. Width, 7¼ in. (All objects in Candia Museum).

9. Female bust, found at Elche. This limestone bust, originally painted, from the ancient Ilici, now Elche, near Alicante, in Spain, is regarded as a Greek work, showing Phoenician influence, of the fifth and the beginning of the fourth century The absent pupils of the eyes were inset, of some other material; the back is hollowed out, after the fashion of a money-box. Height, 21 in.

a b

10. (A) Woman's head. Terra-cotta; the work of the Yoruba. Discovered by Frobenius in the Congo basin.
(B) Wooden figure of Man on horseback. Yoruba. Height, $9^3/_4$ in.; diameter of bowl, $6^3/_4$ in. (Museum für Völkerkunde, Leipzig).
(C) Massa village at the confluence of the two arms of the Logone, to the south-east of Lake Chad.

c

chequer-boards of gold, silver, ivory and rock-crystal, and many other objects of this true 'luxury culture', were exported to the Greek mainland. To the Greeks of that time this art must still have seemed utterly alien. It was in tune neither with their simple methods nor with rustic character (Fig. 7c).

But soon they entered Crete as conquerors, destroyed the palaces, and took possession of the southernmost outpost of Europe. The subject race continued to exist under its foreign masters, but, impoverished, enslaved and enervated by the comfort of a long period of civilization, they were capable of producing nothing new. This final period of Cretan art is characterized by a curious rigidity, as though the flourishing naturalism of an ancient culture were slowly dying of its contact with the military spirit of the conquerors. Hence the fact that the art of Knossos was followed by no further progress, but only by the geometrical art of the early Greeks. After the Dorian migration there was an end of Cretan art. It was an anticipation of things to come at the point of separation between Europe and the ancient cultures of the East.

So, in its prehistory, the conception of Europe expands until it signifies the world, and we see that art and its forms borne upon a succession of recurring waves, and that new forms of life and art are always the product of fresh contacts between peoples. Even the remarkable female bust from Elche (Fig. 9) is a creation of the prehistoric world. In her Spanish-Iberian costume she gives us a glimpse of the veil which ends in a point on the head, in an object which bears a resemblance to the modern Andalusian comb, which was worn on the head-dress, as we may see it worn in the great stone sculptures of Cerro de los Santos. The dress is Iberian, but the whole bearing is Oriental, for the life of historic evolution was carried to Europe by two currents, one flowing broadly from the Near East, while the other came from Africa.

Chapter III

AFRICA

*

We have already seen that Europe, in the Ice Age, had a completely different appearance from its present one, and that the Mediterranean area was more directly connected with it. We must now see what consequences are to be drawn from this. As far as the evolution of arts is concerned, we are dealing with a territory which we may call Eurafrica, which includes modern Europe, Africa, and a large part of the Near East.

In prehistoric times this area was united by land-bridges; it was also more clearly separated from Central Asia by inland seas in the South and North-East, since there were wide stretches of water between the Black Sea and the Caspian. Later, Asia was to draw gradually nearer, and Africa farther away, but the old geographical unity of the Eurafrican area persisted into the period of the Roman Empire, which made it a political unity as well. Europe was only the north-western fringe of a greater cultural whole; both geographically and spiritually Egypt was much closer to the Greeks, and Carthage to the Romans, than were the peoples and countries of the north.

Between the two oldest centres of the Mediterranean basin, Spain and Egypt, lies North Africa. The early Palaeolithic Age, like that of Western Europe typified by the hand-axe, was followed by an age of Capsian art. Next came a period of continuous development, which, with easily recognizable differences in various regions, extended from the Atlantic to Egypt, and from the shores of the Mediterranean to the northern Sahara. Large areas of the latter were still covered with meadowland and watered by streams, and some parts of it remained fertile into historical times.

How far Capsian paintings influenced the finely incised drawings which we find, towards the close of the Old Stone Age, on the shells of ostrich eggs, it is difficult to determine; yet from then on it is possible to speak of native industry in Africa. Wood, leather, or other perishable substances have of course disappeared, and all that remains is a large quantity of stone implements, and fragments of the ostrich eggs that served as vessels before the invention of pottery. Linear patterns, dots, etc., often appear as ornamentation, and show some connection with the European Neolithic Age, as do the innumerable megalithic monuments which cover the whole northern edge of the African Continent. In Algeria and Tunisia dolmens, menhirs, and stone circles can be counted in thousands. The dolmens are often in the form of a table or crude altar, but round sepulchral towers of various heights are not uncommon. The identity of the men who built the mysterious ruins between the Limpopo and the Zambesi, of which the remarkable stone buildings at Zimbabwe are good examples, and the date when they were built—are questions not yet solved. Here we find fortress-walls over thirty feet high, skilfully built of granite cubes without mortar, and inside them an intricate system of chambers and corridors. Numerous remains of mine-workings and smelting furnaces show that here, in this early period, men sought for gold.

In the art of the Sahara, after the beginning of the Neolithic Age, a particular style of pottery was so characteristic that in a certain sense one may see in its primitive technique the beginnings of this art. The clay was plastered on to the inner side of a basket, so that a vase was produced, on whose outer surface the pattern of the weave remained, even after firing, when the mould had been detached. To the vessel thus formed a neck was attached, ornamented very simply with the finger-nails or a pointed stick, just as in the early European Stone Age. The people who produced the oldest art and culture of North Africa were closely related as a race to the ancient Egyptians; even to this day the people of North Africa are uniformly Hamitic, except for those who migrated there in the Middle Ages.

Superimposed rock paintings and drawings from the Western Sahara.
The oldest, with the mammoth, date from the Stone Age,
while the next, with Libyan symbols and a dromedary,
date from the fourth century A.D., are the work of Berbers;
finally Mussulman figures have been scratched by primitive artists

Although the course of the Neolithic Age in North Africa can be more or less followed by means of various specimens of pottery discovered there, and while the rock-paintings and drawings—which are often superimposed—provide a concise history of early African art, there is a conspicuous gap when we look for an epoch to correspond with the European Bronze Age. Ancient bronze objects are so rare in North Africa that the very existence of a Bronze Age there has been disputed, though this seems most improbable when we remember that the region lay between the two oldest and most important bronze cultures of the Mediterranean, and was closely connected with both. Moreover, Egyptian inscriptions recording the victories of Merneptah (1225—1215 B.C.) tell us, as do the inscriptions of the later Pharaohs, that spoil from Libya included swords and other metallic weapons.

The account which follows does not lead up to the early culture of Egypt, but will deal first of all with the 'primitive' art of negroid Africa, the Ethiopia of Herodotus. A later chapter will be devoted to Egyptian art.

The Real Dark Continent

Even if Africa had been a unity at some earlier period, this would eventually have been disrupted by the drying up of the Sahara. The Mediterranean cultures affected the northern edge of the continent, but a separate development was beginning in the south. Palaeolithic stone implements are found in the southern-most point of Africa, where the art of the Bushmen, a survival of the Old Stone Age, is still practised to this day. Like Palaeolithic man, the almost extinct South Bushmen of Africa are hunters, wandering over the plains and forests. About 4 ft. 7 in. in height, they have the very narrow loins and spirally curled hair, which is so often represented in Capsian art. The extent of their wanderings was once very wide, for paintings ascribed to them are found over almost the whole of South Africa. The Bushmen are undoubtedly a very ancient race: Homer, Herodotus and Aristotle speak of dwarf peoples. Even in the nineteenth century, they still stalked, climbing trees and hiding in the foliage, and killing their quarry with bow and arrow, or by leaping down upon it. They had no villages, but slept in caves or holes in the ground, and lived entirely on game, fruit, and edible fungi. They knew nothing of metal-working or pottery, and their implements were of roughly chipped stone. It is therefore natural to compare the Bushmen's drawings with those of the Palaeolithic Age, and to try to prove, as a general proposition, that under the same conditions the same sort of art would emerge today as 20,000 years ago.

The case is not quite so simple. If we examine these pictures—for example, the drawing shown on page 37, in which a hunter, concealed in the skin of an ostrich, and armed with bow and arrows, is stalking a flock of ostriches; or another, which shows little Bushmen driving off a herd of stolen cattle, and pursued by taller enemies —we find a power of composition and of logical narrative entirely lacking in

Palaeolithic art. Again, their technique is unlike that of Palaeolithic rock-paintings; as well as incised drawings, where sharp stones were used, with extraordinary sureness of hand, to engrave smooth rock surfaces, there are polychrome paintings of a very different kind, coloured with mineral pigments mixed with fat or marrow. The latter are mostly found in the east of South Africa, while the former, the so-called petroglyphs, are found chiefly in the west. But no rigid limits can be drawn; the technique was determined by the nature of the materials available at the moment.

Still less is it possible, in the present state of our knowledge, to date the pictures with any accuracy. It has not even been established beyond question whether the Bushmen are really responsible for this art, in spite of the evidence of Europeans who insist that they have found Bushmen actually at work upon such drawings. The stylistic differences of the African rock-paintings seem rather to indicate an art developed through many centuries and by many races as a natural means of expression.

Rock-painting by Bushmen. Ostriches, and on the right a man disguised as an ostrich, holding a bow. Colours blue, black and white

Many of the Algerian rock drawings (page 38, top), of which the inner surfaces are often smoothly polished (probably to make them take the colours more readily), show animals which wandered away from North Africa after the Ice Age—such as the rhinoceros and the giraffe (page 35); but there are later drawings (page 38, bottom) belonging to an entirely new culture, which reveal the new spiritual impulses, the new migrations and mingling of races, which now affected this continent.

The small, light-skinned Bushmen who still survive in isolation on the waterless plains of South Africa, together with the dark-skinned Pygmies of the inaccessible virgin forests of the centre of the continent, may be taken as the most ancient racial elements in Africa; but they are submerged today by two other larger groups.

Outline drawing deeply incised in a smooth wall of rock. Tiut, Algeria. (Germany)

The compact, rectilinear northern half of Africa is inhabited, to the south of the Sudan, by the Sudanese Negroes, while the triangular southern half is the land of the Bantu Negroes, a younger and not entirely homogeneous ethnic stratum, mixed in the East with more Hamitic blood than the true Negroes, and in the West with less. It is now generally assumed that the Hamites made their way into Africa toward the end of the Northern Ice Age (which in Africa was a rainy period) from the steppe country of Western Asia in a number of waves, entering not only the coastal region of the South but following the natural routes of emigration, especially the Nile valley, and penetrating far into the west and south of the continent. The basis of their economic life is cattle-hunting, while the Negroes cultivate the soil with the mattock and hoe.

From the earliest times broad streams of culture have flowed into the interior of Africa from the Mediterranean and from Asia. Across the narrow straits of Bab-el-Mandeb a great wave of migration swept westwards to Lake Tchad. The Hyksos, about 1800 B.C., and the Arabs, in the seventh and eighth centuries A. D., the most widely separated in time, may be noted, as two of a long series of races who have contributed to African art and culture.

Even the earliest architecture, in its more highly developed forms, reveals alien influences. The Negroes themselves do not use stone as a building material, but clay; with this they developed an extraordinary range of forms, especially in the cities of the Sudan, which contain as many as 200,000 inhabitants. These cities show a highly

Cattle-raider wearing an ass's mask. Scratched in sandstone.
North-west Africa, Sahara. (Frobenius)

developed architecture, with vaulted roofs and domes; their great mosques and palaces, with massive containing walls and imposing towers, are all built of clay. Islam, which invaded this region in the eleventh century, has here, in combination with the native art, created marvels from nothing.

In such purely African buildings, uninfluenced by the outer world, as the villages of the Massa (Fig. 10c), we see an exceptionally beautiful architecture, perfectly natural in its execution, whose pure lines run unbrokenly upwards. Farther north and south, where the clay contains a greater proportion of sand, it no longer permits of this accomplished style of architecture, which roofs its houses with a dome, admitting light through a window at the apex, so that they somewhat resemble, on a small scale, the Pantheon in Rome. The symmetrical steps which form the base of the buildings, which often reach a height of more than twenty-five feet, are continued up to the apex, and produce an effect of natural articulation. These houses are the work of the potter rather than the mason, being shaped entirely by hand; their colour is a pinkish grey. Sometimes, instead of the simple articulation of the wall from the ground upwards, we find buttresses shaped like long isosceles triangles, which become narrow vertical mouldings. These houses are arranged in picturesque disorder, and their bases often touch, but never intersect; sometimes a smooth-walled tower, rising among them, diversifies the groups of conical forms.

In Africa, as in all parts of the world, the round house was the first architectural form; for wherever man, either for reasons of security, or to get a better view, built a mound, in order to live upon it, there was naturally a circular space on its summit; this was reduced to a quadrangular form later, when the building was divided into rooms, and the need arose for gangways or corridors. This is true of all primitive peoples, and the oldest buildings everywhere confirm it. A gradual development took place from the tent to the beehive hut, and then, even in Africa, to the domed structure, often with cylindrical vaultings and roof (this page). The form of building mentioned above, in which clay is the only material, is the most remarkable architecture produced by the Negroes without foreign influence.

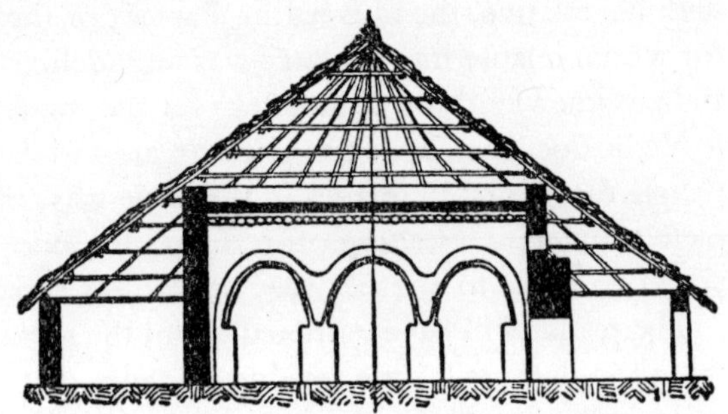

Section of vaulted building at Mokwa, Western Sudan

If in this survey, which does not deal with ethnology, but with art, the western half of the African continent is especially prominent, it is because the eastern half, with its mainly agricultural population, conspicuously lacks artistic ability. These Negroes of the East draw, as a rule, more clumsily than European children, and their decorations are unimaginative and undeveloped; the West, however, conspicuous for its love of art and sense of style, is extremely rich in human and animal figures of all kinds.

Idols and Masks

In every primitive representation of the human figure one sees that the origin of all sculpture was the mask. This is true of European art: among the prehistoric relics of Greece and Crete are large, flattened, disc-like faces, with no backs to the heads, just like those which are found in Bosnia or Rumelia. The wooden pole on which the mask was originally carried can be seen surviving in the unhumanly long necks of many ancient European images (Fig. 6a).

Contrary to general opinion, the existence of idols implies an advanced stage of intellectual and material culture: their worship occupies an important place in the history of religion, the evolution of which goes together with that of art and culture. Mythology and the history of art are mutually explanatory; both show that idolatry does not necessarily indicate a low stage of culture, any more than its condemnation does a high one.

Among civilized peoples, idolatry is not coincident with particular racial affinities or definite fields of culture. We have only to compare the image-worshipping Hindu with his relative, the idol-hating Parsee; or the idolatrous Phoenician with the Jew. for whom relapse into idolatry was an indelible disgrace. The ancient religion of the Indians knew nothing of idolatry, yet the modern Brahmins, who profess adherence to Vedic doctrines, are among the greatest idolators in the world. Though outwardly people may worship images in the same way, the images themselves may have completely different meanings for them; for one worshipper they are no more than symbols, while to another they are beings capable of rational behaviour.

The reader will have gathered, from the survey of the older Stone Age of Europe, that though there is little reliable evidence that this period was acquainted with idols or images of gods, in the later part of the Neolithic Age there was an increased belief in the magical power of objects and symbols. Almost all the Negroes of the East Coast of Africa, the Kaffirs and the Bechuanas, are today, in this respect, on much the same level as the people of the Old Stone Age; they do not practise iconolatry, but believe in tutelary spirits, and in a multiplicity of powerful and mainly evil beings, who live in hollow trees or other hiding-places.

The cultural region of West Africa coincides with an ancient matriarchal culture, founded economically on a primitive agriculture, carried on without the help of the plough or of draught-animals. Its religion is a pronounced ancestor-worship, which in art expresses itself indefatigably in the form of masks and images of the dead. These masks play an important part in the cult of the dead; hence, for the most part, they must not be judged by purely aesthetic standards, since they have—as elsewhere in the world—to fulfil religious purposes. In Africa they are used in dances which

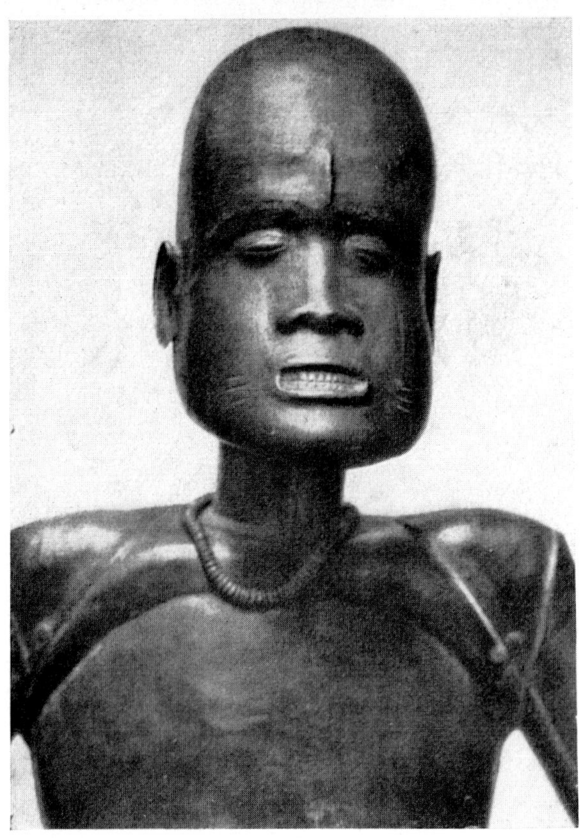

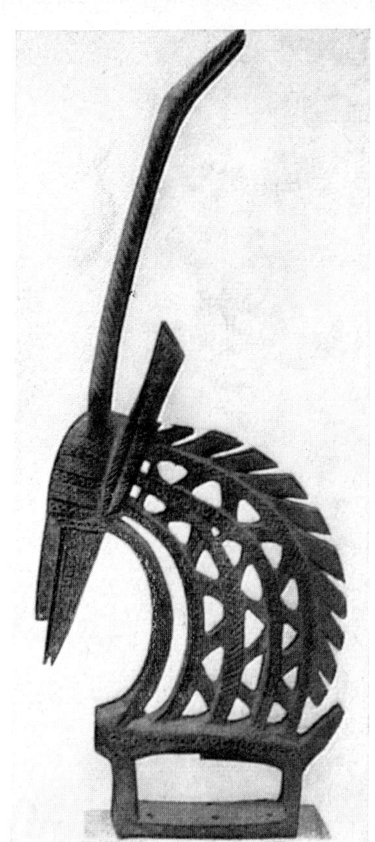

11. (A) Bust of a brass figure from Dahomey. (Ratton Collection, Paris).
(B) Stylized Antelope. Crest of a mask from Senegal.
(C) Lion, of sheet silver, riveted. Dahomey. (Ratton Collection, Paris).

a

b

c

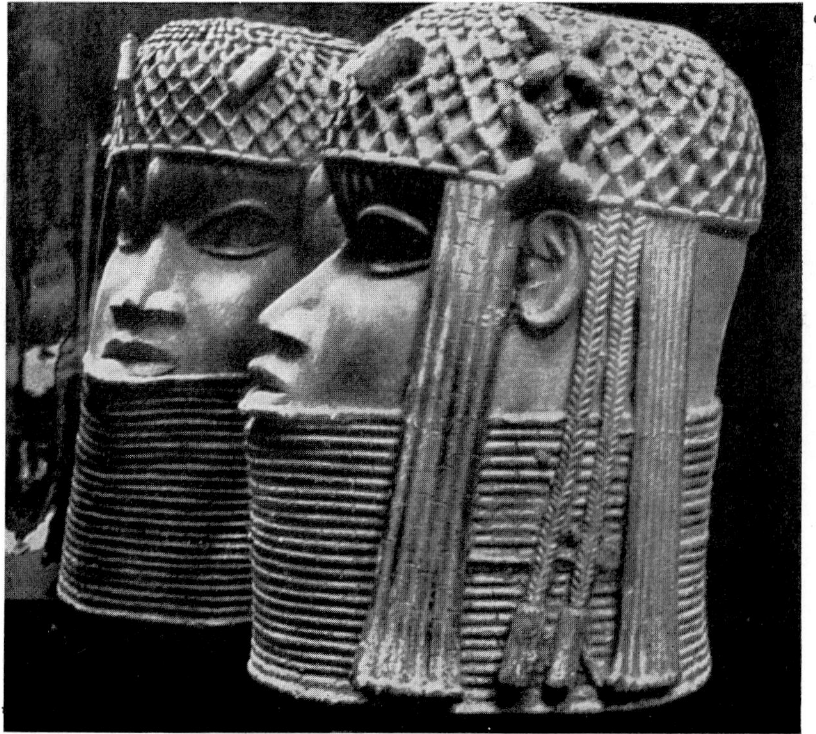

12. (A) Girl's head with head-dress and necklet of strings of coral beads. Bronze cast from Benin. Height, with base, 19 in. (Museum für Völkerkunde, Berlin). (B) Three children with vessels in their hands. Bronze plaque from Benin. (British Museum). (C) Bronze head from Benin; richly ornamented with strings of coral beads. The original is in front; the head at the back is an image in a mirror.

13. (A) Parents with child. Large colour-box in carved wood, from New Zealand. (Stephen-Chauvet Collection, Paris). (B) Wooden Mask from New Caledonia. (Musée de Trocadéro, Paris). (C) 'Gona'. Shield with ancestral image. Gulf of Papua, New Guinea. (Stephen-Chauvet Collection, Paris). (D) Wooden Club, Polynesia. Marquesas Islands. (Musée de Trocadéro, Paris).

a

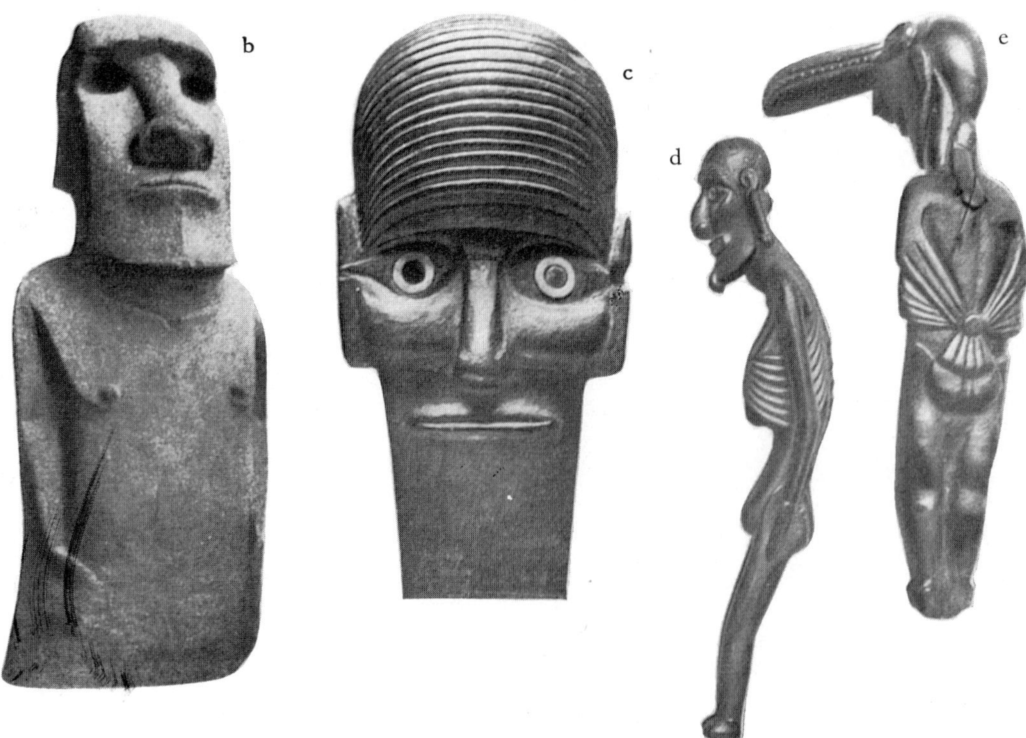

14. Art of Easter Island. (A) Landscape made at the time of the European discovery of the island. One can see how these gigantic stone images were hewn out of the cliffs and then detached and set up. Drawing by De Bar from a sketch by Pinart. (Stephen-Chauvet). (B) Stone image brought to England in 1868 on board the *Topaz*. Height, 7 ft. 6 in. (British Museum). (C) Butt-end of an oar or ritual staff of the old inhabitants. Length of whole, 5 ft. 5 in. (Stephen-Chauvet Collection, Paris). (D) Characteristic Wooden figure. Height, 17½ in. (British Museum). (E) Bird-man, connected with the island cult (cf. text p. 53). Height, 11.8 in. (British Museum).

are supposed to promote fertility, or as war-masks to terrify the enemy. We cannot, therefore, judge of their expression without the most accurate knowledge of the way in which they are used; this is especially the case on the West Coast, where the whole tribal power is often in the hands, not of the chieftains, but of secret societies.

Primitive Art

This West African ancestor-worship, ubiquitous and all-powerful, is expressed in more ways than by masks, for there are races among whom every article of daily use is decorated with figure motives: on spoons and forks, stools, drums, wooden caskets, on all parts of the house, even on the snuff-boxes—everywhere there are human figures, faces, eyes, hands and other parts of the body, carved in the round or in relief. There are also images of animals; for, together with ancestor worship, totemism is one of the oldest cults in the world. Through totemism man feels himself related to the animals; he sees, too, that animals have many powers—for example, that of flight—which he himself has not, but which he tries to attain by means of friendly relations with the animal whose emblem he adopts and to whose protection he confides himself.

The art produced by African culture, like that of the other primitive peoples, springs from a deeply religious attitude, which modern humanity regards—often very unjustly—with contempt. Before its never-failing abundance we see how narrow-minded is the traditional survey of art, based only on knowledge of civilized countries, which is apt to regard itself as the history of the art of the whole world. It is true that the economy and the thought of peoples living under natural conditions are primitive in form, but their art is the complete expression of their world, undivorced from other manifestations of life. It is more intimately interwoven with the life of these peoples than is the art of the white men with theirs. We, with our ideas formed by European rationalism, cannot easily understand the primitives. Human life, as history teaches us only too plainly, is something more than a function of the intellect, and the observer of African art, if only he will venture to surrender himself to his feelings rather than to his sense of cultural superiority, will find himself confronted not by the Negro, but by the eternal human creature who peoples this planet with his millions of individual existences and desires.

Typical West African chieftain's throne, with seat and base, a massive supporting-pillar, and four lighter legs. (Togo)

The art of the Negro is often called heavy, clumsy, and oppressive. It is said to have a 'cubic' character, comparable with the power of ancient Egyptian architecture and the mighty mass of the African continent itself. Such parallels are all too easily drawn, and the author cannot unreservedly agree with this characterization of

African art. It is true that many of the chieftains' thrones (page 41) are excessively heavy, and the figures of horsemen (Fig. 10b) are squat and massive, but in such objects there is always some deeper reason for this, either the importance or the purpose of the object itself. Such shapes are by no means dictated by the general character of African art. It is a mistake to regard the art of the Negroes, or of any primitive people, from a purely aesthetic point of view; one must always remember the extent to which this art is the expression of faith, and how far it is bound up with religion. Even where Europeans can find no meaning in these productions, there is always some thought, always the incessant activity of the imagination, behind them. It is often a religious earnestness, a religious solemnity, which gives these masks and images an expression which the white man wrongly interprets as a comical grimace.

Where the spirit of jollity and the love of life is expressed in the art of the Negro, there, too, appears his innate sense of humour. The naïve *joie de vivre* and untamed energy of a primitive people may be seen not only in Africa, but in the United States, where the spirit of the Negro has engendered much of what the European regards as 'genuinely American' life.

The Art of Benin

One of the finest, most surprising, and most curious incidents in the history not only of African art, but of the art of the whole world, is the art of Benin. Springing into existence among simple agricultural tribes, it was not wood-carving, nor painting, nor any merely industrial art, but the art, refined to the last degree, of casting in bronze by the *cire perdue* process. In this the preliminary model consists of a core of hardened sand or clay which is covered with a thin coating of melted wax; this (when the finishing touches have been given to the wax) is covered with a coat of clay. After the core has been fixed by means of pins the wax is melted and run out, and the empty space left by it is filled with molten bronze. The outer husk has now filled its purpose, and can be broken, and the rough casting is polished and touched up with punch and chisel.

Until 1897 nothing was known of the existence of this culture, since for more than a century no European had so much as set eyes on Benin, with the exception of Sir Richard Burton, the daring traveller who visited the holy places of Mecca and Medina in disguise. But he said nothing of works of art and it was generally believed that any white man must die if he beheld the face of the king of Benin. Sixteenth and seventeenth-century accounts of the existence of great organized military States in Upper Guinea, which even mentioned the native art of casting in bronze, had long been forgotten, as the empty spaces on old maps of Africa show.

The Negroes themselves had closed their country to the outer world, since the white man had destroyed their kingdoms, stolen their women, and carried away their men to America as slaves. The powerful state of Benin was hermetically closed, and would perhaps have remained unknown even longer, had not a British commissioner taken it into his head to pay the king of Benin a visit, in spite of opposition. The reward of his enterprise was that, on the 3 January, 1897, he and his escort—numbering more than 200—were massacred. A punitive expedition was organized, and warships were sent; by the 7 February a powerful fleet lay at the mouth of the Benin River, and on the 18 February, forty-six days after the massacre, the capital was razed to the ground. The arrival of the white invaders interrupted a festival, celebrated by innumerable human sacrifices, crucifixions, and other atrocities. The most appalling cannibalism was practiced in Benin at this time, and the blood with which bronzes, ivories, and the very walls of the terrible city, were spattered, was not evidence of the cruelty of a single king or of one inhuman government. In the adjacent Negro States an unrestricted lust for murder prevailed, and religion had taken forms such as history has rarely recorded, only paralleled by the human sacrifices of the Aztecs. The British White Book relates that by the altars in Benin were found roughly carved cudgels for killing the victims, whose blood ran down the altar steps.

Drawing engraved on an ivory beaker from Benin. Lille Museum

Even if we wished to assume that such a brutal people could have developed so vital an art, we learn from the White Book that the best bronzes were found in one of the storehouses of the royal palace, beneath the filth of generations, and that the finest bronze plaques and magnificently carved elephant tusks were lying about in a state of partial decay, while the few tusks of more recent date revealed no carvings.

It is evident, then, that here we are dealing with an art of some antiquity, no longer valued by a degenerate people.

In the circumstances it is not surprising that as more and more of these treasures arrived in Europe scholars were for a long time unwilling to attribute an art of such astonishing technical perfection to a Negro people. Von Luschan, director of the Berlin Völkerkundemuseum (Ethnological Museum) acquired nearly one thousand of these works of art, and the British Museum about five hundred (Fig. 12). Thanks to Von Luschan's researches, there is no longer any doubt that all these are products of a purely Negro art, and that although the art of other African tribes shows signs of alien influence, that of Benin is unaffected by Indian influences, or by imported articles. The style of these bronzes is purely African and is closely related to the art of Joruba, as well as to that of Dahomey (Figs. 11a and 11c) and Ashanti.

The ancient connection between these two adjacent countries, which finds expression in the tradition that the kings of Benin came from Joruba, is so clearly revealed in their art that they may almost be regarded as a homogeneous province. The same images of the gods appear; the ram, the catfish, the snake and the lizard are represented as totems; and such figures of horsemen as we see on the bronze plaques are found again in Yoruba (Fig. 10b).

Drawing on an elephant tusk from Benin. (Von Luschan)

According to Frobenius, whose works are widely read, the art of Benin, like that of the whole of Upper Guinea, is the dying echo of an ancient, vanished, and otherwise unknown culture, which he calls the 'Atlantic' culture, and whose art, he thinks, was degraded and 'negrofied' in the Negro countries. To support this view he proposed dates for the Yoruba heads (Fig. 10a) as far back as the middle of the first millennium B.C. If this were so, there would be an interval of more than twenty centuries between them and the closely related art of Benin; for in the latter we see Europeans represented, one of whom has a pipe in his mouth (page 43, right). This representation, like that shown on page 44, is not among the most ancient examples of Benin's art, but the earliest examples cannot possibly be dated so far back. Only one thing is certain, that the native metal-work of Benin was already known before the first arrival of the Portuguese in 1472. In 1484 Diego Cao, with Beheim of Nuremberg, the friend of Columbus, discovered the Gold Coast, and in 1553 the Portuguese were followed by the English. From an account published in 1599 we learn that bronze and lead, swords, daggers, articles of clothing, and even hats, as well as coral and unwrought iron, were being imported.[1] From this we know that the people of Benin had early acquired a knowledge of ironworking, and that we are dealing with a developed and civilized country. As early as 1732 we learn, from another source,[2] that Benin was even then decadent; this was confirmed by later travellers. What the British destroyed in 1897 was only a husk, from which the living art had long departed. These facts, together with the native tradition that in the year 1485, under King Essige, a fair-skinned man came into the country with the Portuguese, who made bronze plaques for the king and taught his art to the natives —easily explain the representations of Europeans, and many other things. Struck[3] is perhaps right in putting the culmination of the art of Benin in the sixteenth and seventeenth centuries and assuming an 'archaic period' from about the middle of the twelfth to the middle of the fourteenth century, while describing the 150 years between that point and the year 1500 as the 'early period'.

According to tradition the power of the rulers of Benin extended southwards across the Congo as far as Angola. In fact, the art of the Bakuba in the southern basin of the Congo is closely related to that of Benin, and confirms the tradition that these people also came from Benin, as their neighbours the Baluba may have done. Religious iconoclasm, however, gave the art of the latter little opportunity of development; the ancient images of their ancestors were destroyed, and only in the east of this Negro kingdom, which escaped the frenzy of the iconoclasts, did sculpture of the human figure survive. Here the ancestral images which were found are among the best which Africa has produced.

All these countries of the African interior were, and to some extent still are, sanctuaries in which an ancient art took refuge after it had gradually disintegrated, in the coastal regions, under European influence. Art cannot survive unaltered as a visible expression of a culture which has been destroyed or altered by conquest—as may be seen in all parts of the world; in America no less than in Africa.

Modern Negro Art — The Fetish

Just as human influences were hardly able to alter, but only to enrich, the art of

[1] Hakluyt II, Pr. 2. [2] Barbet.
[3] Zur Chronologie der Benin-Altertumer, Ztschr. f. Ethnogr. Vols. 5 and 6, 1923.

Benin, so the African's robust artistic feeling and sence of form survive even now. Over vast areas, primeval forest affords the basis of a homogenous and essentially unalterable way of life. In the regions once covered by the ancient Congo kingdom, the kingdom of Lunda and the kingdom of the Karembe, African art, at its best and most genial, flourishes to this day. There the Negro expresses his sense of humour, in wall-paintings, and even more in ivory carvings. When he first made the acquaintance of Europeans he at once began to cover elephant tusks with spiral processions of figures, in which sailors, naval officers, scientists equipped with spectacles and butterfly-nets, bedizened chieftains, and grotesque animals appear one after the other, as they did to the curious eye of the artist. To this day the Negroes often display in their drawings their innate sureness of touch, a quick perception of the characteristic, and a keen observation of Nature. Such paintings as are found on flat rock-surfaces, or the walls of caves, in crevices of the cliffs, or in the houses, represent, especially in South Africa, battle-scenes, hunters, the domestic animals of the Kaffirs, and every possible kind of wild creature. Erotic scenes of a very unrestrained character are not unknown, but plants and ornamental motives are rarely represented. Where European influences have not been at work the pictures are painted in red, ochre, white, and black. The drawings are made with hard stone on soft slate.

The art in which the Negroes, above all those of West Africa, achieve the most astonishing results is that of sculpture. Today, as always, it is inspired by the worship of the dead. In the ancestral image the dead man lives on; his descendants seek his advice, his aid, and his protection, and provide for his needs by offering sacrifices before his image. Such a carving becomes an actual *fetish* after the priest has provided it with a magical nostrum, the *ngilingili*, which is usually introduced into a hole bored in the region of the navel, or preserved in a little box in the same region, which is preferably closed with a shell or a scrap of looking-glass. The characteristic features of Negro sculpture are the emphasized heads, over-large and carefully executed, with their jewelry, coiffure, and tattoo-marks—all things which help to create the personality—and the too short legs; hands and feet receive only summary treatment. Wood—apart from bronze castings, and the occasional use of ivory—is the chief material. Only in the grass-lands of Cameroon does one find also a highly-developed pottery, which produces the clay pipe-bowls in the form of heads, known as Bali pipes; in the rest of Africa the work of the potter is left almost entirely to the women, who produce only simple utensils for use in the house. One does occasionally find other articles of baked clay, but the wooden model is always recognizable.

Carved figures are often studded all over with nails or scraps of iron, which are hammered in to stimulate the fetish. How far this custom can be attributed to the influence of the Christian churches, with their reliquaries and crucifixes, it is difficult to say; but these figures are most widely distributed where the Christian missions of the sixteenth century were most successful, and where numerous images and pictures of the saints were imported. Still less can we decide how far the representation of the

Madonna may have influenced the various representations of mother and child in Negro sculpture; for wherever a foreign influence makes itself felt, its transformations and adaptations are conditioned by the permanent stock of native forms. The freely creative artistic personality is as little known in Africa as among other primitive peoples. The cohesive force of common religious ideas, of family crafts and tribal industries, is too great to permit of such individuality. Even in ancient times the art practised in Benin and in the kingdoms on the Congo was a universal court art, produced by a definite caste. Hence there was hardly ever any breach with tradition, and African art, in so far as it is still based upon a native culture, has an enduring life of its own.

Chapter IV

AUSTRALIA AND OCEANIA

*

SOUTH-EAST of Africa is the great island of Madagascar, of which only a very small proportion of the inhabitants are Negroes, the population being mainly Malayan-Polynesian. Here, almost on the coast of Africa, begin the art and culture of a largely tropical world of islands, which stretches over the enormous distance of 15,000 miles, more than half of the earth's circumference, its central point being Australia, while the most easterly of its islands—Easter Island, which belongs to Chile—is already in the shadow of South America. In considering its art it is convenient to regard the islands of the Malayan Archipelago, lying between Asia and Australia and to the south of the Philippines—Sumatra, Java, Borneo and Celebes being the chief among them—not as a part of the purely Oceanic area. They are thoroughly steeped in the art of Asia, and, as Indonesian Islands, are more fittingly included in the chapter on Indian art. The rest of the great swarm of islands surrounding Australia are divided into Polynesia, Melanesia and Micronesia.

Polynesia is the 'polyinsular' region which includes, with innumerable other islands, the Samoan Islands, the Pacific Sporades, the Society Islands, Tahiti and the Marquesas; the whole assuming the shape of an enormous triangle, with New Zealand in the west, the Hawaiian or Sandwich Islands in the north, and Easter Island in the east. Micronesia, the region of little islands, includes the many small islands north of the Equador, from the southernmost point of the Philippines to the Gilbert Islands, including the Mariana Islands, the Caroline Islands, and the Marshall Islands. Lastly, Melanesia takes its name (the 'Black Islands') from the dark skin of its inhabitants. It includes New Guinea and the adjacent area, as far as the Fiji Islands, the Solomons, the New Hebrides, and New Caledonia.

The Art of the Australian Aborigines

The Australian aborigines are among the most primitive peoples of the world. They apparently wandered from India, over a land-bridge which then existed, and when once the ocean had begun to isolate their little continent they were thrown upon their own resources, under conditions which were extremely unfavourable to their general development. On this lost continent, the culture of the Stone Age survived almost to the present day.

When Europeans first arrived in Australia the natives knew nothing of pottery,

15. 'Tiki'. Ancestral figure enthroned; on richly-carved wooden panel, with spiral ornamentation. New Zealand. (Moris Collection, Paris).

16. (A) Head of Wooden statue. Polychrome carving from New Mecklenburg, Melanesia. (Barton Collection, Paris).
(B) Wooden figure with Dragon from New Guinea, Melanesia. (City Museum, Bremen).
(C) Dance of Bats. Painted in black, red and yellow on 'tapa' (bark-cloth). Dutch New Guinea.

17. (A) Leather cuirass of Haida workmanship, painted black and red. The beaver is represented in the stylization and duplication peculiar to Indian art. Text p. 59. Height 27 in. (Museum für Völkerkunde, Berlin).

(B) Drawings scratched on objects made from the tusks of the walrus; the work of Alaskan Eskimo. Arrow-straightener in the form of an animal, 6 in. long.; tobacco-pipe, 12¾ in. long. (Museum für Völkerkunde, Berlin).

a

b

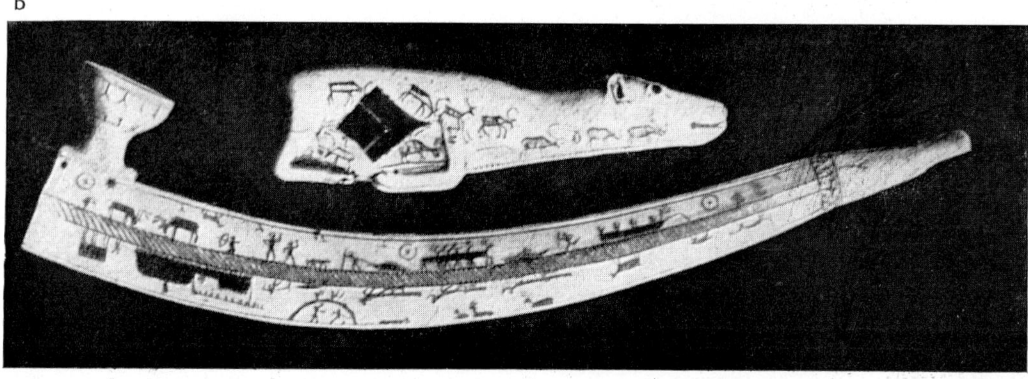

18. (A) Stone figure of late Huaxtec culture, found at Vera Cruz, Mexico. (American Museum of Natural History, New York). (B) Mayan Calendar. Text p. 63. Monolith in the ruins of Quiriga, Eastern Guatemala. Height, 11 ft. 2½ in. (C) Inner courtyard of palace and doorway at Mitla, the necropolis of the Zapotec kings, in the Mexican state of Oaxaca.

or the use of metals; they had only the most primitive huts, often nothing more than a wind-break; in New South Wales they even lived in caves. In circumstances very like those of the European Neolithic Age an art developed which in many respects resembled the art of Neolithic man, hovering on the verge between naturalism and stylization.

In 1839 Grey discovered paintings in the sandstone ranges along the Glenelg River. One of these (page 50), which loomed overhead on the roof of a cave, represents a human head, surrounded by a halo; a stiff yet eloquent representation, such as always appears at the end of a naturalistic epoch. The face is firmly outlined, the eyes and nose are represented by a single line; the mouth is lacking, as is so often the case in European Neolithic drawings. The reddish hair glimmers palely about the head, and the white spots represent pearls, or shells, or other adornments. Precisely because of this simplification, the figure, only faintly outlined, with fine red streaks on the body, has an impressive actuality, despite its remoteness from life. Further developments were to come.

Spencer and Gillen, in the Warramunga district of Central Australia, found ancient rock paintings consisting merely of circles and straight lines, in white and brown, the rock background being of a reddish colour. All these decorations had their meaning: the concentric rings indicated resting-places, and the connecting lines, as Strehlow was able to prove, represented tracks.

Figure with Kangaroo. Rock painting from North-West Australia (Grey)

Besides these prehistoric paintings, one finds in Australia, as well as among the Papuans in the interior of New Guinea, the Andaman islanders, and the many primitive tribes who must be regarded as the earliest immigrant population, an art of a totally different kind. It appeared wherever an even passing contact with Europeans gave rise to new experiences and resulted in a sudden rejuvenation, and forgetting of old traditions. The half-savage artist applied himself to his art with intense delight in the representation of life, and a surprising talent.

The Dutch explorers often spoke of the natives' incredible skill in drawing: given pencil and paper—things they had never seen before—they sketched animals or human beings with a firm and skilful touch, and with an accuracy which excited the greatest astonishment. A member of the 'Fly' expedition left a note-book behind in which they drew an astonishing caricature of the owner, complete with hat and tobacco-pipe.

The Australian Blackfellows are fond of depicting scenes with a number of figures; these are delightfully fresh in conception, and are often drawn on the most curious materials, if necessary even in sand. Slabs of smoke-blackened bark are

Head with rayed Halo in red and yellow. Painting on the roof of a cave on the Upper Glenelg

sometimes used (page 51) with the thumbnail serving as a pencil; on the inner side of opossum skins lines are scratched and filled in with fat and charcoal; rocks and the walls of caves are painted with clay, ochre and charcoal. On lonely islands in the ocean whole picture-galleries have been found, where generations of fishermen have occupied their leisure in covering smooth surfaces of rock with spacious pictures of men, birds, fishers, lizards, crabs, and beetles.

Melanesian Art

Sailing north-west from Australia, one comes to Melanesia, in many ways the most interesting region of Oceania, and the richest in works of art. Here we see the contrast between the Melanesian aborigines, dark-skinned and with crinkled or wavy hair, and those of Micronesia and Polynesia, light-skinned and with smooth or wavy hair, who during a long history have often intermarried with other races. Among the dark-skinned Papuan tribes (mainly inhabiting the interior of New Guinea and also the isolated islands to the north-west), and the Australian blackfellows we find signs of artistic progress in the long-established plastic representation of men and animals.

During the European Stone Age, favourable climatic conditions in Central and Southern Asia caused light brown or yellow-skinned peoples to evolve; as the so-called Old Malays came southwards in their great double boats, or catamarans, to the Archipelago, and from there made their way farther east, the cultural encounters thus caused resulted in great artistic productiveness. The shores of all the Melanesian islands, as well as of New Guinea itself, were largely overrun by the Malayan newcomers and an awakened people, with some knowledge of agriculture, though owing to the fertility of Nature they had little need to practise it, gave themselves up to a delight in artistic creation which found its expression in wood-carving of almost unsurpassed quality.

Every household utensil, every tool, every post, every flat surface in this region is decorated, and nowhere does primitive art seem to have flourished more luxuriantly. In New Caledonia the natives decorated their bamboo staves with incised drawings of, among other things, the richly decorated gable-ended huts of their chieftains, totemic animals, and the liveliest scenes of tribal life. Here a man is beating his wife; there hunters shoot their arrows; while other figures stand in rows or dawdle about, wearing the cylindrical straw hats which Captain Cook so well described.

Putting on one side the horrible 'modern' industrial productions of these islands, where European influence has almost destroyed the old techniques, one is often surprised by the number and variety of the objects, often connected with a definite craft or calling, which are produced with the poorest tools, such as stone chisels, coral rasps, shells or bones, and mineral pigments or vegetable juices. Differences of style, in various districts, are often strongly marked, changing with differing religious beliefs and observances. Belief in wood-demons and all sorts of spectres and hobgoblins leads to the strangest creations, effigies and frameworks in human form, covered with bark-cloth, and masks (Fig. 13b) which cannot have failed to impress the traveller. No less magical, and with a refined sense of proportion, are the numerous 'tapas' of painted bark-cloth (Fig. 16c), which are used instead of woven mats. Other images are ancestral figures, connected with the cult of the dead, such as the 'Uli', uncouth statues with great helmeted heads (Fig. 16b), small bodies and even smaller legs. On painted shields, as well (Fig. 13c), we see stylized ancestral figures; the 'Ship of the Dead', which we have seen in prehistoric European rock-paintings (Figs. 3b and 3c), and which sometimes appears in the rare rock-paintings, such as were found in a grotto on a small island off the western coast of New Guinea (page 54), derives from ancient Indonesian mythology.

These peoples, and this entire culture, spread from India through the island world in waves of migration, of which all record has perished. Recent research increasingly

Section of a Soot-drawing on Bark, the work of Australian Blackfellows
(Brough Smith)

emphasizes ancient Chinese influences on the art of this region; but the most decisive influence was certainly that of Indian sculpture, and the bird-motive, so often found in it, occurs in a thousand variations throughout the whole of Oceania. In the extreme west of New Guinea, where a Melanesian-Papuan element came into sharp collision with the Indonesian, the Melanesian art has an inexhaustible inventiveness and an irrepressible delight in decoration; one never ceases to marvel that black and naked cannibals should have produced this art which, with a vitality astonishing in this luxuriant tropical setting, created its little counterfeit worlds on a hundred islands, and yet, to the discriminating eye, is clearly distinct from the old Australian-Papuan art, as well as that of Micronesia and Polynesia.

Micronesia and Polynesia

Micronesia, and especially Polynesia, at first sight seem poor in art compared with the Melanesian area: contact with Europeans has resulted in the disappearance of many things, and only the relics preserved in museums—mostly statues, feather mantles, and other personal adornments—testify to the great artistic achievement of the past. These regions, like Melanesia, were an ancient Indian colony. The present inhabitants arrived by way of Indonesia, coming into contact with an older population, in many respects related to the Australians.

Repeated intermarriage with the races gave rise to a conception of the cosmos in which grotesque belief in magic, and worship of the sun and moon, exist side by side with ancient ancestor worship. Totemism, prevalent in Melanesia, is less so in Micronesia, while in Polynesia it seems hardly to exist. The social hierarchy is everywhere sharply defined, and is preserved even where the ancient culture has disappeared. Chiefs, freemen, and bondsmen are more clearly distinguished than in Melanesia, where they are often fellow-members of the secret societies. In Polynesia the chiefs were powerful almost to the point of being gods, and the conduct of the individual was prescribed by rigid convention. Wood and stone were the only materials known, until the Europeans introduced metal; though isolated words in the native language are a distant recollection of the metals of Insulindia, or even of the primeval Indian homeland.

Formerly, natural taste and sense of colour brought the manufacture of bark-cloth, and the crafts of plaiting and weaving, to a high degree of perfection. Owing to the great distances between the islands, the old Malayans, once they had left the Asiatic mainland, received no fresh stimuli without; during this long isolation from the rest of the world, very strongly marked differences in style developed in the art of individual islands. In the decoration of flat surfaces, the inhabitants of the Marquesas Islands, and above all the Maoris of New Zealand, show a much greater sense of order. This includes tattooing and articles of personal adornment. The word 'tattooing' comes from the native *tatau*, meaning, roughly, 'order'. As the leading principle in the organization of design, this constantly asserts itself; in Samoa it almost stifles all other artistic motives, in a wealth of arbitrary decoration.

Easter Island

One of the most remarkable and mysterious expressions of Polynesian culture is found on lonely Easter Island, on the eastern edge of Polynesia. The island was so named by a Dutch expedition under Admiral Roggeween, who landed there at Easter 1722. On this island—remarkable in more than one way—the Dutchmen found, to their great astonishment, innumerable gigantic stone figures (Fig. 14a), the largest of which was nearly seventy feet high. Over 550 such stone images were counted, almost all consisting only of enormous heads, without trunks or arms. Later expeditions which set out to visit Easter Island were unable to find it, so the mystery was increased. Various names were given to it as the ships came and went.

When in 1816 the poet Adalbert von Chamisso came to the island, on his voyage round the world on the *Rurik*, the natives prevented a landing. In 1862, however, they were conquered and enslaved, some being sold on other islands, and some doomed to labour on the Peruvian guano deposits. Since on this occasion their king and their priests perished, the inscriptions which were found on large wooden tablets were mostly indecipherable. Only from fragmentary traditions is anything known of the strange bird-worship which was practised here. Besides the king, there was elected every year, as among many other ancient peoples, a captain or war-lord, known here as Tangata-Manu, or the 'Bird-Man'. To secure the fittest man for this office, it was the custom for a number of picked men, at the beginning of July, while the people watched from the shore, to try to fetch a sea-swallow's egg from a neighbouring crag, the sea-swallow being regarded as a lucky bird. This required an extremely powerful swimmer, who alone could survive in those dangerous waters, and the attempt was rarely made without loss of life. The first one to bring an unbroken egg ashore was elected leader of the people. Unlike the king, he wore his hair closely shorn, and for a year lived in a cave especially prepared for him, where he was waited on by the people. Such figures as those in Fig. 14e refer to this cult, while others (Fig. 14b) have carvings on their backs which show that an unique hero-cult was practised on this island.

Nevertheless, one can hardly call Easter Island an inexplicable curiosity, for it fits into the general survey of Polynesian art and culture. The volcanic island is almost entirely bare of trees, and the colour of the red tufa, and the ease with which it can be worked, must have appealed to the artistic faculties of the people, leading them to make ever larger and larger images. Easter Island is thus a good example of the way in which material and environment can produce a special kind of art. The Melanesians often finish their carvings in a few hours, in order to paint them in bright colours for some festival; but Polynesian idols are of durable wood, and those of the Maoris are true works of art (Figs. 13a and 15). Those of the ancient inhabitants of Easter Island seem to have been made to last for eternity, on this forgotten corner of the globe; these stone figures are unique and expressive works of art, comparable with the prehistoric monuments, the dolmens and menhirs, of Europe. They have always been regarded with astonishment and wonder, since they are far superior to the simple stone monuments of Tahiti and the other South Sea islands.

Research has also solved their greatest secret, that of the writing on the 'speaking boards' (found at first singly, then in greater numbers), as consisting of pictorial signs and symbols whose significance is linked with the general scheme of Polynesian culture.

The Ship of the Dead
Rock-picture in a cave on a small island just off the west coast of New Guinea

It was long believed that even the Maoris were ignorant of the art of writing, until the Treaty of Vaitagi, which the Maori chiefs concluded with England, showed that the

Specimen of script on a 'Speaking Board' from Easter Island

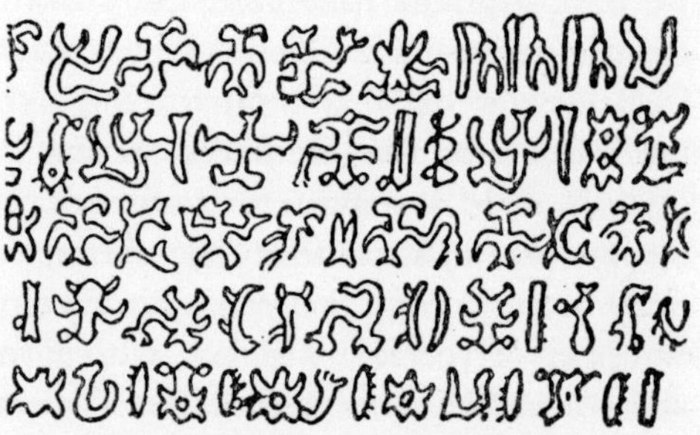

Signatures of two Maori chiefs to the Treaty of Vaitagi

native New Zealanders had written characters of their own. These characters have inherited something from ancient India, and perhaps from the very first writing of the human race, as we may see by comparing the two illustrations above with the oldest seal-impressions from the valley of the Indus (Figs. 26b and 26c).

Chapter V

AMERINDIAN ART

*

America had its own art and culture long before it was discovered by Europeans; this, one of the many mysteries of what was truly a 'New World', led to many misunderstandings.

The native Americans are still called 'Indians', for the original error of their discoverer, who believed that he had landed in India, is perpetuated in many languages. In German, at least, there is a difference between *Inder* and *Indianer*, but in French and in English the same word is used for the natives of Hindustan and the aborigines of America, so that to avoid confusion one speaks, paradoxically, of an American Indian.

Much the same thing happened when the Spaniards, sailing from the Antilles to the mainland, and coming to the great peninsula which lies between the Gulf of Mexico and the Caribbean Sea, asked the natives what the country was called. They replied, in their own language, 'I cannot understand you', which sounded to the Spaniards like 'Yucatan'; and this sentence is still preserved, and the name of the peninsula is like a symbol of eternal misunderstanding.

When, at the beginning of the sixteenth century, the white explorers, shortly after Columbus had landed on the Bahaman islands of Guananani, penetrated into the mainland, in Yucatan and elsewhere, they found the New World in a condition not unlike that of Europe at the time of the migration of the peoples. Alongside great and highly developed Empires, comparable with Rome and Byzantium, were a number of younger and less settled peoples, some no more than savages. On the other hand, the conquerors found a peculiar civilization, with a network of highways such as they had not previously seen anywhere else, with its gigantic buildings, pyramids like those of the Nile valley, and a wealth of finely-wrought vessels and ornaments of gold and silver.

The differences between the ancient civilization of Mexico and Peru, and those of the rest of North and South America, have led to the belief that the American Indians could not all have had the same origin; but more recent research shows plainly that all Amerindian art and mythology has a common Asiatic source. Hence the term 'Red-skin'[1], found in most European languages, is no less inappropriate than 'Indian'.

[1] It is possible that the term is not derived from the painting of the face, as some authors have suggested, but from the fact that the Spanish explorers spoke in their reports of *hombres colorados*, or *gente colorada*. Foreign translators, consulting their dictionaries, found that in Spanish the colour *red* is called *rojo*, but also, as the most vivid colour, *colorada;* overlooking the fact that *colorada* more commonly means 'coloured', and that the old explorers were simply speaking of 'coloured people'.

Actually, the American Indians, like all peoples of Mongolian descent, have a complexion containing no red, but ranging from the lightest to the darkest brown; they show, as well, other easily recognizable Mongolian characteristics—prominent cheekbones, straight black hair, and a scanty growth of beard.

They must have come from north-eastern Asia, across the Bering Strait, which was once probably dry land. It seems fairly certain that these Asiatics, the first real discoverers of America, had not progressed beyond the culture of the Stone Age at the time of their arrival in the New World. They knew nothing of agriculture, nor of keeping flocks and herds; drinking milk, grinding meal by means of querns or millstones, the use of the wheel—in, for example, vehicles or the making of pottery—were quite unknown. These discoveries were made in the Old World long after the close of the Stone Age; the immigrants would have brought them to their new home if they had not left Asia earlier. Today, the general opinion of American research is that the first immigrants came from Asia at a very early period, followed by many other migrations, until finally, perhaps about 3000 B. C., a sedentary culture evolved in the favourable climate of Central Mexico. Though it may have been a long time before Tierra del Fuego was reached, and the newcomers settled in South America, it is none the less clear that Amerindian culture was a spontaneous growth on American soil.

The Eskimo

The Eskimo, like the other Arctic peoples—Lapps and Samoyeds, Yakuts, Koryaks and Greenlanders—still maintain the ancient connection between North America and Asia. These peoples live under the most difficult conditions. In Arctic North America, where the March temperature falls as low as 36^0 C. below zero, both fauna and flora are very like those of the Ice Age. Agriculture is impossible, and they live like the men of the Palaeolithic Age, wandering in deserts of ice and snow, without metals, without flocks, and without pottery. Except for a few inland tribes, the Eskimo are a coastal population, scattered across the whole of the Arctic region of America, on the mainland as well as on the islands, and on both coasts of Greenland. Formerly only their southernmost outposts, in Alaska, reached the northern limit of the trees. Thus, for the purposes of art, wood is almost entirely excluded, for such pieces of driftwood as they find are used for making things which could not be made without it—weapons, boats, sledges, etc.

Leather and bone are materials of which the great land and sea mammals yield unlimited quantities, and Eskimo art consists, above all, of fine carvings and engravings on walrus ivory (Fig. 17b). These show a considerable facility for drawing, but little feeling for decoration—as in the art of the Ice Age. The figures, represented with the greatest verisimilitude, are usually shown hunting, fishing, and sledging. Bone carvings of the human figure are found, even among tribes living under the most unfavourable natural conditions, especially in Alaska. These, too, are comparable with European productions of the Palaeolithic Age.

Indians of the Forest and Prairie

The nearest relatives of the Eskimo are the inhabitants of the great forest region of the north and north-west. This once stretched from the Upper Yukon, across the basin of the Mackenzie and the Canadian lake district, to the Atlantic coast, and was inhabited mainly by Athabascan and Algonquin Indians, with a sprinkling of Iroquois and Hurons, who came from the country about the lower Ohio and the Mississippi, and possessed a somewhat higher culture, for the regions between the Ohio and Florida formerly belonged to the various families of the Sioux, whose forefathers erected the great earthern structures, the 'Mounds', found in these parts, and who have left evidences of a fully developed agriculture, permanent settlements, and other signs of a higher social life. The art of these south-eastern Indians took the form, especially, of pottery and textiles; their plaques of copper repoussé, figured vases, and other objects, obviously derive from the high civilizations of Central America, while their silver ornaments are influenced by European models.

The art and culture of the prairie Indians who form the background of the nineteenth century 'Wild West' stories, are a comparatively late phenomenon: the introduction of the horse, of which the Indians were originally quite ignorant—their only domestic animal of any size was the dog, and in South America the llama—turned the inhabitants of the prairies into nomads.

Over the whole of this enormous area, especially the south-west of the United States—New Mexico, Arizona, Colorado, Utah, Nevada, and California—are found numerous picture-writings of the Plains Indians, mostly on gigantic blocks of stone forming part of the detritus of the Ice Age, which give one instructive glimpses not only of the mental world of the Indians, but also of the earliest art of a hunting people in the first days of their culture.

These pictures are scratched in the rock and filled in with black, white, red and yellow pigments: the black being obtained from a mixture of soot and clay, the red and yellow from ferruginous minerals, and the white from infusorial earth. The fat, employed as a medium, was got from beaver's tails or the hooves of the antelope. Here again we have a method used in the Ice Age. The art of the forest and prairie Indians as a whole—their weaving, pottery, and carving in wood, bone, horn and stone—can be described briefly, since the lines it follows are already familiar to the reader.

Special mention must be made of the tobacco-pipes, the 'pipe of peace' which is mentioned in so many tales of Indian life. This is found among all the prairie tribes, usually in a simple form; only rarely is the bowl inlaid with lead or tin, or the stem decorated with carvings. The earthenware pipes of the Iroquois are usually trumpet-shaped, while the bowl is sometimes decorated with a human or animal head, and sometimes shaped like a human figure, with the face turned toward the smoker.

In their extensive use of birchbark and of the hair or bristles of different animals in weaving, we rarely find anything beyond technical dexterity. The ancient colour, in so far as colour is still used in Indian art, has been replaced by crude aniline dyes;

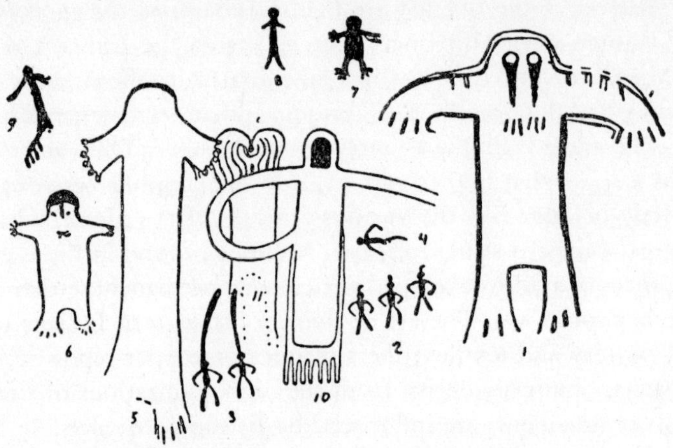

Rock-painting of Algonquin Indians on an erratic block of granite near South Fork, Tulare River, California

1: God, with traces of tears. His arms end in drooping fingers, the Indian sign for rain. The streaks running down to the breast from the eyes have the same meaning, i.e. tears. 2, 3 and 4: Persons of different ranks, denoted by the different height of the head-dress. No. 4 is already dead of starvation, and is therefore shown prostrate. 5, 6, 7, 8 and 9 are making the sign of denial, one or both hands being held out, empty. 10 says, with his right hand, 'I myself', while the left indicates the direction in which the person concerned set out. 11. Incomplete, and can hardly be interpreted. The whole painting is about sixteen feet wide and eight feet high.

just as the modern Indian beadwork, in which glass beads are used, merely imitates the old forms, and by no means replaces the ornaments which they once applied to the skin side of their buffalo cloaks, or to shields, moccasins, or other articles of clothing. The present-day creations of the North American Indians are industrial products, revealing modern influences, and are not comparable with the still vital and original creations of the Negroes. What the Indians produce for the alien industrialist, and for European and American collectors, is not the business of the art-historian. It is barely the shadow of the richly imaginative past, of which the men of today have no understanding; living in the State of Minnesota, they forget that originally this name meant 'the heavenly-hued water', while Idaho meant 'a light above the mountains'—a light which has long been extinguished for the Indians of North America.

The Indian Art of North-West America

In the long and narrow region inhabited by the north-western tribes, which runs from the south of Alaska to the North American state of Oregon, we do not find a primitive art, but, in this region of secret societies and totems, a phase of development which had reached a particular degree of richness when Captain Cook and George Vancouver reached this coast towards the end of the eighteenth century. To understand this art we must discard all our notions of the befeathered Indians of the plains, for a very different people inhabits this region of fjords, islands and mountains, with shadowy forests and waters. Thanks to unending conflict with animals, to hunting, and fishing from the rocking canoe, these tribes preserved their vitality longer than did their brothers of the eastern plains. Their faith in magic and totemism arose out of their contact with Nature, with the ocean, with its beauties, wonders and perils, and their struggle against great extremes of temperature.

In this setting such imaginative peoples as the Tlinkit and Haida Indians evolved an individual art, expressed in drawings and decorative patterns, in stylized and realistic sculptures, and finally, in architecture; its special character is due to the perfection of its decorative motives, which are the basis of all Indian art. In the Haida leathern cuirass (Fig. 17a) one is impressed by the peculiar eye-shaped motives, and closer examination reveals a beaver, represented twice in profile, looking right and left, and between the two heads, with characteristic incisors, is a cylindrical chieftain's hat. The broad tail, thrown backwards over the body, reveals its scaly texture in decorative detail, and an oval formation at its root contains a human face. On either side of the upper half of the tail one sees, inside the rectangular outline of the body, two ravens' heads, and, at the feet, rounded forms which now represent, not eyes, but joints, a formal element frequent in Haida art. Since the eyes themselves usually have eyelids, they are not difficult to distinguish. In this decoration we see the Indian's delight in representing the internal structure of men and beasts, a characteristic of all Indian art. Thus, transparent figures often occur, which show the heart and other important organs.

Knowledge of this decorative art helps us to understand the rich, three-dimensional carvings and totemism of these Indians, as well as the nature of their secret societies, the significance of their wooden masks and ancestral figures, which are often very fine, and, finally, their great timber houses. These latter are richly decorated and supported on piles, with massive gable-ends, before which they set up their brightly-coloured totem-poles, bearing images of their ancestors. The builders of these houses are the only North American Indians to use sculpture in their architecture. Their carvings are as distinctive, in the plastic art of the Indians, as the famous Chillat blankets in the textile art. As to metals, silver was used for ornaments, while the native copper, found in Southern Alaska, was made into richly ornamented plaques, used as a form of currency.

The Hopi and Pueblo Indians

Totem-pole of Haida Indians

In the south, in the wide borderland between the United States and Mexico, is the ancient, but still remarkably vigorous culture of the Indian tribes, mostly settled in Arizona and New Mexico, but who have also penetrated some way into Mexico itself. These tribes, known in Europe as the Hopi and Pueblo Indians, have lived there for over two thousand years, and have gradually evolved an urban culture, with many-storied fortresses in which whole tribes can live, and many circular buildings. In the fourteenth and fifteenth centuries this culture was at ist height, with extensive irrigation systems, fine pottery, and an astonishing variety of woven and plaited fabrics.

Since Douglass's introduction of the *tree-ring calendar* we have been able to date the productions of these peoples fairly exactly. The principle of this calendar is as follows: Ancient conifers (Californian redwood, *Sequoia sempervivens* or *gigantea*) were sawn through, and the annual rings thus revealed were found to agree exactly. Since even living trees go back beyond the Christian era, this ingenious method provides an excellent way of dating ancient works of art; for in accordance with the degree of rainfall—which is remarkably uniform over all this area—the annual rings varied in thickness. So we now know that pottery first appeared in the Pueblo country in the fourth century A.D., and from this we can draw further conclusions. With the help of the hieroglyphic records of the Aztecs, the Mayan chronology, and other results of excavations in South America, we are now able to arrive at an increasingly accurate chronology of American antiquities; today we can indicate the century, and often the decade, in which an event took place, or a work of art was made, whereas earlier we had to be content with guesses, which were often only accurate to within five hundred years.

The Art of Ancient Mexico

Mexico, the thoroughfare between the northern and southern cultures, was itself bound to be the home of a number of important cultures. These influenced the barbaric tribes which wandered into the country across the plains, or dwelt in the primeval forests. An Indian Pompeii, caused by the eruption of the Volcano Ajurco, not far from Mexico City, has preserved a very early phase of the archaic culture, such as one finds from El Salvador to Vera Cruz, which, with its jade images, merges into the nameless and buried cultures that arose in Guatemala as well as in south-eastern Mexico.

Here the most brilliant age of Central America flourished, which culminated in the valley of Mexico, in the great city of Teotihuacan, and farther south in the cities of the 'Old Empire' of the Mayas. This period was marked by the invention of writing. This culture must be regarded as the result of the foundation of great empires or federations of cities, enduring for centuries: it has left traces in its temples, palaces, playing grounds, tombs, urns, idols, ceremonial masks, wall-paintings, hieroglyphics, rich decorative work in every possible material, and magnificant pottery. We do not know why it declined even before the European invasion. There may have been war, or a change of climate, or the soil may not have been able to nourish an increasing population; but there is no doubt that the legendary Toltec empire, and the civilization which arose in Yucatan, in the 'New Empire' of the Mayas, was only the twilight of older civilizations. Once again the historical pattern was repeated;

Page from the Aztec hieroglyphic manuscript, Codex vaticanus B. The god of the planet Venus is hurling a spear at the king's throne. Round the inner margin are Aztec ciphers

new peoples invading an ancient culture and installing themselves as its masters. In this case they were the Aztecs, a small but vigorous race of hunters from the north. For just under two hundred years they were the ruling power between the two oceans; from the time of the foundation of the capital city of Tenochtitlan, now Mexico City, in 1324, to their surrender to the Spaniards in 1521.

Aztec art was certainly influenced by the tribes who preceded them; but their warlike nature added to the old conceptions a savagery quite new in Central America art. They used the ancient forms to express the terror of death, and an appalling cruelty; the eternal tragedy of the world, in which life becomes death, has nowhere been expressed in so inevitable and brutal yet magnificent a way as in Aztec art. Their pyramids were not sepulchral monuments, like those of the Egyptians, but slaughter-houses, sacrificial altars from which flowed rivers of human blood.

Aztec picture-writing (Aubin collection).
To the left of the blossoming tree, whose trunk is broken through (the symbol of the original home of the peoples) is the serpent-headed Earth goddess; to the right, the figure of Itzpapalotl, the Obsidian-butterfly

In central or South America the stepped pyramid was generally made of bricks of sun-dried clay, or in any case it was encased in such bricks. But we need not suspect Egyptian influences, or other fantastic relations. For in ages which knew little of mechanics the inclined plane was the only means of raising heavy burdens, and all over the world men hit upon the same or very similar solutions. Something more will be said of Indian pyramids in the section dealing with South American art.

The hieroglyphic books of the Aztecs, some of which are left, in spite of the Conquistadors' iconoclastic zeal, were actual books, with pages of deerskin or of agave fibre, with a thin coating of lime, doubled and folded. Most of the manuscripts are religious and magical, with many forms of the calendar, which contain the cosmic order, the prophecies, and the innumerable gods of the ancient Mexicans; but there are also lists of tributary payments, registers of landed property, and other more practical informations.

As well as the Aztecs, we have fairly exact knowledge of the Mixtecs and the Zapotecs; for in the valley of Oaxaca, the war between the Mixtecs, whose culture was related to that of the valley of Mexico, and the Zapotecs, who had cultural connections with the south, had gone on for many centuries, and the Conquistadors found these peoples still engrossed in their traditional feud. The Mixtecs had a more refined culture, which is evident in all their relics; goldsmiths' work, carvings in wood and bone, hieroglyphic manuscripts, and fine, many-coloured pottery. The Zapotecs were decidedly inferior, though even their ancient images are better than the late, decadent creations of Mayan art (under Aztec influence) found in the ruins of Cintla. Comparison of Fig. 18a and the figure on page 63 makes this very evident.

The greatest achievements of the Zapotecs were architectural: the cities of Monte Alban and Mitla show great originality of conception and equal ability in execution. The Zapotecs were more engrossed with the idea of survival after death than any other ancient American people. This interest was expressed in countless tombs and mausoleums, many of which (Fig. 18c) are of such stupendous size that they have no parallel on American soil.

Indian figure from Cerro de los Idolos in the ruins of Cintla in the State of Tabasco

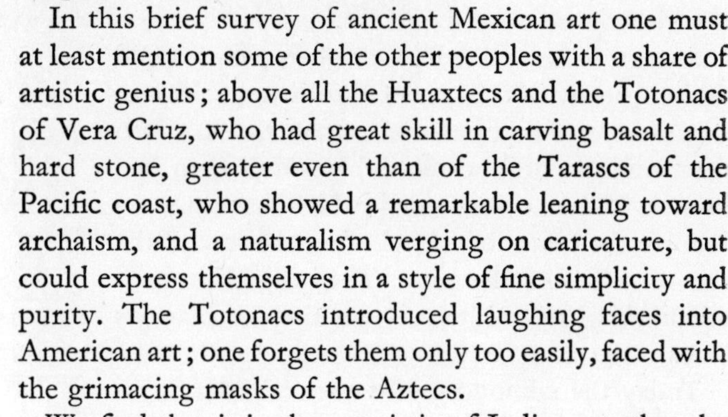

In this brief survey of ancient Mexican art one must at least mention some of the other peoples with a share of artistic genius; above all the Huaxtecs and the Totonacs of Vera Cruz, who had great skill in carving basalt and hard stone, greater even than of the Tarascs of the Pacific coast, who showed a remarkable leaning toward archaism, and a naturalism verging on caricature, but could express themselves in a style of fine simplicity and purity. The Totonacs introduced laughing faces into American art; one forgets them only too easily, faced with the grimacing masks of the Aztecs.

We find that it is characteristic of Indian art, that the details are always naturalistic, even when the whole work is inspired by a conception of quite another kind. Wherever a mythical being is represented, his various parts are reproduced with almost photographic exactitude. Eventually, however, every motive was translated into a decorative form. This is the fundamental form of expression, and the decorative technique is one of rhythmical repetition: one finds not only a striving for symmetry and balance, but also the urge to cover every available surface with ornament. Not until the period of decadence did this die out. Then religious feeling congealed into a hieratic pose; everything was overwhelmed by detail, and the passion for filling every empty space resulted in overcrowding. This is obvious in the later 'colonial' style, and in popular art, where European influence did not have much effect.

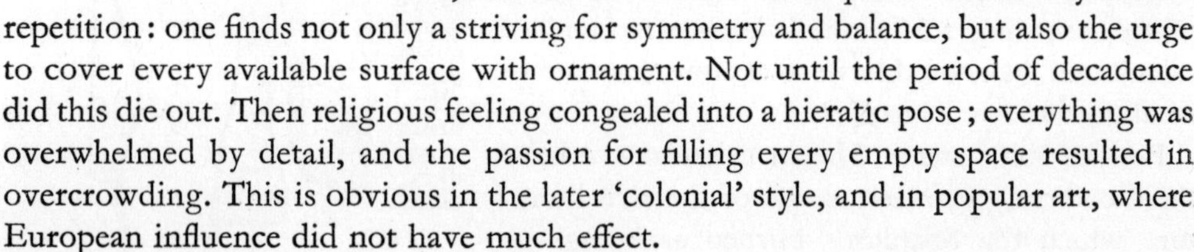

The Art of the Maya Peoples

In southern Mexico, and farther south, in what are now Guatemala and Honduras, and as far down as San Salvador, even before the Christian era, were the Chorti, Cholti and Tzental peoples, speaking three closely related idioms. Not only the ruins of huge cities, but also the steles, the Mayan calendars (which were often a considerable height (Fig. 18b), and bore, as well as two faces looking east and west, a wealth of ornament on head and chest) tell us, in the hieroglyphs with which they are covered, that in this area, until about the eighth century A.D., existed a highly individual civilization. Copan, Palenque and Tikal were the three most important cities of the 'Old Empire' of the Mayas. There was constant, unhindered intercourse between all parts of the country; this is proved by the uniformity of art and architecture, in which Amerindian civilization perhaps reached its height.

Some time before A.D. 1000 there was a rapid decline; many of the cities fell to invading forces and most of the population retreated north into the peninsula of Yucatan, which until then had been a Mayan colony, and which was now to become the centre of a kind of renaissance of the art of the Old Empire. The calendars conscientiously record the foundation of various cities.

Today the complicated Mayan calendar is no longer a mystery and its only difficulty is its correlation with the European calendar. This can be done by relating it to the rest of American chronology, as shown by the tree-ring calendar and by geological research. The best estimate is that of Thompson and Teeple, according to which the Maya date 11 — 16 — 0 — 0 — 0, 13 Ahau 8 Uo,[1] fell on the 3 November, 1539, while according to Spinder's earlier method of calculation we should have to assume this date to be almost 260 years earlier.

Besides this ancient Mayan calendar we have three codices, pitiful remnants of the rich literature which the Spaniards burned as being the work of the devil. The hieroglyphs here, unlike those on the stone steles, have the cursive character of handwriting, and it is clear that the Aztec symbols (page 61) are clumsy derivations of them. Thus, with the Aztecs the numerals are indicated by dots alone, while the Mayas used strokes as well, one of which sometimes stood for five dots. Centuries before the Chinese, they had

Male Mayan figure on a stele at Tzendales. The series of hieroglyphs on the left gives the Mayan date 9 — 13 — 0 — 0 — 0, 8 Ahau 8 Uo

[1] That is, a day which lies 11 cycles of 400 years and 16 cycles of 20 years after the beginning of the Mayan chronology, and which bears the calendarial signature 13 Ahau 8 Uo.

19. Front of the 'Temple of the Warrior', at Chichen-Itza, in Yucatan, the ancient Indian city founded by the Mayas and afterwards conquered by the Toltecs.

20. (A) Zapotec figure with fish symbol in the right hand. Funerary urn from Zaachila, in the Mexican State of Oaxaca. (University Museum, Philadelphia).
(B) Earthenware vessel from Azcapotzalko, Mexico. Relief produced by scratching away intervening material. (Natural History Museum, Vienna).
(C) Three-legged earthenware bowl of the Cholula culture, painted mainly in red and black. Imported into the Mixtec country and found at Nochiztlan. Oaxaca.

21. Earthenware vessels, Chimu. (A) Jug, early style, with a mythological scene painted in black on a whitish ground. (Musée de Trocadéro. Paris).
(B and C). Heads of the mature style: (b) with handle, (c) without handle, entirely 'in the round'. (Gaffron Collection, Berlin).

a

b

c

22. (A) Head of a great stone statue, from Tiahuanaco. Relief modelling, with incised details. Height, 5 ft. (National Museum, La Paz).
(B) Blackish-grey amphory in pure Inca style. Height, 9½ in. (Zürich University).
(C) View of the Inca fortress of Machu Picchu in the Cuzco highlands.

even a special sign for zero, in the form of an empty mussel-shell, and they established the positional value of numerals by means of an elaborate ventigesimal arithmetic, in which the moon stood for twenty. Although many of the Mayan manuscripts are lost, a few Spanish translations were saved, which give us a rough outline of the events of more than fourteen centuries.

Maya hieroglyphs in the form of cursive handwriting. (Seler)

From these, and from archaeological discoveries, we know something of the early period of the Old Empire of the Mayas; of the time of transition, when the city of Piedras Negras was founded; and of the culminating period when the greatest progress was made in sculpture and architecture; and also something of the New Empire, when the most important cities in Yucatan—Chichen-Itza, Uxmal and Mayapan—formed a triple alliance, under which the country for two hundred years experienced a sort of renaissance, although its art was more grotesque than that of the Old Empire.

On the figure on page 66 we see the mantle of the Mayas. Like a coat, as a rule it was thrown over the shoulders and covered the whole body, though sometimes it was gathered up round the hips, so that the ends hung over the arms. Such mantles, with rich fringes, are still worn by the Mayan women. Similar figures occur also in Yaxchilan, and even on various steles in Piedras Negras, suggesting a connection with the old culture.

At first the Mayas expressed themselves in sculpture and ceramics, but in their best period architecture predominated. The connection between architect and sculptor must have been very close, for some buildings are nothing more than enormous masses of sculpture. From the sixth century onwards the Mayas gradually attained complete mastery of their material and as stone-cutters they achieved extraordinary technical triumphs. Like the Egyptians, they rarely produced free, three-dimensional figures, preferring sculpture in high relief. The relief became and remained the principal form, and even when a sculptor did produce a figure in the round, it was obviously conceived as a relief.

Originally all the figures were painted; though now this colour has mostly disappeared, one can see that it must have greatly reduced the impression of profuse over-ornamentation given by the bare stone. The tranquillity of Mayan art influenced their neighbours, the Huaxtecs, and inspired works of art (Fig. 18a), the humanity of which, even in the remoter regions affected by this influence, was entirely different from the frantic savagery of Aztec art.

Kneeling figure of Mayan woman, richly clad, holding a sacrificial vessel. Stone relief from Yaxchilan, in the Mexican State of Chiapas

Much of the charm of Mayan sculpture and paintings is due to the surprising dexterity with which they dealt with perspective. They show a refined feeling for the abstract quality of line, which may be seen also in the later frescoes preserved in Tulum and Chichen-Itza (below). Our present knowledge of earlier Mayan paintings is confined to those applied to ceramics, where the potters felt themselves restricted to traditional, religious motives, though not so strictly as the artists who illuminated the manuscripts.

When we consider such Mayan art, and above all such architecture as has survived, we see how far the Amerindians were removed from all that we imply by the word 'primitive'. In architecture they had progressed as far as the vault or dome, built of overlapping stones. Independently of any Old World influence, they had developed the pillar, which we find at Chacmultun in Yucatan, not merely as a wall decoration, but as a free-standing, supporting column with a well-developed capital. In the illustration on page 67 we see them coupled, and in the eastern wing of the palace at Labna, as at Chichen-Itza (Fig. 19), single. The art of the Yucatan peninsula is not the best produced by this Indian people, but only the echo of an art and culture destroyed and concealed by time and the encroaching jungle.

Recent excavations by archaeologists from the United States, using aeroplanes which make possible a more comprehensive survey and enable tools and provisions to be carried to the most out-of-the-way places, give reason to hope that before long new treasures of Mayan art may be brought to light.

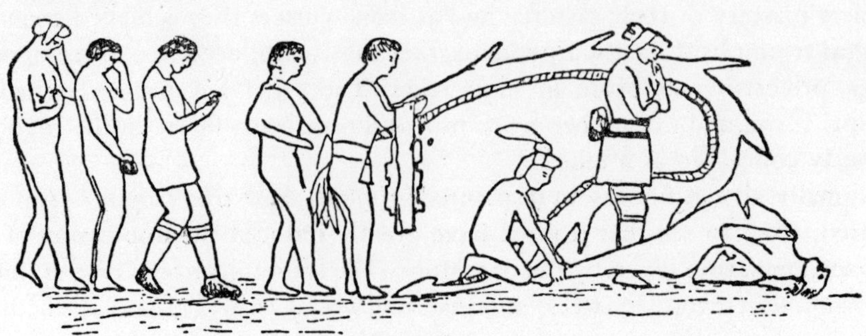

Sacrifice.
From the frescoes in the Temple of the Jaguars, Chichen-Itza, Yucatan

Between the culture of the Mayas and the second great achievement of the Indians, that of Peru, is the isthmus of Panama, leading to the gold-bearing lands of the south and growing ever narrower towards the south and east. In this country, still not properly explored, which was the home of an ancient civilized people, the Chorotegs, the two continents bartered their products. Among the finds at Chiriqui are gold images of eagles (made by the *cire perdue* process), which were worn on the breast. These suggest the art of the ancient people of Columbia: the Quimbaya, in particular, produced ornaments and trinkets of beaten, as well as cast, gold. Today they are the pride of many museums, though their magnificence is dimmed for us by regret, when we think how much this metal was to contribute to the extermination of the great and original culture of the countries of the South American Andes.

Pillars of Mayan architecture. Ruins of Labna, North Yucatan

The Empire of the Chimu

As the Aztecs were merely *epigoni*, who took over an older culture which they did not altogether understand, so the great Inca empire in Peru—most fascinating of all to European imaginations—superseded an ancient Indian culture whose artistic productions can be dated about a thousand years earlier. These people lived along the various watercourses which run down from the Andes to the Pacific. In these fertile valleys, in a coastal region of sand and shifting dunes, there arose, at the beginning of our Christian era, flourishing cities where were produced works of art which are among the highest achievements of the American Indians.

These included the magnificent portrait heads from the valley of Chicama, and the earthenware vessels which, though they have not yet emerged from archaic confusion, represent, in clear line drawing, scenes from the mythology and the solar and lunar beliefs of these people, and from which we can draw fresh conclusions as to their evolution. They record the history of a thousand years of artistic development which culminated in the empire of the Incas.

These vases were shaped by hand, not on the potter's wheel, out of reddish or black clay; this was covered with a thin coat of another colour, generally whitish, through which the design was traced in thin lines of reddish or blackish brown. We can distinguish three styles in the art of the Chimu; an early one, in which simple forms were filled with richly imaginative and fantastic motives (Fig. 21a); a mature one, beginning about A. D. 500, to which most of the heads belong (Figs. 21b and 21c); and finally, a late style, degenerating into the empty and playful.

In early Chimu art we find various fundamental elements which determined the imaginative world of the Indians and influenced all their artistic activities; above all, symbols which we can only understand if we know something of their religious significance. In the hieroglyphic books of the Aztecs and Mayas they are obscured by the ideas of the highly-developed priesthood; and many symbols later bore definite political and religious significance, and are often difficult to identify. In the early productions of the Chimu, however, they appear plainly, as until the fifteenth century A. D. they were faithful to the worship of the moon, which in most parts of the world preceded a solar religion. Thus we find the dog symbolizing the moon, as it did among the Tlinkit and Haida peoples; the serpent, as in Mexico, has to do with the interior of the earth which the Maya knew as Votan—a word reminiscent of the original significance of Wotan in Germanic mythology. At the same time, in Chimu art we often find a goddess in the form of a snail, or with shell-like armour; and in Mayan art she appears as an old Moon-goddess, sitting, humiliated before a young and victorious Sun-god.

Water-bearer. Old Peruvian earthenware figure from Pachacamac. Height, 8 inches

The primitive lunar cult of the Indians was soon accompanied in this dry region by worship of water and the ocean, to which these people, who were fishermen as well as farmers, owed much of their food. The longing for life-giving water, for fertility, runs through the whole Chimu mythology. They created vast irrigation systems, the most famous of which are in the valley of Nepena, where the Chimu made reservoirs in the rocky cliffs, more than 1,000 yards long, and fed by channels running as far as twelve miles into the hills. By the simplest technical means, masterpieces of engineering were created, which not only led water to the parts of the valley where it was wanted, but also provided enormous agricultural terraces with the necessary irrigation, the supply being exactly regulated by a system of channels and sluices.

In the Chimu empire, which extended, at its greatest, over the whole northern coast of Peru from the Gulf of Guayaquil to the frontier stronghold of Paramonga on the Rio Pativilea, a large population was crowded into comparatively few fertile coastal valleys, and imposing cities were built, consisting of enclosed tribal settlements. The capital city of Chan-Chan, near Trujillo, had more than 200,000 inhabitants, and the remains of its houses, streets, squares, aqueducts, palaces and pyramids cover an area of nearly six square miles.

The Indian pyramids, unlike the Egyptian, do not aim at perfect symmetry, the ground-plan being, in many cases, not a square, but a rectangular parallelogram (below). A height of 200 to 220 feet, and a width of 600 to 700 feet, are not unusual in the numerous pyramids of the Chimu; while among the less plentiful buildings in Old Mexico the pyramids of Cholula have bases nearly 1,700 feet long, longer than the largest pyramids of the Nile valley. When these pyramids were temples they usually had, both in South and Central America, a flight of stairs leading to the platform at the top, where the sacrificial altar was placed. There are also great fortresses built in terraced form, and castles, on whose stepped terraces verandahs were built, supported by the twisted trunks of the algaroba tree; rooms, with doorways hung with heavy curtains, led off these shady corridors.

Representation of a Verandah on a jug shaped like a stepped Pyramid (Chimu)

There was a time when these Indian cities were beautiful, with green parks and gardens setting off the triangular pyramids and the severe rectangular masses of the palaces. The walls of sun-dried brick, coated with white cement, were decorated in the same lively style as many of the Chimu painted vases. Other walls were more thickly coated with cement, and these displayed—as in the Chimu capital, and in the Hall of the Reliefs in the palace at Mitla (Fig. 18c)—geometrical arabesque, moons, draught-board and rhomboid patterns, modelled in the stucco, as well as the heads of snakes in a rhythmical repetition by no means monotonous or mechanical, since it was nourished by a live faith. The decorative patterns on buildings or vases often change suddenly from geometrical forms, and even form leaves and flowers, into animal heads; this is not surprising, since with these peoples abstraction and realism were not irreconcilable, but merged into each other as a matter of course. The Indians did not see the mystery of life in organic from alone. They felt that it was just as much inherent in geometrical structures; these, whether the crystals of a snowflake, or the orbits of the planets, or the pattern on the back of a snake, were all designed by Nature.

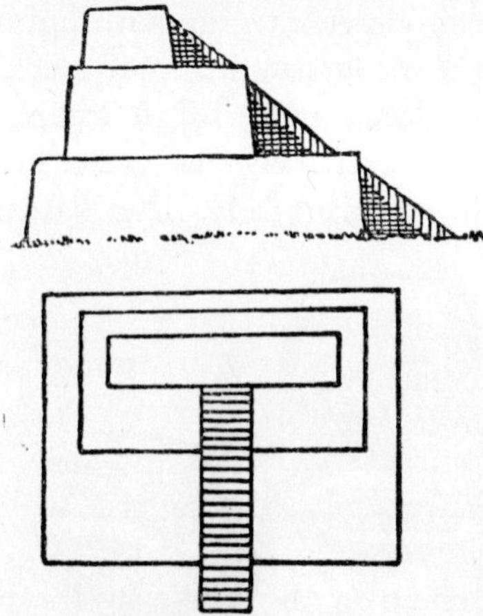

The Pyramid of Etén

While Chimu art, in the north, was able to evolve, unspoilt and uninterrupted, elsewhere it was affected to some extent by outside influences; for more than a thousand years where, along the central Peruvian coast, great temples were erected round Pachacamac, near the modern Peruvian capital, Lima; and farther south, in the neighbourhood of Ica and Nazca, where the Chimu came into contact with the highland tribes.

In Pachacamac, under the influence of religion, and a largely hieratic government, rigidly stylized and exaggerated forms developed, which were at their best in the seventh and eighth centuries; these were influenced by the art of Tiahuanaco, in the Peruvian highlands—which we must later consider more closely—for since this developed at the point where the South American Andes are easiest to cross, it naturally had a strong influence on the art of the coast.

The Art of Nazca

Near Ica and Nazca, in the valleys of the Chincha, Pisco, and Rio Grande, the people of the coast came in contact with more warlike tribes. This contact produced a certain savagery, reminiscent of the greater change which took place in Aztec art. On the many earthenware vessels which have been found, mostly as funerary gifts, are demoniacal creatures, in which the figures of Chimu art are recognizable, inspired by a new imagination.

While the northern artists conceived their sculpture above all in plastic terms, the facial urns found at Nazca represent only the nose in relief; the rest of the face is drawn on the vessel. The decorations are painted in vivid colours. The southern Indians were daring colourists, loving colour for its own sake and using it in the boldest combinations; orange-red with reddish-violet, or grey with light yellow. On other vessels they only separate their bright colours with simple black or brown lines. The high quality of this pottery was made possible by an accomplished technique; the earthenware was covered with an extremely fine glaze, on which the colours show, in some places dully, and in some brightly. The Nazca vases are easily recognizable when they have spouts, as these are separate, connected by a supporting bridge; whereas on the northern coast the two spouts unite in a hoop, at the top of which is a single nozzle.

As this account shows, the productions of these coastal Indians, apart from architecture, were mainly pieces of pottery, usually not more than six to twelve inches, though sometimes as much as forty

Various forms of ancient Peruvian ceramics produced before the beginning of Inca rule

inches, in height. Clay, being easy to get, was preferred to stone, both for building and for sculpture. The use of copper, and—not later than the third century A.D.—of bronze, was well known to the coastal Indians, who used them, as well as gold and silver, for things of daily use and for ornaments. They had an admirable textile art as well, achieved on the simplest of looms; its decoration and technical execution will bear comparison with the achievements of any country.

The saltpetre in the soil, and the dry, hot climate, have caused many of these products, buried with the dead, to be found beside mummified bodies in a state of good preservation. The delicate ornaments, made of the bright feathers of the humming-bird, such as are found elsewhere only in Mexico and on certain South Sea islands, have even been found.

Brightly-coloured South Peruvian vases, with plane representation of its symbolical decoration

Tiahuanaco

If we leave the Peruvian coast and climb the Andes, which rise to a height of 23,000 feet, above the level of eternal snow, we come, after passing through habitable highland valleys, into a harsh and inhospitable region; there, in the southern highlands, more than 12,000 feet up, is Lake Titicaca. Twice as big as Lake Geneva, it looks today like a forsaken sea. Three hours' walk from its southern shore, in a bare, flat, narrow valley, is a waste of ruins in which the most impressive objects are an artificial hill, Ak-Kapana, and a square surrounded by great stone pillars—the Calasasaya. On its eastern side a flight of stairs, made of six blocks of sandstone about 26 feet wide, leads up to a sanctuary, made up of pillars and stone walls, which great heads and figures, carved of trachyte, are set; when found they bore traces of the paint which had once covered them. Among the ruins an even larger sanctuary can still be traced, which once contained four monumental blocks of stone, shaped like altars or sarcophagi. Among the ruins also are great statues, carved from gigantic blocks of volcanic rock (Fig. 22a), and several monumental gateways. The finest of these, the so-called Gate of the Sun, has a frieze with three rows of bird-like figures, gazing up at a central deity, who shows traces of tears on his face.

Here we have an example of the art of a late archaic period, which has puzzled scholars, for these buildings seem never to have been completed, and stand today as solitary witnesses to a prehistoric culture. We have no historical knowledge of any people to whom they can be definitely attributed. Research has merely shown that we are dealing here with two consecutive stylistic periods, which are known as Tiahuanaco I and Tiahuanaco II.

If we compare the latter with the art of Pachacamac (page 70), we at once think of the coastal regions. It seems more than likely that the same great Indian empire flourished here in the seventh and eighth centuries, and that its influence penetrated far into the mountains, where, in the many Indian ruins, and in the ceramics of the higher valleys—of which the chief discoveries were made at Recuay and Chavin—there are remains of an art which, as the Recuay style, and the Chavin style, absorbed the great tradition of Mexico and the Maya countries. They date from a time when the Indians were discarding the primitive moon-worship for that of the sun, and the more intellectual were progressing from this towards pure monotheism. While we may regard the Recuay, and also the later Ica, as more local styles, the Chavin style extends over the whole of the border region lying between the coast and the highlands, a region which the Spaniards called *Ceja de la costa,* the eyebrow of the coast. This style, which can be traced back as far as the first centuries of the Christian era, shows a connection with Colombia and with the Central American cultures, as well as with their most precious possession, the art of writing. Close examination of the Echenique disc (on this page), with its rows of teeth so typical of Tiahuanaco art, clearly reveals its calendarial and hieroglyphic character, similar to that of the golden disc found in the graves of the Maya people of the Quiché, at Zacualpa, in the mountains of Guatemala. The number twenty appears in the outer ring of the Echenique disc; and, as in almost all parts of the world, the divisions of the calendar correspond with the number of the letters in the first alphabets.

The Echenique Disc

The Art of the Incas

As late as the eleventh century, the Incas only ruled in the small valley region round Cuzco, in the Peruvian highlands. Not until the fourteenth century did their empire expand far beyond the present Peruvian frontiers, to include the coastal regions and mountains, from the old kingdom of Quito in the north to a line well within Chilean territory. The art of the Incas was comparatively late. While Chimu art, at the concluding phase of a declining culture, was expiring in fatigued and insipid forms, the new Inca art was inspired by an ambitious nationalism. Though it used many of the old forms, these were refined in the fire of the new solar religion, which superseded the previous idolatry; although the Incas, astute administrators, always kept a pantheon for the old gods in the temples of Cuzco.

Golden head-ornament from Chongoyape, near Lambayeque, Peru. One-third natural size. Chavin style. Cf. text p. 72

The buildings of the Incas were not built of brick, but of stone, quarried in the mountains. The attempt, made five hundred years earlier in Tiahuanaco, was at last accomplished; but it was not the former archaic, inhibited spirit, but a well-organized military state, that built the castles of the Incas at almost the same time as the knights of Western Europe were taking shelter behind their towers and walls. Goethe congratulated the New World on its good fortune, saying that America was luckier than Europe, in that it had no fortified castles; but discoveries made since the middle of the nineteenth century show a very different picture, particularly since 1911, when Bingham discovered in the jungle the Inca city of Machu Picchu (Fig. 22c), whose white granite stronghold now rises from the Peruvian plateau.

A stern and austere spirit built the Inca cities, the strongholds such as Ollantaytambo, and the temples and palaces of the capital, Cuzco. Their beauty lies in the precision of their construction; stones were so accurately cut and polished with copper tools that they could be fitted together without mortar, so closely that there is not room for even a knife-blade between them. Decoration is restricted to fine stepped patterns, while the frequently occurring stone crochets facilitated the lifting of blocks.

In ceramics we find the same restrained decoration and noble perfection of form. On the amphora in Fig. 22b the serpent, once the central motive of many symbolical scenes (Fig. 21a), now merely rouses a faint reminiscent shudder. The art of the Incas combined the glowing life of the tropical coast with the austerity of the mountains.

When, towards the middle of the sixteenth century, the Inca empire, the last of the great Indian States, was defeated, not without a struggle, by Spain, the invaders melted down the gold and silver images and plaques which adorned temples and palaces, and sent them to Europe as loot. A great Indian art perished, for the art produced today in this region, which is still inhabited by millions of Indians, is not worth mentioning, having neither vitality nor originality.

The Primitive Art of South America

Finally, we must still consider the art of the other regions of South America, which were inhabited by primitive tribes; above all, the primeval forest region of Brazil, where Nordenskjöld made many archaeological discoveries, and which, as 'Amazonia', does not entirely coincide with the lower basin of the gigantic river. The mountain Indians had always dreaded the primeval forest and its diseases, just as the inhabitants of the tropical lowlands avoided the mountains. Thus, in spite of the political power of the Incas (except in the lower spurs of the Andes in the north-west Argentine, where Debenedetti made some interesting discoveries suggesting northern influences), a primitive art survived, with idols, figures of stone and earthenware, and urns. These derive from the same sense of form as did the art of the northern prairie Indians.

Generally speaking, South American art, whether in its masks or its decoration, is distinguished from the art of North America by its greater tranquillity. In so far as the nomadic tribes of South America produced any drawings, they laid emphasis on the details which seemed to them of special importance. This explains the 'mixed profile' (page 66 and Fig. 21a), the combination of side and full-face in the case of human beings; and of plan and elevation, in the case of buildings; and above all, the representation of things which exist but are not visible, which often produces those interesting pictures, like X-ray photographs, in which the ribs, or the heart, or other important organs are shown (as we have already seen is the case in drawings by North American Indians). In feather ornaments, sculpture, carving, weaving, plaiting and ceramics, religious subjection, and the principles of repetition, concatenation, and symmetry, form the basis of Indian art.

Chapter VI

THE ANCIENT ART OF THE NEAR EAST

*

THE earliest of the series of great civilizations in the Near East was that of Mesopotamia, though geologically speaking this country round the Tigris and Euphrates was of comparatively recent origin. During the Ice Age the Persian Gulf reached as far as Mosul, nearly 500 miles farther north than it does now, and it was only afterwards that streams, descending from the Armenian mountains, brought down material which was to form the rock on which stood the cities of ancient Babylonia. In the north of plain, on the Tigris, lay Nineveh, Nimrud and Assur, the cities of the Semitic Assyrians, and in the centre, on the Euphrates, were the cities of the ancient Babylonians, Uruk, Nippur, Sippar and Akkad, also subject to Semitic influence at an early period; while in the south, in Ur, Larsa, Eridu and Lagash (of special importance in the history of art), on the shores of the Persian Gulf, which *c.* 5000 B.C. still extended some 120 miles farther inland than it does today, lived the Sumerians, a non-Semitic people. In the East, more towards India, on the Kerchah, the last of the greater tributaries of the Tigris, stood the ancient Elamite city of Susa, whose archaic art goes back to the fourth and perhaps the fifth millennium B.C. In Elam, where the Persian empire was one day to rise, copper weapons and mirrors were already used as early as this, and ceramic art had reached a high degree of perfection (cf. vases on this page).

Prehistoric vases from Susa. Black painting on fine, yellowish earthenware. About 3200 B.C. Louvre

In recent excavations near Mohenjo Daro and Harappa (Figs. 26b, 26c) relics have been found of a common, ancient culture, which connected the cities on the middle course of the Euphrates and the Persian Gulf with those of the Elamites and the first inhabitants of the Indus valley.

Elam, Sumer and Akkad are the names which occur at the beginning of the history of Near Eastern art. From these places came a vital art, and one of *white* humanity. We should not be misled, by the geographical conception of Asia, into thinking of Asiatics in this connection; here only the white race was to be found, for after the Ice Age the Negroes were cut off by the Sahara, and the Mongolians, though expanding in many directions, were kept back by the still ice-covered mountains. Moreover, ancient Mesopotamia, as well as Egypt, was part of the same wide area, extending from southern Spain to the Indus valley, which offered favourable conditions of life at a very early period, where white humanity advanced from the Stone Age to civilization. Here art still shows the common features which were later to develop in various different ways. Even if we agree with the poet and speculative thinker, Friedrich Hebbel, who gave much thought to the origin of art, and who wrote 'In art as in all things living there is no progress, only variations of the stimulus'—it was precisely these variations that in the Near East constantly gave art new motives and means of expression.

The history of ancient Mesopotamia is one of conflict, in which the states and cities of the Sumerian south and the Semitic north, ruled by kings, princely priests or governors, strove for supremacy among themselves and with their eastern neighbours, the Elamites of Susa. The features of their art were by no means determined by political considerations; for even their religions changed about as their civilizations blended. To avoid confusion, the most important thing is to distinguish clearly, in a very involved and still frequently obscure history, the individual styles and periods.

Sumerian Art

The third millennium B.C. shows the art of the Sumerians—whom we must probably regard, after cautiously considering all the relevant facts, as the oldest civilized people of Mezopotamia—in an archaic phase (Fig. 26a). The heads of the figures, even when their bodies are turned towards the observer, are always in profile, and the eye, under a strongly-marked eyebrow, occupies the greater part of the face. The feet remain flat on the ground; the upper part of the body is bare, and the lower part is clad in a bell-shaped garment, decorated with tufts of fur. Bird-like heads and figures with flat feet are found in the earliest representative art, which always represents the male Sumerian with close-shaven hair and beard.

About 2400 B.C., after the destruction of Lagash, begins the age of Gudea (Fig 26d), which may be described as the golden age of Sumerian art. Gudea seems to have been a priest and sage rather than a warrior. The devastated temples of Nina and Lagash were rebuilt in renewed beauty, and Ur, too, rose from its ruins under its third dynasty (2478—2358 B.C.). Various vessels of pure gold, the helmet of one of the kings of Ur, and the costly head-dress of the queens, of gold adorned with precious stones, are surviving evidences of a newly-developed splendour. Important examples of Sumerian art were found among the ruins of Lagash, and are now in the Louvre. As well as archaic bronze figures of men and women, there are figures of various sizes, representing Gudea and King Urbau. Their attitude is still constrained with hands and feet pressed together, but for the first time these figures have genuinely human bodies and one of them is of considerable height. Gudea sometimes holds a plan, and sometimes a measuring-rod; a sign of the increasing importance of architecture.

The idiom of this earliest architecture was derived from the local clay, which could be used in bulk for building walls when it was firmly compressed, or cut into bricks. These were often sun-dried, though they were sometimes fired, and, for important purposes, even glazed. Usually they were stamped with the name of the royal builder. Expensive stone, which had to be brought from a distance, was used only for the thresholds of doors, for occasional supports of buttresses, and for sculpture. Any comprehensive discussion of the details of Mesopotamian architecture must wait till later, since we have too little certain knowledge of the early period; for succeeding generations often rebuilt, so that the really ancient was often obliterated.

Much of our knowledge of the earliest period comes from ancient Sumerian inscriptions on buildings and statues. From a rudimentary script, which indicates a connection with the Indus valley (cf. Figs. 26b and 26c with 26e), the Sumerians evolved forms which called increasingly for straight strokes, and so led to the so-called cuneiform script (Fig. 26d), which presently became predominant in the Near East, and was used for several languages.

Ancient Babylonian Art

Farther to the north, under the rulers of Isin, of Amorite origin (2357—2132 B. C.), who assumed the titles of Kings of Sumer and Akkad, Semitic forms became predominant: the Sumerian baldheads are replaced in their paintings by long-bearded figures with curly hair, whose slender figures already show approximately correct proportions.

In addition to stone bas-reliefs, cylindrical seals are found of great artistic significance. Most of these were cylinders only an inch or two long, often set in gold, and worn as ornaments or amulets, strung on a cord passing round the neck. In spite of their size, they are among the most informative survivals of antiquity. They usually represent the heroic deeds of the mighty Gilgamesh, who fights with all kinds of hybrid creatures, with lions, and with bulls (Fig. 26f). Sometimes he is holding out to the heavenly bull the vessel which is the source of the Tigris and Euphrates.

The bold modelling of the nude, the elaborate treatment of the muscles, and especially the movements of the animals, are astonishing. This fresh realism mitigates the stiffness of the traditional style in sculpture as well; in the Naram-Sin stele in the Louvre, for example, it reaches a high level of achievement. There the relief is higher than in earlier works; it represents a victory of the over-life-sized, horn-crowned, bejewelled king, who is shown in the act of piercing an enemy with his lance, whose followers—who are smaller, in accordance with their rank—flee for their lives. This is a good representation of a dramatic scene.

The whole of Mesopotamia was welded into a united Semitic empire under Hammurabi, the sixth king of the old Babylonian kingdom (2123—2081 B. C.), and the last relics of the old Sumerian art disappeared. He absorbed the Elamite dynasty of Larsa (2357 — 2095) and established a new code of laws, which covered the whole empire and safeguarded his own power, and in order to establish spiritual unity he accomplished one of the greatest religious revolutions of history. The old gods were deprived of their significance, or completely abolished, and the new god, Bel, or Marduk, was the supreme ruler of Babylon.

Characteristic of the art of this period are the representations of the king. The relief in the Louvre shows him with the Sumerian turban, the hair and beard being worn in the Semitic fashion. The details are well observed, but the general execution is less vigorous and more courtly. Already there are signs of weakness, of a decline of energy which did not renew itself until later in the Babylonian empire. In the meantime artistic initiative passed to the Assyrians in the north.

Assyrian Art

In the second millennium B. C. the city of Assur was the seat of the Sun-god of the same name, while in Nineveh stood the temple of the goddess Ishtar. Of the same stock as the Babylonians, the Assyrians—a people given to war and hunting—took over, not only their religion, their science and their alphabet, but their art as well; they were something more than mere imitators, for from the Hittites, too, who since 2000 B.C. had arisen as a great power in the highlands of Cappadocia (cf. page 83), they had received fresh stimuli, and eventually created an independent art. Our knowledge of its earliest achievements comes from literary sources, since most of the objects unearthed by archaeologists are of a later period.

Relief from the palace of Sanherib at Nineveh. Men with a waggon, which they are pulling across a stream, indicated by wavy lines.
In the background are buildings with cupolas, and conventional hills and trees. British Museum

In architecture the Assyrians, from the first, made more use of the round arch and vault than the people of the south; in many cases the corridors and the long halls of their palaces seem to have been roofed with barrel-vaulting, and from the reliefs discovered (such as that illustrated on this page) one must assume that they sometimes roofed their houses with domes, though as a rule, only flat-roofed houses are seen in their pictures and sculpture, and the inscriptions of their kings often refer to cedar beams, imported for the builders. Very often these were used as pillars, which later on, as various excavations have shown, were covered with metal. Stone pillars seem to have been first used with any frequency in the eighth century B.C. Their earliest use was in small temples and canopies (below), which in Assyria, as in Egypt, played an important part, independently of the larger buildings.

Most of the reliefs discovered are now in the British Museum. From these one can get a good idea of the characteristics of the early Assyrian style. Gods, as well as kings and other dignitaries, are always shown with full beards and long hair, while servants and eunuchs are beardless—though, unlike the figures depicted in Sumerian art, their hair, too, is long. Women are very seldom represented, and when they are, it is lamenting in trains of prisoners, or standing on the walls of fortresses. The figures are always shown in profile; the pupils of the eyes are not indicated, and as a rule there are no eyelids; sometimes the broad-shouldered, rather stocky bodies are clad in richly embroidered garments, but when arms and legs are uncovered they show the artist's delight in the elaborate treatment of the muscles, a characteristic already observed in ancient Babylonian art. In the rare cases where figures of slain or plundered enemies appear quite naked there is little sence of organic structure, although details are often accurately observed.

Under Assurnasirpal (884 — 860) creative art received great impetus. In Nineveh he built a gigantic palace, whose ruins are known as the North-Western Palace. It was at the gates of this that the animals with human heads were first placed, which afterwards, as guardians in the form of winged bulls (page 23), decorated the angles of walls all over Assyria. They were so made that the forepart of the body, seen from the front, was 'in the round', and in order that the side view should give the same effect, the inner fore-leg was represented twice. This is the origin of the five legs, that seem to increase still further the power of these creatures, which have the head of a human being, an eagle's wings, a bull's body, and, in the early period, a lion's paws. Sometimes, until their final form was established, they even had human arms. In the arrangement of the limbs of these colossi the same tendency is seen as in the

Assyrian Relief from the North-Western Palace, at Nimrud. British Museum

figures in the alabaster reliefs (Fig. 25): while the old profile-aspect is retained, care is taken that the arms and legs are always fully visible. Inside the North-Western Palace, the longer sides of the principal halls were covered with two great rows of reliefs, separated by a band of inscriptions. These reliefs represent various incidents in the life of the king in his hunting-chariot striking at his prey, or pouring a libation to the gods over the body of a fallen lion, or in his war-chariot leading his army into battle, or being received by minstrels as he returns in triumph after victory.

Mention should be made of the use of plant motives and patterns in Assyrian art. As well as the rosette, the palm-leaf is seen in a new form, that of a fan of outspread leaves, not found in ancient Babylonian art. Very often, too, the palm is used in representations of the tree of life, in which we see various patterns made of interlacing or braided bands or ribbons. In the illustration on this page, above the tree, is the god Assur, with the symbol of the life-giving Sun, whose function it is to ripen the fruits of the earth; while in other representations winged genii stroke the flower-tuft of the date-palm in order that they may bear good fruit. Formal conjurations, or actions expressing the desire for a fruitful harvest, constantly occur.

The God Assur with the disc of the Sun, above the Tree of Life. (Breasted)

Assurnasirpal's son, Salmanassar II, continued his father's work of erecting temples, and built the so-called Central Palace in Nimrud. On all four sides of the great Black Obelisk, perhaps the most important sculptural work of this period which we possess, in five superimposed series, are scenes in which the king's tributary vassals, with their elephants and camels, bring him treasures from all points of the compass.

Assyrian art received a special impetus under the Sargonidae. Sargon II displayed great splendour in the palace of Dur-Sarrukin (page 81), which has not unjustly been called the 'Assyrian Versailles'. The alabaster reliefs, placed end to end, would cover a mile and a quarter. Inscriptions were now felt to be superfluous; the sculptures themselves gave a more vivid record of the life of royalty. Now the artist turned his attention to trifles, representing the pupils of the eyes, and observing details in the background, perhaps a bird in a tree, of which the species now clearly perceptible, whereas previously (page 78) they were represented

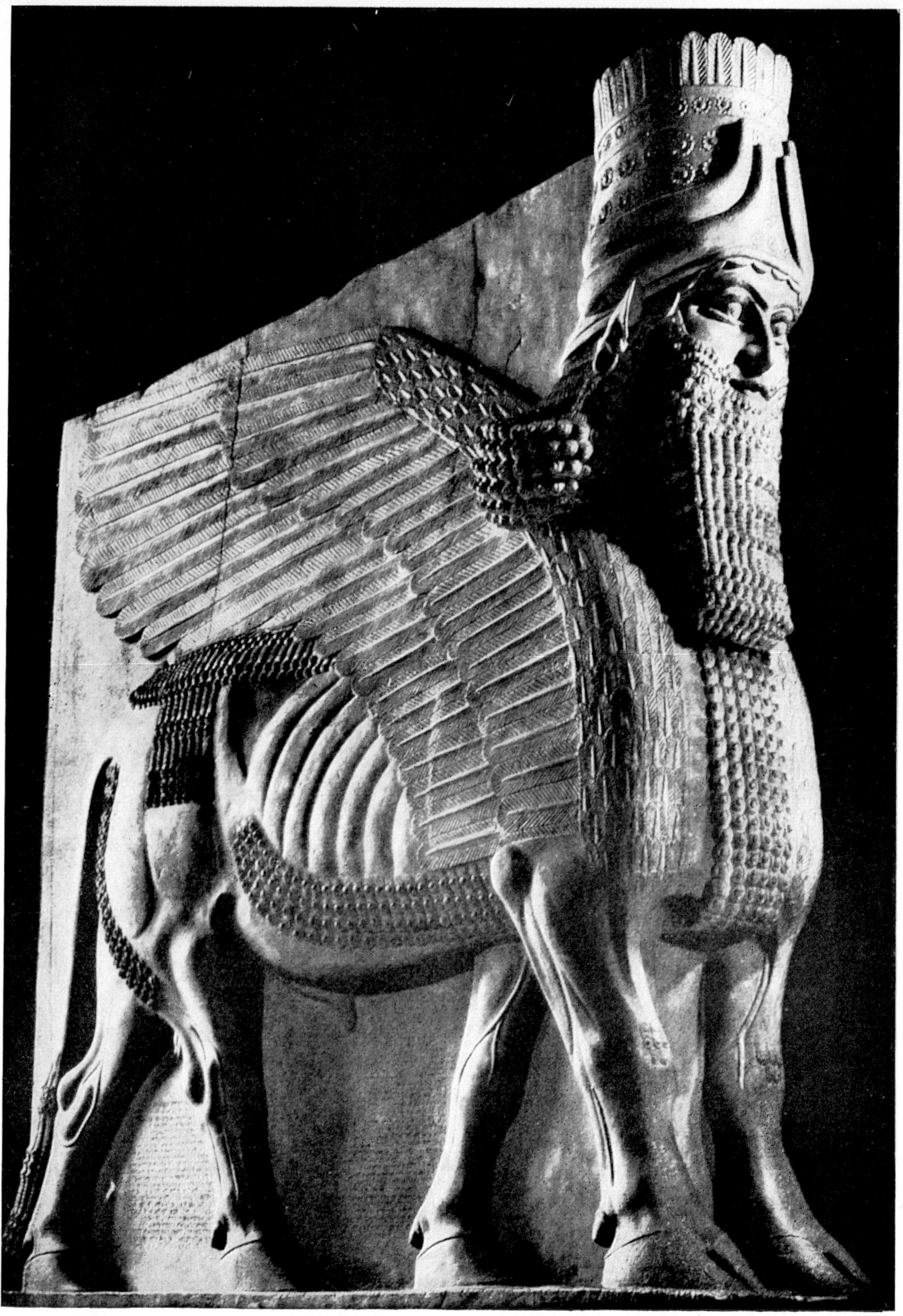

23. Five-footed winged bull from the palace of Sargon II at Chorsabad, near Nineveh. Height of alabaster block, 13 ft. 6 in. Eighth century B.C. (Louvre).

24. (A) Achaemenian capital from the palace of Darius at Susa. Height of whole column of grey marble, 19 ft. Fourth century B.C. (Louvre). (B) Winged Ibex, with hind feet resting on a mask of Silenus. Silver, inlaid with gold. Height, 10.8 in. This was the handle of a great vase. From the end of the Persian era. Fourth century B.C. (Louvre). (C) Assurbanipal hunting the lion. Section of an alabaster relief from the palace at Nineveh. Height, 20.8 in. Seventh century B.C. (British Museum).

25. Four-winged Assyrian god. Height of alabaster relief, 12 ft. Eighth century B.C. (Louvre).

a

26. (A) Part of a Sumerian mosaic, representing warriors refreshing themselves after a battle. Beginning of the third century B.C. (British Museum).

b

c

(B and C) Impressions of ancient seals from the valley of the Indus, which suggest an early connection between the Indian and Sumerian cultures. Text p. 87. Third century B. C. (Mohenjo-Daro).

d

(D) Seated figure of the princely priest. Gudea. According to the cuneiform script on the robe, the statue belonged to the temple of the god Rin-Gizzida, built by Gudea. The statue, of diorite, was found in two pieces. Height, 17.7 in. New Sumerian era, 2400 B.C. (Louvre).

e

f

(E) Impression—counting as signature—in soft clay, of a Babylonian cylindrical seal, representing Gilgamesh contending with wild animals.

(F) The cylindrical seal in question; natural size. (Cf. p. 77).

conventionally. The walls shone with polished metal, and all the colours of the rainbow. The wooden gates and doors were covered with beaten bronze, which often extended in broad fillets along the walls. The general plan of this palace, which gives a good idea of all such structures, may be gathered from the reconstruction (below).

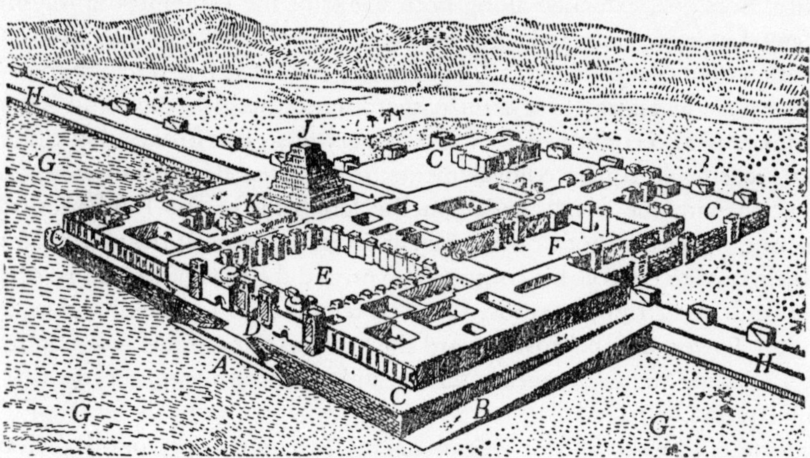

The Palace of Sargon II (722—705 B.C.) at Khorsabad. Dur-Sarrukin, Sargon's citadel, rose above the houses (G) and streets (H) of the city of some 80,000 inhabitants, as a huge mass of brick buildings, whose streets (C) and sloping ramps (B) enabled the king to drive in and out unhindered. From the greater and lesser courtyards (E and F) the halls and apartments, with their flat roofs, were easily accessible. The main entrance (A, D) was strongly fortified, and adorned with glazed and coloured tiles. In the background was an Oriental temple, the Ziggurat (J), which was not built in steps, like the Pyramids, but was ascended by a winding ramp. (Breasted)

Under Assurbanipal (668 — 626 B.C.) the art of Assyria had its last flowering, and rose to its greatest freedom. In energy and power this period cannot be compared with the reign of Assurnasirpal, but the Assyrian feeling for Nature revealed itself more purely. In largely conceived representations of animals and lively equestrian scenes (Fig. 24c) we see the people and their art in a radiant twilight. Under the next ruler, in the year 606 B.C., the Assyrian power came to a sudden end. Babylonia and Persia had formed an alliance, and the last Assyrian ruler, Sinsharishkun, was burned in his palace with wives and his treasures, while the four royal residences, at Nineveh, Dur-Sarrukin, Nimrud and Assur, were razed to the ground. The Babylonians were again supreme in art.

The New Babylonian Art

Under Nebuchadnezzar II (604 — 562 B.C.) Babylonian art reawoke. Babylon above all, but the other cities also—Ur, Larsa, Nippur and the rest—experienced a kind of Renaissance. The king gloried less in war than in the buildings which made Babylon one of the greatest and most luxurious cities of antiquity. According to Herodotus, who is supported in many points by modern archaeologists, this metropolis, with its sister city, Borsippa, extended along both flanks of the Euphrates in the form of a quadrilateral, thirteen miles in length, and covered an area larger than that of Greater New York with its suburbs. A wall, 550 feet high and 140 feet thick, with a hundred gates, with posts and cornices of bronze, surrounded this giant city. This statement of Herodotus was also confirmed by the discovery of a great bronze threshold, decorated with rosettes in square compartments (now in the British Museum).

Connected with the royal citadel on the left bank of the Euphrates were the famous hanging gardens, one of the ancient seven wonders of the world, laid out by Nebuchadnezzar to console his consort who missed the hills of her native Media. On the right bank of the Euphrates rose the great temple of Bel or Marduk, beside which the Biblical Tower of Babel rose toward the heavens. Herodotus's words 'From the outside a winding stair. . . went round and up', describe a ziggurat like that shown in the illustration on page 81.

Very little remains of all this splendour, yet it seems that the new Babylonian art was a kind of classical revival, reproducing ancient forms on a new, gigantic scale. Encaustic tiles of all colours were employed in great quantities; this external brilliance perhaps concealed the fact that this art had little content. It only lasted little more than half a century, for in 539 B.C. Babylon was conquered by the Persians under Cyrus. Although he spared the city and made it the third capital of the Persian Empire, his victory was none the less the beginning of its quick and inglorious downfall.

Asia Minor and Syria

Asia Minor, a land of steppes and mountains, which includes the greater part of modern Turkey, was for a long while mentioned by historians of art—when they were writing of the pre-Grecian era—only in connection with the ruins of Troy, which stood on the Hellespont, near the southern entrance to the Dardanelles. The excavations carried out by Schliemann and Dorpfeld in 1870 — 94 revealed nine layers of habitation, including the Hellenistic, which reach far back into prehistoric ages. The influence of the adjacent Ægean culture, and the Egyptian, is perceptible in the later strata. As well as prehistoric earthenware vases, facial urns, and other discoveries, the most remarkable find was the great golden treasure which Schliemann originally claimed was the treasury of Priam. The Bronze Age stratum contains the ancient citadel of Troy and other buildings, which already reveal the *megaron,* the long, rectilinear, windowless hall from which the Greek temple evolved.

Recent excavations in many places, and the discovery of more cuneiform texts, enable us today to survey the art and history of the whole country. At the beginning of the second millennium B.C. a non-Semitic people, the Hittites, emerged from the prehistoric Stone Age and Bronze Age of Asia Minor. By the beginning of the fourteenth century B.C. they had taken possession of northern Syria, and in the thirteenth and twelfth centuries were the principal power in Syria and Asia Minor until the tenth and ninth centuries, when this region was again split into individual states, and the eighth century, when it was absorbed by the Assyrian Empire. The common civilization of this people is shown by the reliefs discovered, which represent them in their peculiar costume; at first the men are beardless, with pointed shoes, short-sleeved tunics and tall, pointed caps, while the women wear long robes and cylindrical hats; during the Transition period the men's garments are richer and include cloaks, while the appearance of the full beard marks a late period, largely Semitic in character.

The capital of the Hittite realm was Chatti; it lay near the site of the modern town of Boghaskoi. Things found there, and at Uejuk and Sendshirli, on the modern Turco-Syrian frontier, reveal, apart from the costume already described, characteristics of the ancient Oriental style with which the reader is already familiar, figures seen half from the front and half from the side. These Hittite sculptures are not equal to the Assyrian either technically or aesthetically.

Alabaster plaque. Phoenician. Louvre

The great megalithic gateways, like the Lion Gate and the King's Gate in Boghaskoi, should be mentioned; these are adorned with sculptures of the kind just described; also the open flight of stairs, with the bases of pillars, and the gate of the citadel at Sendshirli, where grim, disfigured lions keep watch. However, this art was as far from developing vigorously as was that of the various smaller kingdoms of Asia Minor—Paphlagonia, Phrygia, Lydia and Lycia: at its height it was too closely encompassed by the great artistic output of Mesopotamia and Egypt, and later on it was overwhelmed by Hellenism, and by Islam.

The cultural and political life of Syria had always been dependent on her more powerful neighbours. Owing to their position on the coast, the Phoenicians were the merchants and middlemen of the ancient world; and although they produced no very significant art of their own, disseminated that of their neighbours throughout the Mediterranean area. About 1000 B.C. they not only settled in Cyprus, but also founded several colonies oversea, the most famous of which was Carthage (800 B.C.); as a result of these extensive commercial relations their industrial art reached a very high level. In it were blended all the styles of antiquity: Astarte, renewer of life, the greatest of the Semitic goddesses and the consort of Bel, was most frequently represented, and since her cult was widespread, one may perhaps regard the sculpture in Fig. 9 as a bust of her. Under these circumstances a really individual art was hardly possible, especially since, from the first half of the first millennium B.C., the religion of the Hebrews in Palestine, who were of the same race as the Phoenicians, entirely forbade the use of sculpture. Of the temple which Phoenician architects built for Solomon, a thousand years before Christ, only a few rather doubtful fragments have survived.

The Art of Ancient Persia

After the Indo-Germanic Persians had overthrown Babylon in the year 539 B.C., a single empire covered all the countries of Asia Minor. To what extent the Persians considered this as the climax of the old Oriental civilization is shown by the fact that Aramaic, the most widely-spoken Semitic tongue, was made the official language of the Empire. This Empire was a truly Great Power, with its outposts already on European soil. Greeks and Egyptians were employed at the Persian court, and Persian ships sailed as far as southern Italy.

There was little room for the development of individuality in the Achaemenid empire. The king's secret police controlled governors and officials, and even where art was concerned, he was omnipotent. This art occurs at the end of an evolution of more than three thousand years, but it is, historically speaking, comparatively recent; we speak of it as 'old' only to distinguish it from the later Persian art, which comes under the heading of Islamic art. Under these circumstances, old Persian art was a court, not a popular art; it was not without distinction, though it did not survive the government from which it drew its sustenance. It only flourished for about two hundred years, from 550 — 330 B.C., and quickly withered when Alexander the Great destroyed the power of Persia.

Little can be said of the prehistoric period of this art, since the teaching of Zarathustra had no need of images, bidding the ancient Persians worship the God of Light only in the blazing fire. Simple fire-towers, like those still to be seen at Persepolis and elsewhere in Persia, and rock-tombs, are the only works of art surviving from the pre-Achaemenian period.

A relic of the Achaemenian period, the name of Cyrus is seen among the ruins of Pasargadae, while on the walls of Persepolis are displayed the names of Darius and Xerxes, modestly accompanied by those of later rulers. The great palace of Persepolis was begun by Darius and finished by Xerxes. Only a few of its pillars remain, though many of the walls are perfectly preserved. On one of them Darius is depicted in a majestic attitude, in a style of formal and rather empty solemnity. If a later work shows Xerxes with a sunshade above his head, surrounded by youthful, beardless servants, carrying flasks and napkins and baskets, this is characteristic of a more effeminate age.

One of the clearest and most vigorous sculptures of the Old Persian period is the great bas-relief, dating from the reign of Darius, cut in the rock at Bisutun, on the road from Ecbatana to Babylon, which proclaims the feats of the king in three languages. It was by comparison of the characters that Sir Henry Rawlinson and others were enabled to decipher the ancient Babylonian cuneiform script (page 77).

While little is left of Ecbatana, another favourite seat of the Persian kings, many discoveries were made at Susa; its position at the edge of the Mesopotamian plain had for a long time encouraged the manufacture of glazed tiles and bricks which assumed many of the functions of sculpture, this was not a peculiar property of Persian art, but the result of natural conditions.

Among the most famous friezes of glazed and coloured tiles found here, are the archers, two of whom are depicted on this page. Greek historians say that the body-guard of the Persian king numbered 10,000 soldiers, known as the Immortals. Of these 1,000 carried spears with golden knobs on the shafts, while the knobs of the remaining 9,000 were only silver. Among them were the dark-skinned Elamites, who can be recognized on the frieze, with little fortresses embroidered on their garments; they wear laced shoes, and their quivers are covered with panther-skin. No less famous is the 'Lion frieze' in the Louvre, which seems to have decorated the upper part of the palace wall. In all the friezes the figures are reproduced with

Two palace guards: two of a row of Persian warriors. The whole series of figures formed a frieze of glazed bricks, mainly blue, red, yellow and white, on the palace of Susa. They carry spears in their hands, large quivers on their backs, and bows over their left shoulders. Height of the figures, 4 ft. 10 in. Fifth century B.C. Louvre. (Breasted)

absolute uniformity, for this technique contented itself with repeated impressions of the same moulds; the only variation was a change of pattern, so that every other archer in the decoration is different, while the next pair are exactly like their predecessors.

In the minor arts the Persians produced nothing new. Their cylindrical seals follow the ancient models: so do their ceramics, which after the days of the first, Elamite, Susa (this is true of the whole of the Near East), are not of any great interest to the art historian. The use of the wheel—in making pottery and in vehicles—was always known to them.

As far as we can judge, the Persian Empire's greatest artistic achievement—owing to the means at its disposal—was in architecture. Spacious terraced gardens and earthworks, easily-trodden flight of stairs, and great rows of richly decorated pillars were necessities to the splendour-loving court; but when we consider the details (Fig. 24), we become aware of a feebly imitative spirit, subject to many different influences. This weary and debilitated art (cf. Fig. 24b) could not hope to influence the West, or even to survive at all, at a time when Greek art was beginning to spread. Only in the East did Persepolis and Susa seem like a reflection of heavenly glory: the earliest Buddhist art in India was bewitched by the splendid luxury of Persia, and owed much to its influence.

Chapter VII

INDIA

*

Something has already been said (page 75) of the cultural relations between the Indus valley and Mesopotamia. Recent excavations at Mohenjo Daro and Harappa have revealed the foundations of large cities, with a by no means primitive brick architecture, as well as many lesser antiquities; all these, like the cylindrical seals already mentioned (Figs. 26b and 26c), indicate a connection with Sumerian art, and also a cultural connection, during the Old Bronze Age, with the Mediterranean area. Among the things found, which date back to somewhere between 3000 and 4000 B.C. cylindrical seals, archaic limestone figures of men, and terra-cotta statuettes of women, deserve particular mention.

In the second millennium B.C. India was occupied by a white race which came from the north, crossed the Indus and gradually pushed on to the Ganges, subduing the darker, aboriginal population—the Dravidians—and spread its culture through the whole peninsula. The immigrants, who had left their home for the south, had long passed the level of Stone or Bronze Age culture; they knew all the commoner metals, and had some knowledge of agriculture and cattle-breeding, and a complete alphabetical script.

The hymns of the Rig-Veda date back to the period when they were still in the valley of the Indus, and before they had elaborated the caste divisions which were to be so characteristic of the later India: the ruling castes of priests and warriors, and subject castes of servants and workers. These hymns tell us of Indra (page 88), the War-god, who loved the intoxicating *soma*; beside, and in contrast with, whom—like the indispensable priest at the side of the earthly king—stood a kind of spiritual Brahmanaspati, with the power of magical formulae, and all secret knowledge; they tell also of Agni, the god of the hearth, and Varuna, the guardian of the cosmic system.

The Christian conception of the infinite power and sublimity of the Divine, before which man is as nothing, was entirely unknown to the Indians, as it was to the Greeks. Just as the Homeric poems do not scruple to make the gods objects of derision, so in the Rig-Veda we find songs which make sport of the drunken Indra. This humanizing of the Divine in ancient Indian mythology was of great significance in the later developments of Indian art.

Naturally, no memorials worth mentioning have survived from the ancient Brahmanic era of the Vedas, since it was a nomadic period. The colourful works of art described in the heroic poems would perish only too easily in a tropical climate, owing to the nature of their materials; they were mainly of wood, or were fragile constructions of earth and brick, covered with plaster. Consequently, we have no very clear idea ot the Indian art which preceded the introduction of stone buildings about the year 250 B.C., at which time a thousand years of Buddhist supremacy began.

The God Indra on the three-headed Elephant

Buddhist Art

In the sixth century B. C., at the foot of the Himalayas, Gautama was born, an ascetic, and a seeker of truth. At the age of thirty-six he received enlightenment, and, as Buddha, sought the Way of Deliverance, through the knowledge that alone releases man from the eternal circle of rebirth. Full of compassion for humanity, he first proclaimed his doctrine—the essence of which is almost identical with that expressed in the Christian beatitudes—in the park at Benares. Buddhism, like Christianity, had a long time to wait before it had the power of the State behind it. King Asoka (272 — 231) first made it the State religion. He was its greatest patron, and in his empire, which stretched from the delta of the Indus to that of the Ganges, and far into the heart of the Indian peninsula, he is supposed to have erected 84,000 stupas.

From then onwards, the *stupa*, the symbol of final deliverance, originally a burial-mound, which even in the ancient Brahmanic era could be either round or quadrangular, became the characteristic Buddhistic monument. In Asoka's reign the stupa of Sanci (eighty-four feet in height) was erected at the northern foot of the Vindhya hills, in the centre of India. The smooth stone enclosing wall is still without decoration, while the gates are richly ornamented (Fig. 27a) and show that the old imagery was by no means effaced by the new doctrine. Stupas were built of sun-dried bricks, and most of them were later cased with stone. Only some were built over relics—the majority were tombs. These domed monuments are symbols, commemorating the earthly pilgrimage of the Master, who became more and more of a God as time went on. From a high, square foundation rises a hemisphere, whose form—that of a bubble—is intended to suggest the evanescence of earthly things; on the flattened top of this rests a centrepiece or finial, rising in several stages, or a small, square enclosure, roofed with a stone parasol, partly in commemoration of the tree under which the Buddha received enlightenment, and also of the sunshade which the Persian kings carried as the symbol of sovereignty.

As well as the stupa there are often detached memorial columns, known as

7. (A) Northern gate of the great stupa at Sanci. Height, 22 ft. 9 in. Beginning of first century B.C.

a

b

c

(B) Lion capital of a memorial column erected by the Emperor Asoka at Sarnath, Northern India. On the ring that supports the lions we see, separated by the wheel (the symbol of the doctrine of salvation), the Horse and the Zebu Bull, while on the farther side is another sacred animal, the Elephant. Polished sandstone. Height, 7 ft. About 240 B.C. (Sarnath Museum).

(C) Interior of the Cave Temple of Karli. Ground plan (p. 90). First century B.C.

a

b

c

28. (A) Marble temple of Somnathpur, near Mysore. Completed A.D. 1270. See p. 96.
(B) Naga with his wife and serving-women. Relief of the serpent-god on the façade of the nineteenth cave. Ajanta. About A.D. 550.
(C) Pair of royal founders; front of the ancient Buddhist rock-temple of Karli.

29. (A) Celestial beings: Apsaras and servant. From the frescoes in a gallery of the rock-citadel of Sigiriya, Ceylon. End of fifth century.
(B) Avalokiteshvara. Dark basalt, from Binar or Bengal. Height, 37½ in. Eleventh—twelfth century. (Von der Heydt Collection, Ascona).
(C) Yakshi beneath a tree. Sandstone relief from the Surya Deul Temple, Orissa, Konarak. Height, 18 in. Thirteenth century. (Von der Heydt Collection, Ascona).

a

b

30. (A) The eleven-storeyed Gate-town of the Vishnu Temple at Kumbakonam, near the south-east coast of India. Height, 147 ft. A sacred Bull in the foreground.
(B) The blinding of the Bird. Part of the Ramayana frieze on the Shiva Temple of the Lara-Jongrang group, at Prambanam, Java. End of the ninth century.

stambhas. Some have been removed, but others, in the plain of the Ganges for example, are still standing, or lie shattered on the ground. Like the Mayan steles, they were meant to be enduring witnesses of the message which was inscribed upon them, for their smooth shafts are often covered with the texts of Asoka's edicts. Other such monuments expressed their message by symbols alone (Fig. 27b): since the lion, the bull and the other animals which were known to the old religion as Vahanas—the bearers of the gods—are often portrayed on the stones, it is clear that the stambhas were objects of veneration in the days when the divinity was still represented by his or her sacred animal. In this way Asoka enlisted in the service of the new doctrine an ancient custom, which reminds one of the monuments of Persepolis and the earlier Mesopotamian bas-reliefs. The stambhas can be recognized by the smooth shaft, without a base, by the inverted chalice of the lotus, with its doubly curved profile, and by the drum, surmounted by a three-dimensional figure. The shafts of the columns, often more than thirty feet high, could easily be renewed; they are keyed with a copper wedge to the capital, which was originally wide and low, but became even taller and more slender.

Many of the animals on Asoka's columns resemble, in a certain tenseness of treatment, the modelling of the animals on Persian monuments, and, together with the few colossal statues which survive, have the same high polish. The artists of this period still had a rather defective sense of form. The parts of garments which fit closely seem to be pressed flat, both on the body and at the lower hem, where they flutter round clumsy feet.

The most numerous and remarkable of the other monuments of Indian antiquity are the caves hollowed out of the rock, which were often merely *Caitya*, or places of assembly for the faithful, but were also *Vihara*, or monasteries with numerous cells; they were often designed to serve both purposes. The primitive use of caves for worship in the Ice Age was continued in many parts of the world, especially in Egypt, by worship in rock-temples; it was reserved for the Buddhist spirit of withdrawal from the world to enlarge and divide, and decorate with their truly great art, the cave-dwelling of prehistoric man. Only rarely did the natural cave dictate the plan: these Indian temples were deliberately and painfully excavated from the hard rock, so that their purpose dictated their plan. In Buddhist monasteries a great rectangular hall surrounded by small square cells for prayer and meditation, and with a semi-circular apse at one end (page 90), often surprises by its likeness to the Christian basilica (Chap. XIV). The roofs are supported by pillars, which divide the narrow aisles from the great nave, and often follow the curve of the terminal wall, where a small stupa rises from the floor, exactly the shape of its greater prototype, as a hemispherical shrine or reliquary, crowned with an umbrella (Fig. 27c). Later, the umbrella was replaced by a gigantic statue of Buddha, though in the earlier stages of Buddhism the artist refrained from representing the person of the Enlightened One. Light entered these sanctuaries only from the entrance, where there was usually a window-opening—semicircular, or horseshoe shaped, or in the shape of a pointed or four-centred arch. Sometimes this was preceded by an entrance-hall (as shown in the adjacent plan), which corresponds to the atrium of the early Christian churches, framed by overhanging rocks and protected by a much-perforated and decorated screen.

To name only a few of the large number of these structures: the Lomas Hsi caves in the Barabar hills, like the temples of Bihar and Udayagiri in eastern Bengal, date back to the third century B.C., while those of Bhaja, Bedsa, Kondane, Nasibe and Pithalkora, carved out of the hard red granite of the Ghats, were constructed in the second century. Although their chronological order cannot be exactly determined, one can see clearly how, in the evolution of these temples, the architect began by roofing a wooden building pushed, as it were, into the rock (at Bhaja the holes in the rock in which the joists rested are still visible, and in the temple at Karli the wooden rafters are still preserved), but soon ceased simply to imitate the forms of the timber framework. In the later grottoes at Ajanta, which date from the fifth century A.D., there are only faint reminiscences of the carpenter's craft. In the cave-temple at Karli (Fig. 27c)— nearly 140 feet long and 45 feet in width—a row of pillars supports the roof in a solemn and gliding rhythm, reminiscent in a way of ancient Buddhistic art, which ventured to allude to the master only through such symbols as the wheel or the footprint.

The figures which one sometimes finds at the entrances to the caves and at the gates of the stupas have long outgrown the stiffness of the archaic period, and the profile of Mesopotamian art. The unstable equilibrium, caused by the distinction between the supporting and the moving leg, can be noted even in the earliest sculptures. Already the women have the wide hips and the full, spherical breasts which are still among the marks of Indian beauty. Without any misgivings, the artists try to represent all kinds of movements, so that not only do the figures appear boneless and unstable, as is so often the case in Indian art, but looking closer one sees that they are by no means correctly proportioned (Fig. 28c). There is no need to look for Greek models to explain them when we remember what the earliest Mesopotamian art had accomplished—for example, in the statue of Gudea—or if we reflect that the Indians achieved the plastic representation of the human body without any alien influences. It was not until about the fifth century that the so-called art of Gandhara introduced a number of Hellenic forms into Indian art.

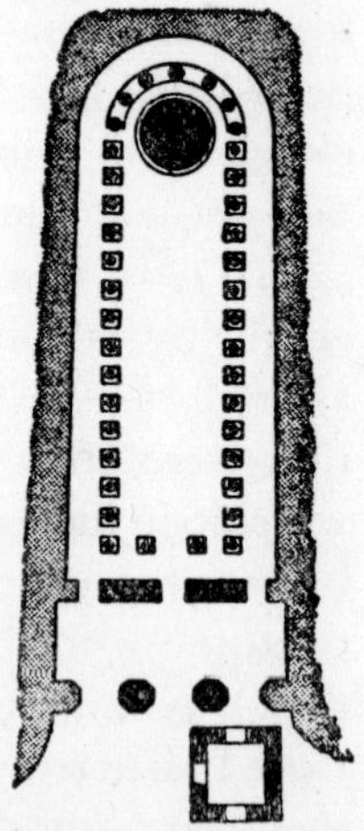

Ground plan of the Cave-Temple of Karli. (Fergusson)

This Gandharan art, originating in Afghanistan, on the north-west frontier, from time immemorial known as Gandharaland, and formerly not considered part of India proper, is really an alien manifestation. It appeared after the invasion of Alexander the Great. Like the provincial Gallo-Roman art in Rome, it was one of the exports of Hellenism. Its effect on the rest of India was not so powerful that one may therefore doubt the independence of Indian art. One cannot dispute the occurence later, in isolated cases, of a certain Hellenistic colouring; but it could not change the character of Indian art.

In the variegated civilization of India, Buddhism was never able completely to assert itself against the ancient beliefs and imagery. Gradually its teaching diverged: Mahayana, 'the Great Pilgrimage', became a sort of folk religion, which after a time bore very little resemblance to the simple teaching of the Master, creating for itself a new pantheon, which was based on the Brahman religion, while Hinayana, 'the Little Pilgrimage', preserved the pure doctrine of Gautama. From the second century A.D. we can distinguish two types of the Buddha. One is an austere and erect figure, with its left hand holding against the hips the upper garment which is flung over the shoulder, while the right hand is uplifted in the gesture which, as Abhaya-mudra, signifies 'Be not afraid!' The other figure is that of the Redeemer, seated with crossed legs in the yogi posture, the left hand resting on the knee, and the right once more uplifted in the Abhaya-mudra. At first the imposing head bore no supernatural emblems, but later on it was adorned with various symbols; such as the urn, which was presently represented by a frontal disc, or little ball, or lock of hair, and which was counted among the thirty-two greater and eighty lesser beauties of the Enlightened One. The standing Buddha is often accompanied by the lion, while in reliefs the seated Buddha is attended by two human figures, each clad in a loincloth and adorned with many jewels—the Boddhisatvas, the disciples of the Teacher. The period of the Gupta empire, from the fourth to the seventh century, was the culmination of Buddhist art. Under the second Gupta sovereign, Samudragupta, the empire covered the whole of northern India and extended far into the south. After a Scythian invasion had been repelled at the beginning of the sixth century, it knew a period of prosperity, when music, poetry and the drama flourished as well as the plastic arts, and there was a renaissance of Sanscrit literature. Now, people began to recall ancient times. Brahmanism exerted an increasing influence on Indian art, simultaneously with, and even through, Buddhism, which it was beginning to permeate. Indian painting now reached maturity; it was an art of astonishing power. All we know of its early history is from tales of richly-painted palaces, where the four quarters of the earth, the sun and moon, mountains and oceans, Heaven and the Gods, were represented. In the Gupta period the narrative picture, and the portrait, were demanded by the ruling class, which surrounded itself with wall paintings and easel pictures, banners, and painted scrolls and wall-hangings. Today, the frescoes in one of the rock-galleries of Sigiriya (Fig. 29a) painted between A.D. 479 and 497, tell us something of this art, so do the wall-paintings of the Buddhist rock-monastery of Ajanta (page 92), which go back, in an unbroken series, from the middle of the seventh to the middle of the fourth century. The walls of the temple, like those of mediaeval European cloisters, were adorned with pictures: in the galleries, as a rule, were those recording the legends of the former existence of the Redeemer; at the entrance to the sanctuary great Boddhisatvas appeared as disciples, and on the walls of the sanctuary itself the miracles of the Buddha were illustrated. The flat ceilings were often painted in imitation of architectural mouldings, and their compartments were filled with a luxuriant wealth of flowers, fruits and animals, and a whole world of celestial spirits. Buddhist frescoes were painted on a carefully prepared surface of wet plaster, their technique being close to the European. A preliminary drawing in hematite was followed by an under-painting in grey monochrome, over which the artist worked with pure mineral pigments. Such painting must have been the result of a long period of evolution. Originally a religious art, it became more and more worldly and refined, the innumerable Buddhist legends providing plenty of subjects.

While the older frescoes and the single figures of Buddha, with their austere style, still breathe the spirit of the Gupta period, which one might call the classical period of India, the later pictures were increasingly filled with life and movement. Palaces, with their entrance-gates, galleries and courtyards, halls and many-storeyed buildings, were painted with evident pleasure in the art of perspective, and isolated glimpses of the countryside are seen, but never a complete landscape. The people, however, are taken from Indian life, with its infinite number of castes and races. In the movements of the languidly beautiful figures, with plump sleek bodies, scantily clad, with their striped veils and loincloths, turbans, diadems, and garlands, the sensuous world of the tropics is expressed, and the ugliness of reality and the dreams of fairyland appear side by side.

Young Rajah, surrounded by Women.
Part of a wall-painting from the Tenth Cave, Ajanta

The spirit of the tropics began to stifle Buddhism; from the seventh century its hold was weakened, and by the end of the twelfth century it had almost disappeared from India proper, though it survived in Indo-China, China and Japan, in Hindustan, and in Ceylon, the citadel of the faith. Here there were few relapses into Brahmanism, and Islam, later, was unable to obtain a footing. In spite of individual pictures of Vishnu and Siva, the art of Ceylon has remained Buddhist since the days of Asoka.

The stupas, or *dagobas,* as they are called in Ceylon, have retained—in Thuparama, Tissamaharama, Mahanaga, and other places, their hemispherical shape. From the end of the eighth to the twelfth century the architecture and sculpture of Polonnaruva was important. It long preserved a tranquil nobility of bearing, and a discreet and austere execution, which remind one of the style of the Sigiriya wall-paintings (Fig. 29a), and which kept something of its vitality until the eighteenth and nineteenth centuries.

Neo-Brahmanic Art

The Gupta period was the classical period of Indian art, in which it reached maturity and perfection; in the following period, together with the shifting of the political centre from the north to the wholly tropical regions of Central and Southern India, this art expressed itself in increasingly rich and exuberant forms. It developed, in fact, into a sort of Baroque, having at its disposal the infinite wealth of subjects provided by the pantheon of Neo-Brahmanism or Hinduism.

The world of this new Indian art was peopled by the descendants of the ancient Vedic gods. In the Gupta period a certain attempt at lucidity of structure was still perceptible, but now a passionate unrest, a riotous activity, a preference for the vast, the wild, and the picturesque were predominant. Previously, the main task of sculpture had been the portrayal of individual figures, but it now turned to large compositions, in which the great epics of the Mahabharata and the Ramayana, with their innumerable legends, triumphantly invaded the plastic arts.

It is often difficult to recognize individual figures such as Vishnu, the ubiquitous Preserver, whose mighty arms embrace the universe. The worship of Vishnu, more frequent in the calmer north, had the greatest affinity to western religions. Krishna, and Rama, the consort of the lovely Sita, were regarded as incarnations of Vishnu. They are the central figures of the two epics. Krishna, who utters the wisdom of the Bhagavad-Gita, is generally represented playing the flute, and his adventures with women are often portrayed. But Shiva, to whom Nandi, the Bull, is sacred, is the most mysterious of the Indian divinities; he symbolizes the male power of creation; he meditates for thousands of years in the Himalayas, or, as Sadhu, wanders through the country. More often than not he is shown dancing (Fig. 31) or with his wife Parvati. He is, at the same time, the god of the strictest asceticism and the god of overbrimming fertility, and appears to mankind both as the destroyer and as the spirit of infinite goodness. In his most majestic representations, as the three-handed

Trimurti, he is Brahma the Creator, Rudra the Destroyer, and Vishnu the Preserver, in one. The forms in which these divinities appear are incalculable and inseparable, and it is impossible to reduce them to a definite hierarchy. Vishnu appears in the form of his enemy, and even that of his enemy's wife. There are countless local divinities, like the Monkey-God, Hanuman, a celibate deity of peculiar power, or Ganesha, the elephant-headed son of Shiva, whom the Indian artists are so fond of representing, and who is regarded by the people as the bringer of good fortune. But, after all, the belief in the transmigration of souls is a sufficient explanation of all appearances; they are only phenomenal forms of the One and Incomprehensible.

The architecture of such a period could no longer confine itself to caves. In the rock temples of Elura, the strangest of all Indian sanctuaries, the hall of the Indra-Sabha temple (illustrated below) is still divided by squat columns, but the general impression is one of space. The pillars stand on tall sockets; their short shafts are topped by massive capitals, expanding at the top, as though supporting the weight of the whole mountain. The Kailasa temple at Elura, named after Shiva's mountain castle in the Himalayas, dates from the eighth century and is the boldest and most wonderful achievement of Indian art. This temple is not inside the rock, but was carved out of it, like an enormous piece of sculpture. Part of the mountain was completely cut

Interior of the Indra-Sabha Temple at Elura

away, and the builders worked at it from both the outside and the inside; the result being a shrine 114 feet in height, covering an area of 272 by 133 feet, decorated with huge reliefs and a bewildering amount of carving.

Cave-temples were not so often hollowed out of the rock, as at Elephanta; but stone temples were built out in the open, containing the statues and symbols of the gods. Externally, these were built in the likeness of celestial palaces; sometimes, instead of resting on terraces, a temple was borne, like a divinity, by rows of lions and elephants, and sometimes it even had stone wheels, like a heavenly chariot. By its inexhaustible and exuberant creative impulse, by its very ecstasy of faith, Indian art, in this architecture, achieved its greatest triumphs. Higher and higher towered the temples and gates, and their superstructures; while the superimposed storeys, with their teeming sculptures, assumed ever richer forms (Fig. 30a).

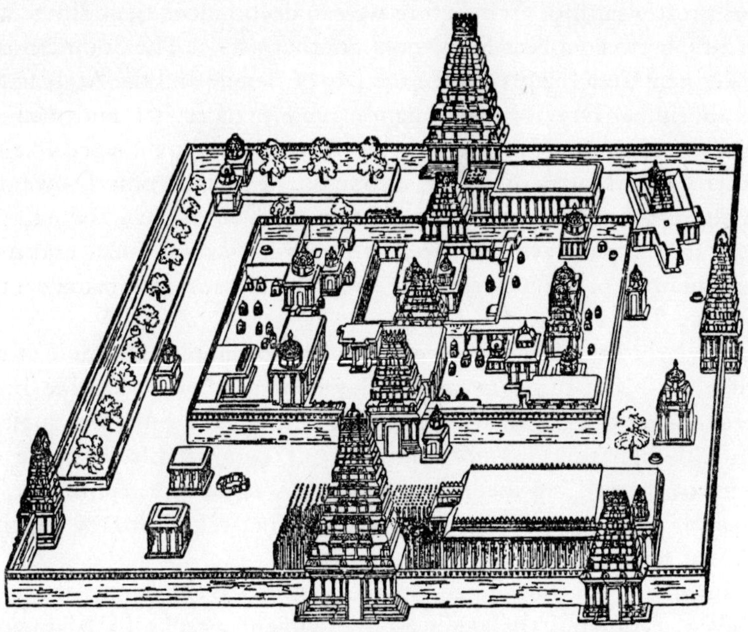

Plan of the Dravidian Temple of Tiruvannamalai,
South-western Madras

As for the general plan of the temple and its precincts, one cannot expect an art so unfettered as this to observe any fixed rules. The temple of Tiruvannamalai (above) is best surveyed from a neighbouring hill, from which it is possible to get some idea of the ground-plan of a great Brahmanic temple. Around the inner shrine the irrepressible fantasy of the architect has laid out courtyards of increasing width, and higher and higher walls. The Hindu must follow a long and mysterious path to reach the sanctuary; courtyards, halls and gateways follow one another, producing a complicated and often entirely assymetrical plan.

Any attempt to classify the architectural forms created by Brahmanic art, or to distinguish any special types of architecture in the temples of individual gods, must be left, as a thankless and questionable task, to the specialist; so must the attempt to distinguish a special Jain art.

The Jains are a religious community founded by Mahavira, a contemporary of Gautama. Although never a very numerous sect, they were able, thanks to their wealth and their piety, to build many magnificent temples on sacred hills. Of these, the white marble temples of Vimala Sha (1032) and Tejahpala (1232) on Mount Abu are the best known; but there are whole temple-cities, as at Girnar or Palitana. In the latter place, since the eleventh century, over 500 sanctuaries have been built, in eleven enclosures.

With this great wealth of architecture we can do no more than differentiate, with some certainty, between a Northern and a Southern style. The Southern is found in the triangular peninsula lying between the Bay of Bengal and the Arabian Sea. Here, where the aboriginal Dravidian population predominates, we find many-storeyed, rectilinear, stepped pyramidal towers, capped with a coping shaped like the upper half of a barrel. The Northern style is characterized by tall conical towers, tapering in a gentle curve, to a rounded point. A good example of this style is the Black Pagoda at Konarak, in the province of Orissa, while in Mysore we shall find magnificent examples of the style of temple typical of southern India, as, for instance, the temple of Somnathpur (Fig. 28a).

This particularly beautiful and serenely-balanced temple was built at a moment when Indian art had paused in its development as though to take breath. The Mohammedan invasions began after the ninth century, and India was subjected to an alien rule. Although this did not entirely stifle national life, and the continued development of the arts, an increasing lassitude was perceptible, manifesting itself in an increasing refinement, and finally, after a brief rekindling of creative fire, in commercialization and general demoralization.

Neo-Brahmanic art, little altered on the whole, survived into the seventeenth century, when it suffered the renewed and violent attacks of Islam, now more powerful than ever; but it has continued until the present day to build many-pillared temples enriched with sculpture. Although its architects have designed the magnificent temples we have mentioned, while its sculptors have created all the innumerable gods and goddesses—not only the great and powerful, but also the less significant deities—the Yakshi (Fig. 29c), for instance, whose versatility and wisdom were often symbolized by the familiar device of giving them several heads and arms—this exuberant and vital art accomplished hardly anything in the decoration of plane surfaces. This disability was inherent in its very character.

In painting neo-Brahmanic art produced nothing comparable with Buddhistic wall-painting. The figures which appear in the wall-paintings of Elura, as early as the eleventh century, are characterized by the curiously angular gestures of their fingers, their pointed noses, eyes, and lips. These paintings were the forerunners of the book illustrations, drawn on palm-leaves (page 97) from the thirteenth century onward,

31. Shiva, dancing. From the interior of the Great Temple of Madura.

a

b

c

32. (A) Pagoda amidst the ruins of Pagan, which extend for twenty miles along the banks of the upper Irrawaddy in Burma. At the entrance are leogryphs, and behind them the portico, a wooden building showing Chinese influence.

(B) Small pagoda, covered with Buddha niches, at Ava, near Mandalay.

(C) Head of a giant statue, in the vicinity of Polonnaruva, one of the ancient capitals of Ceylon. Beside the figure of the Buddha, reposing in Nirvana (45 ft. long) rises the granite statue (nearly 23 ft. high) of his favourite pupil, Ananda. Twelfth century.

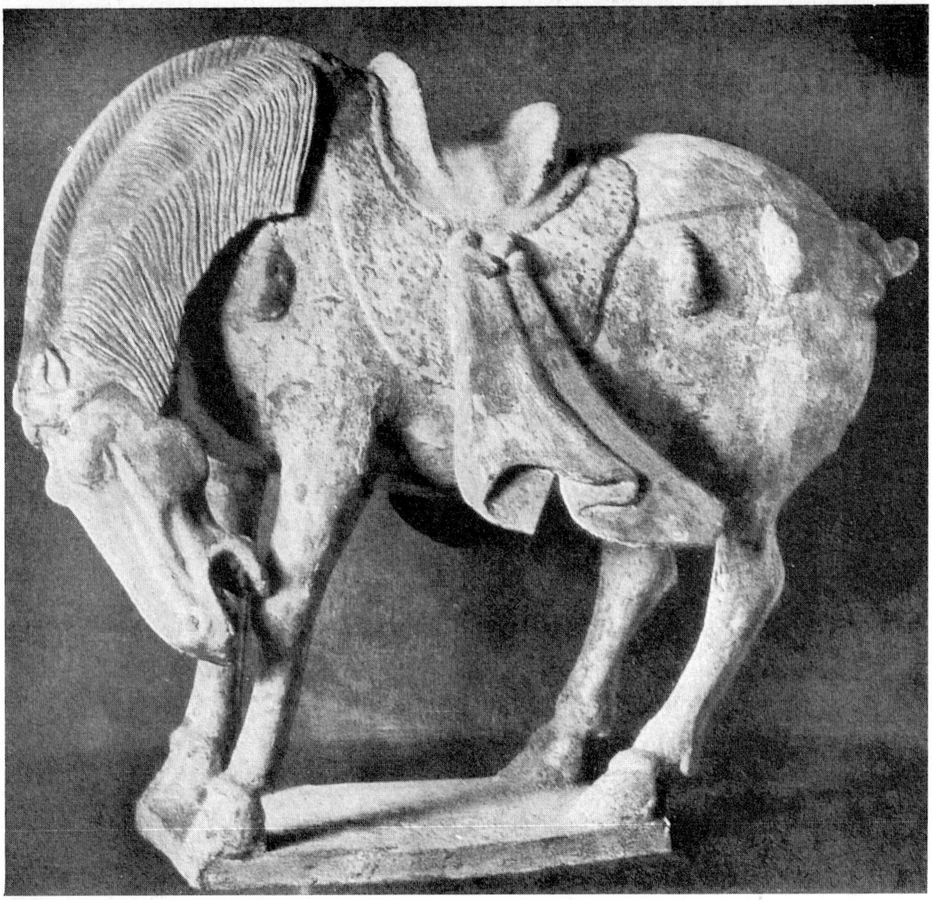

b

c

33. (A) Saddled horse, from a tomb. Painted earthenware. Height, $9\frac{1}{2}$ in. Tang Dynasty. (Coninx-Girardet, Collection Zürich).
(B) Bronze cauldron. An inscription records the names of the donor and the recipient, and continues; 'May sons and the sons of sons, 10,000 years without end, guard it for ever and use it for sacrifice'. Height, $15\frac{3}{8}$ in. Chou Dynasty. (Von der Heydt Collection, Ascona).
(C) Bronze case in the form of a bird. Handle and legs hollow. Height, 13 in. (Meyer Collection: New York).

34. (A) Mandarin, at the end of the so-called Spirit Way. Tombs of the Ming Emperors, to the north of Peking. (B) Bust of a Bodhisattva of the Wei period. High relief, with traces of painting, broken off from a limestone cliff (probably the caves of Kung-hsien). Height, 20 in. (Schlieper Collection, Berlin). (C) Brick pagoda of the Temple of Sung-yueh-sse in the province of Honan. Dodecahedral base, fifteen storeys. According to inscription, built A.D. 523. (D) Colossal figure of Buddha, Wei period. Yun-Kang Cave.

and since the fifteenth century on paper. Long panoramic scenes, whose continuity is often interrupted, are coloured with deep reds and blues, with a nice sense of spatial relations. A fresh development occurred under the increasing Muslim influence, which introduced the Persian art of portraiture and miniature-painting on paper and ivory, which flourished as a glorious derivative chapter of Islamic art in India from the seventeenth century onwards.

Drawing and inscription scratched with a sharp stylus on a slip of bleached and polished palm-leaf

The Northern Border

As a result of the triumphant expansion of Buddhism, the artistic influence of India was felt far beyond her frontiers. The Gandhara art of the north-west frontier was a mixture of Indian and Hellenistic elements (page 90). The sculpture of the Gandhara school above all represented the Buddhistic legends in the idiom of late Hellenic art; while the architecture, as far as stupas and monasteries were concerned, did not, generally speaking, forget its Indian origin, and played with borrowed forms only in the arrangement of columns and their capitals.

A still more remarkable composite art was the product of Hellenistic, Sassanidic, Indian and Chinese influence, in eastern Turkestan. There, on the edge of the Gobi

Portraits of Founders, from the tenth cave at Ming Oei, Turkestan

Desert, from the fourth to the ninth century, several cities of some size had sprung up under Buddhist rule, only to decay in later centuries; today they are buried in the sand. The excavations of Grunwedel, Le Coq and others have revealed, as well as the unimpressive remains of the architecture which flourished around the oases, and the remnants of Buddhist stupas, small temples, great monasteries and individual shrines, a countless number of rock-temples, in the cliffs, in which were paintings of an extraordinary kind. These were mostly carried out in tempera—that is, without the help of a fatty or oily medium. The figures in the illustration on page 97 are recognizable as Buddhistic from the symbols on their foreheads (page 92); but apart from that they are in no sense Hellenistic; they are unmistakable knights, with richly-embroidered surcoats and stockinged feet. Their swords and sword belts are reminiscent of mediaeval Europe, though their faces are definitely Chinese.

Finally, a curious conjunction between the native art and Hellenism took place farther south, in the mountainous country of Kashmir, which, on the whole, tenaciously adhered to Buddhism, until in the twelfth century the art of Islam made its irresistible entry.

In the little Himalayan kingdom of Nepal the Mongolian influence is obvious. Of Nepal it has been said, with some exaggeration, that it contains more temples than houses and more sacred images than human beings. Here, as well as stupas, there are genuine pagodas, of which the earliest date from the fifteenth century. The country served as a bridge, over which Buddhism made its way toward Tibet, over the highest steppe country in the Old World. There we find an even more pronounced mountain architecture: in the forests it combines timber construction with stone walls and high-pitched roofs; while on the bare cliffs the high walls of the palaces and monasteries, built of sun-dried bricks, tower upward like the continuation of the rock. None of these disorderly, close-packed monasteries date back further than the seventeenth century, and this region, explored by Sven Hedin, makes only occasional contributions toward the history of art; as a whole it lies too far removed from the mainstream of development.

In Kangra, as in the whole of the Himalayan region of the Punjab, various schools of art arose in the eighteenth century, which in their pleasant Raga- and Ragini-pictures were symbolical of musical melodies. In the Kangra paintings the artist was fond of contrasting his enamel-like colours with wide, distinctly-mottled surfaces.

Indo-China

With the exception of Ceylon, Buddhism was incapable of retaining its hold in the land of its origin, and today the shrine marking the spot where Gautama received enlightenment is in the hands of the Brahmans. We may read in this, as in the relics of the old Buddhistic art, the verdict of history: that the teaching of the Buddha was not in harmony with the restless spirit of the tropics. As one of the world-religions it was destined to make its way northward into the Himalayas, and farther still—adapting itself to different peoples—into China, Korea and Japan. In Indo-China the more tranquil and conservative spirit of the far East was at work. Its people do not constitute any kind of unity. Mongolian tribes predominate in the north, while in the south the Malay strain is evident. In the same way as Brahmanic art is the clearest expression of the powers and destinies of Hindustan, carrying the European into a completely alien world as he enters its temples which, as they stretch into the sky, defy all the laws of proportion, so it is the more subdued spirit of the Far East that gives the art of Indo-China its characteristic aspect. The light wooden structures of which the reader will learn more in the chapter on Chinese art (Fig. 32a), now appear beside the pagodas; the stupas have become pagoda-like and bell-shaped, and seem content to rest upon the earth, unlike those of Hindustan. Usually, these shrines stand on a stepped structure whose interior, recalling the ancient Buddhistic cave-temples, is pierced by corridors giving on to cells; but externally they have something of the Chinese serenity.

In Burma, where for centuries Chinese, Indians and Malays have constantly intermingled, Brahmanism, as in India, preceded Buddhism. In the ruins of Prome, the ancient capital, one finds stupas of the sixth to the eighth century A.D.; they are round, and often taper like pointed sugar-loaves. Burmese architecture of the tenth to the thirteenth century has left several masterpieces amidst the ruins of Pagan, on the left bank of the Irrawaddy (Fig. 32a), where the finest monument is the Ananda temple which was built between 1058 and 1107. Gilt and painted wooden reliefs adorn the wooden buildings, and even in Mandalay, in more recent times, Burmese architects have reverted entirely to the use of wood as a building material. But in the older pagodas (Fig. 32b), stone is predominant, and in the temples innumerable images of the Buddha, with Mongolian eyes, sit in the innumerable niches.

The many ancient sculptures, in stucco, sandstone and bronze, discovered in Siam, show the familiar Buddhistic figures attended by a partially Brahman retinue. The best examples are in the Bangkok tower, 380 feet in height, which was built in the latter half of the nineteenth century over a mediaeval foundation.

In the eastern provinces of Indo-China, already so strongly permeated by the Chinese spirit that one stands upon the outermost verge of the province of Indian art, the Khmer art of Cambodia deserves special mention. Here, in the earliest times, temple spires played an important part, and series of fairy-like buildings arose in the tropical forest wilderness.

The marvellous temple of Angkor Vat, built between the ninth and twelfth centuries, is one of the best preserved. It was once sacred to Vishnu, whose gigantic statues adorned the entrance. The skilful alternation of galleries and towers of greenish sandstone give the building, which rises in three terraced storeys, a look of compactness in spite of its great size. Inside, bas-reliefs nearly ten feet high extend over a total length of half a mile. In spite of their Indian fluency and exuberance, they have curiously self-contained outlines which remind one remotely of the Chinese work of the Han dynasty, as does the constantly recurring serpent and dragon motive. Together with the sculptures on the soffits and arches of the gateways, these reliefs of Angkor Vat are among the masterpieces of Indian art. Adorned with more than 1,500 square columns, the magnificent building lies at a distance of a mile and a quarter from Angkor Thom, the ancient Khmer capital, whose great rectangular enclosure was surrounded by a moat nearly 100 yards wide, and a wall whose total length was seven and a half miles.

Indonesia

In Prambanan, Indian art is once more in its tropical home. In the early Middle Ages a wave of Indian culture swept over the Sunda Islands—not only over Java, but also over Sumatra, Borneo and Bali. In these islands, so luxuriantly endowed by Nature, the spirit of Indian art spent itself to the utmost, as though determined once more to repeat everything it had ever done. The 'Thousand Temples of Prambanan', or the temple of Borobudur, or the ruins of Mendut, are all encrusted with the figures of the Indian world from the sagas of the Ramayana (Fig. 30b) and the Mahabharata. There Shiva, the great dancer (Fig. 31), dances his way over death and destruction; and though in these statues, and these temples, a thousand enigmas confront us, though walls are crumbling and the pillars falling, though men and gods are sinking into oblivion, Shiva dances and creates new life wherever his gracious feet touch the earth. Behind this radiant art is a history of thousands of years. Indian culture was preceded, throughout the whole of Indonesia, and also in Polynesia, by the ancient culture of Malaya, whose natives had entirely different beliefs concerning life and death; they had long had their own system of tattooing and their garments of painted bark-cloth, and they produced wooden images which represented immemorial conceptions of their ancestors and of the goblins of the forest. What one generally describes as Indonesian, though over and over again it came from India, must be sharply divided, by a line drawn about the beginning of the Christian era, into two different worlds—the world of Buddhism, and the world of ancient Malaysia.

Funerary Boat, from Ridor, Timor, East Indonesia. (Jacobsen. Cf. p. 51)

Even before the Christian era the kind of weaving known as *ikat* was introduced from Asia. It is not a Polynesian production, but is a result of the contact of Hindus and Malays; the same is true of *batik*, and of the stone architecture of Bali, part of which was directly colonized by Indians. Moreover, the shadow-plays and other theatrical performances derive from Indian myths, and many other things in the rich decorative art of Indonesia—for example, the Wayang dolls of painted leather, used in shadow-plays—share equally the qualities of Indian and of Polynesian art, as was explained more fully on pages 48 and 51-2.

Malayan Prince;
Wayang figure from a Javanese shadow-play

Chapter VIII

CHINA

*

The great alluvial plain of the middle Hwang Ho, with its deep river valleys and its continental climate, was the first home of the Chinese people. The ridges between the low-lying areas of agricultural land were covered with undergrowth and trees, which the first settlers cleared by means of fire. For this reason, the divine husbandman, Shen Nung, whom ancient legends credit with the introduction of agriculture, is represented in the earliest paintings as Yen Ti, the Fiery Ruler, or the Lord of Fire. Whether the wars of ancient tradition were against an aboriginal population, or other immigrant tribes, it is difficult to say; but it is clear from the river beasts and sea monsters which are named in legends and represented, with various winged creatures, on ancient bronzes, that the enemy came from the sea. The Miao people seem to have been gradually pushed back into the Yangtze basin, while the Chinese took possession of the region of the Yellow River; the legends confirm this in their own way, when they say that the princes of the Miao, 'The Four Great Malefactors', were 'expelled by the Sacred Sovereigns'.

Nevertheless, a conflict of cultures took place, the results of which lasted through the whole later evolution of the people, and affected the development of Chinese art. The matriarchal system of the conquered, and the patriarchal system of the conquering tribes, form together one of the fundamental elements in the history of primeval China, which is in many ways not unlike one of the ancient American cultures. In a common aversion from milk, in the use of knotted strings as the first form of writing, in the worship of the heavenly bodies, and in a tradition of origins in which the Canidae play an important part, we can see the Mongolian affinity between these peoples—as we also do when comparing the bronze vases of the Chinese, and the hieroglyphs of the Mayas (cf. Figs. 33b with 18b and Fig. on page 64). Unlike the Mongoloid aborigines of America, the Chinese had tamed cattle from the beginning, and harnessed horses, though they only later learned to ride them from their western neighbours.

Chinese tradition dates the invention of writing in the twenty-sixth century B.C. Long before the invention of the paintbrush, as early as the first millennium B.C., they were scratching their script with a stylus-like implement on soft clay, and later still on bones, pottery, bronzes, and early stone sculptures. The characters were pictorial symbols, almost always representing concrete objects. Most of the chief parts of the human body are found among them, as well as the most important animals, some plants and trees, the sun, the moon, and the oldest implements and weapons. These images reveal that the magnetic compass was already known to the Chinese at this period, that they understood the art of firing bricks, that they used wheeled vehicles and boats, that they had many kinds of vases and other vessels, that their houses had windows, and that they wore richly embroidered clothes.

Chinese Antiquity

The autenticated history of China does not go back as far as is often thought; it begins considerably after that of Egypt or Mesopotamia. A fixed point, from which calculations can be made is the 29 August, 875 B.C., when an eclipse of the sun was seen. From this the dates of the two oldest dynasties can be calculated; the Hsia dynasty (2205—1766 B.C.) and the Shang dynasty (1766—1122 B.C.)

We need not accept literally the tradition that the potter's art was invented about 2250 B.C. by the Emperor Shun. Recent excavations have found a primitive form of pottery whose painted and geometrical patterns reveal a decorative impulse of a kind which the reader has already seen (cf. the vase from Susa, page 75), though in China the vessels were not beakers, but were usually earthenware tripods like those of the Stone Age, and before long were being cast in bronze (Fig. 33b). Ancient Chinese records speak of these tripods so often, and in so much the same terms, that there is no doubt that they are among the most ancient ceremonial objects.

The decoration on the oldest of these bronzes indicates the earlier use of another material, wood, which was carved with a knife (chip-carving): signs of the influence of this technique can often be easily recognized (Fig. 33c). The earliest wooden vessels, however, have long ago perished, and apart from fragments of a hard, whitish pottery, and a few articles of jade and bone, all of the same kind, bronzes are the oldest relics of Chinese art.

Besides the heavy tripods—the *Ting*, used for cooking flesh offerings—the bronzes most commonly found are the *Tsun*, or vessels for sacrificial wine. Dishes with handles have also been found, to hold offerings of grain, and many other ceremonial objects, such as the bells, known as *Chung* which can be recognized by rows of knobs by which they were suspended, and which, when struck, emitted a variety of tones.

In the Chou dynasty (1122—255 B.C.) a typical period of feudal civilization began. The house of *Chou*, established in the extreme west of China, produced fresh blood and fresh ideas. In a highly developed patriarchal system, cities now became centres of a power, within which the old family system continued for a long time. Smaller towns were ruled by counts, and cities by feudal princes; over all was the capital of the Great King, to whom all were subject. Under the Chou dynasty the basic principles of government were established, as well as the religious philosophy which for nearly three thousand years was to influence the art of the whole Far East. The ancient demons, gods and fabulous beings in the centre of the earth, who were represented on the bronze vessels, gradually became forgotten. Heaven was now the seat of the supreme God, who looked down upon mankind, rewarding the good and punishing the wicked. His representative on earth was the Son of Heaven, especially deserving this title, since his deceased ancestors were considered to surround the Supreme Ruler. Art and urbanity, rather than the fear of monsters and sinister gods, were now the powers that influenced men. In the religion of the Chou dynasty was a cheerful faith, although it did not ignore the darkness of its primitive background. Something of the same kind happened later on in Greece, where the bright daylight world of Homer stands out against a darker, and only half-forgotten, background. The Chinese nobles, who surrounded their sovereign as a result of court custom and feudal service, regulated their lives by a code of chivalry rather than by any primitive law. As they looked up to the Great King, so he looked up to the Lord of Heaven, whom he worshipped as a father. Ceremonial symbolized this imperial system: when the Son of Heaven received the princes he turned his face to the south; and the sacrifice offered to the Lord of Heaven in front of the gates of the capital epitomized not only humanity's communion with Him, but also the community of mankind. This great festival was the foundation of morality. Confucius recognized this when he declared, long afterwards, that he who understood the meaning of the Great Sacrifice understood the order of the universe as though it lay in the palm of his hand. To understand Chinese art one must always remember this conception of the universe. In a country where ancestor-worship rules both living and dead there is little difference between past and present. This explains the 'suspension' or 'standstill' of Chinese art for long periods, which Europeans, accustomed to other standards, often observe with some disapproval.

Mediaeval China

Things were never quite at a standstill in China. By about 1000 B.C., the predominance of the cities had caused some change in the old ways of life; merchants assumed leading positions, and a few centuries later the power of the empire began to decline The Tartars from the north-west invaded the country, and with a most un-Chinese brutality—perhaps in accordance with a Scythian custom—they made cups of the skulls of their enemies. In this conflict with a young race, a new China was made at the cost of much blood and travail, destined, in the true spirit of ancestor-worship, to save the treasures of antiquity for the future. The strong, imperialistic, military Chin dynasty (255—206), under its emperor Shi-huang-ti, built the 2,000-mile Great Wall of China along the frontier, a much greater architectural achievement than the Roman Wall in England, built three centuries later and only one-tenth of the length. It is understandable that only a few works of art should have survived from this period of invasion and migration; but the Chinese spirit, and Chinese art, emerged purified and refined from their ordeal. By the time of the Han dynasty (206 B.C. — A.D. 220) people were already valuing the ancient bronzes and seeking to preserve them (page 106).

In Han vases the basic form became more and more important, and to this the decoration adapted itself; whereas the ancient bronzes were often only the pretext for whimsical and fantastic ornament. The artistic activities of the Han period were still influenced by bronzes and other objects discovered in ancient tombs: jewellery, weapons, vases and mirrors are mostly of bronze, as well as ceremonial objects of jade, and specimens of pottery—the first Chinese pottery to be glazed—and even lacquered articles, which imply the existence of an ancient tradition.

The best examples of Han art are the stone slabs recently discovered in tombs in the province of Shantung, on which scenes crowded with figures, are represented in flat relief. It is clear from these that Chinese architecture of the Han period differed very little from that of today. We see houses with several storeys, spacious rooms, and pointed roofs with projecting eaves, the cross-beams being supported by separate posts. Sometimes there is a breastwork between the posts—still a favourite method of building in China, as walls do not carry the weight of the roof, but are simply inserted between the supports: very often they are not even fixed, so that they can be altered at any time. This description, of course, refers to the houses of the upper classes; the people lived in modest huts or cottages.

The individual quality of Chinese sculpture became more apparent after the introduction of Buddhism, which brought to China a new pantheon. For four hundred years the country remained in comparative peace under the Han Emperors, until a fresh invasion destroyed its unity, dividing it into three parts: the kingdoms of Han, Wei and Wu, over which various northern and southern dynasties (A.D. 220—618) ruled for four hundred years. This disunity opened the frontiers to external influences, and whereas previously only occasional apostles of Buddhism had set foot upon the soil of China, now the doctrine began to spread, though one must not exaggerate its influence. It had, as a popular faith, to win its place in a decaying hierarchy without destroying the structure of Chinese society. Just as Christianity, also originally a popular movement, gave fresh life to the Middle Ages, enriching traditions with a new imagery, so was it with Buddhism in China. In the east, religious centres, of a kind hitherto unknown in China, were established; between A.D. 455—462 the first four caves of the rock-temples of Yuen-kang, near Ping-cheng, the capital of the Wei kingdom, were completed. The idea of cutting sanctuaries out of the living rock was new to the Chinese, but artists took to the idea with the greatest satisfaction. Buddhism inspired a new kind of sculpture (Fig. 34d). Although many Chinese pilgrims had seen the architectural wonders of India, Indian art was soon to suffer a Chinese transformation: Buddha himself acquired Mongolian features; his garments became more austere and lay flatter against the body, and his whole form lost the sensuous quality which distinguishes Indian art. An entirely mediaeval constraint appeared in these figures, whose faces often wore the wooden smile (Fig. 34b) which appears in all early art as the first experiment in facial expression, and which, as the 'archaic smile', is found both in Greece and in mediaeval Europe.

Rubbing of a flat stone relief of the Han period, representing an unsuccessful attempt to recover a sacred bronze vase.
Wu-liang-tse, Shantung

When, in A.D. 494, the Imperial residence was transferred to Lo-yang, the still more magnificent rock-temples of Lung-men were made, in a region not far from the capital under the influence of the old Chinese culture, and work was still going on there as late as the middle of the eighth century. The cliff-grottoes of Tien-lung-shan, in Shangsi, with their delicate and sensitive sculpture, introduced a kind of Early Renaissance in China, which under the Tang dynasty developed into a really classic art.

The Period of Culmination

Under the Tang emperors (618—907) the political and cultural development of China was expressed in an exceptionally splendid art. China dominated the whole of central Asia; the nomads willingly submitted to her suzerainty, and now for the first time even Tibet was subjugated. Embassies visited remote western countries, and the Chinese, becoming self-conscious, began to produce a more sophisticated art. A new attitude to Nature accompanied this change: landscape painting, of which

Wang Wei (698—759) was the reputed originator, was now, for the first time, recognized as a proper art-form, and it was, indeed, one of the greatest and most original creations of Chinese art.

Chinese painting, as well as sculpture, had placed itself at the service of Buddhism, and Indian painting, also then in its maturity, as is shown by its brilliant achievements at Ajanta and Sigiriya, was bound to influence Chinese artists. Wu-Tau-tzu, who might be called the Giotto of the East, advanced, at this time, from a careful and constrained representation of detail, through a freer and more calligraphic style of brushwork, to a pure water-colour technique, which anticipated what was to come. Chinese painting, as a whole, will be described in a special section, and this reference must be enough at this point; similarly, architecture will not be discussed now, on the strength of the scanty relics of this period, but together with that of a later period, which repeated all the forms which were first created during the golden age of the Tang dynasty.

On the other hand, many masterpieces of Tang sculpture survive, not only in China and Korea, but also in Japan; since A.D. 645 the island empire, under Chinese influence, had adopted not only Chinese political organization but the whole of Chinese culture. The consciousness of power which characterized this period was expressed not merely in the minor arts (Fig. 33a), but also by such colossal figures as the great stone images of Buddha in the rock-temple of Sock-kul-am, near Kyong-yu, in Korea, which look down on the ocean from their mountain-top; or the many ferocious guardian deities and heavenly commanders (Fig. 38a) in which we can already see a transition to a baroque and picturesque style, which reached its full development under the Sung dynasty.

After the dethronement of the last feeble Tang emperor no fewer than five dynasties succeeded one another in a few years (A.D. 907—960). Historians have attributed this repeated change of rulers to increasing refinement of manners, an impotent Court, and the intrigues of women. In fact, the causes lay much deeper: during the sixth, seventh and eighth centuries Buddhism—know also as Foism, since in Chinese, Buddha is called Fo—was the prevailing doctrine, but toward the end of the Tang period, in the middle of the ninth century, there was a strong reaction. More than 45,000 Buddhistic temples and cloisters are supposed to have been destroyed, and the Indian doctrine did not recover its influence for 400 years.

In China, as in Europe, the Baroque style made its appearance in connection with a powerful religious movement. After an impetuous outburst of individualism in the period of the Five Dynasties, China returned, under the rule of the Sung dynasty (960—1279), to the old foundations of her culture. The philosophy of antiquity and the doctrines of the Confucian school dictated the pattern of life, and with tireless diligence the past was investigated and its relics preserved. Inside Buddhism, which still to some extent survived, the Chan sect, the school of self-submersion, predominated, and Taoist mysticism laid a new emphasis on the importance of personal experience. In solitary landscapes poets and painters could forget themselves, in the bamboo thickets, or in contemplation of the everlasting life of the waterfalls. This great and noble period of the eleventh and twelfth centuries may have produced a few statues (Fig. 40d) and pictures which—very doubtfully dated—have been attributed to the painters Mi Fei, Hui Tsing, Li Ti, Hsia Kuei, Ma Yuan, Yiu-Rien-Tsien-Tun (page 111) and others. Since the history of Chinese art, of the Sung period alone, records the names of eight hundred painters, whose most famous works were afterwards frequently reproduced, it seems better, instead of confusing the reader with a jumble of names and dates, to make a general survey of Chinese painting.

Chinese Painting

To understand Chinese painting it is as well to acquire some familiarity with Chinese handwriting which is closely related to painting.

When the European looks at the strange characters standing in vertical rows and reading downwards and from right to left, he asks whether these characters are letters, words, or pictures. The answer is that they are none of these. If this were a purely pictorial script it could only describe visible and palpable things. Among all the systems of writing employed by civilized peoples at the present time, the Chinese is unique, for it consists, not of symbols for sounds, but for ideas. It is, so to speak, the still formless quantity that constitutes the basis of word-formation. In spite of a few attempts, made under European influence, the Chinese never took the final step toward the invention of an alphabet; not even when, during the translation of the Buddhist scriptures, problems arose to solve which an Indian, about A.D. 420, invented a Chinese alphabet of forty-two letters.

The Chinese word and the written symbol for writing, also signifies drawing. Chinese artists like—even more than the early Greeks—to include a written text in a picture as a finishing touch. Few Chinese paintings are without such decorative additions (Figs. 37a and 37b), giving the artist's name, and the date of the painting, with comments on the style, and often including a poem inspired by the subject of the picture. The Chinese show themselves to be genuinely painter-poets. The greatest value is attached to beauty and individuality of calligraphy, and its inclusion in the picture is taken for granted. To them, line is all-important; the quality of calligraphy or painting is determined by the quality of the line, which may be heavy and broad, or light and elegant, or strong and precise. Anyone who looks at paintings in the company of Chinese will see how their eyes are fascinated by the outlines, and how the connoisseur judges by the certainty and vigour of their execution. In their curves, angles and sinnous fluency, suavity and sensibility, brutality and strength, uncertainty or decrepitude are alike expressed.

Colour is not unknown to the Chinese artist, but he uses it always in a linear fashion in flat washes and spots, distinguishing three manners of applying it: the

Kou-shan manner in which the outlines of the picture are drawn with brush-strokes in black ink, while the intervening spaces are coloured; the *Mo-ku* or 'boneless' style, so called because it lacks the lines which should be the framework of the whole, which is closest to European technique, in which the artist uses only flat washes and spots of colour; and the *Hsieh-yi*, which consists only of lines and indications, almost always in ink—that is, in black and white—which is a style of drawing rather than

草書	行書	楷書	隸書	篆書
山	山	山	山	山
水	水	水	水	水
魚	魚	魚	魚	魚
鳥	鳥	鳥	鳥	鳥
靜	靜	靜	靜	靜
淑	淑	淑	淑	淑
貞	貞	貞	貞	貞
烈	烈	烈	烈	烈

Principal forms of Chinese script. The column on the extreme right gives the basic form of the logograph; on its left are the forms of a late period; in the middle are the characters in general use today. Farther to the left are the somewhat more fluent characters of the cursive script, while those on the extreme left are the greatly simplified characters of the so-called 'grass script'

painting, and which Chinese connoisseurs have always considered the most distinguished style. Though these pictures are entirely in black and white, they are regarded as the pinnacle of art. It is difficult to realise the pedantic way in which Chinese schools of painting have, in all periods, dealt with the linear structure of a picture: for example, in drawing mountains there are sixteen different ways of distinguishing the lines, accordingly as they suggest wrinkles, rifts and folds, or the veins on the petals of a lotus, or the course followed by trickling raindrops, or the twists of an 'unravelled rope', etc.

This preference for outline explains the way in which the sea, lakes and rivers are represented; there is no attempt to suggest reflection, or movement, or atmospheric values. The surface of the water is generally shown by very faint lines, or sometimes by a blank; in the favourite subject of a boat or group of vessels, there is never really any water, and one is often conscious of its absence under the many bridges which occur in Chinese pictures. In European painting the sky and the play of colours in the atmosphere give the picture an appearance of depth and reality; but one finds in Chinese paintings only an expanse of bare silk, or a faint brown or yellowish tinge on the paper.

Three of the Ten styles of Drawing practised in East Asiatic art. (Anderson)

In the famous treatise on painting which Kuo Hsi wrote in the eleventh century, he says: 'The appearance of the clouds in landscape pictures differs with the seasons: in the spring they are quiet and gentle; in the summer dense and brooding; in the autumn thin and scattered; in the winter grey and gloomy. The forms and the relations of the clouds come to life if one does not exactly imitate all details, but only reproduces the prospect broadly as whole'. These are the boldest words to which a master of the still predominantly 'picturesque' period of the Sung dynasty would dare to commit himself. Anyone trying to draw an analogy from the European 'picturesque' would find himself baffled by a completely alien sense of form. The instructions given by Kuo Hsi, which do little more than recommend a simple omission of detail, reveal more of the methods of Chinese art and of the Chinese conception of life than the longest treatise. Curiously enough, the unpicturesque quality in Chinese painting is especially expressed in the by no means infrequent representation of rain and mist. It is typical that the latter is not used to pull the picture together, but to break it up, as it is a simple means of giving depth to the landscape by separating particular portions of the picture. When water, other than rain, can be represented by brush-strokes, the artist begins to enjoy himself, and for this reason, falling water is one of the Chinese painters favourite subjects. Anyone with any knowledge of Chinese landscape knows the ubiquitous waterfall.

Much the same is true of trees. The artist prefers to take them individually, reproducing, with the greatest delicacy, the leaves or needles, the trunk, the boughs, and the smallest twigs. Grasses, plants and flowers, bamboos, rushes, a spray of blossom against the sky, or a bird perching on it, have always fascinated the Chinese painter, who reproduces with infinite care every detail of the tree's foliage or the bird's plumage.

Another peculiarity of Chinese painting is that reflections of objects in water are never represented, however natural it seems to us do so. There are creatures of all kinds on the shore, and the mountains rise beyond rivers and lakes, but there is no image of them in the water. Nor does the Chinese artist paint shadows. Even in the brightest sunlight, a tree, or a man in the middle of the road, or a building, casts no shadow, though the Chinese painter does see the shadows *in* an object—the dark rift in the cluff, the underside of a bridge, and so forth. The lighting of a picture is usually uniform: very often a moonlight scene can only be recognised because the moon is visible somewhere in the sky. Such an art could never take for its subject sunrise or sunset, with their sharp contrasts of light and shade.

Bamboo Thicket on the Shore. Painting by Yiu-Rien-Tsien-Tun. About A.D. 1200. (British Museum)

The Chinese explain this absence of shadows and reflections by saying that their paintings represent the inner reality of things, while shadows and reflections are merely impalpable appearances. By European standards of superficial, representational realism Chinese painting does seem at first sight indifferent to reality; but Su Tung-po declared that he who judges a picture by its resemblance to the subject judges it as a child, and a widely-read classical treatise on painting tells us that art creates something that lies beyond form.

The Chinese disregard of chiaroscuro clearly owes something to the essentially linear character of their art, influenced by their technique with its use of finely-pointed brushes.

Lord Macartney, who headed a British embassy in Peking in 1796, describes how, when the Chinese looked at the pictures which the Europeans had brought and saw the lights and shadows on the faces of the people in them, they at once asked whether these people were darker on one side than on the other. The courtiers regarded the shadow on one side of the nose of a portrait as a serious physical blemish, and a few mandarins observed, with Chinese politeness, that it must be of course the result of an accidental injury. All agreed that the European style of painting was extremely unnatural.

As far as the technique of Chinese painting is concerned, the earliest pictures were painted on silk, which is still used whenever possible. After a preliminary priming with a mixture of size and alum, it takes ink or paint equally well, and its dull, silvery lustre gives the picture a peculiar charm. In time, however, silk becomes brittle, and is less durable than paper, which was used as early as the fourth century. The Chinese use thick, finely-fibred and well-sized sheets of paper, not the very thin stuff which we know as 'Chinese paper'. The most frequent medium is the familiar 'Indian' or Chinese ink, which can easily be thinned with water, so that a very faint wash is as easily produced as the deepest black. Other colours are mixed with size, and must, like Chinese ink, be applied very thinly, otherwise they flake off. The scroll-paintings, with a roller at top and bottom, are not only hung on the wall, but are often unrolled and spread out on the floor. Here we have further evidence that this art is a means of conveying ideas, in which writing and painting are very nearly the same thing. This is true even of wall-paintings, which were painted with water-colours or distemper on whitewashed walls.

The connection between painting and calligraphy is connected with the fact that in China, from the moment when art was first mentioned by historians, there are records of scholars, statesmen and generals who were also celebrated painters; while in Grece, as in Rome, and in India, as in Europe, the artist usually comes from the more restricted tradesmen or artisan class. At the court of the Sung Emperors painting was thought one of the noblest occupations, and the Emperor Hui-tsung was considered one of the greatest artists of his day.

The Harvest

The rich seed-time of Chinese art, which came to perfect flower under the Tang and Sung dynasties, yielded its harvest, after a short interval (according to the scale of Chinese history), under the Ming dynasty, which lasted nearly three hundred years. In the interval occurred the Tartar-Mongolian Yuan dynasty (1280—1368). Under the name of Yuan Shi-tsu a Mongolian Khan ascended the Dragon Throne, and Peking became the capital of a State which in brilliance and power excelled even that of the great Tang Emperor, and united almost half the world's inhabitants under its sceptre. This dynasty soon fell, and we can only guess at the essential features of the art of this period.

Hung Wu, a man of the people, was the illustrious founder of the Ming dynasty (1369—1644). In 1421 Peking became the residence of the Ming Emperors, one of whom—Yung Lo—began in 1403 to complete the building programme begun by

a

35. (A) View of the 'Hall of Annual Prayer', in the Temple of Heaven, Peking. From the marble sacrificial terraces rises the dark red lacquered wooden building, with its triple roof of luminous violet-blue, the colour of heaven. Built in 1420, restored at later periods.
(B) Typical Chinese use of wood in architecture of the main hall and the belfry of the Temple of Confucius at Wanhien, province of Szechuan.

b

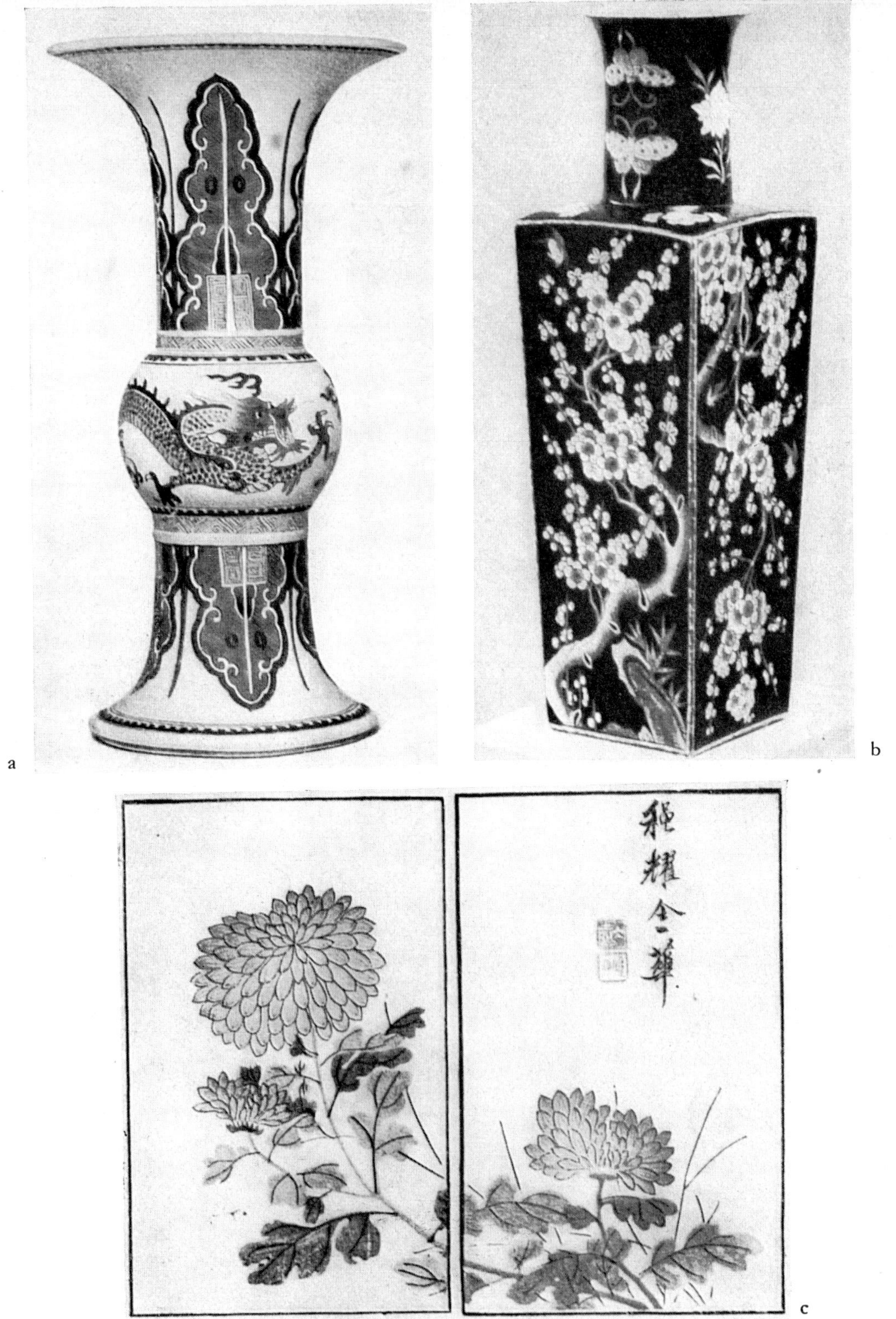

36. (A) Porcelain beaker with sapphire-blue painting under the glaze. Text p. 117. Height, 13½ in. Kang Hsi period of the Ching Dynasty. (Eumorfopoulos Collection, London).
(B) Porcelain vase of the 'Black Family'. Height 19½ in. Kang Hsi period. (Steiger-de Mestral Collection, Zürich).
(C) Golden Chrysanthemum, the Chinese symbol of faithful friendship and indefatigable fulfilment of duty. Colour print from the Manual of Painting of the Brain-of-Mustard-Seed-Garden. Text. p. 115.

37. (A) Chinese Landscape. Painting by the Master Wang Chien-chang. Ming Period.
(B) Han-shan and Shin-te, the Jesting Sages, in servants' clothing. Monochrome painting in Indian ink, on paper. Ascribed to Shubun. Text p. 123. Height, 39 in. (Collection of Count Tsuguaki, Tokio).

a

b

c

38. (A) Head of one of the twelve Heavenly Commanders in the Shinyakushigi Temple at Nara. Text p. 120. Coloured. Height of the whole clay figure, 5 ft. 7 in. End of eighth, century.
(B) Part of the gigantic figure of a divine gatekeeper, in the 'Temple of the Azure Clouds' on the western hills outside Peking.
(C) A Dragon sporting with the 'Pearl of Perfection'. Polychrome ceramics on the 'Nine-Dragon Shrine', in the park of the Northern Lake, in the once Forbidden City of Pekin.

the previous dynasty; although succeeding generations added and demolished many buildings, the last capital of old China, which looks back upon a past of more than six hundred years, must be regarded as a creation of the Ming period. With its walls and gates, and its palaces and temples, it is the greatest surviving memorial of Chinese architecture, which for many centuries changed very little; for Marco Polo, who from 1271—92 lived at the court of Kublai Khan, in 'Khanbaligh', tells us that even then a traveller entering the city by one of its gates could see the opposite gate, straight in front of him in the far distance. A wall twenty miles long encloses the imperial residence, which runs north and south. Over each of the many gates is a massive, temple-like superstructure, which serves the purposes of defence, and is, as a rule, dedicated to some divinity, under whose protection the gate lies. The Temple of Heaven (Fig. 35a), which stands in delightful woodland solitude in the southern quarter of the city, dates, with its rounded forms, from the time of the Emperor Yung Lo, while the temples in the hills to the east are older still. The Lama-temples in the extreme north-east corner show the typical Chinese style of woodwork, which can be seen in all parts of the country (Fig. 35b). Besides the Yellow Temple, and the Temple of the Azure Clouds, which dates from the year 1366 and is, even in its accessories (Fig. 38b), one of the most characteristic products of Chinese art, mention should be made of the pagoda, 182 feet high, at Palichuang, west of Peking. This was first built in 1578, and in form does not differ essentially from the pagoda of Sung-Yueh-see (Fig. 34c), which is a thousand years older. The same is true of the other pagodas, while the so-called 'five-towered' pagoda of Wuta-sse, on the way to the Summer Palace, confirms Marco Polo's account and suggests, with its entirely alien architecture, the close relations which always existed between Chinese and Indian art. The Summer Palace itself was the favourite residence of the late Dowager Empress and is a modern construction, whose halls and ceremonial gateways, open summer-houses, palaces and pagodas, with coloured faience decorations, reproduce the ancient forms.

The centre of Peking was the 'Purple', once the 'Forbidden', city, enclosed by a wall six miles long. Even here the earthly dwelling of the Son of Heaven is widespread and close to the earth, with immense courtyards and pillared halls, whose only decoration are the superimposed roofs, rising one above the other like steps and covered with glazed and gilded tiles, with richly figured terra-cotta ornaments on the upward-curving corners. The Winter Palace, dating from the eleventh century, is the oldest part. Here, on the 'Northern Lake', the present and the past become one. To walk past the temples, over the bridges and through the ceremonial arches of the Nine Dragon Wall, is to fall completely under the spell of Chinese art (Fig. 38c).

Near Peking are the tombs of the Ming Emperors, lying in the hollow of the hills. The dead, like the living, have spacious dwellings, where for hours one can wander from the five-centred arch of the entrance-gate, along the 'Spirit Avenue', between groves of pine and cypress, past the lonely 'Houses of the Dead', and along other avenues, lined with figures, larger than life, of animals and mandarins (Fig. 34a)

The Ming Emperors fostered the national character of their dynasty in their attitude toward sculpture and architecture, by reviving ancient traditions, often producing a deliberately archaic effect, while in painting they also cherished the heritage of the past. Under Tung Chi-chang (1555—1636), equally famous as a scholar and as a painter, a work in three hundred volumes was produced, which remains the standard work on the Northern and Southern schools of painting. Of the 1,200 painters' names which the history of Chinese art records during the Ming period alone, the greatest, or at least the best known, are Wu Wei (1458—1508), Chiu Ying (1522—60), Shen Chou (1427—1509, below), Weng Cheng-ming (1470—1567), Chen Chi-ju (1558—1639), and Wang Chien-chang (1598—1677, Fig. 37a).

For the first time the experiment was made of printing a book in several colours from wood blocks. The simple black and white woodcut was known as early as the ninth century, and the lithotypic print (page 106) in the seventh century, but the fine experiments in the new art could not have been made until the second half of the sixteenth century, though we do not know whether it was at once applied to pictures. The first polychrome prints were in 'The Picture Gallery of the Ten-Bamboo Hall' (1622—27) by the Master Hu Cheng-yen, who called his studio the Ten-Bamboo Hall because of the clumps of bamboo round it. This publication, and a collection of exceptionally fine letter-papers, decorated with woodcuts printed in five colours, which he published twenty years later, was one of the finest productions of the Ming period.

Shen Chou. Landscape of the Ming period.
Fifteenth century. After the Chich-tse-yuan hua-chuan of 1679

The next masterpiece of colour-printing appeared during the Ching dynasty (of which more will be said presently). This was 'The Mustard-seed-Garden', a comprehensive encylopaedia of Chinese painting; its first volume was issued in 1679, the second and third in 1701, and the fourth did not appear until 1818. Its name is probably a reference to a Buddhistic parable comparing the whole infinity of the ten thousand universes to the tiny mustard-seed. It contains dissertations on landscape-painting—perspective, painting rocks, placing of figures in landscape, and other subjects. Nearly all the examples given are admirable reproductions of paintings by old masters (Fig. 36c).

These two masterpieces of Chinese printing give an excellent survey and interpretation of Chinese painting. The 'Ten-Bamboo Hall', above all, fascinates by the clarity and freshness of its illustrations, and the free and unconstrained arrangement of the whole work. The pictures were probably repainted for it, following older prototypes only as far as was expected by Chinese conservatism. It contains roughly equal numbers of pictures and sheets of calligraphy, and was so designed expressly for the pleasure of recluses, scholars and poets; it is rarely that it becomes didactic. The 'Mustard-seed-Garden', on the contrary, is more educative, with reproductions of pictures by the older masters strictly ordered with a view to training the copyist. This is clear even in the colouring, the accurate drawing of the outlines, and the technical delicacy and exactitude of the printing, which is in some ways better than that of the 'Ten-Bamboo Hall', though, in point of artistic feeling, it is often inferior. In their perfection these two books have never been excelled in China, though in the matter of technique they were often equalled; towards the end of the nineteenth century the polychrome woodcut became commercialized.

Our recital has almost reached the present day, and to bring it up to date we have only to record that in 1644 the Ming dynasty fell and was followed by the Ching dynasty (1644—1912), whose emperors were not Chinese but Manchu. It is wrong to condemn this period wholesale, as one of decay; the conquerors were autocratic, but they were undoubtedly lovers of art.

The two great rulers, Kang Hsi (1662—1722) and Chien Lung (1736—93) are not unlike their western contemporaries, Louis XIV or Frederick II. Equally great as generals or administrators, they were also aesthetes and, having unrestricted power, they suppressed many movements of an independent character, but provided art with fresh stimuli. Thus the five and a half centuries of the Ming and Ching dynasties may really be considered a unity.

Almost everything left in China, temples, palaces, statues or pictures, dates from this period. The conception of Chinese antiquity, of its philosophy and cosmology which saw everything as the expression of one cosmic and religious order, obtrudes itself upon the mind as one surveys these last two dynasties, and rounds off a history of many thousands of years.

Glass and Porcelain

Man has always been fascinated by glass. Brittle and transparent, it nevertheless has certain affinities with metal. For like metal, it is softened by heat and can then be moulded, and, just as metal can be coloured by alloyage, so glass can be coloured by metallic oxides.

It is not surprising that with the traditional Chinese experience of bronze-casting, and with such highly developed technical methods as were employed under the Ching dynasty, the art of the glassworker should have reached a new perfection.[1] The Chinese, used to bronze, preferred vessels with thick walls, for them the charm of glass was not so much in its fragile transparency as the depth of its reflections and rich glowing colour. To increase this effect, layers of different coloured glass were fused one over the other, and ornamental motives engraved in the topmost layer. Glass vessels were mostly used in decoration; above all, to hold flowers in the imaginative and symbolic arrangement of which the Chinese have always delighted. The orchid, with its mysterious fragrance, is the emblem of the virtues of the solitary scholar and of the charm of woman; the straight stem of a bamboo, the regularity of its knots, and the strength of its leaves, are symbols of the inviolability of custom; while plum-blossom and chrysanthemum are symbols of loyal friendship and the fulfilment of duty (Fig. 36c).

As well as the new art of glassblowing, and the old arts of bronze-casting and lacquering, that of porcelain, in this later period, became more and more important. Something has already been said of the simple ceramics of Chinese antiquity (page 103). Such recent discoveries as one may, with a clear conscience ascribe to the end of the Han period, still resemble their bronze originals in their greenish and brownish glazes. Only after this period, during which grey or red earthenware was still in general use, does one come across the hard-fired, ringing pottery which anticipates many of the qualities of porcelain.

Sung pottery is distinguished by an exquisite sense of form and line; the decoration is often incised in a white glaze over a dark ground. Porcelain did not become supreme until the Ming dynasty. A sense of colour, like that found under the Tang dynasty, combined with a perfection of technique for which no difficulty was too great, produced remarkable results. The wall-tiles, ridge-turrets, and vessels of the Ming period, covered with coloured enamels, gleamed with a number of novel tones, while the old colours acquired a fresh brilliance. A most superb 'family' was that of the Lang-yao porcelain, whose monochromatic glaze, coloured with oxide of copper, was subjected to a high temperature, while lead glazes were applied to porcelain already fired in the kiln and given a second firing at a lower temperature, the result being the so-called bisque enamel, with luminous hues of turquoise blue,

[1] The first history of glassmaking is still wrapped in obscurity, since all peoples who worked in bronze and clay must have known something of the formation of fusible slags and their applicability to glazing, and something of manufacturing articles by pressing and casting. Even in the Hallstatt graves glass beads were found.

green, yellow, and dark violet. But the most revolutionary improvement was the invention of a method of painting with fireproof colours, independently of glazing proper, so that the colours could be applied before firing. While the technique of blue under-glaze painting was possibly understood in the Sung period, the magnificent developments which made Chinese porcelain famous throughout the world were initiated under the Ming Emperors, in the kilns of Ching-tu Chen, in whose neighbourhood a clay occurs which is rich in kaolin. Once the usual tones of green, yellow and violet were accompanied by iron-red and blue, a premonition may have been experienced of the later 'five-colour painting'.

The preliminary drawing demanded great skill, for the porous, quickly-absorbent porcelain clay requires infallible certainty of touch. If the Emperors of the Ching dynasty are better known to the Europeans than the other Emperors of China, this was partly because the many kinds of porcelain made under the Ching Emperors carried their names all over the world. Kang-hsi (1662—1723) porcelain did not differ fundamentally from that of later Ming period, but further refinements of the old technique produced wares whose glaze, in its impeccable purity and whiteness, is clearly distinguishable from that of the earlier products, with their faint greenish tint and the slight scars that often covered their surface. Blue and white under-glaze painting in particular produced magnificent results (Fig. 36a), with amazing depth of tone, so that the eye is constantly surprised and delighted. Moreover, the under-glaze painting was often enriched with a red produced by oxide of copper, and here, by varying the heat of the firing, the most surprising results were obtained. The *sang de bœuf* glaze of this period, to which every conceivable colour seemed attainable, may be compared, in its luminous depth, with the peach-bloom glaze, with its delicate tints of green and red, while a tender, cloudy blue was a favourite ground for paintings in gold over the glaze.

The Kang-hsi period saw the final and complete development of 'five-colour painting'; *Famille verte,* with luminous green enamel providing the dominant tone, with iron-red, cobalt blue, manganese violet, antimony-yellow and copper-green; *Famille noire* (Fig. 36b), whose softly gleaming ground, with its depths of glistening black, is an almost incredible achievement. Until the middle of the eighteenth century the ceramic art continued to flourish with undiminished vigour; but the *Famille rose,* which the Chinese were fond of calling a 'painting in foreign colours', gradually came to the fore, while the blue and white painting was gradually forgotten.

During the sixty years' reign of the Emperor Chien-lung (1736—96), when three thousand kilns, it is alleged, were at work in Ching-te-Chen alone, astonishing results were still obtained, but there was no further progress—only repetition. Under the two following Emperors, Chia-ching (1796—1821) and Tao-kuang (1821—56) there was increased production, but an obvious artistic decadence had set in, and it was almost a natural denouement that the imperial manufactory should have been destroyed in 1853 during the Tai-ping rebellion. The products of the factory rebuilt by the Emperor Tung-chih do not concern the historian of art, but rather the historian of the mechanical arts—an expression first employed in the industrialized Europe of the nineteenth century, but perfectly relavant here, though hitherto such things had been unknown. It is not the hands and the method of production that make an art, but the creative spirit. With their always admirable workmanship, the productions of this late period interest the historian only inasmuch as they have swamped the collections of every quarter of the world with an enormous number of forgeries—of reproductions passing as ancient porcelains.

The possessor of such products may console himself with the fact that by far the greater number of Chinese bronzes which have found their way into Europe were produced in the nineteenth century. The greatest experts estimate that of the reputed bronzes of the Sung period barely two per cent are genuine. Students of Chinese antiquity speak of at least six great orgies of destruction by Chinese rulers, when innumerable bronzes were melted down—to say nothing of other casualties. The old Chinese coinage is in hardly better case. In Tsingtau, during the war of 1914—18, Japanese foundries were working day and night for years, melting down the bronze coins purchased up-country at ruinous prices, in order to sell the metal at a great profit to the warring powers.

Chapter IX

JAPAN

*

THE oldest Japanese historical works, the *Kojiki*, a 'Record of Ancient Matters' (A.D. 712), and the *Nihongi*, 'Japanese Chronicle' (A.D. 720), begin their chronology with the Emperor Jimmu, who is supposed to have united Japan under him in 660 B.C. In prehistoric times the Japanese people, from the Asiatic mainland, invaded Nippon, the Land of the Rising Sun, and dispossessed the aboriginal inhabitants of a chain of islands with great natural advantages. Korean records speak of continued relations with the mainland, and it was by way of Korea that Chinese writing and literature were introduced into Japan in the third and fourth centuries. Works of art also were imported; many early Chinese bronze vases and mirrors, which found their way into Japan, have been discovered in Japanese tombs and dolmens.

Chinese-Buddhistic Art

By about A.D. 500 the Japanese had become an established race, who lived by rice-growing, fishing and hunting, but were in other respects at a primitive stage of development. The population was divided into family communities, governed by chieftains. The Mikado, as high priest of Shintoism and ruler of the most powerful clan, enjoyed certain prerogatives, from which he managed eventually to derive effective dominion. On this evolving power the splendid Chinese civilization of the period, and the cult of Buddha, had great influence. The Japanese were naturally disposed to absorb the culture and religion of the more advanced mainland. During the Suiko[1] period (552—645) Buddhism took a firm hold in Japan, and the old clan system became a centralized bureaucratic State after the Chinese model, with Chinese laws and ceremonial. The Mikado received the Chinese titles of Tenno, 'Heavenly Ruler', and Tenshi, 'Son of Heaven', and Chinese culture pervaded every side of Japanese life. This explains why, in the history of Japanese art, the earliest names are those of the Chinese masters, the most famous of which is Kuratsukuri Tori, a grandson of the Chinese Shiba Tatto who brought a portrait of Buddha to Japan. By about A.D. 600 there were already more than four hundred Buddhist temples, and one can imagine how eager artists were to provide all these with portraits of Buddha. The works of Kuratsukuri Tori are something between the rigidly constrained, superficial sculptures of Yuen-Kang and the looser style of Lung-men. In these early

[1] The periods' of Japanese history are distinguished sometimes by the names of dynasties, sometimes by the names of capitals.

sculptures (Fig. 40a) Japanese Buddhas of the fifth and sixth centuries are often to be distinguished from Chinese Buddhas of the same period by their pouting lips and somewhat broader noses. Such slight differences are not really enough to enable us to speak of an individual Japanese style; especially as the technique of the bronze portrait required a broader treatment. Examination of the surviving works of art must, on the contrary, lead to the conclusion that in the whole of this period, the so-called *Hakuho period,* no new Japanese style was formed, but that the Japanese continued to adopt Chinese forms.

In A.D. 710 Nara was made the permanent capital (hitherto the Imperial household had transferred its seat with every change of government) and the Nara period (710—784)[1] began; Chinese art now acquired, in the new Imperial residence, a central foothold in Japan, and the Chinese artist Chien-chen, whom the Japanese call Kanshin, created the Toshodaiji temple, one of the finest monuments of Tang art. The same is true of other temples and their sculptures (Fig. 38a): they stood on Japanese soil, but were built by Chinese architects. Whenever the Japanese did co-operate, they were apt pupils, and it was due to them that in Japan, as in China, the art of the Tang period produced so many masterpieces.

Some of these temple statues were of wood, but they were mostly cast in bronze or copper, and often gilded. Most of them are of Buddha, not only in his original character, as Shaka, but, in earlier times, as Minoru, the coming Redeemer of the world, and Yakushi, the great Saviour; and later as Amida, the Lord of the Western Paradise, and Roshana, whose majesty and wisdom exceeded even those of the Enlightened Ones. Besides the Boddhisatvas, one often sees Kwannon, the Goddess of Mercy, by the side of Buddha; while in her incarnation as Yakushi she is often accompanied by the Moon-god Gwakko, and the Sun-god Nikko. Indra and Brahma, the great Brahmanic gods, are often demoted as warriors, to annoy the ancillary spirits of Buddhism; they are then known as Nio. Their coloured images are generally to be seen in the outside niches of the temples, before whose gates the Heavenly Commanders (Figs. 38a and 38b) keep watch. Lively, muscular temple-guardians were set up beside them, figures from an older period, almost incorporeal in their flatness, with heads and gently smilling faces standing out against a perforated, flaming halo. In the Jogan period (A.D. 794—890) it is not possible to distinguish with certainty between Japanese and Chinese works, and the reader must refer, for this period, to the chapter on Chinese art.

Formation of the National Style

In the Fujiwara period (890—1160) Japanese art was finally liberated from the overpowering Chinese influence. In China the Tang dynasty slowly decayed, to be followed by various others, but in Japan the Fujiwara clan remained in power for

[1] The whole of this period is often described as the *Tempyo period,* which should really be restricted to the years 729—766.

a

b

39. (A) Landscape with Bridge. Coloured woodcut by Hokusai, no longer entirely unaffected by European art (1760—1849).

(B) Two lovers. Coloured woodcut of the Hishi-Kawa Moronobu school. The hair is dressed in the fashion of the Genroku period. Ascribed to Morofosa, but is probably the work of Moronobu (1658—1717), regarded as the originator of the woodcut in Edo, the Eastern capital, the modern Tokio. (Strauss-Negbaur Collection, Berlin).

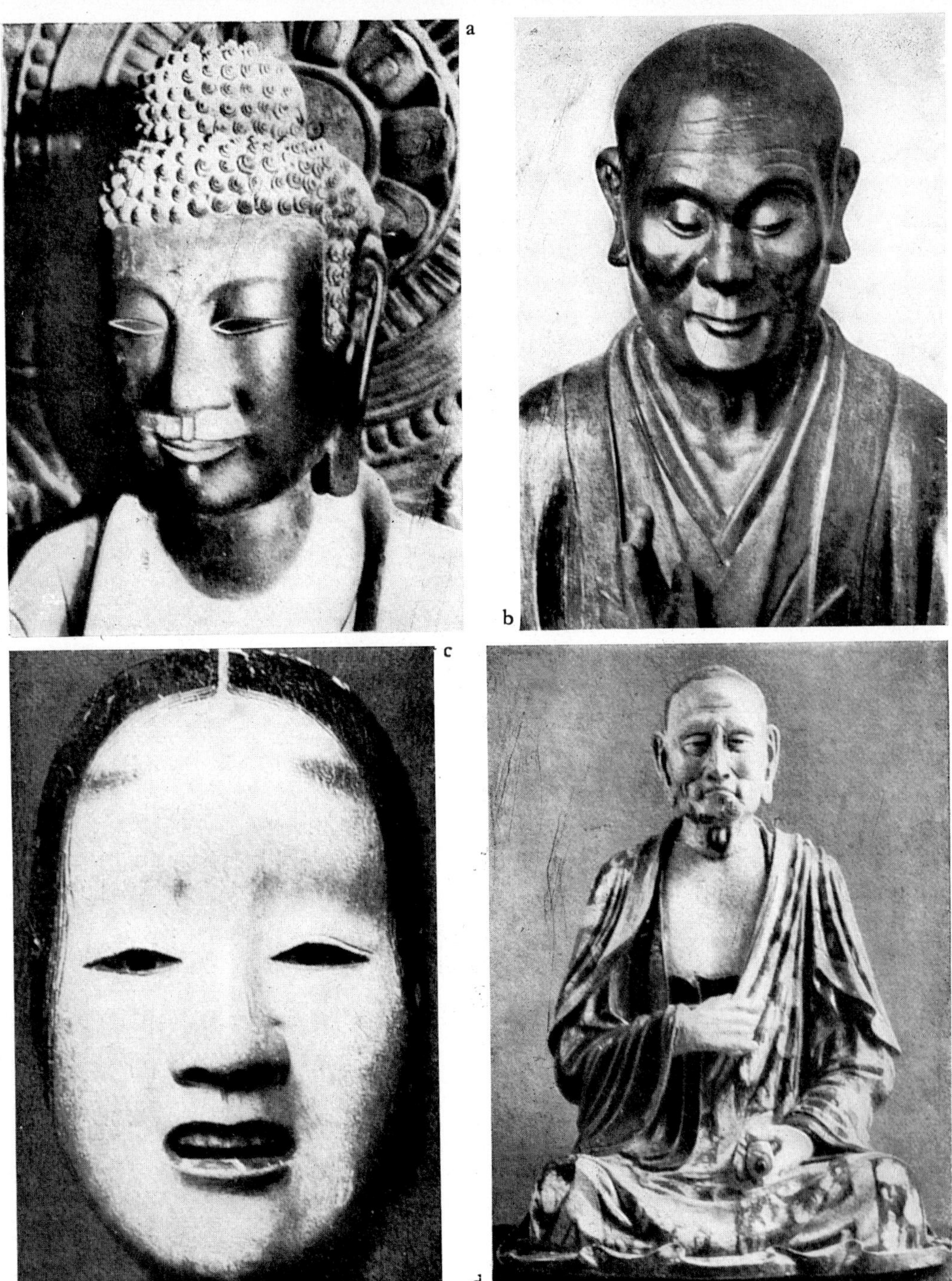

40. (A) Head of Buddha, by Kuratsukurino Obito Tori. Part of a bronze group, originally gilded, showing Buddha with companions. Dated A.D. 625. The whole figure is about 5 ft. high. Included for the purpose of comparison, it stands halfway between the austere, conventional, insipid sculptures of Yuen-kang and the freer style of the early Lung-men.

(B) Portrait of a Priest. Black lacquered wood. Height of whole figure, 20 in. Ashikagu period, 1334–1573. (Mercanton Collection, Lausanne).

(C) 'No' mask, 'Deigan'. Work of the wood-carver Echi Yoshifune. About A.D. 1400. (Reinhart Collection, Winterthur).

(D) Lohan. Included for the purpose of comparison. Chinese. Life-sized figure of glazed terracotta; colouring yellowish white, brown, and green. From a temple in the neighbourhood of I-chou, province of Chili, destroyed during the construction of the western Manchu tombs. Probably eleventh–twelfth century. (Metropolitan Museum, New York).

41. Sethos and the Sun-god. Limestone relief in the sanctuary of Abydos. On the solar disc above the head of the god is a scarabaeus. Nineteenth Dynasty.

a

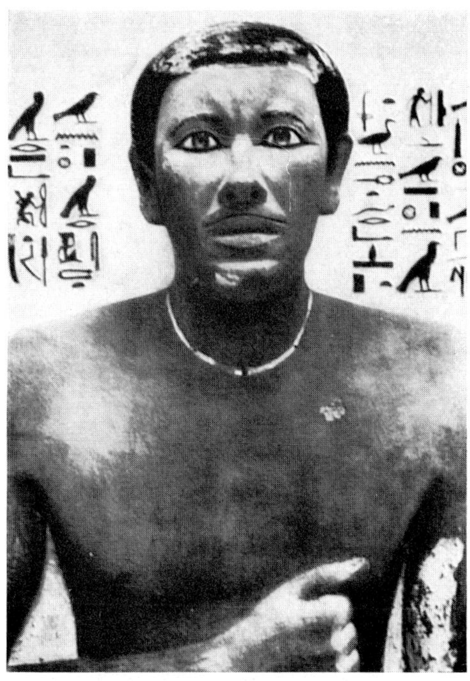

b

c

d

42. (A) Prince Rahotep. Painted limestone statue from Medum. Eyes inset, Body yellowish brown, hair black, beard and amulet grey. Height of seated figure, 3 ft. 11 in. Fourth Dynasty. (Cairo Museum).
(B) Nofret, wife of Rahotep. Seated figure of painted limestone. Eyes inset. Skin pale yellow, hair and eyes black, white fillet round the head, with design of flowers in red and green. Height, 3 ft. 10 in. Fourth Dynasty. (Cairo Museum).
(C) The Sphinx, Gizeh. Height, 65 ft.
(D) South-western aspect of the pyramid of Chephren at Gizeh. Limestone. Height, 442 ft.

almost three hundred years. The images of Buddha grew suddenly plumper and more human, with no loss of majesty. Both in sculpture and painting, there was an increasing tendency towards individualism, and consequently towards a national style; this may really be said to have been begun by a painter, Kose-no-Kanaoka, about A.D. 890, and is known as the Yamatoe style.

The long scroll — pictures, so popular in China during the Sung period, which were never seen as a whole, but could only be examined slowly, bit by bit, were called Makimono in Japan, where they were filled with wild and passionate scenes: the most celebrated of these are attributed to Mitsunaga.

The world revealed in these pictures is not unlike Europe at the end of the Middle Ages, when Christendom had become really European: the visions of Dante could have found a place in this new Japanese panorama. There is no doubt that Buddhism, after various compromises with the Japanese spirit, had become a national religion.

The twofold nature of the Japanese character, in which self-control and warlike ferocity exist side by side with a certain effeminacy and refinement, is reflected perfectly in the art of the Fujiwara period. For as well as the picture books which represent the most appalling tortures, there are those attributed to Takayoshi Tosa— simple narratives, representing in rich and delicate colours, and with unprecedented emotional power, the joys of a peaceful life in the sunlight of peaceful islands. As in the Renaissance, so in Japan at this period, beauty and ugliness, good and evil, are very close to each other. The Heike period (1160—1185) was a time of conflict and confusion, in which the increasing individualism of the age did much to humanize art.

In the Kamakura period (1186—1333) the 'Zen' sect, a typical reformation movement, brought the former scholastic theology to an end: images ceased to be enthroned in unapproachable solemnity. The kindly Zizo, the favourite divinity of the new faith, appears not as a celestial saint, but as a man of gentle and friendly appearance, like a brother of the Kwannon, who is now endowed with all the charms of human womanhood, quite unlike her Indian prototype. This new sense of reality approached more and more closely to the human, and consequently there now appeared for the first time genuine portraits, giving the impression of absolute truth to nature. Takanobu (1140—1204) is regarded as the undisputed master of the portraiture of this period; he was followed by Nobuzane Fujiwara (1177—1265) and Yoshimitsu Tosa (1292—1330).

To an even greater extent than the Chinese, Japanese architecture of this period remained a carpenter's art. In a country where earthquakes are frequent, and which is exceptionally rich in timber, a wooden frame was, and still is, the natural form of construction. Many buildings have no permanent walls at all, and often the outer walls are replaced by sliding screens of wood, which can be removed at will, and inside, fixed or folding screens are used as partitions. The gabled roof with widely projecting eaves was not originally curved as it is today; something between the hipped roof and the gable roof was the so-called 'Irimoya' roof, in which a hip-side thrust itself against the lower part of the gable. This roof, which appears on the oldest Shinto temples, was developed to its most refined form during the Kamakura period. The temple of Kibitsu-jinja, near Okayama, begun in this period, but not finished till 1390, shows the final and improved form of the roof. From the ground plan one can see how much this kind of temple was capable of variation and elaboration. There was really no essential difference between the house and the temple, since in either the ground plan could be easily altered by combining simple units. The natural colour of the wood, which in places of importance was often reinforced with plates or ornamental nails of bronze, provided, in the simple and elegant perfection of its carving, the decoration of the interior.

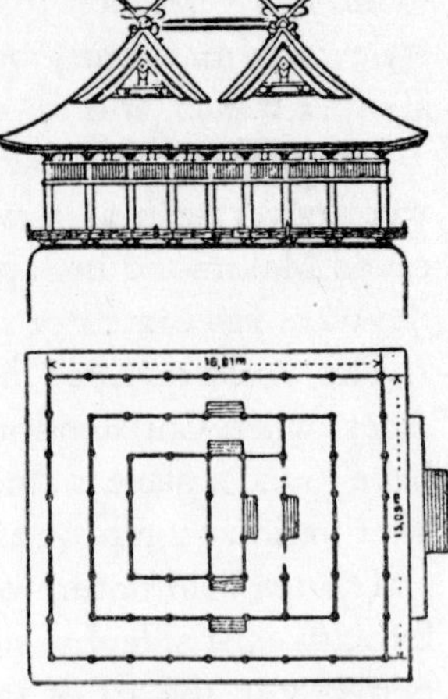

Side elevation and ground plan of the temple of Kibitsu-jinja, near Okayama. (Baltzer)

The Buddhist temple introduced into Japan, together with the pagoda, the curved, tile-covered roof. The outside colouring of these Buddhist buildings was usually warmer in Japan than in China, but in both countries the favourite colour for temples is a brilliant red. But it is really the beauty of the park-like grounds round the larger temples and houses, with their tall trees and flowering shrubs, their waterfalls and groups of rocks, their fountains, statues, and stone lanterns, that makes these Japanese buildings examples of true landscape architecture, in a very different way from the Indian rock-temples.

The Modern Period

The Ashikaga period (1334—1573) was a time of internal conflict, which reduced the country to a state of ruin. These sufferings brought about a profound inner change; in art new forms appeared, which are still current. In religion, the Zen sect, the Protestants of Buddhism, were most favoured by the rulers of the period; their priests and artists, looking once more to China, created a kind of Chinese renaissance, particularly apparent in the Zen cloisters and temples. This austere doctrine denounced all exaggerated ornament, so that interior gilding, and the coloured paint or wash on the outside, quickly disappeared, and Shintoist temples became increasingly Buddhistic in form.

It was in accordance with this spirit that the superimposed double roofs of Buddhist architecture should be replaced, as in the Kibitsu-jinja temple in Okayama, by juxtaposed gables connected only at their base (above). An ingenious expedient, like that which was found in Europe by the Cistercians who, when the strict rule of their Order forbade the building of lofty towers, contrived to give their louvre-turrets or belfries a form so stately and imposing that they could not fail to impress. Palaces and temples in this period were often in the same building, for the austere doctrine of the Zen monks was in full harmony with the idea of the ruling caste of the Samurai. It was significant that among the minor arts all kinds of metal-work, such as sword-hilts and guards, received the most attention and skill.

Of the creative arts, painting, as almost always in Eastern Asia, took first place. In the Ashikaga period it was supreme. Religious art, with its images shining with gold and bright colours, retired into the background, while Chinese landscape painting took its place. The master responsible for this was Shubun, of whom very little is known: it is not even certain whether he came from China, or whether there were two painters of the same name, of whom one was Chinese. In any case, another wave of Chinese art, this time of the Ming period, broke over Japan. This time Japan gave, as well as took. Sesshu (1420—1506) was the pupil of Shubun, but one who excelled his master; under his influence, Kano Motonobu (1476—1559) gave Japanese painting a style of its own and became its classical master.

The European who is not a specialist in the art of Eastern Asia, finds it difficult to disentangle the different schools and movements, but generally speaking it may be said that at this period Japanese art had shaken off the influence of the Middle Ages and was turning towards a new realism.

The tea-ceremony, which was one of the ceremonials of the Zen sect, produced new and beautiful forms in pottery. Tea, and the room in which it was drunk, received special treatment in Japanese art. As before, the forms which were to be so valued in Japan came from China and Korea; but it was Japan that first associated them with the personalities of definite artists. The lives of individual tea-masters cannot be written, but their creations, on the border between fine art and mechanical art, deserve adequate mention at a period when the history of Japanese art begins to merge in the history of the art of the rest of the world.

In 1543, during the civil wars, a junk with three Portuguese merchants on board cast anchor off the little island of Tanegashima. The Portuguese began commercial relations, which led to an extensive trade. In 1549 the first Jesuit, Francisco Xavier, arrived in Japan. Many points in common between Christianity and Buddhism, even in external matters, caused the new religion to make rapid progress. In art a type of black-clad priest now appears; as the illustrations show (Figs. 40b and 40d), this figure differs from its Chinese prototype. In 1502 Japanese embassies were sent to the Pope and to the courts of Lisbon and Madrid, and towards the end of the sixteenth century there were more than half a million Japanese Christians. This must not be forgotten when the art of the Toyotomi period (1573—1603) is considered. The pronounced assimilative instinct of the Japanese caused many features of Japanese art to come closer to European conceptions. The Japanese became more understandable and accessible. To this day many people regard Japanese works of this period, especially the coloured woodcuts, as the height of Japanese art.

In 1614 persecution of the Christians began, but Japanese art and life had already been deeply influenced.

During the Tokugawa period (1603—1868), a wave of international feeling and expansion was followed by one of seclusion. In Tokio, Matahei Iwasu (1578 — 1650) founded the Ukiyoe school, which dealt only with contemporary life, in a popular and easily intelligible way. The woodcut, which in China had been used only as a method of reproduction, now became a means of expression in itself. Hishikawa Moronobu (1638—1717) was the first draughtsman to draw with the express intention of having his drawings cut in wood, and was the founder of the original woodcut (Fig. 39b) in Japan. What Moronobu began was carried on by Kaigetsudo Ando (1688—1715), Okumura Masanobu (1685—1764) and Suzuki Harunobu (1725—1770), and was finally completed by Utamaro (1753—1806), Hokusai (1760—1849), and Hiroshige (1797—1858), to name only a few of many artists (Fig. 39a).

This Japanese art of woodcut, a very recent development, became widely known in the West during the nineteenth century; its bright colouring—which was to some extent borrowed from abroad—gave rise to a completely false idea of the generally colourful nature of Eastern Asiatic art; an idea which is in fact true only of a very small section.

Chapter X

EGYPT

*

When the reader, after an historical circuit of the world, comes back to Egypt, he finds himself again in the ancient Eurafrican region which we dealt with in the first chapter, and which was the birthplace of the art and civilization of white humanity.

Various general ideas from the previous chapters will help to explain the oldest art in the world, the art which originated in the valley of the Nile. There, under favourable conditions, the cultural evolution which can be observed in all parts of the world, from the Stone Age onwards, produced an art which goes back as far as the fifth millennium B.C. Discoveries made in the last few decades enable us to see far beyond the age of the Pyramids, long regarded as the earliest important monuments of human evolution.

Gold-plated handle of flint knife of the predynastic period

In graves, to which little attention was formerly paid, but of which there are large groups in many places, especially near Abydos and El-Amra, the dead have been found, wrapped in leather, linen or matting, with their knees drawn up and their sunken heads supported by their hands, in just the same position as the Indian mummies along the desert edges of the coastal valleys of Peru. From these ancient burial chambers, the earliest Egyptian graves, the gifts that were made to the dead have been recovered. These are mostly earthenware vases, made without using the potter's wheel; many are in the form of human beings or animals. These vases are usually remarkably unstable, and have many other points surprisingly like prehistoric American vases, but there is little danger of confusing them with the latter.

In primitive religion the serpent, as the creature of the earth, continually recurs in association with a circular symbol; for example, in the Egyptian knife-handle illustrated on this page, dating from about 4000 B.C., or the Chinese dragon with the pearl (Fig. 38c), or the Indian symbols (Figs. 21a and 22b), or in the story of the serpent and the apple in the Garden of Eden. The same is true of the Moon-goddess and the Sun-god, the dogs or jackals that guide the dead, and the eagle or falcon that ascends into Heaven.

In Egypt, which offered exceptionally favourable conditions at the end of the Ice Age, a highly-developed art and culture appeared very early. After a preliminary phase, to which the above-mentioned tombs belong, the rudiments of writing appeared about 5000 B.C.; the people no longer used pictures as a means of communication and perpetuation, but had got as far as using pictorial abbreviations as a verbal, if not as a phonetic script. Short inscriptions are found on bones or wooden tablets. Impressions of cylindrical seals have also been discovered, like those described in the chapter on Babylonian art; these were used in Egypt for stamping the clay seals of wine-jars. These early symbols already contain the elements of the Egyptian hieroglyphs.

While the oldest statuettes, in their substantial proportions, show no technical or artistic advance beyond the Stone Age, the decorative reliefs on the earliest Egyptian rouge-palettes, made of slate and used for cosmetic purposes (especially for the preparation of the green pigment used for outlining the eyebrows), reveal an astonishing quality of draughtsmanship.

Many of these palettes, like the example illustrated on this page, were produced in the beginning of the historical period, when a king of Upper Egypt, Menes, united the whole of the Nile valley under his rule, and founded the so-called Ist Dynasty about 3300 B.C. After the Ice Age, the once green desert areas were largely uninhabitable, and the population was bound to collect in the still uncultivated Nile valley. Cultivation of the soil required a compacter community, and the ancient traditions of the founding of the kingdom are based on economic necessity.

During the IInd Dynasty, which is supposed to have begun about the year 3000 B.C., one can see, from the relics discovered in all parts of the country, that a uniform Egyptian style was developing. Not only did the Nile produce suitable conditions for civilization to emerge, but it also united the Egyptians and gave them the necessary energy for creating the first great monumental art. It also gave them the material; for while in the almost contemporary

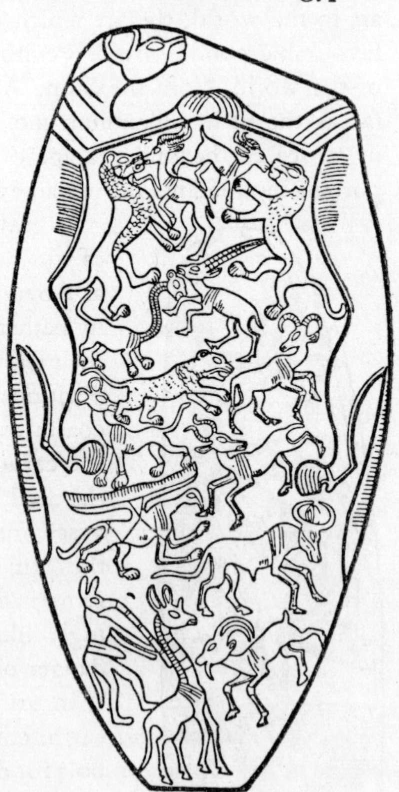

Back of an ancient Egyptian rouge-palette. The hybrid and playful forms of the animals are interesting. Predynastic period. About 3600 B.C. Ashmolean Museum, Oxford

civilization of Mesopotamia the only building material available was clay, the Egyptians could, from the very first, develop the art of building in stone. Excellent limestone came from the edge of the Libyan desert, while in Upper Egypt there was a compact sandstone, and in the extreme south, near Assouan, reddish granite was found.

The Old Kingdom

While under Menes the centre of gravity of the kingdom lay in Upper Egypt, under the IIIrd Dynasty it shifted downwards into Lower Egypt. On the escarpment of the western desert, not far from the site of the modern village of Saqqara, King Zoser instructed his architect, Imhotep, to build the first stepped pyramid to be made entirely of stone; this was 195 feet in height. It seems that the calendar based on the solar year should be ascribed to Imhotep, who until a later period of Egyptian history was paid divine honours. This was first introduced somewhere between 2781 and 2776 B.C., so that the IIIrd Dynasty can be dated with some certainty.

The monument which Imhotep erected for his sovereign is perhaps the oldest of all the Egyptian pyramids. In six enormous, superimposed terraces, successively diminishing in diameter, it still clearly betrays the cubical form of the tombs known

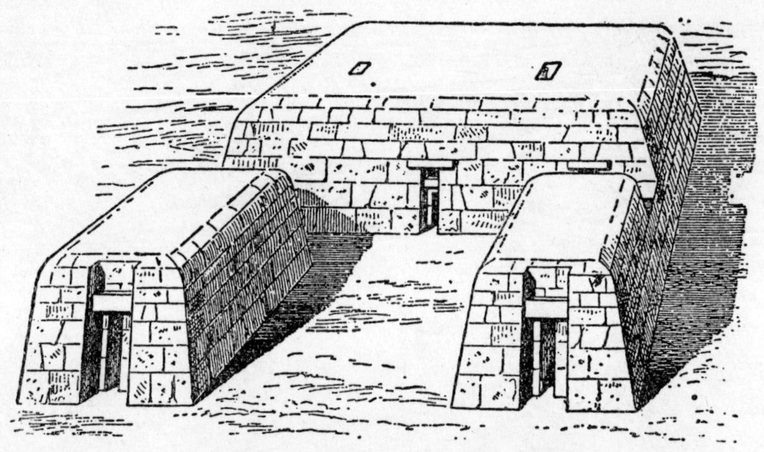

Egyptian Mastabas at Gizeh.
(Reconstruction by Perrot and Chipiez)

as mastabas, which later on, as the less ambitious tombs of the magnates, formed avenues and isolated groups beside the pyramids. The mastaba was a simple structure (above), consisting externally of a rectangular block with sloping sides. The artistic value of these simple tombs consisted in the flat, painted reliefs (page 128, also Fig. 43c) which decorated the inside walls, and sometimes the outside of the doorways, which were walled up after burial. Later, the mastabas were often divided into several chambers and connected by corridors.

She-ass, accompanied by Foal, carrying corn.
From the interior of a Mastaba

The step-pyramid of Saqqara was followed by the so called 'bent' or 'curb' or 'kneed' pyramid of Dahshur, the sides of which were broken at an obtuse angle, until King Snofru, the successor of Zoser and the first ruler of the IVth Dynasty, erected yet another sepulchral monument at Dahshur, whose smooth, unbroken sides—the final form of the pyramid—rose to a height of 320 feet. His son and successor, Cheops, laid at Gizeh the foundations of the greatest pyramids on earth, of whose appearance, in antiquity, the accompanying illustration will convey some idea.

From a base 760 feet square the Cheops pyramid rises to a height of 472 feet. Three and a quarter million cubic yards of stone were needed for its construction. To judge from the little that is left of the limestone casing, it seems originally to have been painted in various colours. Close behind the pyramid of Cheops his second successor, Chephren (Fig. 43a) built his rather smaller pyramid, (Fig. 42d) cased with rose-pink granite, which, like the huge granite monoliths used in the temple attached to the

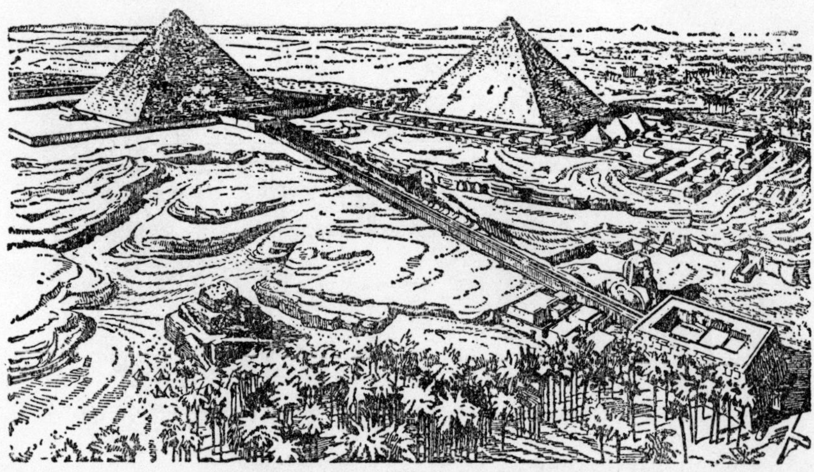

Reconstruction of the Pyramids at Gizeh. On the right, the pyramid of Cheops; on the left, the pyramid of Chephren. In the foreground, on the right, is the granite gatehouse in the valley—flanked by the Sphinx—proceeding from which is a covered corridor leading from the city on the hill to the pyramid (surrounded by a wall) which contained the tomb of the king. Before the pyramid was a courtyard in which the funeral rites were performed; from this the interior of the pyramid could be reached. Smaller tombs for the royal family and the dignitaries of the realm surrounded the great pyramid. On the left, in the foreground, is a pyramid in the course of construction; sloping ramps lead up to it, for the transport of material. These ramps consisted merely of sun-dried bricks, and were removed when the building was completed. (Hoelscher)

a

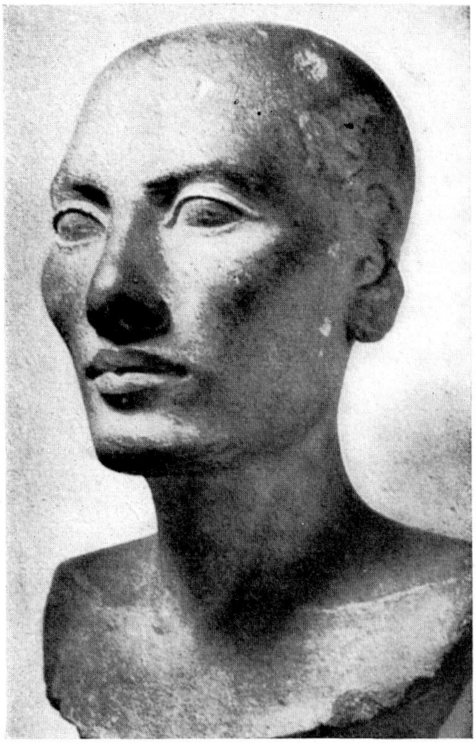

c

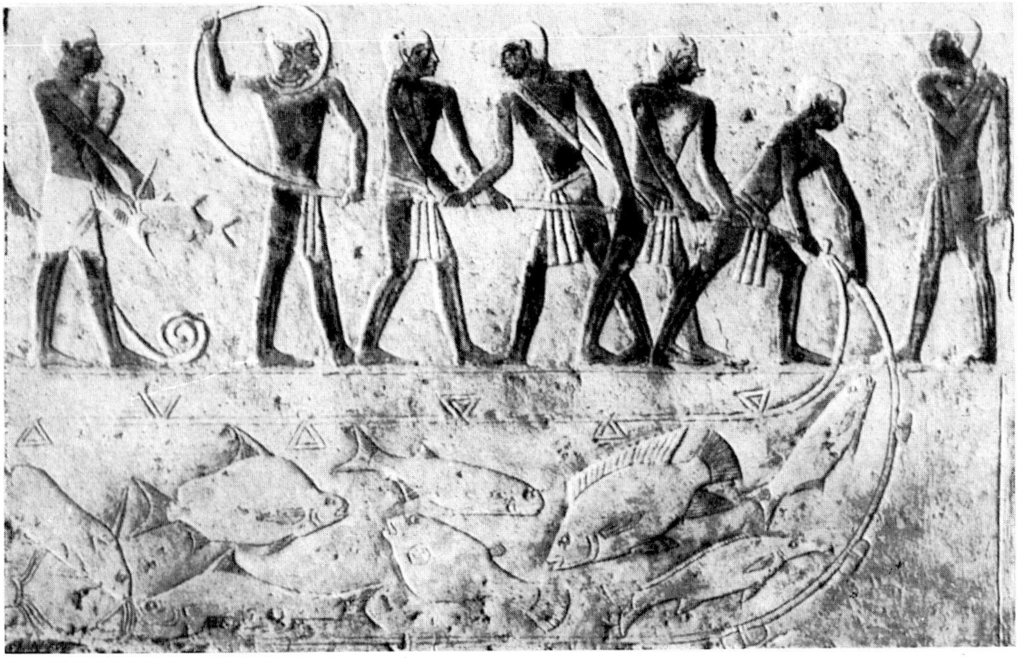

43. (A) Chephren, protected by the Falcon. Part of a statue from the Valley Temple of the Chephren Pyramid. Height of the seated figure of diorite, 5 ft. 6 in. (Cairo Museum).
(B) Limestone bust of Fourth Dynasty. Complexion, reddish ochre; eyes painted. Height, 13½ in. (Louvre).
(C) Fishing scene, on the mastaba of Akhuthotep. Various species of Nile fishes can be clearly recognized.

a

b

c

44. (A) Clustered sandstone columns in the temple of Luxor.
(B) Colossal columns at Karnak; one hundred men could stand on the capital of each column.
(C) Façade of the Rock-temple of Abu-Simbel with the seated figures of the King (Rameses II), hewn out of the sandstone. In a niche over the entrance is the statue of the Sungod with falcon's head. Nineteenth Dynasty.

45. (A) Model bust of Queen Nofretete, from the studio of the sculptor Thutmosis in Amarna. Eyes of rock-crystal, crown blue with many-coloured band and yellow frontal insertion: brightly-coloured collar. Limestone. Height 19 in. (State Museum, Berlin).

a

b

(B) The ancient lunar deity Chons, with crosier, scourge, and a sceptre made up of the symbols of life, duration, and happiness. On the forehead is the symbol of sovereignty, the uraeus; on the chin the divine beard. Upper part of a granite statue from Karnak; 8 ft. 6 in. high. Probably Eighteenth Dynasty. (Cairo Museum).

(D) Youth bearing offerings; with three flowering heads of papyrus and a head of lettuce. Limestone relief on the eastern wall of the colonnaded hall at Karnak. Seventeenth Dynasty. Time of Tutankhamen.

(C) Sesostris I and the god Ptah, regarded as the first of the gods, the creator of the world, and therefore the patron of artists. Part of the relief decoration of a limestone column, 10 ft. 6 in. high. In the two left-hand corners, and in the upper right-hand corner, are the symbols of the Key of the Nile. Text p. 135. Twelfth Dynasty. (Cairo Museum).

c

d

a

b

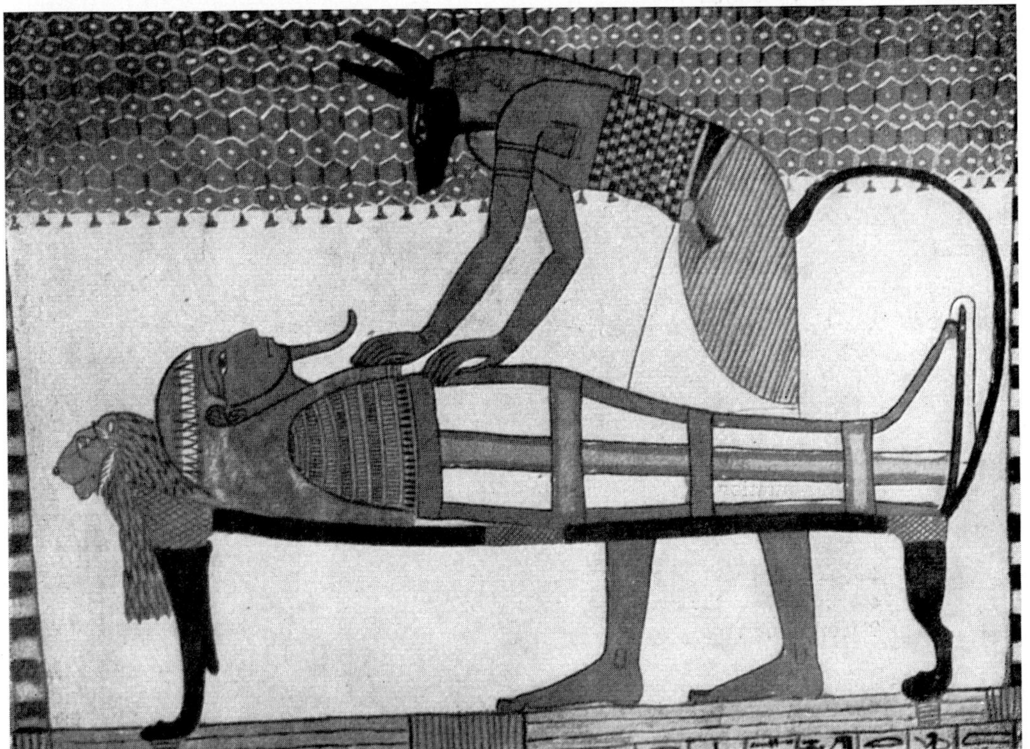

c

46. (A) Geese. Part of a painting on plastered surface in a tomb, Medum. (Cairo Museum).
(B) The dog-headed god of Death, Anubis, clad in vest and apron, examining the mask and binding of a mummy lying on a bier in the form of a lion. Wall-painting on plaster in the tomb of Sennudjem at Karnak. Height of Anubis, 28 in. Nineteenth — Twentieth Dynasty.
(C) Reapers in the Kingdom of the Dead. One sees the wooden Egyptian sickle, in which toothed flakes of flint are inset. Part of a wall-painting on plaster in the tomb of Sennudjem at Karnak. Height of man, 11.8 in. Nineteenth — Twentieth Dynasty.

pyramids, must have been brought all the way from Assouan, some 600 miles away. The Sphinx (Fig. 42c), the crouching lion with the king's face which gazed toward the rising sun, was cut out of a natural ridge of rock some 200 feet in length; this was also the work of Chephren's architect.

While the Sphinx, in its present state of preservation, gives only a faint idea of the great impulse towards sculpture which took place at this period, we can follow its development more clearly in other surviving works. At Medum, in a tomb of the beginning of the IVth Dynasty—if not of the end of the IIIrd Dynasty—were found painted limestone statues of Prince Rahotep (Fig. 42a) and his wife (Fig. 42b). These seated statues, though still somewhat archaic in style, show an attempt at verisimilitude which clearly was nothing new. The figure of King Chephren (Fig. 43a), which Mariette dug up from the colonnaded hall of the valley temple—in which there were twenty-three other statues of kings, all over life-size—has, in spite of its solemn and impassive dignity, an artistic vitality and freedom which is most notably expressed in the admirable way in which the tutelary falcon is joined to the head. When this art was not constrained by the austere solemnity which it owed to the deified kings, it showed, by the close of the IVth Dynasty, a pronounced realism. Sculpture became so lifelike that the hard but lifelike modelling of the Asiatic features of the limestone bust in Fig. 43b remind one of the constant invasions of Mesopotamians into Egypt at about this time.

The ideas, so clearly expressed in these sculptures, must have influenced the whole of Egyptian life. When, about 2550 B.C., a new royal family, the Vth Dynasty, ascended the throne, a great change took place in Egyptian religious ideology. The obelisks of Abusir and Heliopolis were erected; the cult of earthly majesty withdrew before that of the Sun-god Ra, and the dimensions of the pyramids were reduced to more human proportions. Such limestone statues as those of 'scribes', to be seen in various collections, impress one as being actual portraits, and wooden statues like that of the so-called 'Magistrate' in the Cairo Museum evidently attempt complete verisimilitude.

It is not only in statuary that there is this attempt at truth to nature; it occurs also in the paintings and reliefs (Figs. 46a, 43c and page 128) of the period. From these, even more then from the hieroglyphic records, so numerous under the VIth Dynasty, which were dictated by the moods and desires of the moment, one can divine the spiritual attitude of the period and the coming development of the Middle Kingdom. It is significant that towards the end of the Vth Dynasty the tombs of the nobles became more and more richly decorated, while, at the same time, asserting their independence, they withdrew from the burial-places of the kings. The Pharaohs of the VIth Dynasty removed their seat to Saqqara, which since the days of Menes had become a great city, and about the year 2900 B.C. was given the name of Memphis, after the pyramid of King Pepis I.

The new class of landowners and the great nobles had more and more of their own way in the newly-formed feudal governments. About 2300 B.C. the VIth Dynasty, with its unrestricted individualism, brought to an end the old world of monumental art and spiritual unity—and with them the Old Kingdom itself.

The Middle Kingdom

With the increasing power of the individual nobles and the emergence of a wealthy middle class, the sovereignty of the Pharaohs of the VIIth to the XIth Dynasties became almost nominal. Few works of art have survived from this troubled interim period. Instead of building pyramids, simple rock sepulchres were excavated in the cliffs at the edge of the desert. From an architectural point of view the rock-tombs of Beni-Hasan are particularly interesting, since in the pillars of their porticoes and sepulchral chambers we can trace the history of the Egyptian column.

The Old Kingdom had only the simple square column; but now the number of their sides increased, and in Beni-Hasan we already find sixteen-sided columns. Since these facts were slightly hollowed, we have already the basic form of the later Doric column of the Greeks. The so-called Egyptian 'Proto-Doric' column has also a round base-plate by way of pedestal, and a square abacus at the top, which takes the weight of the joists of the roof or ceiling. Before long there were clustered columns, with lotus-bud capitals (page 131, left). This lotus-bud capital is the earliest experiment in first expanding and then reducing the column, an expedient which the Greeks later applied to the entire column, with magnificent results.

The power of the Pharaohs began to increase again, and in the XIth Dynasty the sepulchre of kings Mentuhotep III and IV was built in Thebes. Shaped like a temple, its chambers, reached by long shafts, lie deep in the rocks, while at the entrance, inside a spacious courtyard, are two wide terraces, one above the other, supported by columns and crowned with a pyramid. The upper terrace alone is supported by no less than 140 octagonal columns. The princes of Thebes at last succeeded in restoring the unity of the kingdom, and when, in about the year 2000 B.C., Amenemhet I, the founder of the XIIth Dynasty, seized power, an age of renewed splendour dawned upon the Nile valley. This Middle Kingdom, as it was called, made its power felt far beyond its frontiers. The ships of the Pharaohs sailed to Punt, the land of incense on the Somali coast, and about this time the first Egyptian statues were set up in Crete. The sculptors of the Middle Kingdom preferred a darker hard stone to the light, pinkish kind which had been used previously; statues and figures in reliefs (Fig. 45c) alike became more slender. A receding forehead and a larger mouth give the faces a rather voluptous and African appearance, but under Amenemhet III the artists reverted to nobler forms. The grey granite statue of this king, now in the Cairo Museum, is one of the finest of the few surviving monuments of the period.

Generally speaking, the art of the Middle Kingdom was inferior to that of the

Old Kingdom, but in some ways it prepared the ground for the artistic achievements of the New Kingdom. In Beni-Hasan, instead of painted relief, actual wall-paintings appeared for the first time; not frescoes, but tempera paintings. The colours were mixed with gum tragacanth and water, and applied with a hair-brush or a slip of reed. In a tomb of the XIIth Dynasty were found pictures of glassblowers, which show that about this time, if not earlier, this art was known.

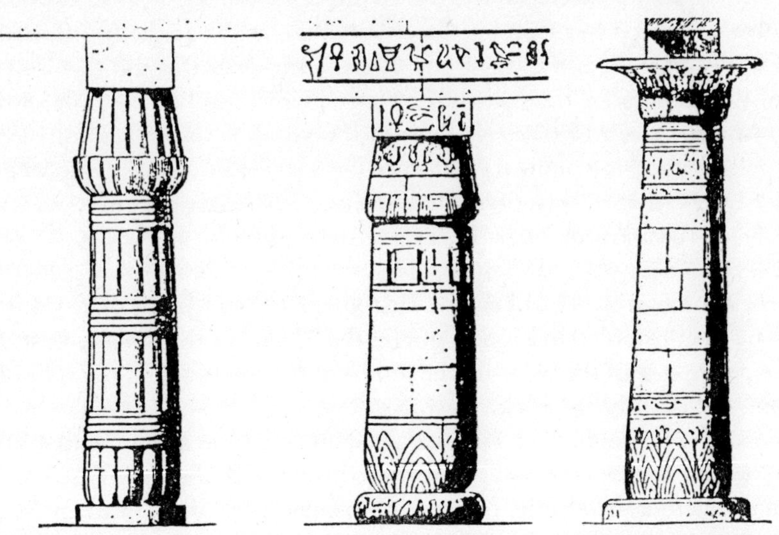

The evolution of the Egyptian column from the Middle Kingdom to the New

Apart from the fact that little sculpture of the Middle Kingdom has been preserved, the culture of this period seems to have expressed itself better in literature. Political and social changes, and the closer relations between peoples, had confronted the Egyptian intellect with questions which could not be answered through the plastic arts, but rather by means of the highly-developed hieroglyphic script. There was only a brief interlude of literary activity, since after 1788 B.C., under the XIIIth Dynasty, fresh disorders took place. During the period of the great migrations, in the second millennium B.C., the people known as the Hyksos, or 'shepherd kings' invaded and conquered Egypt, and under the oppressive government of foreign rulers Egyptian art was stifled for nearly two hundred years.

The New Kingdom

During the XIVth, XVth and XVIth Dynasties Egypt was under foreign rule, with its capital in the Nile Delta, until the princes of Thebes, the XVIIth Dynasty, began the war of liberation which Amasis, the founder of the XVIIIth Dynasty, brought to a victorious end about the year 1580 B.C. With this begins the New Kingdom, which lasted for about five hundred years after the expulsion of the Hyksos, and became the centre of a world power embracing the entire area of the old Oriental civilization. A result of this struggle with the Hyksos, in the course of which the Egyptians became acquainted with the horse, was that the New Kingdom became a military State, eager to make conquests, and its Pharaoh a warlike sovereign with a great army, whose strength was based on well-drilled, chariot-borne warriors. Egypt now advanced her frontier towards Nubia, as far as the fourth cataract; the Syrians were overrun, and to their surprise the Egyptians found themselves on the banks of the Euphrates, the 'backward water', which, unlike the Nile, flowed from north to south. Queen Hatshepsut revived the voyages to the land of Punt (below) on a large scale, and in commemoration of her success built the magnificent terraced temple of Deir-el-Bahri, west of Thebes, in a semicircle of precipitous rocks. Thebes, the centre of the movement of liberation, was henceforth the capital of the new empire.

The rock-tomb which had become customary in the Middle Kingdom was now adopted by the Pharaohs. In a lonely gorge, the 'Valley of the Kings', west of Thebes, on the opposite side of the Nile, are the tombs of the rulers and dignitaries of the New Kingdom, cut deep in the rock.

Tutmosis I, who died about 1520 B.C., had already built there the first of the great temples, which were eventually to spread throughout the valley of the Nile, and whose remains today give it its peculiar atmosphere. The walls of the palaces and the

Loading the ships of Queen Hatshepsut, the first great queen of history (1500 B.C.). On the walls of the temple of Karnak. The inscription states that never yet has such a quantity of African treasures been destined for one prince as the contents of the five sailing-ships which the Queen had despatched to Somaliland. (Breasted)

tombs are covered with coloured reliefs and paintings, which constitute the greatest superficial area of painting ever achieved by any race. In them is reflected the whole history of the New Kingdom, which carried on an active exchange of goods and works of art with Crete, Syria, and the rest of the ancient Oriental world. Egyptian influences began to invade the Near East, while, on the other hand, the subject Syrians influenced Egypt through their gods, their art, and their music. Under these stimuli the Egyptian spirit, which had remained almost unchanged for centuries, began to expand in new directions.

The greatest change took place about 1360 B.C., under Amenophis IV, who replaced polytheism by the monotheistic worship of the solar disc, Aton. For a little while the old worship of Amon was violently persecuted. The king laid the foundations of a new royal residence in Middle Egypt—in the neighbourhood of the modern Tel-el-Amarna—at some distance from Thebes, the city of the old religion, and at the same time changed his name to Akhnaton. This was accomplished by an artistic revolution, the results of which may still be seen at Amarna. The bust of Akhnaton's wife (Fig. 45a) shows a degree of female emancipation previously unknown in Egypt. Neither the religious nor the artistic reformation had any lasting effect. The king's successor and son-in-law, Tutankhaton, was compelled, by the powerful adherents of Amon, to change his name to Tutankhamen. A weakling, who achieved undeserved fame through the treasures brought to light on the discovery of his tomb in 1922, he could only look on while the religion of Amon was re-established, and the memorials of the heresy of Amarna were as far as possible obliterated. Tutankhamen was compelled to acknowledge the ancient gods and to return to Thebes, which was restored to its position as the capital of the kingdom by the general Karemhab, who had long had actual control of the country, on his ascending the throne as the founder of the XIXth Dynasty. The kings of the XIXth Dynasty created a new imperial army, which included foreign mercenaries from all parts of the world (below).

The external traffic of 'Thebes of the hundred gates' was mainly with Karnak and Luxor, on the right bank of the Nile, while on the left bank of the river the necropolis, with its rock-tombs and royal temples, rose from the steep escarpment of the desert. As an architect, Rameses II was second only to the builders of the Pyramids. In the royal temple of Amon, at Karnak, founded by Amenemhet I in the XIIth Dynasty, and continued by nearly all the sovereigns of the XVIIIth and XIXth Dynasties, he completed the colonnaded hall on a scale greater than anything previously attempted. 4,550 feet long and 1,820 feet wide, it is the greatest monument of Egyptian religious art. There are still proto-Doric columns in the great hall, but in the colonnades, which, like the hall, date from the XVIIIth Dynasty, there are eight-stemmed papyrus columns with closed umbels and sharp chamfers; presently

Negro, Asiatics, and Libyan. Sketch in the sepulchral chamber of Sethos I, XIX Dynasty, Karnak

a closed, bell-shaped capital appears, which, in the great columnar hall of the XIXth Dynasty, and on the twelve smooth, round columns, sixty-eight feet in height, of the central hall (Fig. 44b) expands into an open umbellate capital. The other 122 columns, which once supported the roof of the hall, which is 328 feet long and 164 feet wide, have the closed papyrus-umbel capitals above smooth but richly carved shafts. It is almost impossible to make out the original plan of this temple from the ruins, owing to the many subsidiary chambers and separate buildings which were added during the long period of its construction.

The columns of the beautiful ruined temples of Luxor also display the closed papyrus capital, though not in its finished shape, but in the more primitive bundled form (Fig. 44a). These temples and sepulchral enclosures were not only in Thebes;

Reconstruction of a temple at Karnak with the massive tapering gate-towers, the so-called pylons, the courtyard, and the colonnades

there is not room here to list all their ruins and remains. Rameses II built a vast sepulchral temple, with lofty central nave and lower aisles, on the left bank of the Nile, as well as temples in Tanis and Bubastis. The great rock-temple at Bet-el-Wali, whose transept is still supported by proto-Doric columns, is of unusual design; a great avenue of sphinxes leads up to the temple at Es-Sebua, and in the temple of Gerf-Hussen colossal statues of kings lean back against the lofty columns. At Abu-Simbel the temple itself is entirely inside the hill, while against the façade stand four colossal images of the king (Fig. 44c). This art was already in its decline when the XXth Dynasty, under Rameses III, built a temple to the Moon-god, Chons (Fig. 45b), near the great temple of Amon. It is remarkable for nothing but its simple form, and for that reason is often mentioned in histories of Egyptian art. Nothing new or original was now produced, and only the old forms were dully repeated.

When we consider the sculpture of the XVIIIth Dynasty (Figs. 45a, 45b and

45d) we see the results, in the New Kingdom, of a development, which had already begun in the Middle Kingdom (Fig. 45c). These figures, despite their distinction of form, are not entirely free from a certain pose; when we compare the portrait of Nofretete (Fig. 45a) with her over-long neck, her slightly sunken breast, and large ears, with the classic heads of the Old Kingdom (Figs. 43a and 43b), she gives the impression of a decadent creature, despite her air of fashionable elegance.

Art had run its course in Egypt in a longer period of time than that which divides us from the ancient Greeks. There was no further renaissance. In the best works of the New Kingdom, such as the relief representing Sethos I (Fig. 41), we can see its limitations: it could do no more than reproduce the same attitudes, the same profiles, and the same symbolism—in which the uraeus on the heads of the kings (Figs. 45a and 45b), with the looped cross, the Key of the Nile (Fig. 45c), which was the emblem of eternal life, and the scarabeus (Fig. 41), the symbol of the earthly life and the origin of humanity, were constantly repeated. After the XVIIIth Dynasty there is no intensification, but only a widening of the stream of Egyptian art; it is only consistent that in the course of this multiplication the paintings on papyrus, as the oldest miniatures or book illustrations, should now, as a new kind of plane representation, court comparison with the old wall-paintings. The outlines were drawn in red or black with a fine reed-pen, and were often filled in with colour, applied with a brush; but the moment this art sought to shake off the old fetters it relapsed into the primitive. The wall-paintings of the XIXth and XXth Dynasty (Figs. 46b and 46c) return to old formulae, which compare very badly with the lucid art of the Old Kingdom (Fig. 46a). There was no faith to give this art a fresh impetus.

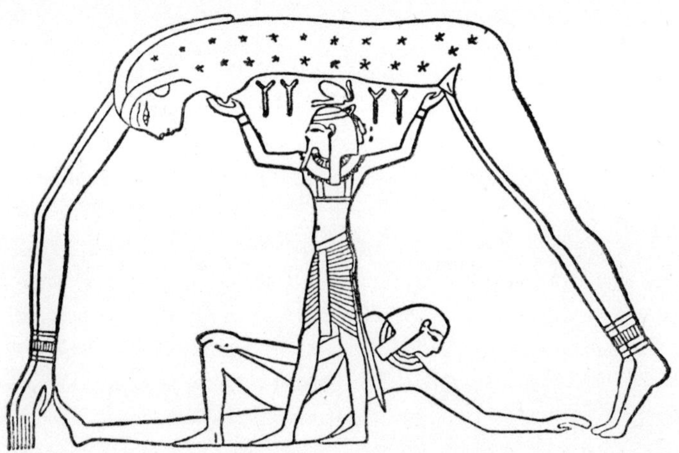

The Goddess of Heaven, Nut. Beneath her star-besprinkled body are the four props of the heavens, and the god of the air, Shu; at her feet is the earth-god, Geb. Often represented on the wooden sarcophagi of Egypt

The late period, especially in the more important productions, like the statues of Sen-Mut, had returned to the stereotyped style of sculpture from which ancient Mesopotamian art could never entirely break away.

What could be done, in the millennia before the rise of Greek art, was done in Egypt, in an area smaller than Switzerland, at a very early period and for a very long time. This art never reached the point of representing object in correct perspective. The art of the ancient East is not so much a matter of 'progress' in the representation of spatial relations, as the expression of the philosophy of peoples who could never free themselves from the dark background of life; they realized the awfulness of eternity, and their art was inspired by dread rather than by joy. The formal elements of Greek art had already been prefigured in the ancient East, but it was for the Greeks to give humanity not only freedom of thought, but freedom of form, and an art that was truly victorious over matter. But in Egypt the clock of history ran down: the art of the latest period, which dragged on from the XXIst Dynasty to the XXXth Dynasty, and on to the age of Hellenism, did much in the way of imitation, and did it well, but it was no longer creative. In the last period of Egyptian art we see the grinning countenance of the strange, often ugly and dwarfish god Bes (page 139), the symbol of a period which had lost its old faith in the great cosmic order of the universe.

47. (A) Late archaic female head of the Akroter-Sphinx in the temple of Aegina (Glyptothek, Munich).
(B) Herakles, drawing his bow, from the eastern gable of the Aphaia Temple, Aegina.

a

b

c

d

(C) Kore with outer garment laced over the shoulders. Found to the west of the Erechtheum in 1886. The chiton can be seen at the throat. The forearms were usually inset in these statues, as may be seen from the round recess on the right upper arm. There are flowers on the diadem; on the head was a pin or wire to prevent birds from fouling the face. Attic island marble. Height, 32 in. End of sixth century B.C. (Acropolis Museum, Athens).
(D) Attic Vase in mixed style, with red and black figures. Represents Herakles, under the protection of Athene, capturing Cerberus by cunning, Hades having surrendered the hound to him on the condition that he does not touch it with his hands. Herakles entices the hound with his right hand. Cerberus here has two heads, and bears on the top of each head the serpent of the underworld; the tail too ends in a serpent. Height of vase, 22 in. Sixth century B.C. (Louvre).

a

b

(B) Head of t statue of a Gre athlete; the n row olive-wrea about the he shows that he w the winner of contest at Oly pia. Found Benevento Italy. Height, in. End of fi century B.C. (Louvre).

c

d

48. (A) Head of a charioteer. The whole statue, 5 ft. 11 in. in height, was found at Delphi in 1896, in front of one of the longer sides of the temple of Apollo. According to a disputed inscription, it was probably a votive offering made after winning a chariot-race at Delphi about 470 B.C. The eyes are filled with glass, which in this rare instance has escaped destruction; they give the face its profound and fiery vitality. The fillet on the head was once inlaid with silver; the lips were covered with silver foil. (Museum, Delphi).

(C) The Orpheus relief; one of the most celebrated works of the late classic period—fifth century B.C. Orpheus, Eurydice and Hermes are shown, returning to the upper world along the desolate paths of Hades, at the moment when Orpheus, forgetful of his promise, turns to gaze upon Eurydice. Hermes gently takes her hand in order to lead her back to the underworld. Reproduced from the best Roman copy of the lost original. Height, 4 ft. (National Museum, Naples).

(D) Part of the front of the so-called 'throne' found in 1887 in the Villa Ludovisi. Parian marble. Height of the fragment about 3 ft. 3 in. The bath of Hera. (Formerly assumed to represent the birth of Aphrodite.) The goddess, attended by two nymphs, emerges from the spring of Canathus. (National Museum, Rome).

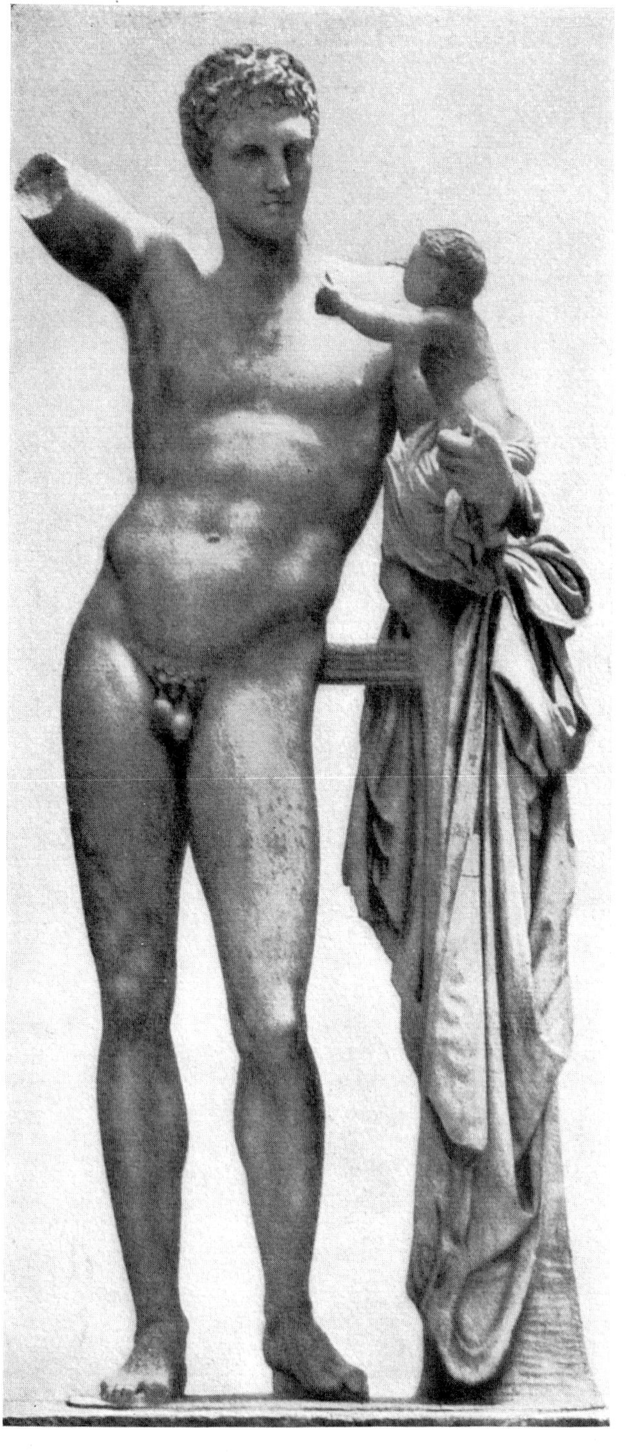

a

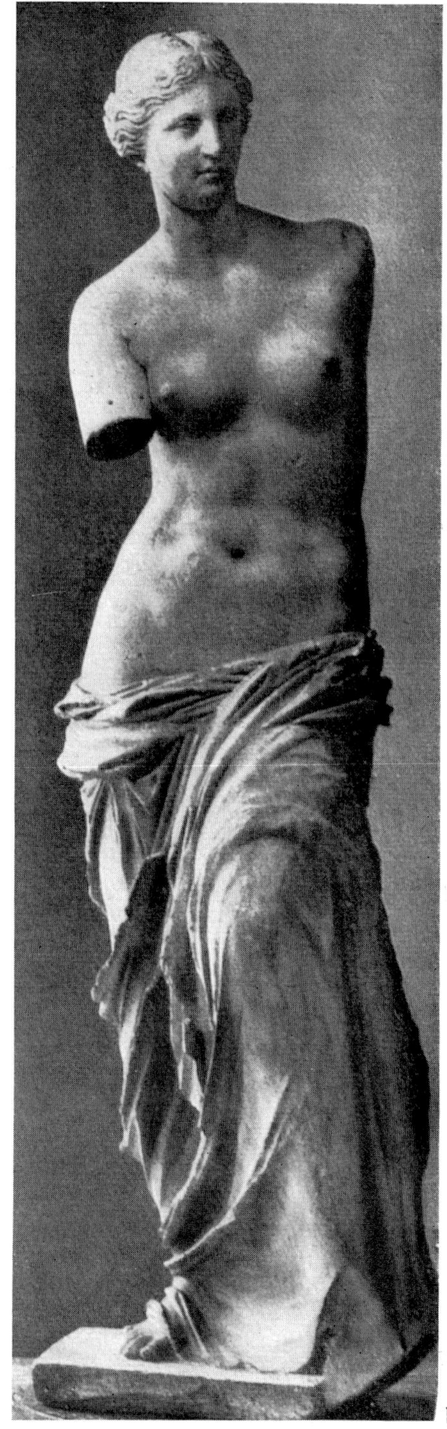

b

49. (A) The Hermes of Praxiteles. The uplifted right hand may perhaps have been offering, enticingly, a bunch of grapes to the boy Dionysus (represented as a miniature adult and not as a child). The stump of the arm, and the left leg, just above the foot, were restored by a Roman artist.
(B) The Venus of Milo. The Aphrodite discovered in 1820 on the island of Melos. Height of the figure, which consists of two blocks of marble, joined in the region of the loins, 6 ft. 8 in.

a

b

c

d

50. (A) North view of the Temple of Poseidon.
(B) Part of the Assembly of the Gods, from the eastern frieze of the Parthenon. Probably Poseidon, Apollo and Artemis. (Acropolis Museum, Athens).
(C) Panel from the Western frieze of the Parthenon. Plaster cast.
(D) South-eastern aspect of the Temple of Nike, Athens.

Chapter XI

GREECE

*

In the thirteenth and twelfth centuries B.C. the great migrations which had been sweeping across Asia since the second pre-Christian millennium brought Hellenic tribes across Thessaly into the Peloponnese, and Greeks ousted the Pelasgian or Achaian Mycenaeans.

The Æolians settled on the north of the west coast of Asia Minor and in the adjacent islands, especially in Lesbos. The Ionians took the middle portion of the same coast and the Ægean islands: while the Dorians, in about 1100 B.C., took the Peloponnese and the south-west coast of Asia Minor, and the more southerly islands, such as Crate, Melos, and Rhodes. A few centuries later Greek colonies were started in Sicily and Lower Italy. *Graecia magna* was born, at a time when the other powers, above all Egypt and Babylonia, had reached the later stage of their development.

The Homeric poems date from about 900 B.C. In 776 B.C. began the calendar based on the Olympic Games, and from about 700 B.C. the influence of the oracle of Delphi was felt as far afield as Phrygia and Lydia, whose kings sent votive offerings to the 'Navel of the Earth'. Greece was the birthplace of a new humanity, whose way of life, during the next fifteen hundred years, determined the features of antiquity.

At the same time, one must not imagine that Hellenism was something entirely new, or that art and culture did not exist before the arrival of the Greeks. Recent research has gradually dispelled this ancient misconception; for as soon as Egyptian, and fifty years later, Babylonian, scripts were deciphered, a new written history of human civilization appeared.

In the art of Greece the white man first discovered his individuality; this discovery was made in southern Europe and under the influence of the older civilizations of the East, and we must not fail to examine the twofold European and Asiatic legacy which the art of Greece had inherited.

The Inheritance from Ancient Europe

The Greeks, when they came into the country, had iron as well as bronze, and in place of the free and individual idiom of Mycenaean art at the time of its maturity they brought the geometrical motives of ancient Europe. The first four hundred years of Greek art are called the geometrical period, from the kind of ornament applied to jewellery, weapons, and tools, to minor works of art in clay and bronze and above all, to pottery.

The painted earthenware vases of the earliest periods, the work of a people who inhabited the land before and during the rule of Mycenae, first appeared in the ninth and eigth century, and were still being produced in the seventh century. At a very early period the inscriptions on them included the artists' names. The finest were found outside the Dipylon, the double gateway of the old burial-ground of Athens, on the site of the old potters' quarter, and are decorated in what is known, therefore, as the Dipylon style. This reached its height between 850 and 750 B.C., and consists of a dark brown ornamentation painted with varnish on a background of light reddish-yellow clay. As in the art of neolithic Europe, zig-zag lines, wavy stripes, crosses and circles combine to form patterns, and these, unlike the similar Boeotian vases, which are perhaps older still, already show the key-pattern of which the later Greeks were so fond (Fig. 52a).

The late Cretan-Mycenaean art was bound to influence the development of Greek art: motives from northern Europe came in contact with others which had long ago absorbed Oriental elements, while Asiatic motives combined with Greek geometrical patterns, and all sorts of Eastern animals and fabulous creatures crept into the Greek decorations.

Comparable with these geometrically decorated vases are the earliest earthenware

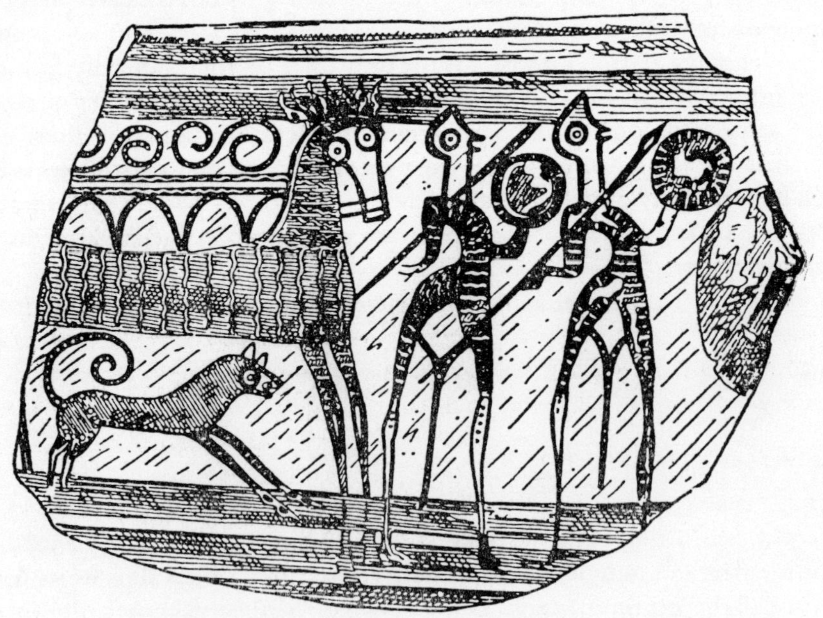

Fragment of a painted vase from Tiryns. About one-third actual size.
Cretan-Mycenaean culture. National Museum, Athens

effigies of women, found in tombs in Boeotia and Mycenae (Figs. 6a and 6b), which combine motives of pre-historic ornament with the bird motives common in Oriental art; with their often exaggerated long necks and lipless faces these are conceived entirely in the spirit of prehistoric art. They show the dislike of any empty space characteristic of all primitive art; often the early Greek potter makes a virtue of necessity, when he fills empty spaces with his geometrical patterns.

Oriental Influences

To understand what is original in Greek art one must realize to what extent the Hellenes, once they had settled down in Greece, took their place in the then highly civilized Mediterranean world. The gigantic walls built by the ancient rulers of the land rose above their simple villages. Black-bearded traders brought glassware and jewellery from Egypt (below), and other benefits of civilization, garments hitherto unfamiliar, for which the Greeks had no names. Thus, the Greek word *chiton*, for a tunic, is derived from the Phoenician word *keton*. The Phoenicians, on their side, had learned much from the Egyptians, and ended by bestowing on Europe the greatest gift she had ever received, that of the alphabet.

As early as the middle of the second millennium B.C. the Phoenicians seem to have developed an alphabet of twenty-two letters, but without vowels, from Egyptian hieroglyphs. They were first people to use symbols representing *sounds*, like the letters of our own alphabet, rather than *things*.

Golden jewel from Ægina. The Egyptian god Bes with birds and duplicated asps, on a little ship ending in lotus-blossoms

By the twelfth century B.C. they had already given up using clay tablets, and were importing papyrus from Egypt. When the Greeks adopted the alphabet, after 900 B.C., they began to use the signs for some of the Phoenician consonants, which did not occur in Greek, to denote their own vowels. About 700 B.C. the knowledge of the alphabet was so widespread among the Hellenes that the first inscriptions began to appear on vases.

A later geometric style, about 750—700 B.C., was followed by an Orientalized style, whose formation was largely due to the art of the Phoenician metal-worker. The palmetto and the lotus-blossom, the double volute of palm-leaves (as shown in the adjacent illustration), and various other Oriental patterns, find their way into Greek painting. Lions, tigers, sphinxes and gryphons begin to replace European animals. The effect of the black design on a yellowish ground is often heightened by the addition of red, brown or white. The bodies of the men are usually brown, while those of the women retain the brighter colour of the ground. Very often we see the so-called 'kneeling run', where an effect of speed is obtained by making one knee of the runner touch the ground. The chequer-board pattern seems to have come from the Greek cities of Asia Minor.

Cretan influence appears next in the Proto-Corinthian style of vase-painting, in which geometrical and old Asiatic patterns are combined. Favourite subjects were the heroic battles of antiquity. Silhouettes appear as well as outline drawings; while over the blackish-brown varnish on the pale ground the details are added in dark red. The old dipylon vases were often as tall as a man, but many small earthenware oil-flasks were now produced as well. In the pure Corinthian style an individual national style makes its appearance, a style of archaic black-figure vase-painting.

Early Greek painting on a Rhodian earthenware plate, representing Hector and Menelaus fighting over the body of Euphorbus. British Museum

Archaic Art

From the middle of the eighth century B.C. the Greek world made great advances, both internally and externally. The legendary age of the kings, and the earlier feudal age, were things of the past, and the *polis*, or city-state, became the main political unit. As soon as their art had shaken off the geometrical style and reverted to Oriental forms, infinite possibilities were created, and the soil was prepared on which classic Greek art was later to flourish.

Between 750 and 550 B.C. nearly all the coasts of the Mediterranean and Black Sea were colonized from the Greek seaports. Most of the Greek tribes took part in the founding of these settlements, which became independent centres, and for hundreds of years defied the aggression of foreign peoples. From Spain, across Lower Italy and Sicily, the colonial area stretched as far as the southern coast of Russia, where the Greeks came into contact with Scythians, exchanging the products of Ionian industry for the corn of south Russia. Byzantium was founded by the Greeks, as was Cyrene, on the African coast, and Naukratis in Egypt.

It was entirely in keeping with the spirit of the age that the Greeks, for the first time since the fall of Mycenae, should have produced a great monumental art. A new art of sculpture was developed from Egyptian models. Stone temples were built to shelter the colossal images of the gods; their elements were eastern in origin, but they expressed the Greek spirit, less by an overwhelming effect of enormous masses, than by the perfect harmony of individual parts.

Between 590 and 560 B.C.—a period of great significance for the whole of humanity—Solon, one of the seven sages of Greece, created the juridical State, and prepared the ground not only for political, but for intellectual liberty; but what was created in that fortunate age, later generations of Greeks and Persians destroyed.

Nevertheless, many works of the sixth century B.C., in marble, bronze and earthenware, have been preserved. In 480 B.C., the Persians razed Athens and the Acropolis to the ground, burning the temples and destroying the sacred images. The art of destruction had not become so refined as it did later, so when the Greeks had finally conquered the Persians, the temples were rebuilt, even finer than before, as a thank offering to the gods. Since they would not offer the old, damaged statues, they buried them in the sacred precincts, or used them in raising and levelling the ground for the buildings of the classic age. In 1884, in the so-called 'Persian dump', most of the sixth century statues which the Athenians buried on the Acropolis about the year 470 B.C. were recovered.[1]

Like other works of early Greek art, these were not statues in the sense of portraits, but *agalmata*; by which untranslatable word the Greeks meant anything ornamental, anything regarded with pride or joy, whether a wreath, or a tripod, or the figure of a youth or maiden. The statues of gods are distinguished from those of humans only by the external emblems of their power.

Attic Lekythos

From excavations in various places we can form a definite idea of the appearance of the cities of ancient Greece. The narrow streets were lined with small, simple houses. In the middle of the city was the *Agora,* or market-place. The buildings followed the lie of the land, or old highways; new quarters added themselves to the city which increased by a natural growth, and only after the seventh and sixth centuries B.C., when the population had increased, was there any methodical town-planning. The city was surrounded by a stout wall, often enclosing considerably more than the inhabited area. Sparta alone was too proud to protect her cities with walls, priding herself upon the invincibility of her warriors, until in a single day, at the battle of Leuktra, her military glory perished.

Thrones and banqueting-tables set in the open-air were the forerunners of the temples to the invisible deities; they were given houses only after the Greek heroic poems had completely humanized them. The private houses of the Greeks were built of bricks

[1] These were exclusively works of the period, 600—480 B.C., but it may be assumed that still earlier votive offerings may have been built into the foundations of the Parthenon, or buried in heaps of refuse not yet examined, when the Acropolis underwent alteration at the beginning of the sixth century.

and timber. In Greece, as in Asia Minor, there were ridged roofs as well as flat roofs. This was a natural result of the method of timber construction; the earliest pediment sculptures on the Acropolis were carved from the native limestone, in fairly low relief, with the woodworker's tools, the saw, the drill, the gouge and the rasp.

Apart from a few paintings on tiles and vases, few relics of archaic Greek painting have survived. Between painted bas-reliefs and paintings on flat surfaces there was little stylistic difference. On some steles, the life-sized figure of the deceased, portrayed in outline only, stands in majestic calm, with a beaker in the right hand. The feet, in the antique manner, are still firmly planted on the earth.

Herakles attempting to wrest the tripod from Apollo. Plane representation of an early red-figured Amphora from the workshop of Andokides. Text page 143. Sixth century B.C. Antiquarium, Berlin

The earthenware vases of this period reveal an ever-increasing sense of form, and may be divided into definite groups. A common form is the *lekythos* (page 141), slender jugs or vases with handles, developed from a form of small vase, for holding incense or unguents, and employed during the funeral rites. They became larger and larger, until at last they were used to decorate the tombs. The *aryballoi* were globular vases which served the same purpose. The *amphora* was used for storing liquids, the *hydria* for fetching water, the *krater* for mixing wine, the *kyathos* for ladling the wine from the *krater,* and the *oinochoe* for pouring, while people drank from the *kylix,* or cup, and the *kantharos,* or beaker.

During the sixth century red-figure vase-painting (above) was developed, while the black-figure painting reached its highest point of grave and austere perfection at the close of the archaic period (cf. Fig. 52a). The black figures stand out against a white ground; the eyes of the profile heads are still almond-shaped, as though seen from in front. Their development is most clearly shown in the vases with decorative inscriptions, restricted mainly to Attica; one of the finest of these is the so-called Francois-vase, after the name of its finder, now in the Archaeological Museum of Florence. This is signed with the names of the potter, Ergotimos, and the painter, Klitias. This style, which, may be described as early archaic, is followed by a more austere style in which the yellowish ground is reddened by adding colouring matter to the clay, while the figures are painted in glossy black, scratched away where lines are to be drawn upon them, and small ornamental details are painted over them in colour. These vases show scenes from the daily life of the Greeks and of their gods, while ornamentation is confined to the neck and foot and rim of the vase, and to the handles. The greatest master of this style of Attic vase-painting was Exekias. Together with his name, that of Nearchos appears in the inscriptions, as potter and painter both, while Amasis and Nikosthenes were doubtless merely the proprietors of the studio. Under Asiatic and Ionian influence the forms of the vases gradually became rounder; the garments of the figures developed pleats and folds, and as a great innovation a bird appeared, fluttering among interlacing boughs. Nikosthenes was the chief maker of vases at the end of the black-figure period; Chariteros, Timagoras and Tychios were others.

With the *red-figured* vases began a period of complete freedom and maturity. The whole ground of the vase was now covered with glossy black varnish. At first only the outlines, but later the whole figures themselves were scraped away, revealing the red ground, and the brush was used on the inner surfaces.[1] In the studio of Andokides (page 142) both black and red figure vases were produced, the two styles often appearing on the same vase. Epiktetes, one of the most famous painters of the early red-figure style, whose favourite vessels were drinking-bowls, only occasionally produced black figures; he was really a linear draughtsman rather than a painter, and restricted his work on the inner surfaces to the most necessary details (cf. Fig. 47d).

As in the painting, so in the sculpture of the second half of the sixth century B.C. we can see the progress from early archaic uncouthness to archaic austerity. Pausanius names Gitiades of Sparta, architect and maker of bronze statues, as the best of the Doric school; Dipoinos and Skyllis may be regarded as his pupils, and later, Klearchos of Samos. These are the sculptors of the strictly archaic, Doric statues, most of which are described as statues of Apollo, and which today are among the greatest treasures of our museums. They are all figures of the same type; the shoulders hang lifelessly, but the arms are beginning to free themselves from the body, and the knees are becoming less rigid.

After the age of the Tyrants an inward ferment began in the whole of the political and intellectual life of the Greeks. Their urge to freedom expressed itself, politically, in the introduction of republican constitutions, and, artistically, in the gradual

[1] When large black patches—representing, for example, the hair of the head—threatened to merge with the background,a thin red line was drawn between the two. There are no longer any touches of white in the red-figured vase painting, and dark red is used only for accessories.

discarding of many restraints. The Greeks were beginning to become gravely conscious of their own great intellectual powers.

The Doric island of Ægina now came to the fore with her own artist, her own special school of art,and it was the Æginetic and Peloponnesian schools that perfected the treatment of the nude body in art. One of the earliest of the Æginetic artists was Kalon; then came Onatas, with his son and pupil Kalliteles, who were working shortly after the Persian wars. In Sikyon, Kamachos was the most celebrated painter, and Ageladas is named as the leading artist of Argos towards the close of the sixth century. The groups in the pediment of the temple at Ægina (Figs. 47a and 47b), today the pride of the Munich Glyptothek, were conceived as bronzes, and given bronze accessories and touched with colour; here the epic heroes were for the first time represented in sculpture, naked, with helmet, shield and spear. Artists had become aware of the beauty of the body. Such representations of bodily postures as now appear were formerly quite inconceivable. The 'Archaic smile' and the vague, awkward look, gave place to an attempt to reproduce lifelike and animated expressions.

Bas-reliefs in the late archaic style, like that illustrated in Fig. 48d, became more numerous. The sculpture of this period was usually in soft, brownish limestone, painted in bright and varied colours.

Solon was followed by the Tyrants. Peisistratos tried to give Athens the brilliance of the princely courts of the Hellenic Orient. In the second half of the sixth century the art of the Ionian islands invaded Attica, where such masters as Enchoios, Aristokles, Antenor, Kritos, Nesiotes and Hegias were working; the latter is believed to have been the teacher of Phidias. The consequent juxtaposition and conflict of Doric and Ionian ultimately produced the classic art of Athens. The Acropolis, like the citadels of other Greek cities, was enriched with more votive gifts, and on low pedestals, or on tall and slender pillars, stood the effigies (Fig. 47c) in which late archaic art evolved a modified kind of rococo. Several stately figures of girls, the slender and aristocratic *korai* of this period, with the gloss of well-preserved marble, and painted in brilliant colours, were discovered in the 'Persian dump'.

In this period, which saw the beginnings of Greek tragedy, sculpture found a new means of expression. The eyes gaze solemnly from the resolutely impassive face. Attic dignity is combined with the Ionic sense of the possibilities offered by the noble material—marble.

To all these works the remnants of colour, without which the art of Greece was unthinkable, still lend an appearance of life. The idea that the Greek statues had nothing but the pure white of their marble is quite mistaken. In the astringent gravity of these early Greek figures is the temper of the generation that endured the assault of Persia. In the fifty years between the Persian and Peloponnesian wars, Greek art developed to its full maturity. Before we consider the works of this classic period, it will be as well to take a backward glance at the development of the temple, which was almost the only architectural monument of the Greeks.

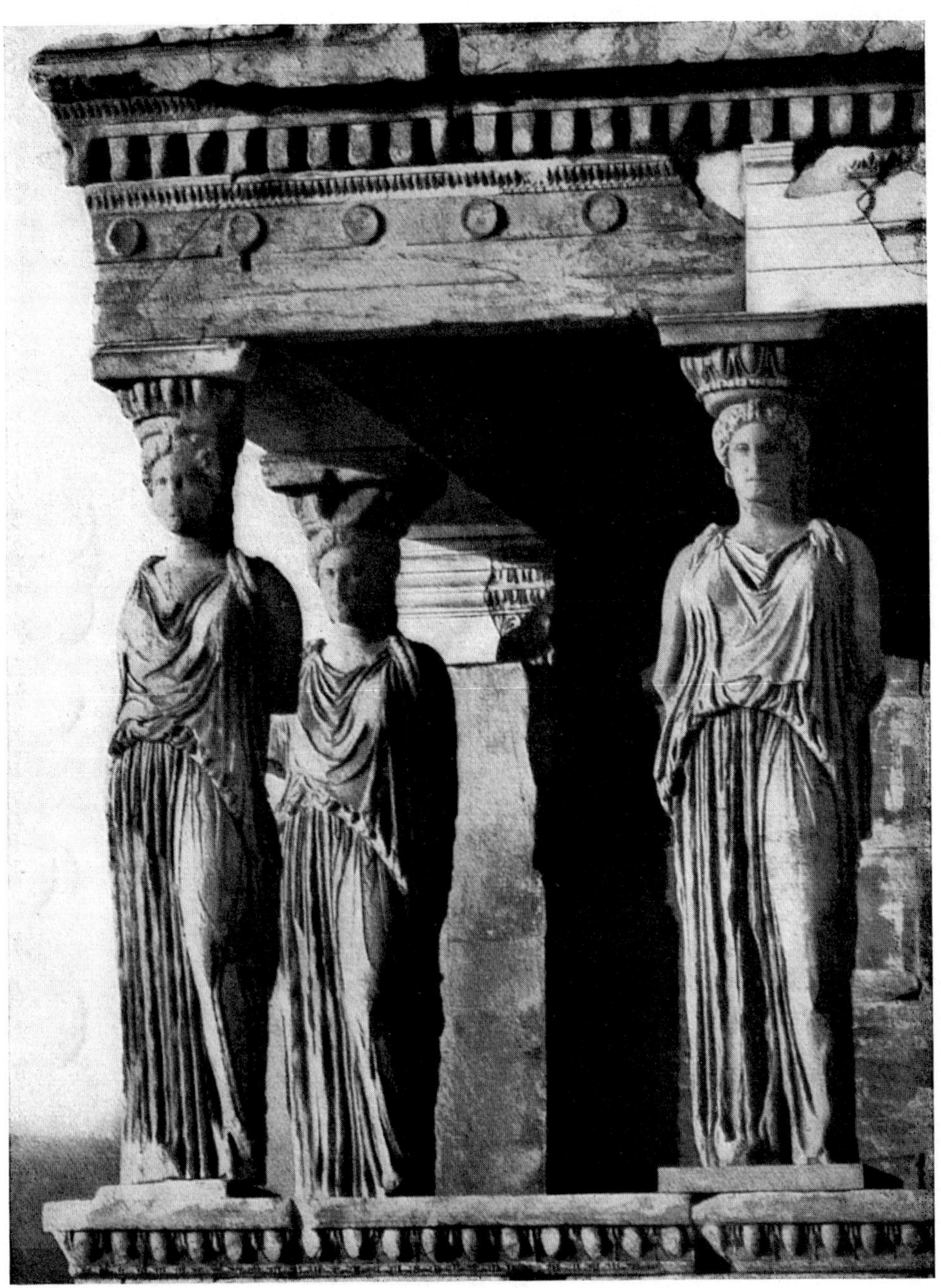

51. Part of the southern side of the Porch of the Maidens. Erechtheum, Athens.

a

b

c

52. (A) Figures on a black-figured vase. Middle of sixth century B.C.
(B) Drawing on a white lecythus. End of fifth century B.C.
(C) Galloping quadriga, with Hermes. In the chariot, Echelos abducting Basile. Double-sided Attic relief. Found in Phaleron, 1893. Height, 40 in. End of fifth century B.C. (All in the National Museum, Athens).

a

b

c

53. (A) Wounded Galatian. Probably a copy in marble of a bronze statue of the second century B.C. Time of King Attalus I of Pergamon. Height, 34 in. (Louvre).
(B) and (C) A scene often represented in the first century B.C. Maenads and satyrs dancing round Dionysus and Ariadne to the music of the double pipe. Relief on the sides of the 'Borghesian Vase', found in Sallust's garden in Rome. Pentelican marble. (Louvre).

a

b

54. (A) Rustic idyll. Marble relief of the time of Claudius, with the sacred precinct in the background. First century B.C (Glyptothek, Munich).

(B) Dionysos, with Icarius. Reproduction of a Hellenistic work of the third or second century B.C. The four masks unde the table on the left show that the host is a dramatic poet. The introduction of an architectural background was imitate in many Roman reliefs. Height of marble relief, 30 in. (Louvre).

The Greek Temple

When sacrificing to their gods, the Greeks assembled in the open air before the altar. It was therefore not essential, except when there was actually a sacred image, that every Greek sanctuary should be housed in a temple. Hence the nucleus and basic form of the temple (right, *a*) is always a simple chamber, and to this the temple was restricted in the case of many small sanctuaries; the inner chamber had only to shelter the sacred image and a few of the more precious votive offerings, while of the congregation only the priests entered it on the occasion of special ceremonies. Behind a fairly deep portico, supported by the frontal columns of the side walls, the *antae*, lay the entrance, through which the inner chamber received its light, for the other walls were windowless.

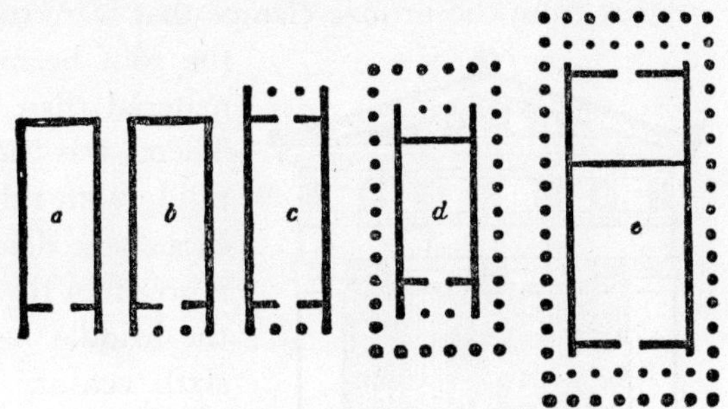

Development of the Greek Temple

Even in the earliest period this simple form did not content the Greeks, and presently (*b*) columns were placed in the portico, between the antae, an arrangement which often recurs in the ancient treasuries (page 146). Sometimes a second portico was built before a back entrance (*c*), giving rise to the double porticoed temple. Finally the *cella* was surrounded with columns, which supported the gabled roof, as in the Temple of Zeus at Olympia (*d*).

The internal divisions of the Greek temple are not necessarily expressed by the exterior. No religious service required the enlargement of the inner chamber, since the rites were always celebrated in the open air. Around the city churches of the Middle Ages people went about their everyday affairs, and the worshippers trod on consecrated ground only when they entered the church precincts; but the Greek temple was already in the centre of a sacred precinct, divided from the outer world by walls. Greek art, therefore, could devote itself entirely to perfecting the physical form of the sanctuary.

The temple kept the features of a house, and centuries of evolution culminated in the form which finally crowned the Acropolis with the incomparable perfection of the Parthenon (*e*).

It was not the beauty of the site alone that determined where a temple was raised, as a modern observer might suppose when he sees the remains of a temple to Poseidon on the cliffs above the sea, the temple of an island goddess on a gentle slope overlooking the shore, or that of a city goddess on the heights of the citadel, where it obviously expresses the sovereignty of the divinity over her realm. Sometimes a sacred spring has brought the sanctuary down into a narrow valley, while the ridge beside the valley is unoccupied, and the city temples were very often placed along the streets.

The temples were always of hewn stone. When they were not of marble, but of limestone, they usually had a coat of dazzling white plaster, so that they stood out plainly against the landscape and did not blend picturesquely with it.

Apart from the bronze clamps that were sunk into the stone, and the timber of the roof beams and the coffered ceiling, no other material than marble or limestone was employed. There was no amorphous binding material, no filling with rubble; no stone had an accidental shape or a shape determined in the course of the work, as is so often the case in the most perfect buildings of the Middle Ages. While the archaic temple of the sixth century was still long and narrow, with a heavy superstructure resting on massive pillars, which threatened to sink into the earth under their oppressive burden, the later temples gradually achieved a perfect repose of balanced stresses.

Front of a Doric treasury

Styles

When one speaks of styles in connection with the Greek temples one is not referring to entirely different forms of artistic expression, but to one and the same expression of the Greek spirit, which, in accordance with the difference between the Doric and Ionic temperament, manifested itself in the various orders of architecture.

The Doric temple originated in the Peloponnese; it was built of simple limestone, covered with white stucco; the triglyphs (page 147, left, *f*) and the dripstones depending from them were black, and the ornamentation was red and blue. The bold decoration of the cornices of the eaves mitigated the stiffness of the triangular pediment. The ridge ornament was often in the shape of a Gorgon, whose distorted face was supposed to strike terror into any evil spirits that might approach the building.

At first the contrast between support and burden, between vertical and horizontal, was still plain. Without bases, as though they had pierced the three layers of the substructure, the massive columns and antae stand in front of the old Doric treasuries, such as that of Megara, at Olympia, or the Athenian treasury at Delphi. With a strong base, since the shaft tapers rapidly only in its upper two-thirds, the Doric column carries the weight of the superincumbent beams as though it had grown where it stands. The impression of strength is increased by the shadows of the sharp-edged chamfering. The columns of the oldest temples have, as a rule, only sixteen such grooves; later on there were twenty or more, which gave the column an appearance of stability and strength and dispelled the idea of any possibility of fracture.

At the top of the column is the cushion-like *echinos* (*c*), the most significant member, in which the support and the load encounter each other. Narrow rings, the so-called *anuli,* the relic of an earlier garland of leaves, prepare the eye for the horizontal. The transition from the circular *echinos* to the architrave, the main beam (*e*), is effected, aesthetically and technically, by the square *abacus* (*d*).

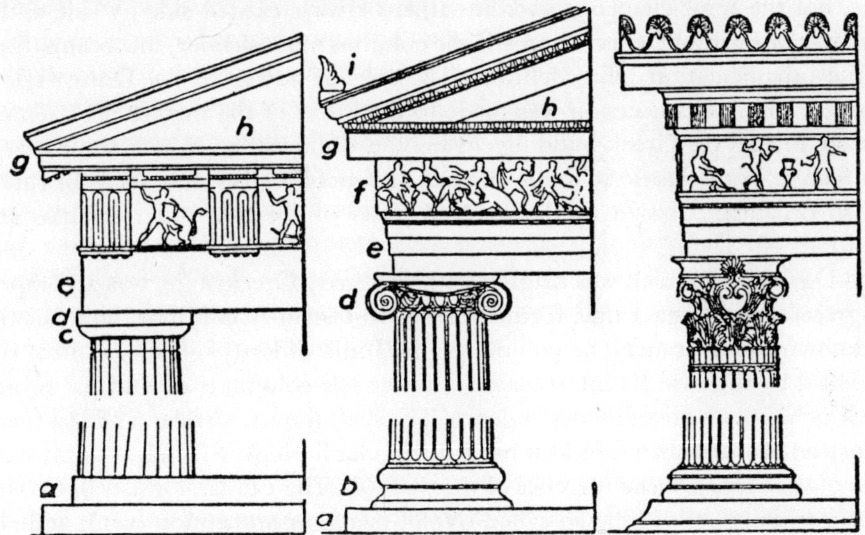

The Doric, Ionian and Corinthian styles in the Greek Temple

This balance of horizontal and vertical occurs again in the coloured strip of ornamentation oo the frieze (*f*), where the sharp-edged *triglypas* once more tend upwards, but are restrained by the *metopes,* the sculptured figures between them. Whatever force of aspiration still remains is then captured by the shallow pediment (*h*), which rises, with the *cyma recta,* above the *geison,* the cornice (*g*). The triangular field of the pediment, the *tympanon* (*h*), is filled with decorative sculpture.

We can trace the evolution of the Doric style from its beginnings on the surviving temples of Sicily and Lower Italy. The so-called Temple of Hercules, at Girgenti with the still ponderous capitals of the antae, and tall, clumsy entablature; the second temple at Metapont, the old temple of Pompeii, and the temple of Selinunt—all these show a development which took place after the eighth century. It was then that Rome began to extend her influence, and that the Hellenes, in one tremendous effort, carried Greek civilization far into Italy, until it outdid Greece itself in wealth and activity.

In Italy, the true South begins at Naples. In the Gulf of Salerno, at the northern limit of the compact settlement area of the ancient Greeks, lies Paestum, the Greek

Poseidonia, with three temples in an excellent state of preservation. The finest of these is the large and important temple of Poseidon (Fig. 50a), which stands near the older so-called basilica, and which once impressively overlooked the city.

The long, dark building can be recognized from a long way off. From whichever side one approaches it, the temple keeps the perfect serenity of the Doric style. There is no other surviving Doric temple to equal it. For the Parthenon is not, strictly speaking, Doric, but Attic: individual details, and the general effect, are Doric, but the Ionic element which in Athens always existed side by side with the Doric was not without effect—it made the columns more slender, the beams lighter, and the ornamentation more delicate. The solemn power of the Doric style was tempered, and due concession was made to the lustre of the marble. The temple at Paestum, like all the Greek buildings in Italy, is of limestone, which emphasizes the great feature of the Doric style, its emphatic sobriety. Only a few strips of carefully finished ornamentation in the beams and joists of the two older temples are of sandstone.

The Doric style, which was originally the ordinary Greek style, was accompanied by a graceful and elegant one, formed mainly in Ionian Asia Minor, which is therefore known as the Ionic. The column of the Ionic order (page 147, centre) is distinguished by the base (*b*) interpolated between the column itself and the substructure, which gives it greater independence. The shaft is more slender, and less tapered, and instead of sharp chamferings it has semicircular flutings, which leave only narrow ridges of the original circumference of the shaft (*d*). The capital consists of two parts, the ornamental portion, the so-called ovolo, cyma, or anthemion band, and above this, supporting the architrave, the volute, which has an elastic appearance, owing to the central thickening. The Doric echinos (*c*) bears up strongly against its burden, while the Ionic voluted capital seems gracefully to yield to it; in it the Doric abacus(*d*) is compressed into a thin plate, together with the so-called Lesbian cyma. Even the architrave loses something of its weight, jutting out slightly in three layers (*c*), and is joined, in the original Ionic order, to the cornice (*g*) by the so-called dentils, in which one still sees the ends of the wooden joists, reproduced in stone; the Attic order discards the dentils, and in the new temple of Athene Nike (Fig. 50d) replaces them with a splendid and richly ornamented frieze (*f*).

A masterpiece of the Ionic style, the Erechtheum still stands on the Acropolis. Under one roof it combined the ancient cult of the city goddess with that of the territorial god, Erechtheus. The natural shape of the site led up to a building which was larger and higher than the ordinary, simple temple, and contained a flight of steps, which, in the Caryatid Porch (built after the Peace of Nicias in 491 B.C.) (Fig. 51) bridged the difference of level in an ingenious manner. The inclusion of human figures in an architectonic system, which was only tentatively attempted in the Treasury of the Knidians at Delphi, finds here its most satisfactory solution.

The Greeks of that period must themselves have realized the more virile character of the Doric style, and the slightly feminine nature of the Ionic; for in the Ionic Erechtheum Caryatids are used, while in the Doric temple of Zeus at Agrigentum, begun after 480 B.C,. male Atlantes, giants four times life-size, stand between the half-columns.

It seems best, for the sake of clarity, before considering the classic style itself, to describe very briefly the characteristics of the so-called Corinthian style, which did not appear in Greek architecture until the fifth and fourth centuries, considerably later than the Doric and Ionic styles, which had already reached perfection in the first half of the sixth century, and may be regarded as contemporaneous. When the Corinthian column was introduced the Greek temple was already past its height, and only departed from the established form when the site or the special demands of the local cult made it necessary. Differences in the dimensions, and in the number and order of the columns, had always occurred, and no Greek temple was ever exactly like any other. For example, the round temple was known very early; it may even represent the oldest form of temple, since it goes back to the prehistoric round house. This form was used only for small buildings, which as a rule protected the round altar-hearth; in the market-place of Athens citizens who had deserved well of the State were feasted in such temples.

The most important innovation effected by the Corinthian style was the introduction of the acanthus-leaf, which henceforth often replaced the palmetto. The invention of the Corinthian capital (page 147, right) is attributed to the sculptor Kallimachos of Corinth. The need for a capital which should be richer than the Doric and less one-sided than the Ionic (meant to be seen only from directly in front), was bound to arise in the second half of the fifth century, with the more luxuriant taste of the period. It is true that the defect of the Ionic capital—the fact that its overhanging volutes were unsuitable in corner columns—was later remedied by setting them at an angle. But the Corinthian capital gave more scope to the imagination, and to the love of display, so that it became typical of the later Hellenistic period and of Imperial Rome. There was no longer any question of an order of architecture in the old, strict sense of the term, and the further development of this order of columns, which really belongs to a much later time, was continued into the Byzantine and Romanesque periods.

Classic Art

The oldest style of Greek art—the geometrical—prevailed from the time of the Doric migration, and reached its maturity in the ninth and eighth centuries. Then, under the influence of Eastern forms, it gradually lost its rigidity and its more essential characteristics, and a new style—the archaic—began about the year 700. In the sixth century, when the black-figured vase-painting reached its maturity, the development of the red-figured vase-painting had already begun. A transition from the early to the mature archaic style took place simultaneously in sculpture—as, for example, in the pediment group at Ægina—and in the fifth century we see the advent of classic Greek art.

At about this time the Carthaginians and the Etruscans had formed an alliance in the Western Mediterranean, and in many places Greek supremacy was imperilled. They were equal to the occasion in 490 B.C. when the Persians sailed into the Ægean, and after various conquests on Attic soil made a landing at Marathon. There, to the amazement of the world, the Persians were defeated in open battle, the Hellenic lance triumphed over the Persian bow, and the free citizen over the serfs of the Asiatic despots. Marathon and Salamis heralded the great age of Greece, the glorious maturity of Athens.

The two decades from 450 to 430 B.C. have been called the Periclean Age. Its artistic achievements have established the fame of the Greeks for ever, even though today people often find it more difficult to appreciate these works than did the last few generations.

It is easier to understand the old, archaic forms, whatever province of art they belong to, and whatever people produced them; for these are always simple and striking. In Greek art, the magnificence of its later maturity is also easily appreciated; the baroque of antiquity is in harmony with the European baroque of the seventeenth century, for both originated in a similar development of the sense of form. The classic art of the Greeks is by no means so easy to understand, for with Winkelmann's formula of 'noble simplicity and silent majesty' in mind, one is in danger of slipping into a classicistic way of considering the masterpieces of Greek art, and of forming a conception of a Greece that never existed.

The great museums and collections, and the enormous numbers of reproductions of ancient works of art, and Roman copies, are all infected by a way of looking at them very different from the Greek way. Only under the clear serenity of the southern sky, when man was liberated from the fear of life, could these simple, unmysterious, and unself-conscious forms originate, which in the delicacy of their proportions, and in the combination of their individual parts, achieved a harmony whose ultimate perfection can be clearly grasped only after close examination and careful measurement.

The character of this classic Greek art, which has neither the stiffness of the archaic or the violence of the 'baroque', can still be seen in those buildings which fate has preserved on the Acropolis. The long, flat crest of the great limestone rock that rises precipitously on the two long sides and falls away steeply at the back, so that only in front, at the narrow western point, is it possible to make the ascent from the city, was fashioned by Nature to be the fortress and the sanctuary of Athens (page 151). The ancient city, with its low houses, which did not attempt to emulate the dignity of the fortress-temple, lay round the rock, on which the gleaming marble temples rose into the deep blue sky in immaculate symmetry. That which was shaped by human hands rose superior to amorphous Nature, and the Greek was proudly conscious of the power of the human intellect. On the summit of the rock the mighty structure of the Parthenon towers over all, but beside it the Erechtheum and the Propylaea stand each with its own independent life, unlike the citadels of the Middle Ages, where all the components are fused together and absorbed into their natural environment.

About the middle of the second millennium B.C., when the Mycenaean civilization was still flourishing on Greek soil, the Acropolis was the seat of the princes, and where, later, the earliest of the temples stood, a royal chapel may have been dedicated to the cult of the goddess. After the Doric migration the sacred precinct would have been filled with simple altars and statues; but the first temples cannot have been built until the seventh century, when the rule of the kings was already a thing of the past.

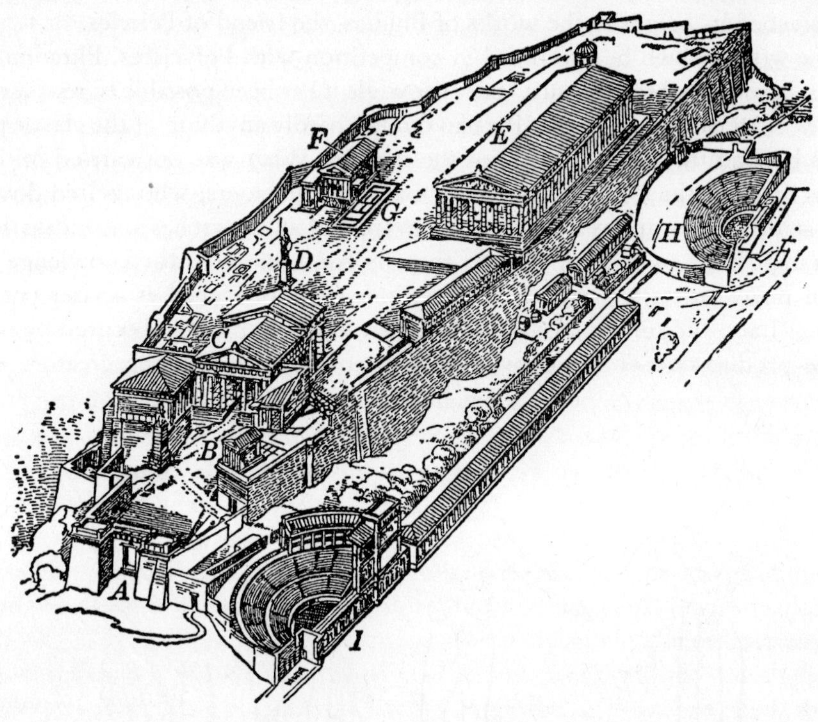

Reconstruction of the Acropolis of Athens. Behind the lower entrance-gate (A), which was erected only in Roman times, one sees on the right (B) the Temple of Nike (Fig. 50d), and proceeding through the Propylaea (C) and passing the bronze statue of Athena (D), one finds the Erechtheum (F) on the left, beside which, at an earlier period, rose the Hekatompedon (G), while on the right is the Parthenon (E), and beyond it the small Roman temple. From the Parthenon one looks down into the Theatre of Dionysos (H), with the sacred precinct. One sees the Asklepieion beside this, against the wall, and passing through the long hallway of the Eumenes one reaches the Odeion of Herodos Attikos (I) of the first century A.D. (Breasted)

Pericles, in 477 B.C., undertook to restore the Acropolis, as the most essential feature of a comprehensive building programme; it had been devastated by the Persians, and he commissioned Iktinos and Kallikrates to replace the old Parthenon by a building of Pentelican marble. The new temple was completed in the year 438 B.C. Phidias's chryselephantine statue of Athena was exhibited there, three times as large as life. Classic Greek art had now reached its highest development; it was an art in which strength and grace, simplicity and splendour, were effortlessly combined.

The Parthenon, 230 feet long, was not one of the largest of Greek buildings; it had a predecessor in the Doric Temple of Zeus at Olympus, of which Libon is said to have been the architect. The pediment groups and metopes of this older temple are of Parian marble, and compared with those on the temple of Ægina they show clearly, in the grouping of the figures, the progress made by the art of this period, which reached its height in the works of Phidias, the friend of Pericles.

Of the works which he produced in competition with Polycletes, Phradmon and Kresilas, hardly anything has survived; for while it has been possible to recover many examples of archaic art from the 'Persian dump', hardly anything of the classic period remains beyond the ruins of some of the temples. What was not carried off by the Romans or Byzantines was destroyed by barbarian invaders, who melted down the bronze statues for weapons and tools. So, in spite of all researches and excavations, it is often impossible to find any trace of the original works, and for knowledge of the work of many artists we have to rely on imitations produced at a later period in Greece or Italy. Judgments of classic Greek art have often been obscured by the fact that the productions of the copyist have been attributed to the creators of the

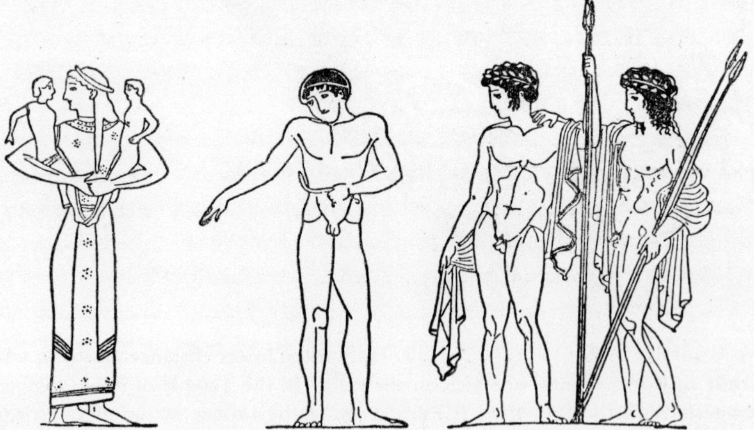

Evolution of bodily attitude in Greek vase-painting. On the left, the strictly archaic profile attitude of a woman with children, on a black-figured vase in the Berlin Museum. In the middle, and on the right, figures from two red-figured vases in the Bonn Museum show the relaxation of the attitude in an athlete using the strigil, and the free play of the limbs and garments in the figures of Castor and Pollux

originals. Study of the few authenticated works of this period enables us to guess how much of the magic of the originals has been lost in the process of translation (cf. Figs. 48a-c and 52c).

One of the most magnificent works of Phidias—or at least, of his school—the decorative sculptures of the Parthenon, the 'Elgin Marbles', are today one of the most precious treasures of the British Museum. The names of Alkamenes, Agorakritos and Kolates, artists of the school of Phidias, have been preserved by posterity. Myron, his son and pupil Lykios, and Strongylion, an excellent animal sculptor, together with Styppax and Kresilas, constituted a school of their own. Demetrios stood alone as a portraitist, of whom Quintilian said that he was more concerned with likeness than with beauty.

In the second half of the fifth century the Peloponnesian sculptors proudly claimed equality with the Attic artists, and the name of Polyclitus is hardly less famous than that of Phidias. This Peloponnesian master was above all a portraitist. Patrocles, Daedalos and Naukydes, with many others, must be regarded as belonging to his school.

The Greeks of this period, however, regarded painting, rather than sculpture, as the highest of the representative arts. Aristotle considered that the highest qualities of art were embodied in the monumental wall-paintings of Polygnotus; among whose predecessors was Mykon. He had a rival in Panaenus, with whom Onasias, about 450 B.C., produced some much-admired wall-paintings at Delphi.

The question, whether the wall-paintings of Polygnotus were actual frescoes on a limestone basis, or tempera paintings on marble, or even easel-pictures painted on wooden panels, cannot be determined; but in any case easel-paintings became popular a little later; they were at first tempera paintings with the brush, on wood coated with chalk, but afterwards wax paintings on marble panels, the wax being applied with the spatula, were more common.

Apollodorus of Athens was known as the first skiagrapher or shadow-painter, and also as the first easel-painter to introduce the gradation of colour in accordance with light and shade, the most important development which Greek painting had undergone since its first beginning; for flat stylization was suddenly changed into the representation of physical and spatial depth.

Many factors combined to bring this change about. The germs of landscape painting, which made their appearance at this time, may perhaps be found in the flourishing art of scene-painting. The richer the Greek world grew, the wider became the range of its art. Temple architecture, which was always predominant, was gradually seconded by an always more versatile secular architecture. The Greek theatre, in which the players, as well as the chorus, appeared on the ground level, sought the backing, where possible, of a hillside; and presently, facing the audience, and before the 'scene', a moveable, decorated wooden screen, the proscenium was erected, which was destined to be covered with painted decorations.

Music now began to play an even larger part, and Pericles built in Athens a special hall for musical contests. Of this nothing is left except brief descriptions. Race-tracks were provided for foot-races and were described as stadia, because the *stadion*—a Greek measure of length, which was about 215 yards—was regarded as the normal length of the track, while the race-course for horses and chariots, the hippodrome, was considerably longer. The training-grounds on which the young men prepared themselves for their contests, the gymnasia and palaestra, were richly equipped with colonnades, assembly-rooms, courtyards, and baths, and before long there were public buildings for conversation—in many of the larger cities—known as *lesche* or 'speaking-rooms'.

In the Greek dwelling-house the pillars faced inwards, not outwards, as in the temples. No Greek house of this period with any pretensions to comfort could dispense with its colonnaded courtyard.

When the Parthenon was almost finished Pericles commissioned Mnesikles to transform the entrance-gate on the west side of the rock into a stately building, the Propylaea, with colonnades on either side of the gate. As in the dramas of Euripides and Sophocles, so in art also the fate of the individual was beginning, by the second half of the fifth century, to interest the observer. Art, so to speak, invaded private life, and the tomb, becoming more intimate in character, underwent a fresh change. Attic art began to discard its old restraints, and Aeschylus complained that the city was overflowing with miserable clerks and scriveners and sycophants, and that people no longer exercised their bodies. Party strife was becoming the ruin of Athens, and the series of wars which are usually described as the Peloponnesian War, wasted the energies of the state for twenty-seven long years, until at last, in the spring of 404 B.C., the city succumbed to the combined assault of the Persians and the Spartans.

The downfall of Athens meant the end of the classic era, although, in the fourth century, its influence was still perceptible; yet, when Praxiteles, an Athenian by birth, produced his masterpieces for other cities, it was plain to see how far the capital of Attica had derogated from its former position. It is true that the masterpieces of the following period, such as the Hermes of Praxiteles (Fig. 49a) or the marvellous torso of the Venus of Milo (Fig. 49b) are reminiscent of the classic age; but they show also, in their transition from the sublimity of the works of Phidias to the serenity of a dreamy sweetness, that Greek art was not what it was. In the fourth century began the transition to Hellenism.

II. Greek Black Figure Vase. 5th Century B.C.

Chapter XII

HELLENISTIC ART

*

THE importance of Greece in the world was out of all proportion to her political power and significance; her influence outlasted even that of the Roman Empire, reaching far into the future.

The reader must first of all understand what is meant by Hellenistic art. Hellenistic art—that is, an art more or less imbued with the Greek spirit—first appeared in the Macedonian empire. Alexander the Great extended his empire as far as the frontiers of India, and there arose in that country the peculiar blending of Greek and Indian forms known as the Grandharan art, of which we have already spoken (page 97). In the various states into which his empire split, his successors founded new royal cities—on the Nile, the Tigris, and the Orontes—and it was there that the civilization and the art developed which are called, in the strict sense of the word, Hellenistic.

The Diadochian[1] cities of Egypt, Mesopotamia and Syria were fundamentally Greek, and the intellectual frontiers of the Old World were gradually effaced. Greece was still the mother country, but when, for a second time, she became subject to Egyptian and Asiatic influences, her art again reflected the life and the activities of the African and Asiatic coasts.

The Roman power, which was established in all the Mediterranean countries after the fall of Corinth in 148 B.C., did not make an end of Hellenism, nor did it originate a new style. The Romans, like the Macedonian kings before them, acknowledged the culture of the conquered Hellenes, who had long been living in southern Italy and Sicily. Intellectually, Rome was subject to Greece; and later, Christian art sprang from Greek-Asiatic roots, not from Roman. Thus, the conception of Hellenism covers the whole world of antiquity, in so far as it was subject to Greek influences. In art, the most significant fact is that no original forms appeared; the old Asiatic and Greek motives were combined in countless different ways. The seed which had been sown for centuries at last bore fruit. Even the production of Greece herself belonged to this new and greater world: in style, fourth century and fifth century Greece are clearly distinguishable, but in the next period, even in Greece itself we can no longer speak of a purely Greek art, but of Hellenistic art.

[1] From the Greek *diadochoi* = successors.

Hellenism in Greece

After the power of Athens was broken, the battle of Chaeroneia, in 338 B.C., struck the final blow at the rest of Greece. In architecture, the Doric style soon lost its leading position, though it was not completely abandoned. Greek culture turned more toward Asia, and the Ionic style achieved fresh triumphs, while the Corinthian style made continual progress. Satyros and Pythios were the architects of the Mausoleum at Halicarnassus (page 157), the majestic tomb of King Mausolus, who was to give his name to all princely tombs. Here we see a combination of architectural motives which was to become more and more widespread. In the Philippeion at Olympia, Philip of Macedonia, between 337 and 334, built an Ionic rotunda whose two-storey inner wall was divided by nine Corinthian half-columns.

Other developments in theatre architecture were making the permanent scene and the auditorium of stone, the usually circular orchestra being divided from the latter by a gangway, while beside the front wall of the *skene* the *parascenia* projected like wings, as for instance, in the Theatre of Dionysos (page 151, H), completed under the administration of Lycurgus. Hardly less splendid were the theatres at Epidauros, the work of the younger Polyclete, and at Megapolis in Arcadia, the largest in Greece.

Painting had now a fuller command of technical methods. The school of Sicyon, under Eupompos and his pupil Pamphilos, put its principles in writing and introduced the teaching of drawing in the Greek schools. Malenthios, Pausias, Aristolaos and Euxinidas, like Aristides or Nicomachos, and Euphranor, who was no less celebrated as a sculptor than as a painter, continued the work of their predecessors. Nikias was regarded as the greatest Attic artist of this period, though Pliny considered Athenion of Manoneia to be his equal. These masters were among those who lived beyond the Ægean, and who may be counted as part of the Ionian school. Apelles was the greatest, and of his competitors, friends or envious rivals, we may name Protogenes, Antiphilos, and Theon of Samos, whose figures were said to 'start out of his pictures'. The usual phenomena of an age of unrestrained individuality appeared automatically. They expressed themselves by allegories and apotheoses, of which the best known—from a later Roman copy—is the picture of Alexander's victory over the Persians (page 158).

In the fourth century sculpture Praxiteles, Skopas and Lysippos were pre-eminent; we might add to these the names of many other masters, but these three in particular stand for the three leading schools of Greek sculpture. Praxiteles was an Athenian, Lysippos a Sicyonian, and Skopas came to Athens from the marble island of Paros. It is now impossible to distinguish between their works, and even the ancients disputed whether the great group of the 'Niobids', which was so admired in Rome, but has only survived in later copies, was the work of Praxiteles or of Skopas. One cannost say definitely whether Leochares, who, with Timotheos and Bryaxis, was one of the colleagues of Skopas, did, after three attempts to make an Apollo, finally create the 'Apollo Belvedere', now in the Vatican.

In the work of these masters we see a gradual tendency towards sentimentality and the pathetic. In the arrangement of figures there is an increasing individualistic naturalism, and more and more attention is paid to refinement of expression. In the perfect rendering of the smoothness of the skin, in contrast to the rougher texture of the hair, in the reproduction of muscles and folds and wrinkles, in, to put it shortly, the rendering of material qualities, the art of Praxiteles, in particular, reaches a height that makes him the greatest representative of his epoch (Fig. 49a). The ever-increasing consciousness of personality was responsible for this realistic tendency in

Reconstruction of the Mausoleum of Halicarnassus. Standing on the great base, Ionic colonnades support a stepped pyramid on the summit of which is the monument of the king and queen, who are enthroned in a chariot drawn by four horses. (Breasted)

the plastic arts from the middle of the fourth century onwards, which resulted in the gradual emergence of the portrait. Lysippos recorded, in his bold and impressive bust, the power and the sovereign will of the young Alexander. This head does not go beyond the limitations of naturalism in its emotional expressiveness, but its modelling is free and unrestrained, with none of the tightness which is still to be seen in the head of the Hermes of Praxiteles. The eyes and the corners of the mouth are tense with restrained passion, and on the forehead, furrowed by the slight raising of the eyebrows, there is a look of suffering far removed from the Olympic serenity of the works of Phidias, or from the quiet and tranquil charm of Praxiteles.

Here, for the first time in antiquity, was a baroque impulse, though these tendencies do not allow us to think of the whole of Hellenism as a baroque movement, like that of the European seventeenth century. The artistic world of antiquity was too large and the spiritual currents that mingled in it were too various. The conflict between the asiatic and the European sense of form was incessant, and the two were continually blending in a synthesis which produced works of the greatest expressiveness. In this connection it is interesting to consider briefly the last of the early baroque waves, which in the second century A.D. created the small round temples in Baalbek and Heliopolis, which surprisingly anticipate later European baroques (page 159). But if we realize that seventeenth-century baroque is a development of Renaissance, and therefore ultimately Greek forms, we can understand more easily such anticipation and repetition.

In the course of the half-century that saw the end of Greek freedom—of which the Peloponnesian War was only one of the causes—the classic art of Greece was declining from its public and universal significance into the quiet felicity of individual expression. The old forms were not discarded. They were still valued, and regarded as standards; whatever significant deviations there are, are due to Oriental influences.

Alexander's Victory. Part of a Mosaic floor discovered in Pompeii in 1831, which is a reproduction of a picture, painted in Alexandria, representing Alexander's victory over the King of Persia

The Mausoleum of Halicarnassus, like the Nereid Monument at Xanthus, followed the Asiatic custom of building tombs of two or more storeys, while the Greeks had always been content with the simple stele or headstone, since it was forbidden by law for any private individual to erect buildings with colonnades and gabled roofs.

In the prosperous seaport and mercantile city of Corinth an increasing appetite for luxury was weaning the Greeks from the austerities of Sparta. Here the Corinthian column, and with it the Corinthian style, had long resulted in a relaxation of the ancient Greek forms. As the architecture of the fifth century was imbued with the Hellenic *joie de vivre,* and had expressed the unity of all existing things, so the imaginative naturalism of the later period began to transcribe the vegetable world in stone. Stylistic motives which were first consciously developed almost a thousand years later, in Gothic architecture, were already present in the acanthus capital. The endeavour to imbue all forms of art with greater vitality expressed itself, in representations of human figures, by increasing animation, while costume became a means of enhancing their physical significance.

Alexandrian and Late Hellenic Art

In the following centuries the art of the world broke through the hitherto customary restrictions. Alexander had stupendous ideals but his desire were unrealized. He had seriously envisaged the merging of the two ruling peoples, the Greeks and the Persians. The celebrated marriage of eighty Macedonian nobles with as many Persian women was not without purpose, nor was the king's marriage with Statira, the daughter of Darius III, and his enrolment of 30,000 young Persians into his army. But when, on the evening of the 13 June, 323 B.C., the king died a premature death in Babylon, it became apparent that his work was only a house of cards. The tumult of conflicting elements that make up the history of the period found expression in its art. The period laboured under stupendous burdens, intellectual as well as material, and as the torrent of life expanded it is not surprising that the mechanical arts assumed an importance which they had never hitherto possessed.

In architecture such a period could achieve nothing but titanic plans, tremendous fragments, and ephemeral creations. This is particularly true of the Alexandrian school. Among buildings, the royal castles were pre-eminent, and by expansion they included whole wards of the cities. In Alexandria there were such buildings as the museum, sheltering the republic of scholars, the library, and a number of sanctuaries, while on the Pharos island which faced the city there stood the first of the world's famous lighthouses, a structure 330 feet in height which gave its name to all its successors.

The small round temple at Baalbek: a typical example of the ancient baroque style of the time of the later Roman Emperors

In addition to the buildings whose components were the column and the joist—and which were now built in several storeys—the domed roof or cupola made its appearance, as an ancient legacy of Babylonian art. Great altars were erected, of which the largest was that at Pergamon (the modern Bergama).

In the century of the first two kings of Pergamon, Attalus II (241—197) and Eumenes II (197—150), a Neo-Hellenic state flourished in Asia Minor on what had long been Ionian soil; and in art, as in science, Pergamon was the rival of Alexandria. The wonderful library of Eumenes II so excited the jealousy of the Ptolemeys in Alexandria that they did not hesitate to prohibit the export of papyrus. In this predicament the Pergamenians invented *pergamena* or parchment, which they employed instead of 'paper'.

Besides these two rivals, Rhodes was one of the principal centres of Greek culture. and was distinguished for its sculpture. The importance of its contributions to the art of the period may be judged from the fact that according to the ancient records a hundred gigantic statues adorned the island, in addition to the famous Colossus. The Colossus, a bronze image of the Sun-god Helios, was set up in the year 284 B.C.; with its height of 104 feet it was the largest statue of antiquity, and regarded as one of the seven wonders of the world. While its creator, Chares of Lindos, was with Eutychides a pupil of Lysippos, two other eminent sculptors were Aristonidas and Philiskos, the latter being also a painter. Among the masters of the first century B.C. Agesandros, Athenodoros and Polydoros are worthy of mention, their common masterpiece being the famous group of the Laocoon, today in the Vatican. The uplifted arm of Laocoon was restored by Montorsoli, and so it appears in photographs. But Overbeck's restoration (as here represented), which expresses the moment of supreme agony far more naturally, and more in the spirit of Greek tragedy, deserves special attention.

Upper portion of the Laocoon group in Overbeck's restoration

The group of the 'Farnese Bull', now in the Naples Museum, is also ascribed to the school of Rhodes. The rearing bull, to which the luckless Dirce is bound, is undoubtedly one of the boldest compositions in sculpture.

If we now take a general survey of the art of this period, we cannost fail to perceive that the art of Pergamon and Rhodes had its roots in the East, while the details, the sober matter-of-fact-ness, and the delight in idyllic subjects (Fig. 54a), represented the final development of the old Greek spirit, which Alexander the Great had dispersed throughout the whole of the East. It lived on in a vast number of local schools of art, which were imbued with the character of the people in whose midst they arose.

Persians and Egyptians, Syrians and Jews came more and more into contact with Greek art, and the hot breath of the East warmed the cool marble of Pentelicus to a new, vibrant life. In sculpture, a rout of satyrs and maenads (Figs. 53b and 53c) reeled through all the regions touched by Hellas, in the still radiantly lovely satyric

55. (A) Head of Caesar. Copy of the early Empire. The only contemporary portrait of Caesar verified by comparison with coins. About 20 B.C. (Vatican).
(B) Marble bust of Roman lady of the time of Trajan. Height, 23 in. Beginning of second century A.D. (Louvre).
(C) Marble bust of the Emperor Caracalla. Height, 10.8 in. Beginning of third century B.C. (Louvre).

a

b

c

a

b

56. (A) Interior of the Pantheon. Text p. 168. (B) Exterior of the Colosseum, Rome.

. (A) The rch of Con- tantine, ome; erected the year D. 312.

a

b

(B) The socket of the column of Antoninus Pius (of which only fragments have survived) representing the apotheosis of the deified emperor and of his consort Faustina. Below, on the left, the personification of the Campus Martius, on which the emperor was burnt, with the obelisk which he had erected. On the right, the goddess Roma, and in the centre, as the principal figure the god Aeon, eternal Time, with the heavenly sphere and the symbol of the Zodiac in his hands. He bears the imperial pair heavenwards; they are accompanied by the two eagles of immortality. Second century A.D. (Vatican).

58. Flagellation and Dionysiac dance. One of twenty-nine scenes in fresco, illustrating the initiation of young women into the mysteries of the Dionysiac festival, painted on the walls of a room in the 'Villa of the Mysteries' at Pompeii. First century B.C.

frolics of Greek legend. As Greece had formed its gods out of the clouds, the winds, and the foam of the sea, so now an insatiable fantasy flung itself upon the heart of Nature, creating works that entered into all her aspects, in which reality and fantasy were equally blended. Only in the late period did degeneration of forms appear once again, when efforts were made toward the composition of reliefs.

In works like the Rhodesian Venus of Milo (Fig. 49b) Hellenism, by combining true nobility of form with the expression of a real psychic life, attained a depth of conception which is sufficiently attested by the artistic power of the late Hellenic era. Beside creations of this kind, it places, with its inexorable love of truth, nourished by the realistic temper of the epoch, the portraits of the Diadochi, and shows the Gaul who stabs his wife and then himself, or Menelaus with the body of Patroclus. In the figure of the wounded Galatian (Fig. 53a) a man of alien race is seen with nobly compassionate eyes; and it is difficult to say how far there is an equipoise in such works between the reckless will of Asia and the Hellenic self-restraint.

A classic ideal still blended its radiance with the twilight of Greek culture, of which the Roman world was gradually taking possession, at first rejecting the Eastern spirit, and thus creating an art which was more European in its orientation.

Chapter XIII

THE ROMAN EMPIRE

*

To find what it was that gave Roman art its particular character—which it often managed to preserve, even after the infiltration of Hellenism—we must go back to its roots, and see what it produced in its earliest phases.

During the great migrations of the second millenium B.C., the Indo-Germanic Italici entered the country and soon split up into two groups, with different languages and customs. The larger remained in the mountains and the broad highlands of the south, while the smaller took possession of the coastal strip on either side of the Tiber. From the latter group emerged the Romans, who were to rule the world for so many centuries. Their language was Indo-Germanic and consequently related to Greek, though not very closely; a sign that the two races had long ago diverged.

In the tenth century B.C. the Etruscans came to Italy from Asia Minor and established themselves in Tuscany. They were an alien people, who, in their dread of evil powers and forces, were great astrologers, reading omens in the entrails of sacrificed animals, in much the same way that the Babylonians foretold the future by examining the liver. From the eighth century onwards, they came into contact with the flourishing Greek colonies in southern Italy (page 137) and, being a sturdy and capable people, they subdued a large area on either side of the Appennines. In considering the art of the Etruscans it is difficult to say what was their own and what was due either to earlier Greek influences or to the influence of their new environment. In any case, the Romans did not produce any art of their own until they had been conquered by the Etruscans; for when Rome is first mentioned the city itself, like its founder, Romulus, bore an Etruscan name. Etruscan, too, were the Royal insignia—the axe in the bundle of rods, the *fasces*. The history of Roman art at first is the history of Etruscan art.

Etruscan Art

Many pages could be filled with descriptions of the Phoenician, Greek and Oriental objects which have been found in the ancient Etruscan cities, Cervetri, Corneto, Chiusi, Orvieto, Vulci, Cortona, Fiesole, Veji, Volterra, and other towns; but more important still are monuments which show how much the Etruscans were influenced by their environment to create an original and thoroughly characteristic style, which the most unpractised eye can easily recognize.

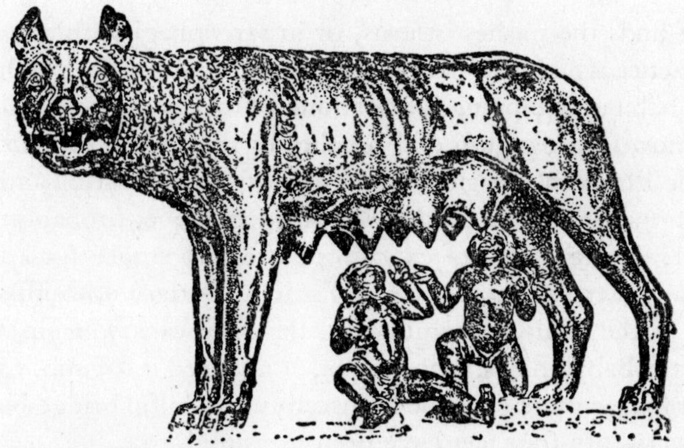

The Roman She-Wolf. Etruscan bronze, about 500 B.C. The twins Romulus and Remus were added in the sixteenth century, in accordance with the taste of the period. Conservator's Palace, Rome. (Breasted)

They seem to have been an active, sober and realistic people, as far as one can tell from the first remote influence of Etruscan art on the art of Hallstatt, in the early Iron Age. Whatever the extent of Etruscan influence in, for instance, the Hallstatt *situla* (page 29), the south of Europe was in advance of the north, where such metal-work was concerned. About the middle of the seventh century B.C. the Etruscan goldsmiths showed an unparalleled skill in granulation—that is, in decorating the basis or background of a jewel or vase, with tiny grains of gold. In the adjacent illustration, which shows the foreign influence at its highest, the entirely original Etruscan conception and stylization can be recognized at once, though it can hardly be interpreted as Hercules being escorted back to Olympus, as has been suggested; it is more likely to represent the soul of one newly dead riding down to the underworld.

This is one of the many scenes found in Etruscan tombs. Where possible, the crypts were hewn out of the rock, and were often given elaborate external façades. In other cases they were roofed with domes, and sometimes even with barrel-vaulting. Very often they consist of quadrilateral free-stone structures, or conical mounds of earth, on a circular foundation. The shape of the tumulus at Cervetri reminds one of the Indian stupa. Inside the tumulus the rooms were copies of those in ordinary houses, the dead lying. with their household goods round them, in alcoves, or on benches against the wall.

Etruscan sepulchral painting on the back wall of the Grotta Campana at Veji

Sometimes one finds their ashes in urns, or in sarcophagi with effigies of the dead on the lid, a practice which was later characteristic of Roman sepulchral art. Thanks to the Etruscan habit of equipping the last home of the deceased with all the necessities of life, we are now in possession of a number of precious *objets d'art* which give a good idea of the Etruscan's mastery of the arts of bronze-casting and stone-carving. An entirely national style was the *bucchero nero* technique, probably suggested by a bronze original; this consisted of exposing pottery to smoke for a long time, producing, after careful treatment, a dark and shining surface not unlike bronze.

In their use of the vault in architecture, the Etruscans were in advance of the Egyptians and the Babylonians, who as a rule only used it for subordinate purposes. Thanks to their frequent use of it, the Etruscans were skilful bridge-builders: in Blera spans as wide as twenty-four feet have been measured.

Plan of an Etruscan Temple (Borrman)

Finally, something must be said of Etruscan temple architecture, which Vitruvius, in his Fourth Book of Architecture, distinguished from the Greek. The ancient Italic temples did not derive, like Greek temples, from the dwelling—house, but from the high place from which the augur observed the flights of birds. From this the Roman podium, with its flight of steps, was later derived. Etruscan religion, different from Greek, required that the temple should be divided into several chambers: the usual plan (above) has three compartments opening upon a portico composed of two rows of four columns, supporting a pediment. Even at a late period these columns were still smooth, as the supporting members of the Etruscan building were originally of wood, encased with plaques of coloured terra-cotta. Even until fairly late in the Roman period marble was not used, and the local *tufa*, a dark and porous volcanic stone, the usual building material, was given a coating of coloured stucco. Consequently, the Italic temple was characterized, for a long time, by a rustic heaviness and crudity, since the materials used did not lend themselves to as much refinement and exactitude as marble. The Etruscan pediment, as one would expect in a northern climate, was steeper than the Greek. We know what the Etruscan house looked like from Vitruvius's description, and also from the many cinerary urns made in the shape of houses. There were gabled houses with closed roofs, supported by piers and columns, and already the later form of the Roman house had made its appearance, with the house built round the central courtyard or *atrium*, and the roof sloping on all four sides toward the *impluvium*, the water-tank or basin. The development of this simple scheme eventually produced many practical and beautiful forms.

Although the expulsion of Tarquin the Proud from Rome in 510 B.C. brought the supremacy of the Etruscans in central and northern Italy to an end, the tradition of Etruscan art still continued, even when, at the beginning of the fourth century B.C., the Romans took the Etruscan stronghold of Veji. Rome continued to extend her sway; shortly after 300 B.C. Chiusi fell, and in 272 B.C., Tarentum. When Syracuse was conquered in 212 B.C., and Bologna in 196 B.C., Italy became Roman.

During the early years of the Roman republic all art was Etruscan in style; but as the Mediterranean basin became gradually subject to Rome, so Rome was invaded by Greek art and Greek culture in proportion to her own invasion of the Greek world.

The Invasion of Hellenism

Many treasures found their way into Rome from Tarentum, Syracuse, Corinth, Athens, and the other subject Greek cities. At this time the first great buildings were erected in marble—such as the peristylar Temple of Jupiter and the Temple of Juno, both on the Campus Martius; these were built by the Greek Hermodorus of Salamis in the year 140 B.C. By this time the great change was completed; the supremacy of Hellenism was acknowledged in Rome, while earlier buildings, like the Temple of the Magna Mater on the Palatine, consecrated in 191 B.C., still belonged to the transitional period. There are rellics of earlier building methods, which adopted Corinthian forms only in their decorative features, clumsy columns whose details were added only in the stucco coating. In the first century B.C. many Ionic temples were built, like the well-preserved temple of Fortuna Virilis in Rome. Also of this period, but Corinthian, is the marble rotunda on the Tiber.

As well as the Fora, or rectangular *piazze* surrounded by colonnades, numbers of 'basilicas' were built for carrying on trade and administering justice. These will be dealt with in connection with the first Christian churches.

Greek influence was responsible for the introduction of the theatre into Italy. The great one at Pompeii was built in the second century B.C. and the first stone-built theatre in Rome in the year 55 B.C. With the general increase of luxury, dwelling-houses became more comfortable, and although, like the Greek houses, they kept their decoration for the inside, they admitted more and more light and air. The old four-pillared Italic atrium was now supported by a greater number of Corinthian columns. In the houses of the patricians a colonnaded courtyard, or *peristyle,* was added (page 173). In Rome, at the end of the republican period, tenement-houses were built, which reached such heights that they had to be restricted by law, at the beginning of the Imperial period, to a maximum of seventy feet. A good example of the *thermae*, or public baths, are those in the Strada Stabiana, Pompeii, built in the second century B.C. They had separate accommodation for men and women, and included cold, warm and vapour baths, and were decorated with all kinds of ornamental friezes.

The dwellings of the dead received no less attention than those of the living. Tombs were richly decorated, and many traditional Etruscan features still survived in a Hellenistic disguise. The oldest monumental sepulchre in Rome is the crypt of the Scipio family, whose entrance is formed by an arrangement of columns over a low round-headed gateway. The monumental tomb of Cecilia Metella on the Appian Way dates, like the small tomb of Bibulus, from the beginning of the first century B.C.

Sarcophagus of Cornelius Lucius Scipio from the family tomb of the Scipiones on the Appian Way. Apparently the work of a Greek artist, with inscription in early Latin letters

The Architecture of the Caesars

Under the Caesars, Rome had at last produced an art which, in spite of its derivation from Etruscan and Hellenistic sources, had unmistakably individual style. It cannot be described otherwise than as an Empire style.

Architecture, in particular, became a new and imposing way of overawing the Plebs, with buildings of enormous and impressive size, divided into vast halls and apartments; 'Golden Rome', in the time of Augustus and his immediate successors (31 B.C. to A.D. 68), was changed from a city of brick into a metropolis of marble. In front of the temple of Caesar rose the orator's tribune; colonnade led to colonnade, triumphal arch to triumphal arch. Obelisks were brought from Egypt, and Roman architects produced innumerable temples and public buildings in emulation of the Greeks. After the fire which devastated the greater part of Rome under Nero, in A.D. 64, the great city, under the Flavians, rose even more splendid from its ashes.

The Flavian Amphitheatre, better known as the Colosseum (Fig. 56b), which was finished in A.D. 80, is in many ways the most imposing building of the whole period. It consists of an oval plan, whose axes measure 620 feet and 510 feet respectively, on which is built a wall divided horizontally into three arcades, each with eighty openings, the lowest of which were doorways. The columns on the ground storey are Etruscan-Doric; those on the first storey are Ionic; those of the second Corinthian; while the top storey, or *attica*, is articulated by Corinthian pilasters and crowned by heavy denticulations. This topmost ring of wall probably enclosed a covered gangway, and it supported, on its inner side, the masts on which awnings were hung in sunny weather. This building is not only an example of the Roman genius for organization, but in its own way, too, it is an architectural and technical innovation over the Greek system of supports and stresses. The way in which the round arch has the structural function, and the columns of different orders have the decorative function, was an application of the Etruscans' extensive use of the vault.

Since the stability of an arch depends on cutting the stone so that the outer edge is broader than the inner, these wedge-shaped stones are a perpetual reminder of the pressure to which they are subjected, so that the arch gives an impression of weight. As soon as this is concealed by covering the joints of the stones, the arch, becoming the so-called archivolt, soars unencumbered into the air. Unlike the Greeks, the Romans, following the Etruscan habit of disguising the wood of their temples, used to disguise the constructive members of buildings; they proceeded, by means of the archivolt, to extend the use of the arch in the arcade, which now became, together with the old systems of columns, an open order in which support and load harmoniously merged into each other. It has this great advantage, that it avoids the straight, heavy beams of the architrave, necessitated by the wide spacing of columns, which are difficult to obtain, and which will often hardly support a superstructure of several storeys: a series of arches which cannot shift laterally, merely gains in stability if loaded. This system was fully developed in the theatre of Marcellus, which was begun in 13 B.C., but the Colosseum is by far its most impressive example. The seats, which accommodated 45,000 people, were stepped around the arena, ascending to a colonnade which constitutes the topmost gangway. The arcaded gangways of the lowest storey were roofed with barrel-vaults, but those of the middle storey with cross-vaults, which were still more extensively used in the Baths of Titus. The arena itself was exceeded in area only by those of Tarragona and Pozzuoli; the arenas of Arles, Capua, Pola and Pompeii are also deserving of special mention.

Surprisingly few ancient Roman theatres have survived; they are distinguished from Greek theatres only by the fact the actors appeared on a raised stage instead of in the orchestra. The best preserved are those at Taormina in Sicily, and at Orange in the south of France.

Trajan (A.D. 98—117) was particularly active as a builder. Under him, Apollodorus of Damascus built the Trajan Forum and Trajan's Column, round whose shaft, 88 feet high, winds a strip of marble relief, 39 inches high, 650 feet long, and containing more than 2,500 figures. These depict, in consecutive order and in detail, the campaigns and victories of the Emperor.

Trajan's successor, Hadrian (117—138), whose tomb, with its circular substructure, afterwards became the Castel Sant' Angelo, produced in the Pantheon, the largest surviving domed building of antiquity, and one of the most original and impressive monuments of Roman architecture. As the illustration shows, the outside of the buildings is in the form of a squat cylinder, held together rather than divided by three string-courses of cornices, and crowned with a shallow dome. The entrance consists of a deep portico, in the style of a Greek temple, consisting of three rows of columns and a fairly steep pediment. By this, the lighter Greek style is reconciled

External elevation of the Pantheon

with the massive forms of Roman architecture, in spite of their very different character. The discord, inevitably caused by the conjunction of the richly decorated portico, with the austere and massive circumference of the rest of the fabric, was mitigated by the ingenious way in which they were combined. A rectangular structure, to some extent reminiscent of the old Etruscan temple (page 164), comes between the portico and the main building, so that the old central entrance of the Etruscan temple becomes the door of the Pantheon, while the side entrances have become semicircular niches, softening the transition from the square portico to the circle of the Pantheon.

The Greeks never used a closed and self-contained space in their temples. But the Romans, who collected images of gods from all parts of the known world, wished to reconcile all contending cults in one magnificent temple. They arrived at the idea, therefore, of designing a dwelling for all the gods—the Pantheon—a circular building roofed with a dome, as a symbol of heaven and earth. The height, and diameter of the interior, are 142.6 feet; the curve of the domed roof, produced downwards, would rest on the ground like a ball (below). The building is lit through an opening in the apex of the dome, the *opeion*, 26 feet across. Up to the edge of the dome the cylindrical wall is divided into two parts, according to the principles of the 'golden section'. One of the niches (Fig. 56a), opposite the entrance was opened when the Pantheon was changed into a Christian church. In the Renaissance the old incrustation of the upper portion of the cylinder was replaced by a new facing, and dummy

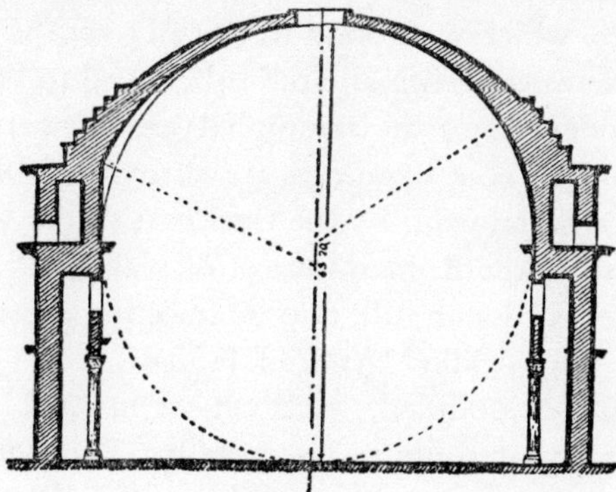

Section through the Pantheon. The radius of a sphere enclosed in the cylinder is the radius of the cylinder and half the height of the interior

windows with triangular pediments were inserted. The coffering of the ceiling is old, and their proportions, calculated for the boldest effect, produce a fascinating illusion; they become smaller as the diameter of the dome decreases, so that the spectator has no uncomfortable feeling of enforced contraction, but feels almost as though the whole cupola was unsubstantial and floating in space.

Art had found ways, unknown to the classic architecture of Greece, of freeing the spirit from its earthy burdens. The Pantheon is the most majestic expression of this tendency to the baroque in the art of antiquity: its effect is produced, not by the essential structure, but by the decoration, which conceals a nucleus of an entirely different character. The impression of the floating dome is not inherent in the structure, but is deliberately evoked. Behind the niches and recesses an extremely complicated system of supports, trusses and relieving arches is hidden. The dome is not really a hemisphere, but much flatter, as may be seen from the schematic section on this page. The decorative lining (right) only hides the structure and the outward thrust, which is taken off the walls of the cylinder (left) by heavy rings of stonework.

Roman architects were equal to any task; the arch, which even in the early years of the empire had been used with admirable effect in many technical structures, such as the still extant aqueduct of Nîmes (page 171), had now become the chief problem of western architecture, and kept it occupied for centuries.

Besides the Pantheon, Hadrian built other buildings in and near Rome. His villa at Tivoli was built between A.D. 123 and 134, and consisted of a group of many individual buildings, offering in miniature an exposition of the architecture of the then known world. Its grounds contained palatial dwelling-houses, bath, theatres, libraries and picture-galleries. Since Rome had become a world-power, Italy had become a great museum of art, and one may regard the collections of wealthy Romans as the prototypes of our modern museums.

The triumphal arches, which were soon to rise all over the empire, were a Roman innovation. As early as 121 B.C. such an arch is believed to have been erected in the Forum Romanum; under Augustus triumphal arches were erected even in the remotest provinces. In all these openings are surmounted by round arches, each of which is made into a barrel vault by the thickness of the walls. A single opening after a time failed to satisfy the Roman love of display, and three arches pierced the later monuments (Fig. 57a). Later still, two intersecting passages were contrived on a square ground-plan, the so-called 'Arch of Janus'.

Pilasters, either single or coupled, were almost invariable additions, framing a surface covered with sculptured figures; a more massive, and often quite plain, addition, the *attica*, provided space for an inscription, as well as a base for the triumphal chariot or statue which crowned the whole. In Athens, Ancona, Aosta, Benevento, Susa, and many other cities, these symbols of Roman sovereignty are still standing.

Composite Capital on the Arch of Titus, Rome

The oldest triumphal arch still standing in Rome is the Arch of Titus, built in A.D. 81. In this the so-called 'composite order', a cross between the Corinthian and Ionic capitals was first used; this opened the way for further transformations. The Romans, with their love of show, had already achieved stronger effects of light and shade in the Corinthian capital by means of deeper carving, and gave the baroque tendencies of the time full play in the matter of protuberant forms. The composite capital, with its picturesque and sculptural richness, was as far as possible removed from the original architectonic conception of the order; later on it was often criticized for the inadequate finish of its details, but this may well have been due to deliberate omission rather than to lack of skill.

The well-known Arch of Constantine (Fig. 57a) was built at a time when Roman art was no longer supreme all over the world, and when the Roman was giving way to the Christian spirit. For a whole century Rome had produced nothing new, and in this arch reliefs of the time of Trajan, Hadrian and Aurelius were included in a mechanical way by an age which had long ago produced its best. The architecture of such new buildings as were erected after the Arch of Constantine was Christian rather than Roman. The illustration below is typical of the undecorated, functional buildings and purely technical structures of the empire, and it remains only to glance at the sculpture and painting of the Romans.

The 'Pont du Gard', near Nîmes in Southern France. This Roman aqueduct was built at the instance of Agrippa, the son-in-law of Augustus, about 19 B.C., and served to convey water to Nîmes, the ancient sanctuary and site of medicinal baths, Nemausus. It is built in three storeys of 6, 11 and 35 arches, rising to a height of 160 feet above the bed of the Gardon, here 270 yards wide. (Breasted)

Sculpture

It had been possible for the Romans, with their dynamic will to power, to canalize in architecture the manifold energies of the ancient cultures. They raised triumphal arches to symbolize their world-embracing sovereignty, but for the very reason that their empire was so extensive, they could not fill it entirely with their own productions. The integrity which had inspired the art of Greece was lost for ever. The Roman could not, like the Greek, be content with portraying only his ego. Moreover, beneath the Hellenistic luxury-art was concealed the deadly seriousness of a power which felt itself created to rule the earth. It would have been strange if these circumstances had not found expression in art.

With Pasiteles, a native of a city of lower Italy, who acquired Roman citizenship in the year 87 B.C. the Hellenistic art of the idealizing portrait came to an end. Nowhere are Roman self-awareness and love of truth shown more plainly than in the later portraits of their rulers, in busts, statues or coins. The spiritualized and resolute face of Caesar (Fig. 55a), the bull-necked, brutal head of Caracalla (Fig. 55c), or the head of a Roman lady (Fig. 55b), all show the effort to achieve truth.

Only in the hair is there occasionally a trace of stylization. In portraiture Roman art produced much that is fine and of lasting value. The barbarian heads that began to appear more frequently have an expressive vitality, which came southwards from the art of the Roman provinces beyond the Alps.

In larger compositions, where human portraits and mythological figures appeared together (Fig. 57b), the latter often acquired a remarkable semblance of reality. At the same time, the wealth of mythological figures was inexhaustible, for the Romans had long been accustomed to regard as their own all the gods of the ancient world. Typical of the last phase of Roman portraiture are the many representations of Antinous, which under Hadrian filled the Roman world. Antinous was a handsome youth, a favourite of the Emperor; in obedience to a medical superstition, he drowned himself in the Nile in order to save the Emperor's life. Hadrian, in his romantic gratitude, had him deified; but Roman art still required verisimilitude in his portraits, so that in all of them he displays the same seriousness, the same full lips, the same wistfully melancholy features.

The wholesale importation of Greek works of art was over by the end of the second century B.C.; but ever since the time of Augustus the older works of Greek art had been incessantly and indefatigably copied. Sometimes, among such figures, one glimpses the Roman spirit, in a certain urban sleekness and in the natural delight of the townsmen in the garlands fondly woven of fruit and foliage, peculiarly susceptible of picturesque treatment.

The Roman relief, like architectural sculpture, pays more attention then the Greek to chiaroscuro effects. His sense of reality, and his desire to produce an impression of space, made the Roman artist portray backgrounds (Figs. 54a and 54b) rather than landscapes in depth.

The attempt to make remoter objects recede by representing them in flatter relief led to a new kind of artistic development, in which details were often sacrificed to the total effect. The Romans were happiest in those works which represented contemporary events with as much reality and truth to nature as possible. Of necessity, the composition of such works was rather prosy, and in order to tell as much as possible a certain over-crowding was inevitable. Frequent undercutting makes for a rich alternation of light and shade, and in Trajan's reign one sees the beginnings of the so-called optical contour, in which a faint relief is strengthened by the shadow in a furrow made by the traversing drill. The restless quality of Roman sculpture was progressively intensified, as an expression of a profoundly troubled age which was seeking for a new purpose in life.

Painting

Roman painting took above all the form of wall-painting. The only easel paintings to have survived in any great numbers are found in Egypt, as wooden panels let into the walls, or as Hellenistic mummy-portraits, which are extremely valuable as examples of the tempera painting of antiquity, and are sometimes of a very mixed technique. They are generally painting of the head and shoulders only (Fig. 59a), the majority dating from the first and second centuries A,D. They have a lifelike expression, and are accomplished and naturalistic representations; it was more than a thousand years before such paintings were again possible.

In Rome the oldest paintings are those found in tombs, and because of the lighting in such places, they are executed on a white ground; they are of mythological or historical scenes, and sometimes bear inscriptions in Latin letters. The few fragments that remain of the wall-decorations of Roman palaces are somewhat later in date. It is hard to associate the various surviving paintings with the few painters' names—such as Fabulus, Cornelius Pinus and Attius Priscus—which have been handed down by tradition. The cities, Pompeii and Herculaneum, which were buried by the eruption of Vesuvius, are of far greater importance in the history of Roman painting.

When, during the greatest heat of summer at mid-day on the 24 August in the year A.D. 79, Vesuvius erupted, Pompeii was buried under masses of lava and thus preserved for future generations. It was in a sense the mediatrix between the Greek and Roman worlds. Wealthy and prosperous, built on a slope above the once navigable Sarnus, it had more than 20,000 inhabitants at the time of its destruction. But until 1748, although excavations had been made at a very early date, it remained unknown and forgotten. Since then, however, houses and streets have been uncovered, revealing in paintings, bronzes, and silver and gold ornaments, a Hellenistic luxury. The city, followed every change in the artistic fashions of the time, so that if we are

Typical arrangement of the Peristyle in a Pompeiian house, seen from the Atrium. (Breasted)

now able to distinguish four styles of Roman painting, covering altogether three centuries, it is mainly on the evidence of the frescoes, discovered in Pompeii.

The first style, known also as the 'incrustation style', coincides with the use of tufa as the chief building material. Its productions were not actually paintings, but imitations in plaster of Hellenistic marble panelling: polychrome 'marbles', divided into panels and friezes, rise from a yellow socle or skirting, and are surmounted, as a rule, by a denticulated cornice. As though to make up for this rather parsimonious ostentation, which is not enriched by sculptured ornamentation, we find, in rooms decorated in this style, as in the Casa del Fauno and the Casa di Sallustio, magnificent mosaic floors, which seem to complete with the gleaming walls (page 158). The 'ancients', as Vitruvius calls the Hellenistic architects, of the third century and later and the Roman architects of the second century B.C., had already made a beginning with this kind of interior decoration.

The second style, which was already practised in Rome before the beginning of the first century B.C., reached Pompeii by the year 80 B.C. It lasted into the Augustan age, and was known as the 'architectural style', because, while it discarded the plastic stucco-work, it imitated the marble panelling in paint. Such paintings make the wall seem to recede from the skirting and cornice, and painted pillars heighten the illusion. Not content with this, the artists presently began to paint foregrounds and backgrounds, with appropriate perspective foreshortenings. In a Pompeiian house you suddenly find yourself standing before a mysterious closed door, while above it the wall seems to open; or you see curtains, and behind them, through an archway, you have an unexpected glimpse of open country. Landscape and figure paintings were pressed into the service of these illusive arts, which did not deny their origin in the Hellenistic art of the theatrical scene-painter, which they betray by their numerous representations of curtains and the frequent introduction of the masks of tragedy and comedy.

In the Villa of the Mysteries the wall becomes a stage, and in the great fresco paintings discovered in 1909 (Fig. 58), executed mainly in red, the cult of the Greek mysteries is revealed in a solemn pageant. In the private living-rooms, and in the paintings on their walls, where the artist's imagination had free play, the spirit and tastes of the period are revealed more fully than in the architecture, where physical limitations of material could never be wholly disregarded. Here Roman art displays an illusionism which many will perhaps find suprising, but which is fundamentally the expression ot a period that marked the close of a great artistic and cultural age.

In this free and picturesque illussionist aıchitecture we see the artistic ideals of the Romans, in which the columns could never be too slender, the ornaments never too rich. In the so-called House of the Odyssey landscapes in Rome one sees the rustic scenes among which the cultivated townsman sought to find his way back to Mother Earth. Nature for the Greeks was only a setting for the personal activities of the gods. Something of this conceptions is still to be seen in the Odyssey landscape in the house on the Esquiline, which is still inspired with the heroic spirit: a flowing spring, surrounded with rushes, with a nymph sitting beside the spring, while on the hillside above sprawls a mountain god. Such ideas survived even into the Christian late antique. In Ravenna the river-god innocently appears beside the Jordan during the baptism of Christ.

Of the third style one phase is called 'Egyptianized', inasmuch as it was transplanted into Italy after the battle of Actium in the year 31 A.B., as its subject matter and decorative motives would indicate; while its basic phase is described as the 'candelabra style', because the walls are often divided into sections by green-painted candelabra, as in the Casa dei Capitelli figurati, in Pompeii. The third style shows a preference for a black socle or skirting; the broader surfaces are red, and the upper portion of the wall white, though violet, blue and yellow often occur. There are good examples of this style in the houses of Caecilius Jucundus and Spurius Mesor.

Most of the houses, however, are examples of the fourth style. In this the juxtaposition of yellow, red and black is frequent, and to these are added blue and yellow, while violet disappears and the cinnabar red of the third style becomes darker and turns to brown. Compared with the cool and refined effects of the third style, the fourth seems warm and living, and excursions into the playful are frequent. In it the artistic spirit of late antiquity is still plainly perceptible.

Section of the relief on Trajan's Column. The Emperor Trajan is sacrificing a bullock to the gods before a bridge newly built across the Danube. Height 27½ in. Second century. Text page 167. (Breasted)

Chapter XIV

EARLY CHRISTIAN ART

*

ANY chapter in a book begins abruptly; but a new chapter of history begins almost imperceptibly. Though many events occur dramatically, and it is said that from that moment something entirely new came into being, we see, looking closer, that they were generally preceded by a long period of preparation. There were many battles, persecutions, and disputes before Constantine the Great, in 324, made Christianity the state religion.

Generation followed generation, and in the Roman empire pagans and Christians lived side by side, sometimes in peace, sometimes not. In its idiom, the Christian art of this period is indistinguishable from Roman. In the catacombs the first Christian symbols were painted on the walls (Fig. 59c), before Hellenistic sculpture had produced its last impressive creations, such as the statues of Antinous (page 172), the paintings in the tombs, and the mummy-portraits (Fig. 59a). Christianity changed not the forms, but the content of art.

The mythology of the ancients was replaced by the stories of the two Testaments. Naturally enough, one of the earliest images was that of the Saviour. Sometimes He is depicted as the Good Shepherd, an example of which is the little third-century marble statuette in the Lateran Museum, showing a curly-haired boy, turning his head aside as he bears the lamb upon his shoulders. Sometimes, as in a wall-painting in the Calixtus catacomb, in Rome, He is represented as the youthful and beardless miracle-worker at the raising of Lazarus (a scene that was often depicted, since the conquest of death was one of the fundamental concepts of the new doctrine). He is also pictured as a child on his mother's lap in a picture in the Priscilla catacomb, which, in its quiet humanity, foreshadows the many pictures of the subject which came later. On the other hand, the Passion was not portrayed in the pre-Constantinian era; and instead of the person of God the Father one usually sees only a hand emerging from a cloud, while Angels are everywhere represented as fully clothed and wingless youths. In the oldest Roman paintings—those in the Domitilla catacomb, which date from the first century—we see clearly how antique vase-painting influenced Christian art; for example, Noah is shown drifting on the sea, alone, in a little chest, in exactly the same way as Danae at an earlier period.

This was a simple and homely narrative art, ingenuously depicting the same animal and human figures which heathen art had long used as decorative motives:

a

b

c

•. (A) Portrait of boy. Painting of the Roman Empire. Painted on wood with wax and resin as media. Found, with any similar paintings, in the Egyptian province of Fayum. See p. 172. Second century A.D. (Metropolitan Museum, ew York).

3) Portrait; head of unknown man. Found at Ephesus, p. 177. Third century. (Kunsthistorisches Museum, Vienna).

:) Assembly-room in the catacomb of Petrus and Marallinus, Rome. Third century.

a

b

60. (A) Interior of the early Christian basilica, San Paolo fuori le mura, Rome. Built at the close of the fourth century; restored nineteenth century.
(B) Basilica of Sant' Apollinare in Classe. Ravenna, sixth century.

a

b

61. (A) Mausoleum of Galla Placidia in Ravenna. Byzantine influence. Second half of fifth century.
(B) Part of the mosaic decoration of the great Omayyad Mosque, Damascus, p. 200. About 715 A.D.

a

62. (A) St Mark's, Venice. Begun 976, enlarged during the eleventh and twelfth centuries; decorative additions continued into the seventeenth century; not the cathedral church of Venice (S. Pietro holds that rank) but a magnificent shrine for the bones of its patron saint.
(B) Interior of the Hagia Sophia, Constantinople, looking eastwards. Sixth century. Text p. 185.

b

in particular birds, but also genii, psyches, and winged cherubs, which, despite their likeness to angels, mus not yet be regarded as such. The Dionysian vine (Fig. 64b) appears particularly often, since Christ had compared Himself to a vine and His disciples to the grapes. The peacock, the symbol of immortality, and the anchor, the symbol of hope, are entirely in keeping with the ideas of antiquity. The Good Shepherd is joined by the fisherman, with rod and line, the Fisher of Men, who also suggests water and baptism. Very old symbols appear; the fish, for example, is a favourite symbol, since the initial letters of the Greek words Iesous CHristos THeou Uios Soter—i. e. Jesus Christ, the Son of God, the Saviour—spell the word Ichthus—fish.

The earliest paintings in the catacombs are still the same as the Roman sepulchral paintings, on a light ground, which have already been mentioned. This early Christian art can be classed with the later Roman styles. In the 'fourth style' it, too, acquired the refinement and delicacy of the end of the latest Hellenistic art.

First Signs of Change

A great transformation, springing from the new impulse towards the transcendental and super-sensual, was gradually coming over the whole of Roman art.

Riegl took the reliefs on the Arch of Constantine (Fig. 57a) as the starting-point of a subtle analysis of the tendencies of late Roman art; he did not deny that the details of individual sculptures were of coarse and immobile character, but he found, in their strictly symmetrical composition, a new kind of beauty, which he called *crystalline,* because it obeyed one of the primary laws governing inanimate matter. Even though we may not agree with him in finding absolute beauty in these laws, this analysis does reveal something new in an architecture where we should not otherwise expect it.

It may be maintained that it is not really a tendency toward the abstract, but rather an attempt to achieve picturesqueness by the neglect of detail, that underlies the elaborate ornamentation of the Arch of Constantine, but this rigid symmetry is none the less significant.

In various other late Roman works of art the tendency is even clearer. The great bronze statue of an unknown emperor—larger than life-size—at Barletta, a portrait head in the Roman Institute of Ostia, and one from Ephesus, in the Kunsthistorisches Museum in Vienna (Fig. 59b), are entirely different from the old Roman portrait statues. These heads have nothing in common with the naturalistic representation, nor with the idealization which existed side by side in Helleno-Roman art, and which could do so because each expressed, in different ways, the same conception of the world.

The Ephesian head looks, not into the every-day life of the Roman world, but wistfully into a remote distance, unmeasurable by any earthly standards. This is really

12

the beginning of Byzantine art, but before we begin to consider this we must discuss the history of the buildings which early Christianity built to serve its practical needs.

The Catacombs

As well as paintings (page 176), the Catacombs contained other objects of interest. The ancient custom of burying various articles with the dead led to relics of Christian life being found in tombs, such as oil and wine flasks, medals, and various other objects of religious significance. The unsettled life led by the Christians during the first few centuries of the new era caused them to take refuge in underground hiding-places, such as the tombs of slaves and freedmen (which incidentally proves that the custom of burial in catacombs was practised in Rome before Christianity). It was natural that they should follow the heathen custom, for in life they formed one community, and in death they wished to be united. The catacombs provided the best opportunity for this, since the Christian belief in a life after death led them to reject cremation; and Roman law required that graves be respected, so that even those of the Christians had some security.

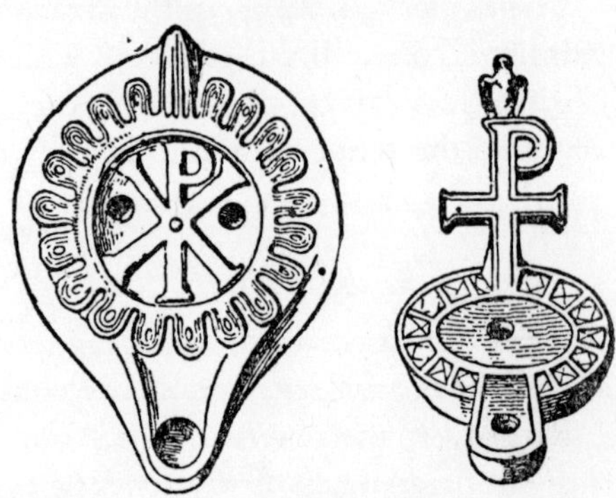

Ancient Christian lamps found in the catacombs

The actual structure of these subterranean cemeteries, most of which lay outside the city, consisted of intersecting galleries, *cinuculi,* from ten to fourteen feet high and twenty to forty inches wide. Small lighting-shafts, *lumaria*, ensured ventilation and gave a faint light. When needed, fresh galleries were driven under those which already existed; so eventually a catacomb might consist of several storeys. Very often, too, new galleries ran through the older tombs.

The dead were laid in sepulchral chambers, *cubicula*, with rectangular openings (Fig. 59c), closed by marble slabs. Inscriptions, or symbols, recorded the names of the dead. Where there was little room the 'cubicula' were excavated at right angles to the galleries instead of parallel with them. In front of graves of bishops and martyrs the galleries were expanded, forming chambers of some size; these graves were further distinguished by an arch, *arcosolium* (Fig. 51c). When Christianity became the State religion the little memorial chambers were enlarged, forming sepulchral chapels, *cellae memoriae,* which were provided with wider lighting-shafts. Eventually, chapels were built over them at ground-level.

Besides the catacombs already named, others deserve mention for their paintings: the cemetery of Pretextatus, and the cemetery of Ostrianum, with the grave of Saint

Agnes, and the tombs of Petrus and Marcellinus, with the fine assembly-room (Fig. 59c). These are the most extensive, and as far as paintings are concerned, the most important; though there are catacombs in Naples and Sicily which are more remarkable for architectural features. A more spacious ground-plan, and tombs carved out of the natural rock, which are sometimes walled in with marble, or connected by short corner-posts with the rock above them, give the Sicilian catacombs a more monumental character; this is largely due to the survival of ancient tradition. In the Roman catacombs there are few sarcophagi, and those are of a simpler character.

The Basilica

After the edicts of tolerance in 312 and 313, there was a great advance in Christian art in the Roman provinces: Egypt, North Africa, Syria and Asia Minor. In Macedonia, Greece and Italy Christian churches were henceforth built in the form of the basilica, and in that of the rotunda.

The basilica is a very old form. The Greek name, *stoa basileios* or *basilike,* 'King's hall', indicates that it existed in the Hellenistic East before it came to be used in imperial Rome, as a secular building connected with the forum, serving as a law-court and a covered exchange. Architecturally, it developed from the necessity of providing large open spaces, protected by a roof supported on columns. The system of lighting was that already used in Egyptian temples, with windows in the upper walls of a central nave, rising above the two side-aisles.

Christianity took over the traditional basilica, and created, by adding such architectural forms as the Roman 'atrium', a long rectangular church, usually running from west to east. Unlike Eastern temples, it was not the house of the divinity, to which only priests had access, but a place of assembly for a large congregation. Consequently, the Christian basilica was decorated inside, while outside it was plain.

The basilica was divided lengthways into three distinct portions. First came an open space surrounded by covered arcades, the fore-court or *atrium* (shown on the right of the illustration on page 180), in which were assembled those who were not yet fully qualified members of the congregation, the various classes of penitents, and the catechumens, pagans and Jews who had accepted Christianity but had not yet been baptised. In the larger buildings the atrium had its own gate opening on to the street, while the font or *kantharos* was in the centre of the court. In the east, but not in Italy, there was an inner vestibule, the *narthex,* adjoining the *atrium*, for the more advanced penitents, pilgrims, and catechumens.

The church itself was a long, narrow building which was usually divided longitudinally into three by two rows of columns. The central section was higher and wider than those at the sides. The rows columns, in accordance with the rules of Roman architecture, were either arcades, with archivolts, or else they simply supported the straight beams of the architraves which carried the upper walls of the central nave. The timbered roof was either open (Fig. 60b), or hidden by a painted and coffered ceiling (Fig. 60a).

The central nave, the principal accommodation for the congregation, led, through a great triumphal arch, to the actual priest's house, the *presbyterium.* There, generally above the grave of a martyr, and approached by several steps, was the altar, under the shelter of the canopy or *ciborium.* This stood approximately in the centre of the semi-circular floor of the apse, which was a niche-like expansion of the eastern wall of the nave, roofed with a cupola, and often windowless. Here, arranged in a semi-circle, were the benches for the priests, and in the middle, at the back, was the bishop's throne, the *kathedra,* from which the word *cathedral,* the name for a bishop's church, was afterwards derived.

An early Christian basilica

The form of the basilica, which we see today in about forty fairly well-preserved fourth-century churches, contained all the seeds of mediaeval architecture. Nevertheless, we must not over-estimate their architectural quality: they were composite structures, carefully and deliberately put together, rather than homogeneous creations. Old architectural forms, and the classical orders, were used without hesitation; for a long while the outside of the basilica remained shabby and plain, while the inside had already begun to glow with mosaics, and to achieve some sort of lucid and harmonious arrangement. After a long time, when bells had been introduced, a bell-tower, or *campanile,* was built beside the church, at first entirely separated from it.

The old church of St Peter in Rome, which early in the sixteenth century was replaced by the present building, was probably built in the time of Constantine the Great. Like the Church of Nativity in Bethlehem, and most of the other larger and more important basilicas of that period, it had a nave and double aisles. As in a temple of late antiquity, a flight of steps led up to a gatehouse which opened on to a courtyard with colonnades, in the midst of which was the font. There were three doors in the façade, opening into the central nave, 325 feet long and 88 feet wide, while two further doors opened into the aisles, whose high roofs leant steeply against the upper walls of the nave, squeezing the windows up toward the upper edge of the great central wall, the inner side of which was covered with superimposed bands of allegorical paintings.

In spite of its simpler ground-plan, and alterations in the seventeenth century, Santa Maria Maggiore, in Rome, with its nave and lateral aisles, bears a strong resemblance to the old St Peter's; as in the latter church, its rows of columns support horizontal beams. These, however, were usually replaced by arcades, as in San Paolo fuori le mura (Fig. 60a), restored after a destructive fire in the nineteenth century; this is the only fourth-century church still standing which can be compared in size with the old St Peter's.

In the fifth and sixth centuries many Christian basilicas were built, their plan being modified in accordance with local needs. Women, in the East, could not sit beside men at divine service and special places had to be provided for them, the most suitable being galleries over the side-aisles; these were contrived by constructing a second floor in each aisle, the space beneath opening into the nave through a further series of columns (Fig. 62b). One of the oldest examples of this is to be seen in the basilica of St Demetrios in Salonica, built mostly in the fifth century.

In North Africa, where Christianity had early been adopted, the apse was often omitted, while the number of aisles was increased; at Matifu there is a basilica with seven, and the basilica of Damus el Carita has nine. A few of the Syrian churches adopted various mediaeval developments at a very early period, and in northern Mesopotamia, from the seventh century onwards, basilicas with domes were built, as at Kefr Zeh, Mar Augen, and Salah.

One of the finest existing buildings of this period in Europe is the church of Sant' Apollinare, in the ancient port of Classis, which was dedicated in A.D. 549 (Fig. 60b). Not far from Ravenna, Sant' Apollinare in Classe stands today in front of a dark pine-wood, a simple brick building in an open field. Beside it is the campanile, a massive round tower. Such round towers usually distinguish the churches of Ravenna from those of Rome, where the campanili were always square.

The Rotunda

The Christian rotunda accompanied the basilica from the beginning; it was a development of Roman architecture, based on traditional forms. As in the Pantheon and many other Roman buildings, the outside received little attention compared with the inside; a practice greatly encouraged by the dome. In theWest, the congregational church was originally a basilica and only smaller structures such as baptisteries and *cubicula* were built as rotundas; but in the Christian Orient, from a very early period, large churches were planned in that form.

In its simplest form, as a baptistery, the rotunda is a single dome-covered room, often with an internal peristyle, in which case the cupola rises above the area enclosed by the ring of columns, and is supported by them. The space between the ring of columns and the enclosing wall constitutes the so-called gallery; in the outer wall niches were contrived at a very early period, as in Helena's tomb in the Roman Campagna, and the churches of San Giovanni in Fonte, at Ravenna, and St George, in Salonica. These niches led to the development, from a circular ground-plan into a polygon, and a combination of the basilica with the disposition of parts required by the rotunda. We find such combinations in the Roman church of Santa Constanza, built at the close of the fourth century, the baptistery of the Lateran, built by Sixtus III in the fifth century, and the church of Santa Maria Rotonda at Nocera, built about 430.

The most important early Christian circular buildings, which in Italy took over the function of true community or congregational churches, are San Stefano Rotondo in Rome, and San Lorenzo in Milan. San Stefano Rotondo, built under Pope Simplicius (468—483), has a ground-plan of three concentric circles, so that it has two galleries. The inmost space has a diameter of seventy-five feet, the upper wall, pierced by windows, being carried on twenty-two Ionic columns. The outer circle of supports consist of eight massive piers and thirty-six pillars connected by semi-circular arches. The columns of the smaller circle give the interior a cruciform shape, which does not appear very clearly in the ground-plan shown below, owing to the faintness of the supporting members.

In the great Roman city of Milan, which even in the time of the pagan emperors exceeded Rome in area, if not in splendour, the church of San Lorenzo calls for

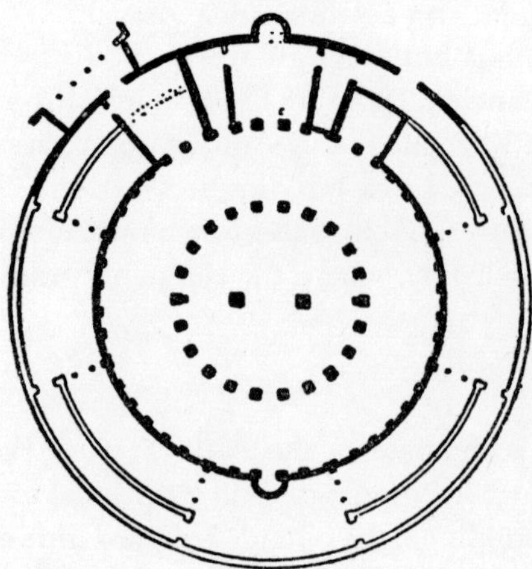

Ground plan of San Stefano Rotondo, Rome

mention as a magnificently spacious building; but as it was built on the foundations of the banqueting hall of an ancient palace, and restored in 1573, it lies outside the scope of this historical survey.

The church of San Vitale, in Ravenna, begun under Theodosius at the instance of Bishop Ecclesius (524—534), is one of the most wonderful rotundas in Italy; but it is only mentioned for geographical reasons, since it belongs to another school of art. Ravenna was a Byzantine colony on Italian soil; from Byzantium she received her inspiration, her materials, and her artists. While early Christian art is closely bound up with Byzantium, the true Byzantine art, as the following chapter shows, can be clearly distinguished from it.

Chapter XV

BYZANTINE ART

*

When Constantine removed his capital from Italy to Byzantium on the Bosphorus, and founded a 'new Rome', which took its name from him and was solemnly inaugurated in 330, the whole form of Roman art began to change.

In Rome the columns and ornamental details of the basilicas were usually obtained by pilfering from ancient buildings; but by the Sea of Marmora there grew up, in the course of the fourth century, a school of original and creative stonemasons. As we shall presently see, a great change must have occured to make possible the Golden Gate of Theodosius, with its flanking towers, and the simple divisions of its white marble façade, reminiscent of Egyptian architecture (page 134). The Near East, and Egypt in particular, had become the stronghold of the new faith. Many anchorites who had fled from the world settled by the Nile, in whose valleys there were innumerable convents. The first western monastery, founded by St Benedict of Nursia on Monte Cassino, between Rome and Naples, in 525, was comparatively insignificant. Its church was a simple basilica, and it was a long while before the influence of the Benedictine Order spread from Monte Cassino all over Europe.

Meanwhile, in Byzantium, many splendid and palatial buildings were built; not only above, but also below ground. The 'Water-halls', or covered cisterns, built in A.D. 528, the 'halls of a thousand and one pillars', as they were called, have actually only 224 columns, which rise from the dimly lit cisterns; but they are hardly less

Longitudinal section of Hagia Sophia, Constantinople

63. Baptistry of St Mark's, Venice.

a

b

64. (A) Story of the Fall. From the Jakobus codex dedicated to Alexios Komnenos (1081 - 1118). (Vatican).
(B) Panel with symbols of Christ, vines and peacocks. Basilica Sant' Apollinare Nuovo, Ravenna. Sixth century.

65. (A) The monastery of St Joseph, at Wolokolamsk, founded in 1479; formerly one of the richest monasteries in Russia.
(B) The church of Peter and Paul, on the banks of the Volga, at Iaroslavl. 1691.

b

a

b

c

66. (A) Saint George. Russian icon from Novgorod. Sixteenth century.
(B) The Mother of God. Icon by Simon Ushakov. 1662. (Leningrad).
(C) A panel of the left wing of one of the bronze doors of the cathedral of St Sophia, Novgorod. The work of Riquinus, bronze-founder. Twelfth century.

impressive than the public water-cellar of the basilica, called after it the *Cisterna Basilica,* with its forest of 420 columns. These, and other smaller cisterns, have prototypes in Alexandria, which often consist of several storeys, supported on columns of white marble and red syenite.

Even in the oldest buildings in Constantinople—those built about A.D. 420 —the heavy domed roofs were supported on the abaci of the columns by the imposts, massive cuboids wider at the top than at the bottom (Fig. 60b), which were later modified in many ways (Figs. 74b and 74c).

Among the magnificent palaces, theatres, race-courses, baths, and triumphal columns, arose the new churches; the largest of these, built in 532—537, and thoroughly renovated in 558—563, was the church of the Holy Wisdom, the Hagia Sophia, one of the most splendid churches in the world (Fig. 62b; also page 184).

In it the architects, Anthemios of Tralles and Isidoros of Miletus, combined the rotunda and the basilica in the most audacious manner. The church became a mosque after 1453, and four minarets were added and the decoration of the interior considerably altered; we must imagine all this away to appreciate the original structure. A courtyard surrounded by arcades, the *atrium,* leads to the *narthex*, roofed with a barrel vault and completely encrusted with mosaics. From this one enters (see sectional elevation) the vast interior, above which the cupola rests on four massive piers, connected by arches. The light enters through its circle of forty windows, and increases the curious impression produced by the shallow cupola, ninety-eight feet in diameter, which seems to be unsupported, floating in the air and about to settle down on the walls.

The impression of the suspended cupola is attained by allowing downward-sloping spandrels or pendentives to make the transition between the wall above the round arches and the wall-surfaces rising to the cupola. The impression of a nave in the rotunda is produced by lengthening the central square towards the entrance and towards the altar by half as much again, these prolongations being roofed with half-cupolas leaning against the main cupola, and by confining the galleries to the longer sides of the building. Complicated though the whole system of juxtaposed and intersecting cupolas appears at first glance, the solution is lucid and logical. Above the medley of arches, conchae and arcades, supported on slender, variegated marble columns, the great sheltering cupola hangs outspread, while the interior surfaces were once covered with the transcendent splendour of mosaics.

Development Phases

Byzantine art is closely involved with the art of surface decoration in mosaic, created by the infinitely patient and careful juxtaposition of innumerable *tesserae*. This art was known to the Egyptians and Persians; it originated in floor-surfaces covered with broad patterns and geometrically shaped slabs of stone or marble. The next stage was wall-decoration, and the smaller the tesserae the richer the designs. Roman mosaic had already produced such works as 'Alexander's Battle' (page 158), but it was left to Byzantine art to perfect this technique by using minute tesserae of coloured and gilt stone and glass, which were encrusted over masonry.

Semper, in his volume on style, associated the peculiarity of Byzantine art with carpet-weaving; this is a purely mechanical explanation, which does not explain why Byzantine art confined itself exclusively to a linear technique, while the ordinary pictorial method was equally possible. The increasing flatness of Byzantine representation is the increasingly lucid expression of a new tendency towards the supersensual, which is more readily represented by the pure abstraction of line.

Just as Roman painting, rather than architecture, revealed the dreams of earlier generations, so Byzantine mosaics were the purest expression of the new Christian faith. What was only suggested in the head from Ephesus (Fig. 59b) was fully expressed in the following centuries.

One thing is certain: the early Byzantine art of the fifth and sixth centuries has already its own idiom, and in the Mausoleum of Galla Placidia in Ravenna (Fig. 61a) the figure of St Lawrence, on the arch over the sarcophagus, shines out against the blue background with a noble and unearthly solemnity. The coloured glass mosaic in this rotunda is not an example of the early Christian narrative art in which a mundane pagan piety was blended with belief in a future life. It is an early example of the true Byzantine style, which for centuries spread from Constantinople over Europe. Its influence was no less great in Russian than in Islamic art, and it left a profound impression on the emerging Romanesque style of the West.

In Byzantine art the transition from antiquity to the Middle Ages was effected very smoothly. When in the eighth century the Byzantine empire was robbed of its eastern and southern provinces by the Arabs it merely closed its ranks. The capital, Constantinople, was by far the wealthiest, most flourishing and most powerful city of the Middle Ages.

Then came the revolt of the iconoclasts. In 726 the pictures in the churches were hung farther from the ground; in 728 they were prohibited; and in 754 the mosaics and frescos were covered with whitewash. It seemed that this meant the end of Byzantine art; but under the Macedonian emperors (867—1057) the so-called Middle Byzantine art began a second flowering, in which Byzantium showed itself superior to all the rest of Europe. The cruciform domed church emerged. The Middle Byzantine form had five cupolas; its original examples in Constantinople were the Church of the Apostles and the Church of St Irene; while in Italy St Mark's, in Venice, is an especially beautiful example.

The influence of this building was all the more effective by reason of its combination, of Eastern and Western elements. In Venice one can study the often misunderstood 'petrifaction' of Byzantine art on European soil. The mosaic decorations of the baptistery of St Mark's are an admirable example of the latest Byzantine mosaic work at the end of the Middle Ages (Fig. 63). They are the work of Byzantine and Italian masters, commisioned, towards the middle of the fourteenth century, by the Doge Enrico Dandolo, who is buried there.

The mixture of the Byzantine and Gothic styles, which had already made its appearance, demonstrates the vitality of Byzantine art even after a thousand years. If the Gothic style appears in the scene of the Crucifixion, on the wall at the back of the altar, where the feet of Christ are fastened with a single nail, or where the Doge kneels beside Mary and John, and Salome, in an ermine-trimmed, long-sleeved gown, appears as a Western princess, these few aberrations cannot conceal the fact that all the other figures are still entirely Byzantine.

The Archangel Michael.
From the mosaics in the conventional church of Daphni, near Athens. Beginning of twelfth century. (Millet)

In Venice, or Daphni (right), or in the celebrated pictures of Hosios Lukas at Phokis, or in the portico of the Koimesis Church of Nicaea, one must avoid seeing in these mosaics, with their admirable linear style, the petrification which did occur, here and there, in the mechanical output of the Mount Athos school. Byzantine art, in its grave and religious earnestness and unworldliness, is more than any other the truly sacred, Christian art.

The deliberate adoption of a plane and linear mode of representation is not necessarily the final phase of artistic evolution; Byzantine art, like Egyptian, adopted this principle from the outset. This Byzantine fondness for a linear style explains why, in the earliest stage of Byzantine art, in continuation of early Roman and Oriental tradition, the first Christian book-illumination should have developed. As early as the fourth century the ancient form of rolled manuscript was replaced by the *codex*, the bound volume of folded leaves. Some of these were written on purple vellum, enriched with gold and silver lettering and coloured pictures. From the *minium* or native cinnabar which was generally employed as a red pigment, the first book-illustrators were called *miniatores*, and in later times the pictures themselves were called *miniatures* (Fig. 64a).

Chapter XVI

RUSSIA

*

It was in Russia that the influence of Byzantine art was most enduring; Russia never had a Romanesque or a Gothic phase, nor any comprehensive renaissance as there was in most European countries. Byzantine art remained almost unchanged in Russia, in spite of wars, racial migrations, and almost two centuries of Mongol rule, until, under the Muscovite Czars, in the fifteenth century, it acquired a more national character. Even when Peter the Great, at the beginning of the eighteenth century, undertook the wholesale Europeanization of Russia a Baroque style emerged, in which monasteries and churches (Fig. 65) kept many Byzantine elements, such as the clusters of domes and the towers with pyramidal roofs, which Russian art, hundreds of years earlier, had adopted, reproducing the native wooden architecture in stone.

In Russia and the Orthodox countries of the Balkans the curious phenomenon is to be seen of peoples making a foreign art their own, and using it to express completely their own faith. They received Christianity, not from Rome, bur from the Greek empire of Byzantium.

The first Christian communities in Russia were formed after the foundation of the Empire by Rurik in 862, during a restless period of conflict with Byzantium, when Russia as a whole was still pagan. But after St Vladimir's conversion in 989, when he ordered the people to break their idols and be baptized, Christianity became the official religion of the State. Novgorod in the north and Kiev and Tchermigov in the south, were the principal centres from which it was propagated.

The Byzantine Foundations

Together with Byzantine Christianity, Byzantine churches appeared in Russia. One of the oldest and finest is the cathedral of St Sophia in Kiev, planned by St Vladimir and built, between 1020 and 1037, by his son Yaroslav. The cathedral was reconstructed in the style of the Ukrainian baroque, and does not now convey much idea of the original plan, with its five naves. It never, of course, competed with the Hagia Sophia in Constantinople; but with its shallow main cupola, and other secondary cupolas, and its two flanking towers at the west front, it was at that time the finest and richest church built in Russia under Byzantine influence.

The cathedral is of particular significance in the history of Russian art, for in it mosaics and frescos have been preserved which show that Russian art, at first, was nothing but a continuation of Byzantine art. In the choir are mosaic paintings on a gold ground which are absolutely Greek in character, with no Slavonic characteristics; historically, these come between the mosaics of Hosios Lukas and of Daphni. Following the Byzantine custom, in the central circle of the main cupola is the bust of the Saviour surrounded by the four archangels, while the majestic figures of the Apostles are on the outer ring, and the Evangelists in the pendentives.

Kiev was not as rich as Byzantium, and consequently the mosaics are often replaced by frescoes, usually of a brownish tone. The Biblical scenes and representations of the saints are purely Byzantine. The fascination of Constantinople is shown by a series of frescoes on each side of a flight of steps, showing life at the imperial Byzantine court; in particular, dancing, hunting, the circus (below), the baiting of animals, and other amusements. These frescoes have suffered from unskilful restoring, but one can still recognize the same style as in the ecclesiastial mosaics, The figures are flat, and shown full-faced, while behind them is an architectural background of section of arches, of stylized gables and domes. These details, and other scenes from the life of the Russian people, show that Slavonic and Byzantine artists were working together as late as the middle of the eleventh century (page 190).

On the other hand, in the frescoes in the cathedral of St Sophia at Novgorod, built, also under Yaroslav, by Byzantine architects, after the pattern of the Kiev cathedral, there is hardly a trace of any original Slavonic inspiration. At first, Russian art followed closely all the developments of the Byzantine. The representations of the Last Supper, for instance, in the conventual church of St Michael in Kiev, finished in 1108, have the same over-elongated figures, with small faces, that are characteristic of Byzantine art at the same period. In the frescoes in the monastery of St Cyril, near Kiev, founded in 1140, the first Slavonic faces appear. Specifically Russian elements appear more obviously in the miniature-painting of the period, as soon as it ceased to be practised exclusively by Greeks. There are clear differences; lifelike animal and plant motives appear together with conventionalized Byzantine faces, and bright reds and blues, always favourite colours of the Russians, emphasize the national character of these illuminations, which lasted into the thirteenth century. The oldest which can be called truly Russian is the

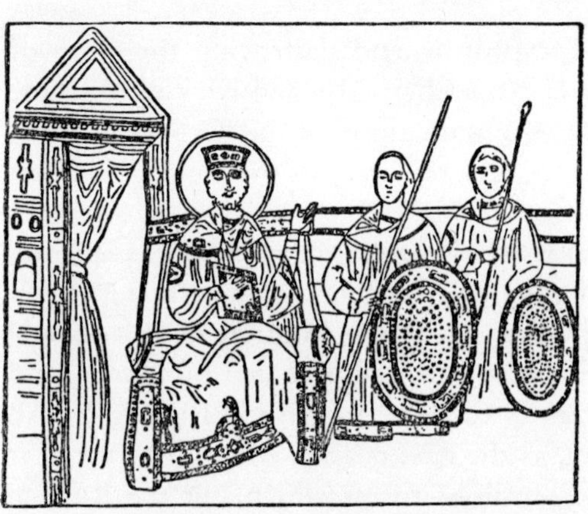

The Emperor of Byzantium at the Circus

'Ostromir Gospel' of 1057, but for the time being there was no continued elaboration of a Russian style, for after 1054 the kingdom of Kiev had split up into various independent, and often hostile, principalities.

Novgorod, in the north, on Lake Ilmen, was alone able, for some time, to remain, like Venice, a republican city state. It traded with the German factories, and belonged to the Hanseatic League; its archbishop was chosen by popular election, which was not subject to confirmation at Byzantium. The main church of Novgorod, the Cathedral of St Sophia, is more solemn in appearance than the cathedral of Kiev; it is higher, and its windows are smaller. The city was open to Western influences, for the so-called 'Korssun' bronze door (Fig. 66c), dating from the latter part of the twelfth century, was made at the Magdeburg foundries. European Romanesque may have reached Russia by way of Novgorod.

The Emperor and Empress of Byzantium, in a fresco on the walls of the cathedral of St Sophia, Kiev. Eleventh century

In 1222 the Mongols, under Genghis Khan, seized the Crimea in the south; and in 1237 the Tartars entered into northern Russia, capturing and destroying the cities of Ryazan, Vladimir, Kolomna and Moscow. In 1240 Chernigov and Kiev were taken, and by 1242 Russia had become part of the Mongol empire of the 'Golden Horde'. The Khan of Kipchak, from his capital, Sarai, on a tributary of the Volga, ruled his Russian dominions as a despot.

Under this Asiatic rule Russian art was affected by many influences, not, as before, only that of Byzantium. In the great Mongol empire, which, in the second half of the thirteenth century, stretched from the China Sea to the frontiers of Poland, and from the Himalayas to Siberia, the eastern Mongols had accepted Buddhism, and the western Mongols Islam, so that a current of Chinese, Indian and Islamic Persian art flowed into Russia. Islamic architecture, as the next chapter shows, had taken at about this time—especially in Persia—the sensuous forms which suit the Russian temperament. Four-centred arches, onion-shaped and heart-shaped domes, blind windows, and niche-like recesses, now occurred frequently in Russian architecture, and the new, bright colouring of roofs and cupolas can also be attributed to Asiatic influences. The numerous spires of the churches shone with red, white and green, and there was an increasing tendency to cover them with gold. In cities like Rostov, which were flourishing centres in the time of the Mongols, the Tartar 'Kremlin', or fortified citadel, appeared, and when the Muscovite Grand Duke, Ivan I, moved his capital to Moscow, and in 1333 was confirmed in his dignities by the Great Khan, the first stone-built churches were built in the city, which always, even during the period of Mongol overlordship, tried to surpass all other Russian centres. The Metropolitan now moved his seat to Russia, and the Grand Ducal power established itself so firmly that in 1480 Ivan III was able to free all Russia from the Tartar yoke.

Muscovite Art

In 1453 the Ottomans, under Mahommed II, besieged Constantinople with a great army and a powerful fleet, and in forty days reduced the ancient city, massacred its dignitaries, and made it the capital of the Ottoman Empire. Only in the monasteries of Mount Athos, on the easternmost of the three prongs of the Chalcidician peninsula, did Byzantine art feebly continue in the hands of Greek and Russian monks. Otherwise, the Byzantine inheritance fell to Russia.

By his marriage to the Princess Sophia, the niece of the last Byzantine emperor, who had taken refuge in Rome, Ivan III formed contacts with Byzantium and Europe. It was he who added the two-headed eagle, the badge of the Greek emperors, to St George of Moscow, and styled himself Grand Duke and Autocrat of all Russia. Under him, and his son Ivan the Terrible (Ivan IV), a new Russian empire was created, and with it a national art.

Ivan IV, who in imitation of Caesar was crowned as 'Czar', regarded himself as the rightful heir of the Roman and the Byzantine empires. The clergy at once invented an ideology which placed the Czars of Moscow at the head of the new world state: all Orthodox countries were to unite in a single Russian czardom, and the Czar would be the only Christian emperor on earth. No fourth Rome could follow the third, but only the kingdom of Christ, which was eternal. In the legend

Constantine Monomach on the throne, with crown, sceptre, pallium and pectoral cross. On the right and left, ecclesiastical and secular dignitaries. Carving on the throne of Ivan the Terrible in the Uspensky Cathedral, Moscow. 1551

of Constantine Monomach, who had separated the Orthodox from the Roman church, the majesty of the title of Czar was constantly repeated. Wearing the Hat and Pallium of Monomach, and dressed in brocade and covered with gold, the Czar sits immovably on his throne. Ivan IV was 'Terrible' only to the unorthodox peoples; for the Orthodox Russians he was the stern and god-fearing ruler. Religion became, as it had been in Byzantium, a powerful factor in political life; richly endowed stone-built churches and cathedrals were built in all parts of the country. From Novgorod, first subjected by Ivan III in 1478, and from Pskov, the clock-tower originated, which was to spread everywhere through Russia. When the Cathedral of the Assumption of the Holy Virgin, which had just been begun by inexperienced native architects, collapsed, the autocrat summoned the Italian Aristotile Fioraventi from Venice, who built the cathedral, in the years 1475—79, on the lines of the old cathedral of St Demetrius of Vladimir. He gave it, as a foretaste of the new Russian style, five shining onion-shaped domes (the so-called 'imperial roofs') with gilded spires and crosses with chains, while the interior was decorated in the Italian style. He was soon followed by other Italians, among whom were Pietro Antonio Solari, Alevisio Novi and Marco Rufo. Between 1484—1507 they built, at the highest point of the Kremlin, the Cathedral of the Annunciation, while Marco Rufo, about 1487, began the so-called 'Faceted Palace', as the chief residence of Ivan IV. In this way the crystalline fashion of cutting and polishing masonry, known as faceting, first practised in the early Italian Renaissance, was introduced in Russia. In Moscow, in so far as the Italians could influence it, there was a Byzantine Italian renaissance; but in spite of this the interiors of the churches remained in the Russo-Byzantine style, as in the third great cathedral of the Kremlin, that of the Archangel Michael. The well-known Pokrovsky Cathedral (Vasili Blazhenny, left), at the lower end of the Red Square, was designed by Barma and Postnik. It is not really typical of its period, for such fantastic complexity is an exception; too many things have been crowded in, to produce an effect of the greatest possible magnificence, and no less than eleven chapels are clustered in a disorderly way under the turrets. The only

The Pokrovsky (Vasili) Cathedral, Moscow. Built 1554 - 60 under Ivan the Terrible

a

b

c

67. (A) The second room in the bath-house of the Imperial Palace in Delhi. Walls and floor white marble; fountain in the foreground. About 1640.
(B) Persian jug in the Minai technique, from Rhages. Text p. 201. Beginning of thirteenth century.
(C) Large hanging lamp, for use in a mosque; with ornamentation in enamel. Surian. Thirteenth century.

a

b

c

68. (A) Court of the Virgins, at the entrance of the Alcazar, Seville, begun by Pedro the Cruel and completed in 1402 by his successor.
(B) Interior of the mosque of Cordova.
(C) The Court of the Lions, in the Alhambra, Granada.

b

69. (A) The Taj Mahal, near Agra, the first capital of the Great Moguls in India. Built 1630 – 48, in white marble, by Shan Jehan, in memory of his wife.
(B) Mosque of Sultan Selim II, Adrianople. West view. 1568 – 74.

a

b c

70. (A) Horseman fighting. Page from a bound volume; originally, perhaps, an illustration to the Shah Nameh, the famous epic poem by Firdusi, Persia's greatest poet. About 1400.
(B) Iskender's fight with the dragon. Part of a gown of Persian brocade. In coloured silks, with gold and silver thread, on a light blue background. About 1600. (Kremlin, Moscow).
(C) Portrait of a Persian prince. Miniature from the school of the Sultan Mohammed. About 1530. (State Library, Leningrad).

fundamental features of Russian art are the division of the many internal compartments into two storeys, and the replacement of the original wooden gable-roof by pyramidal roofs of stone. Even in the days of purely Byzantine art these abstract forms had proved entirely in accordance with its spirit.

The Icons

In the whole of this period there is nothing to be said of Russian sculpture; even when there had been isolated attempts to introduce sculpture into the new national architecture, the old Byzantine dislike of the three-dimensional image persisted. Only in Novgorod, which was more open to Western influences, was there any exception. As early Russian architecture developed from wooden buildings, so the Novgorod school of sculpture was based on wood-carvings. It is significant that Novgorod had to employ a German bronze-founder (Fig. 66c), who was

Group of Russian cavalry. Miniature from the Slavonic manuscript of Silvestrovskiy Sbornik, containing the legends of St Boris and St Gleb

expected to produce bronzes in a flat style, like the few examples of Russian sixteenth-century wood-carving, one of the best of which is the throne of Ivan the Terrible (page 191).

The icon was originally derived from Byzantine mosaics, frescoes and miniatures. The desire to preserve popular legends in permanent form resulted, in Russia, in its development from the Greek image (*eikon*), and form the icon was developed an original Russian form, the painted screen or *iconostasis,* which was established everywhere by the fifteenth century. It became the chief ornament of the Orthodox church, assuming the function of the altar-rail, or of the curtain in an Oriental church. Like the proscenium of the Greek theatre, the iconostasis has three doors; through the centre one only priests may go. It divided the holy of holies from the faithful, in much the same way as the rood-screen in the Western church; but it played a much bigger part in the liturgy, and each individual painting on it had a definite meaning. A certain degree of freedom was permissible only in the representation of garments, in the backgrounds, and in separate small icons which did not form part of the icinostasis.

In the 'Book of the Council of the Hundred Chapters' of 1511 it is laid down that painting should not be done for gain, but only in accordance with the will of God. The painters were anonymous monks, whose work, accompanied by prayer and fasting, was itself a form of worship. With great care they prepared their panels of birch, pine or lime-wood, or more rarely, of cypress, scraping a flat surface in the centre, so that the protruding outside edges made a protective frame. The surface was primed with chalk and size, and the colours were mixed with yolk of egg. Strict rules regulated the palette; in early icons the background was gold or silver, but later, white, green and blue were added. As a preservative, the painting was coated with white of egg, which has an unfortunate tendency to darken.

The finest icons came from Novgorod, which escaped the troubles of the Mongol overlordship. When Prince Andrei Bogolyubski besieged the city in 1198 an icon was carried round the walls, and when the image of the Mother of God was pierced by enemy arrows she began to weep; this incident is the subject of one of the finest of the many splendid icons in the Novgorod museum.

The most famous painting of Eastern Christendom is the 'Vladimirskaja', the 'Holy Virgin of Vladimir', supposed to have come from Constantinople to Kiev, and from there, in 1155, to Vladimir. On the 26 August, 1395, it was solemnly brought into Moscow amid the rejoicings of the people; on the same day the Mongols are said to have been repelled from the gates. There are many legends about this icon. When Napoleon entered Moscow it was rescued from the burning Kremlin and later restored in triumph to the cathedral. Thorough examination has revealed what is left of the original, after six over-paintings and renovations, spread over as many centuries. These remnants, though experts differ on points of detail, reveal the Virgin of Vladimir who, in expression and posture, has always been an archetype in Russian art.

Next to the Virgin and Child, Saint George, the great martyr, is one of the most popular saints in Russian iconology. He is most often represented, not as the conquering hero (Fig. 66a), but as a solemnly enthroned Byzantine figure. All through the fourteenth, fifteenth and sixteenth centuries, which were the classic age of Russian painting, the Byzantine style remained the changeless expression of an unalterable faith, behind which all individual qualities disappeared. For this reason the few painters' names which have been handed down by tradition, such as Rublev or Rublyov, and Dionysios, have remained nothing more than names.

The Gate of the World

During the seventeenth century, Russian faith began to waver, and about the beginning of the eighteenth century Russia suffered a vast upheaval involving the whole intellectual life of the nation. The window which Peter the Great is said to have opened upon the West had never really been closed since the days of Ivan the Terrible, and the wind of doubt blew through it—the breath of the Reformation. During Peter's youth Russian faith declined, and when he came to the throne as Peter the First, a new age began for Russia.

After his first European journeys, which in 1697 led him through Germany and Holland to England, Russian life was entirely reorganized. The old costume was abolished, and anyone with a beard had to pay a high tax. New titles of nobility were created, and men of the people were promoted to the council of their sovereign, who made a bondwoman, Catherine, the first Russian Czarina. The contemporary of Louis XIV proclaimed himself a patriarch of the Orthodox church, introduced Western culture, and founded Latin schools and seminaries in all parts of the country.

Baroque Gatehouse over the entrance to the convent of St Laura, the oldest and most celebrated of Russian monasteries

Regardless of the masses of the people, and the ranks of the Old Believers, who had now become sectaries, he ruthlessly enforced his reforms and made Russia a European Great Power.

Architects were summoned from all parts of Europe—Germans, Dutchmen, Italians, Frenchmen—in order to create the new capital of Petersburg, named after the sovereign; to conjure out of nothingness the world metropolis, as Dostoevsky called it. The first plans were drafted by the French architect Leblond (1679—1719). In 1670 he sent for Domenico, a native of Lugano, known to the Russians as Andrei Petrovich Trezzini, who, amongst other things, built the fortress of Peter and Paul in its earliest form.

The brilliant achievements of the new age brought to a close a period of truly *national* Russian art.

In such buildings as the church of Peter and Paul in Yaroslavl (Fig. 65b) it had sounded its swan-song. It was as though the unrest and uncertainty of a period of change, as though the straining after something new, was striving to express itself in the long, slender throats on which the five 'imperial roofs' of the old Russia reared upwards from a substructure in which new laws were manifested. A painter, Simon Ushakov (1626—86), figured in this revolution. Some have called him the greatest of the Russian Old Masters, the Russian Raphael, while others regarded him as the perverter of Russian art when the innovator sought in his paintings (Fig. 66b) to liberate Russian art from its Byzantine incorporeality. In vain did the priests declare that it did not beseem the faithful to gaze upon such fleshly and sensuous images, and even to adore them The influence of the priest had gone the way of the old Russia.

After the middle of the eighteenth century, having discarded, under Peter the Great, all its Muscovite memories, the new Russia professed its adhesion, under the two Czarinas, Elizabeth and Catherine, to the spirit of Western Europe. So the old national art of Russia was merged into the international Baroque, and therewith into the secular art of the world.

Chapter XVII

THE ART OF ISLAM

*

Just as Byzantine art was connected with a religion rather than with any particular people, so the art of Islam is by no means exclusively Arab, but is based on the spiritual attitude of Islam—which means Submission (to the will of God)—the name given by Mohammed to the religion which he founded and preached. This was the second great attempt to develop and complete the Jewish faith.

Similarities in the character of Byzantine and Mohammedan monotheism produced a similarity in the art of the two religions. In spite of differences in detail, the art of each shows a tendency toward the abstract, with none of that confident surrender to the physical world shown by the Greeks.

It was not caprice, but spiritual compulsion, which made the Jews prohibit images; and this aversion led to the most violent and momentous disputes between Byzantines and Mohammedans. Byzantine and Islamic art, dictated entirely by religion, can only by appreciated if one understands their spiritual and intellectual foundations; and only then can one see how miraculous was the appearance in Europe of the Romanesque style, which enriched Christian art for the first time with a magnificent sculpture.

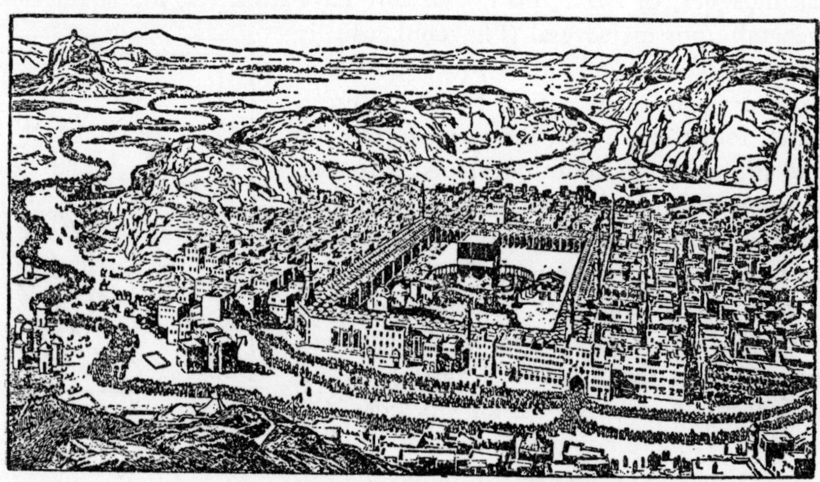

Bird's-eye view of Mecca, with the Kaaba surrounded by cupola-covered colonnades. The simplest form of mosque. (Breasted)

In the Islamic world, it can be seen clearly how a uniform religion, with the same ceremonial requirements everywhere, produced, even amongst the most dissimilar peoples, a remarkably uniform art. Nevertheless, the art of these various countries differed in detail, as did their political development. It is interesting to trace the various manifestations of that art which, together with the teaching of Mohammed, spread over a wide area; but it is necessary first to indicate the common requirements dictated by the spirit and the ritual of Islam.

Architecture and Decoration

The mosque is, above all, the principal form of Islamic architecture. At its simplest it consists of a rectangular court, the *haram*, with a basin in the centre to serve the purpose of religious purification, and often surrounded by colonnades roofed with cupolas (page 197). On the eastern side of the court, in the direction of Mecca, is the house of prayer; of no great height, it is divided by rows of columns. In the wall opposite the entrance is the *mihrab,* a niche or chamber which to a certain extent corresponds to the Christian altar. To the right of this is the high pulpit, the *minbar*, from which a sermon is preached on Friday, and to the left, farther from the wall, the railed platform, the *dikka*, on which is the *maksara*, the seat of honour reserved for the Khalif. The walls and piers are decorated with large plaques (Fig. 62b), on which are inscribed the names of Allah, Mohammed, and the four first Khalifs, and many quotations from the Koran. Candelabra hang from the ceiling, and the floor is covered with carpets or straw matting; but there are no chairs or benches. While the small mosques, or *mesjid*, do not usually have minarets, the larger ones, the *djami,* generally possess several (Fig. 69b), usually rising from the corners of the mosque, though in many cases a single tower stands beside it. From the minaret, four times a day, the *muezzin* calls the faithful to prayer. In its more developed form the mosque was entirely roofed with cupolas, and here the Byzantine example is obvious. Such mosques are often built in conjunction with the tomb of the founder, and with the *madrasah*, or college attached to the mosque, whose professors, in the summer, use the mosque for giving not only theological but also legal lectures, for the Koran includes the Mohammedan civil and criminal code.

Stalactite vaulting from La Cuba near Palermo

The domes are usually pear- or onion-shaped. The arch, when it has to carry a load, takes the old, traditional forms; but for decorative purposes the semi-circle is replaced by the horse-shoe arch, the four-centred arch, or the pointed arch. These different forms will be discussed separately later, when we come to considering the extent of Islamic influence on Gothic architecture.

Islam, however, was responsible for one new creation—the so-called *stalactite vaulting,* which sprouts out of a number of small niche-like vaulting-cells. It derives its name from the stalactite-like formation of the little stucco (or, more rarely, wooden) corbels, which hang from the joins of the masonry or cover the intrados of an arch; in the latter case they are often richly gilded, giving an uncommonly brilliant and picturesque effect. The great decorative value of this cellular mode of construction has always been emphasized, but it also provides a satisfactory way of hiding the corbelling in vaults and other points where a load is taken (page 198).

Arabesque with Kufic script. (Gayet)

In ornamentation the Mohammedan combines the abstract spirit of this religion with a sensuous and elaborate fancy; this striving after a decorative effect is most obvious in the arabesque, called after its inventors, the Arabs. This combines the stylized, organic forms of plants—leaves, shoots and tendrils—with the Arabic script, and is, on the whole, far more exuberant, and at the same time more spiritual, than the ornament of the Egyptians or Byzantines, who tended more towards simplification. The cursive script encouraged this tendency to cover large surfaces with ornament. In its oldest, rectilinear form, Kufic, so called after the city of Kufa (above), it was peculiarly in harmony with the austere spirit of the early Islam; while the later Islam, whose art was more sensuous and mellow, made more use of curvilinear forms (Figs. 67c, 62b).

The Origins in Arabia and Syria

The Arabs began to reckon time from the year of the Hegira (622), the flight of the Prophet to Medina; when Omar died in 644, barely a generation later, the new faith had already made subject the large area between Tripoli, the frontier of India, the Red Sea, and the Caucasus. At this time the Arabs had no art of their own, worthy of the name. The Kaaba, in Mecca, which they had worshipped long before Mohammed's birth, was the earliest expression of a form of worship which forbade any kind of image. Three hundred heathen idols which had been assembled there in the course of time were destroyed by Islam, and there remained only the famous black stone built onto the eastern corner of the cubical edifice. Once—the legend ran—it had been as white as snow; but the sins of humanity had blackened it. The great rectangular courtyard surrounding the sanctuary was given its present form in the seventeenth century, though the 360 gilded cupolas of the surrounding gallery date from the previous century (page 197). On the other hand, the Mosque in Medina built in the year 700, which contains the tomb of Mohammed, is like those described earlier in this chapter.

The first of the larger Islamic mosques with a circular ground-plan was the Mosque of Omar, on the Mount of the Temple, in Jerusalem, which, according to Oriental legends, was the central point of the earth. The famous Dome of the Rock is an octa gonal structure with two series of pillars, of which the inner series supports a large drum, bearing the dome. Here, as in the arcades of the rectangular mosques, the Mohammedans took any columns that were to hand—classical, Early Christian, or Byzantine—placing them without any regard for their type, since they could not lessen the beauty of an architecture which depended, not on the exact ordering of its parts, but on the brilliance of its decorations.

When the Mohammedans built mosques in the countries they had conquered they always made use of local architects; but when, as in Syria, they found Christian churches, they adapted them to the new religion. Thus, the great Omayyad mosque in Damascus was originally an early Christian basilica, with wonderful mosaics (Fig. 61b), and some of the workers employed in its reconstruction, in the year 707, were summoned from Constantinople by Khalif Welid I. In the same way, the mosque of El Aksa in Jerusalem was originally an early Christian basilica, which in its new form was given seven aisles and a cupola.

The Khalifs of the Omayyad period (661—749) removed their capital from Medina to Damascus; but no traces of their seculaı buildings remain there. Elsewhere in Syria we have the earliest examples of their secular architecture in the so-called 'desert palaces'. These always have the same open halls and wide courtyards, in which the nomads felt most at home. The adoption of the old architectural forms the Near East resulted in the building of something like monumental Bedouin camps, which are interesting for their picturesqueness rather than for their architectural qualities.

In the rich decoration of the magnificent desert palace of M'shatta (i. e. 'winter camp') in the land of Moab, near the frontier of the Roman province of Arabia, we see that the prohibition of images, which was based only on the oral utterances of the prophet, was by no means strictly obeyed in secular buildings. The temptation to profit by the skill of native artists was so great, and the *joie de vivre* of the Arabian magnates so imperious, that they could not bring themselves to give up their pleasure in the forms of all kinds of animals, wild and tame, and of individual human figures.

Together with M'shatta, the palaces of Ukhaidir, Kasr-et-Tuba, Kusejr Amra, and also, probably, El Kasr, at Rabbath Amman, date from the time of the Omayyads, when Islamic art was still feeling its way.

The New Persian Art

With the overthrow of the Omayyads in the year A.D. 750 the Arabic overlordship of the Islamic peoples was at an end. The Khalifate was transferred to the Persian

Abbasids (750—1258), who ruled the Mohammedan world no longer from Damascus, but at first from Kufa, and after 762 from Baghdad. Under Harun al Rashid (786—809), the contemporary of Charlemagne, Baghdad became one of the world's most brilliant capitals. By the Tigris and upper Euphrates—notably, at Rakka and Samarra—richly decorated mosques and palaces arose, and round, spiral towers which were the last offshoots of the old Oriental *ziggurat* (page 81).

The arabesque style of Kufa (page 199) gave way to a flatter ornamentation, in which the design repeated itself at short intervals. Combinations of polygons, circles, ellipses and stars replaced the twining foliage of the true arabesque, as well as quatrefoils, trefoils and conventionalized grapes and vine-leaves.

The intimate relation of Arabic and Persian taste in art brought the ceramics of Islam, in the home of the ancient Mesopotamian glazed tiles and bricks, to a perfection rarely equalled and never exceeded. From Baghdad the lustre technique, which was used even for the production of paving tiles, spread throughout Persia, reaching Egypt and Spain. Lustre, or the very thin glaze made from metallic oxides, was produced in an extremely skilful way, a gold lustre being superimposed and lightly fired over a previous glaze of stannous oxide. After turquoise green, the favourite colours were ivory white and cobalt blue, which were often combined on large vases.

In Rhages, a shining city of blue glazed bricks and tiles, the so-called Minai vases were produced (Fig. 67b), which are even rarer than the lustre faïence; they are painted in many colours on a white ground, with occasional touches of gold, and portray horsemen riding almost naturalistic horses; the Asiatic features of the riders on the later examples show the increasingly Mongolian character of the cities of Western Persia.

The Persian poet, Sadi (1175 - 1263), after a later miniature

After the death of Harun al Rashid the Islamic empire disintegrated into various more or less independent Mohammedan States. The empire had contained too many peoples. In the year 868 Egypt became independent; in 969 Sicily became an autonomous Emirate; while from 1070 onwards the Seljuk Turks extended their rule in Syria and Asia Minor. From the beginning of the thirteenth century the Mongolian hordes of Genghis Khan and his successors began to spread over Persia, and by the conquest of Baghdad in 1258 they extinguished the power of the Abbasids.

The new rulers embraced Islam, and Islamic art received a fresh impulse. For the Persians the Semitic faith in God had always been too arid and inflexible, and in the Mohammedan sect of the Shiites, in contrast to the Arab Sunnites, they overlaid original doctrines of Islam with various mystical and pantheistic ideas. Now fresh Asiatic and even Chinese motives found their way into Persian art. Towards the end of the fourteenth century the Mongol Tamerlane (Timur-Lengh), one of the most powerful and terrifying potentates of history, seized the empire of Genghiz Khan; and under his sceptre, in Shiraz, the city of roses, Persia's greatest poets sang their songs. Samarkand, in Turkestan, was for many centuries a brilliant centre of Persian culture. This Persian art is more luxuriant, softer, and more sensuous, more faithful to life, and therefore more inclined to imagery, than the art of the Arabs, Egyptians and Moors.

In architecture Persia produced a softer version of the pointed arch, transforming it into the four-centred arch, which was used everywhere, even in India (Fig. 67a). The minarets grew smoother, slenderer and taller, carrying under the pointed cupola only a covered gallery, which in those unquiet times was used not merely for the call to prayer, but also as a watchman's post. From the ruins and reconstructed fragments of the mosques of Kaswin, Ispahan and other cities the development of the mosque can be traced as far as the fourteenth century. The famous Blue Mosque of Tabriz is one of the most important Persian buildings of the fifteenth century, while in the sixteenth and seventeenth centuries, under the Safawids, a late revival set in, which produced many fine buildings, especially in Ispahan.

Most of the Persian miniatures date from the time of the Safawids. They reflect the brilliance of a Persian art and culture which were already many hundreds of years old, and were undoubtedly the highest that Islam had produced. Such plastic and graphic representation as was possible under Islam was realized in Persia. In the countless manuscripts of the *Shah Nameh*, the 'Book of the Kings', the miniatures (Fig. 70a) tell us of the brilliant and colourful life of those days, of the fighting, hunting and feasting; in the history of the prophet the religious devotion of Islam finds expression; and the many exquisite individual portraits (Fig. 70c) reveal a poetical feeling for Nature which the Persians may have owed to their acquaintance with Chinese art.

In the confluence of all the energies of the East, and the blending of the ancient inheritance of Persia with Mongolian and Indian motives, an art originated in Persia, under Islam, which to the Europeans of the Middle Ages became, as did no other, the symbol of the Oriental fairyland. Moreover, Persia, in the matter of functional building, as the heir of the classical art of Asia Minor, produced not only palaces, castles and mosques, but caravanserais, bridges and baths of truly monumental architecture.

The Textile Arts

Among nomadic peoples cloths of all kinds play the most important part in the household, and, according to the reports of contemporary writers, Mohammed's own house contained a great wealth of woven fabrics. In the tent which served as his presence-chamber in Medina all kinds of cloths and carpets were displayed. The prophet, who, until he was forty, when he ceased to care for earthly things, had worked and lived on the caravan routes as a travelling merchant, never lost his appreciation of beautiful fabrics, and his people bought them for him in the foreign markets. All the colours of the East, especially scarlet and gold, lay outspread on his divan; and the representations of figures which were gathered here from all parts of the world do not seem to have detracted from his comfort.

Europeans were interested mainly in the Oriental carpets. Nothing very definite can be said as to their origin, for carpets are of great antiquity, being among the prehistoric possessions of humanity. For nomads, who could not easily carry household furniture with them on their journeys, the carpet was almost the only substitute, enabling them to do without tables, chairs and bedsteads, as well as many ornamental articles.

The knotted carpet is a surprisingly late development. The oldest relics discovered belonged to the nomadic tent-dwellers of the Tarim basin in Central Asia, and were produced in the fifth or sixth century A.D. The earliest Islamic example is a fragment bearing a Kufic inscription, which must have been made about A.D. 1000. But down to the sixteenth century, owing to the very small number of old examples in existence, we have to trace its evolution in the paintings of European artists.

Briefly, its technique is that short tufts of wool or silk were knotted over the vertical threads of the ground-warp, so that by the serial insertion of weft threads a solid fabric was obtained, while the shearing of the loops produced a level surface. Among the most precious are the silk rugs and carpets manufactured under the Safawid dynasty; but many of the far more numerous wool rugs and carpets are equally beautiful. The earlier patterns are purely geometrical, but these are gradually replaced by geometrically stylized plant and figure motives, evenly distributed inside the ornamented border, while those of the Safawid period begin to show animals among scattered trees, bushes and flowers, while men and fabulous beings inhabit a flowery world.

We can trace a similar development in the other kinds of textile fabrics; especially in brocade, where metallic threads are mingled with silken. A Persian gown of the end of this period (Fig. 70b) reveals a graphic style which is clearly related to miniature painting, and is an excellent proof of the fact that Persian art was able to maintain its admirable standards for a very long time.

The simple sewn or embroidered Kelim carpets, which usually contain a geometrical rosette in an octagonal central field, were produced by the nomadic Turcoman tribes, and like the tufted Bokhara carpets, and the Afghan carpets, come from Asia, beyond the Persian frontiers. Their customary dark red tones, with deeper shades of violet and chestnut brown, cannot compete with the brilliant splendour of the Persian colouring.

Finally, the carpets of Asia Minor must not be forgotten, and above all the

Turkish tufted carpets. These are considerably later in origin. A favourite motive in eighteenth-century prayer-rugs is an arched gateway, enclosed between columns, which represents the *mihrab,* the prayer-niche, against a red background. Of later date are the Smyrna carpets, easily distinguished from the Persian by the longer double tuft of the knotted threads. In their design and colouring they have always paid greater regard to European tastes.

The Islamitic Art of India

Buddhism, under King Asoka, had for the first time united India from within, but under Brahmanism it fell apart, and the second integration was imposed from without. About the year A.D. 1000, the Mongolian peoples who had adopted Islam began their incursions from the north-west. From the beginning of the thirteenth century increasing numbers of mosques appeared alongside the pagodas of the Brahmans, and the imperial Mohammedan palaces rose beside the old royal castles.

The first Mohammedan empire of India was governed, from 1206 to 1526, by various dynasties, which alternately enlarged and contracted their dominions. Three Tartar dynasties in succession governed the empire from Delhi, until in 1398 Tamerlane—more properly Timur-Length, the lame Timur—who in thirty-five campaigns had not only subjugated Persia, but had pushed on to Moscow, and had conquered all the kingdoms of Central Asia in rapid succession, over-ran India as far as the mouths of the Ganges. Cruel and bloodthirsty though he was, he protected the arts and sciences, and in the year 1526 one of his descendants, the Great Mogul Babur, 'the Lion', founded in Delhi and Agra the powerful dynasty of the Great Moguls.

Various buildings in Delhi date from the period preceding 1526; in particular the Kutub minaret, 260 feet in height, and the tomb of King Altamsh; also the mosques in Ahmedabad Djonpur, Kulbarga, Mandu and Pandua. In all these there is a combination of Mohammedan, Persian and early Indian forms. If we follow the line of development we see how the Indian vitality and brilliance gradually surrendered to the much colder and soberer spirit of Islam. The teeming animal motives of Buddhistic and Brahmanic ornament were entirely discarded; only the black columns of destroyed pagodas were used for the courtyards of the new buildings which were erected on every hand.

Under the Great Moguls there was a synthesis of Mohammedan-Persian and Hinduistic forms. Akbar (1556—1605) was, like Asoka, a born ruler by nature; he was tolerant in his treatment of the Hindus, and thanks to his guidance there was a revival of art under Mohammedan rule. Under Shah Jehan (1628—58) it maintained its vitality, and it was not until the eighteenth century that it began very slowly to decline.

Besides Delhi and Agra, Adjmir, Djaipur, Fatehpur Sikri and Bijapur were cities in which magnificent mosques were built, and which had evolved their own

Mohammedan-Indian style. Very often they took over the ground-plan of some old Indian temple (page 95), in which case they possessed several courtyards, of which the innermost enclosed the sanctuary. Often, too, the gateways in the enclosing walls were equipped, after the old Indian fashion, with massive gate-houses. In bath-houses, tombs and palaces the four-centred arch was perfected, and in Bijapur, in the sixteenth century, cupolas were built with the profile of the pointed arch, a daring style in which Mohammedan art competed with European. Akbar's palace of red sandstone in Agra prepared the way for the lucid and classical style which reached its height under Shah Jehan, whose great mosque in Delhi is said to be the largest in the world; while the entrance-hall of his palace, one of the most remarkable examples of its kind, is like the nave of a Gothic cathedral.

Lastly, the Taj Mahal (Fig. 69a) which is often considered the most beautiful building in the world; there is no doubt that it is one of the most costly. Enclosed in a magnificent park, it rises from a square with resected corners in a regular system of chambers, which, connected with one another and with the four-centred niche that shelters the entrance, lead into the octagonal central chamber. Above this rises a twofold cupola; the inner cupola forming a dome of semi-circular section, while the outer cupola rises majestically from a drum. Every part of the building is decorated with inlay of marble and semi-precious stones, and even the windows consist of translucent and richly decorated sheets of marble.

The Taj Mahal is really a work of international art, for architects from all parts of the world were invited to take part in its construction. While it is uncertain how far Europeans may have co-operated in the work, such later buildings as were erected in India in the eighteenth century must be regarded as standing on the frontier of genuinely Oriental art. After the downfall of the Mogul dynasty the influence of Europe became increasingly powerful, preparing the way for a new integration of India by an external power—by the British Empire.

The Mediterranean Basin

In the Magrib—that is, in the West—Islamic art developed differently. Egypt's geographical position made her an interesting connecting-link. After she had become independent of the Khalifate of Baghdad in 868, an Arabic architecture, using the pointed arch, developed under the Tulunid dynasty; this was a consistent architecture, not engendered from the relics of ancient buildings. It surrounded its great courtyards with slender, uniform arcades. When in 960 the Shiite Fatimids from the west of North Africa conquered Egypt and founded Cairo as its capital, they built, in the course of the next two hundred years, a great number of palaces incorporating the pointed arch, all of which today lie in ruins, and of which only fragments have been preserved in the Cairo Museum. From these it is obvious that Egyptian art was dependent on the art of the Near East.

The last independent creations of Egyptian-Arabic art were produced under the Mamelukes, in the fifteenth century. Its buildings, as time went on, became more graceful and ornate, but also more characteristic and attractive. The courtyards were now often covered, and a dim light filtered through stained-glass windows into enclosures whose roofs were supported by stilted arches, pointed, but expanded in horseshoe form. This Arabic style was finally replaced by the much heavier Turkish style when Sultan Selim I conquered the country, and in 1517 turned it into a Turkish province.

Egyptian art was subject to various influences, but countries lying farther to the west, once they had been conquered by Islam, preserved the strict doctrine of the Prophet, as it had been taught in Damascus for more than three hundred years. In the west of North Africa, the true *Magrib*, there stands to this day the Mosque of the Olives, built in the year 732, with its assemblage of ancient Roman and Byzantine columns, and its minaret—here, as everywhere in the West, a massive square tower.

When the Omayyad dynasty in Damascus was overthrown by the Abbasids, Islamitic art was already so firmly rooted in Morocco, and also in Spain, that under the Moors, a people of Arab and Berber descent, a Moorish art was developed, which had a fertilizing influence on the western world.

In Cordova, in the year 786, Abder-rahman I began to build a great mosque, in the usual style, on the site of an ancient church. As the centuries passed it grew ever larger and larger, until at last, in the tenth century, a forest of two hundred columns no longer contented the faithful, and in its final form the mosque had no fewer than nineteen aisles and thirty-five transepts, with more than one thousand monolithic columns of every imaginable kind of stone. These columns of Roman, Byzantine and West Gothic origin are connected by horse-shoe arches; in the two Mihrabs and their adjoining chambers five small arches are contrived in the large arches, while the walls are covered with the most delicate marble inlay.

The luxuriant growth of the Cordova mosque (Fig. 68b) might be regarded as symbolical of the spread of Arabic-Moorish culture on Spanish soil, where in the tenth and eleventh centuries it was often greatly superior to the culture of the rest of Europe. Of the mosque in Seville (which was not, like the mosque of Cordova, afterwards preserved as a Christian church) nothing is left but the minaret—which was converted by the addition of a belfry into a campanile, the Giralda. The Alcazar, the palace of the Almohads, built in 1181, displays the so-called Mudejar style of the fourteenth century, a style adopted by the Christian rulers, who in building their magnificent palaces employed Moorish architects and workmen. Gothic forms of architecture were often included, with Hebraic designs and other accessories. Later alterations have deprived the Alcazar of much of its radiant beauty. Not only Gothic decorative motives, but even Renaissance forms have defaced parts of the old fabric; but individual portions of the great building, such as the Court of the Virgins

(Fig. 68a), are reminiscent of the wonderful Alhambra, or 'Red Palace' in Granada, begun by the Nasrid rulers in 1232. This magnificent building was completed in the course of the fourteenth century, and consists of a number of princely dwelling-houses, combined into a whole by means of communicating courtyards and halls.

The two finest courtyards, the Court of the Myrtles and the Court of the Lions, date from the second half of the fourteenth century (Fig. 68c). The Court of the Lions is so called from the twelve black marble lions which support the wide basin of a fountain. Here, on European soil, late Moorish art has, at last, hesitatingly ventured upon the sculptured representation of animals. Further, the vaulted ceilings of the three niches in the background of the so-called court-room show shadowless figure-paintings, but it is impossible to tell whether they were the work of Moors, or of Christian painters in the service of Moorish sovereigns.

Here, in the Alhambra, the abstraction of Islamitic art produces a beauty whose ultimate effect is always decorative and always avoids reality. Slender, delicate, finely articulated pillars only seem to support a wall that is actually a reinforced curtain hanging between piers.

Granada is still with us, but we can only guess at the Moorish art of Italy. The Christian Normans who were ruling over Sicily by the end of the eleventh century destroyed too many of the palaces and mosques of the Moorish rulers. Yet they themselves later employed Saracenic artists, and besides the country seats of the twelfth century (which are known as La Cuba, La Zisa, Favara and Menani) examples of stalactite vaulting and rich mosaic decoration show traces of Saracen art; so does the Capella Palatina in Palermo, where the Christian and the Moorish chivalry mingled, and where the great spiritual unity of the Middle Ages was consummated. It is hard to say what is Norman and what is Arabic in the cathedrals of Cefalù and Monreale, when Byzantine illusions and Islamitic stalactite-vaulting are combined in these Christian temples.

In concluding this survey of the far-flung and heterogeneous art of Islam we must not forget the art of the Turks, for it has endured longer than any other branch of Islamitic art, testifying to the spirit of Islam down to the present day. The art of the Seljuk Turks, which preceded that of the Ottoman Turks, was an offshoot of Persian art. But in Asia Minor the Seljuks acquired the Byzantine spirit, and at the same time the Ottomans entered upon the scene.

When the Ottoman Turks gained a footing in Europe, and when in 1361 they conquered Adrianople, which was to remain the capital of the Turkish realm until Mohammed II entered Byzantium as a conqueror and the heir to an empire, the two great currents of Byzantine and Islamitic art were joined. In the mosque of Selim II (Fig. 69b), the architect Sinan produced a building in which Byzantine theory and Islamitic taste were blended.

Under the domes and cupolas on the Bosphorus and the Golden Horn the

Christian churches were transformed into mosques, and Justinian's wonderful building, the church of Hagia Sophia, had become a Mohammedan house of prayer a bare three days after the conquest of Byzantium. Constantinople was the meeting-place of Byzantine and Islamitic art. The vast triangular area consisting of Russia, with her Byzantine art, in the north, and the Oriental world of Islam in the south, now saw the advent of the Christian Middle Ages, when the inheritance of Rome was taken over by Romanesque art.

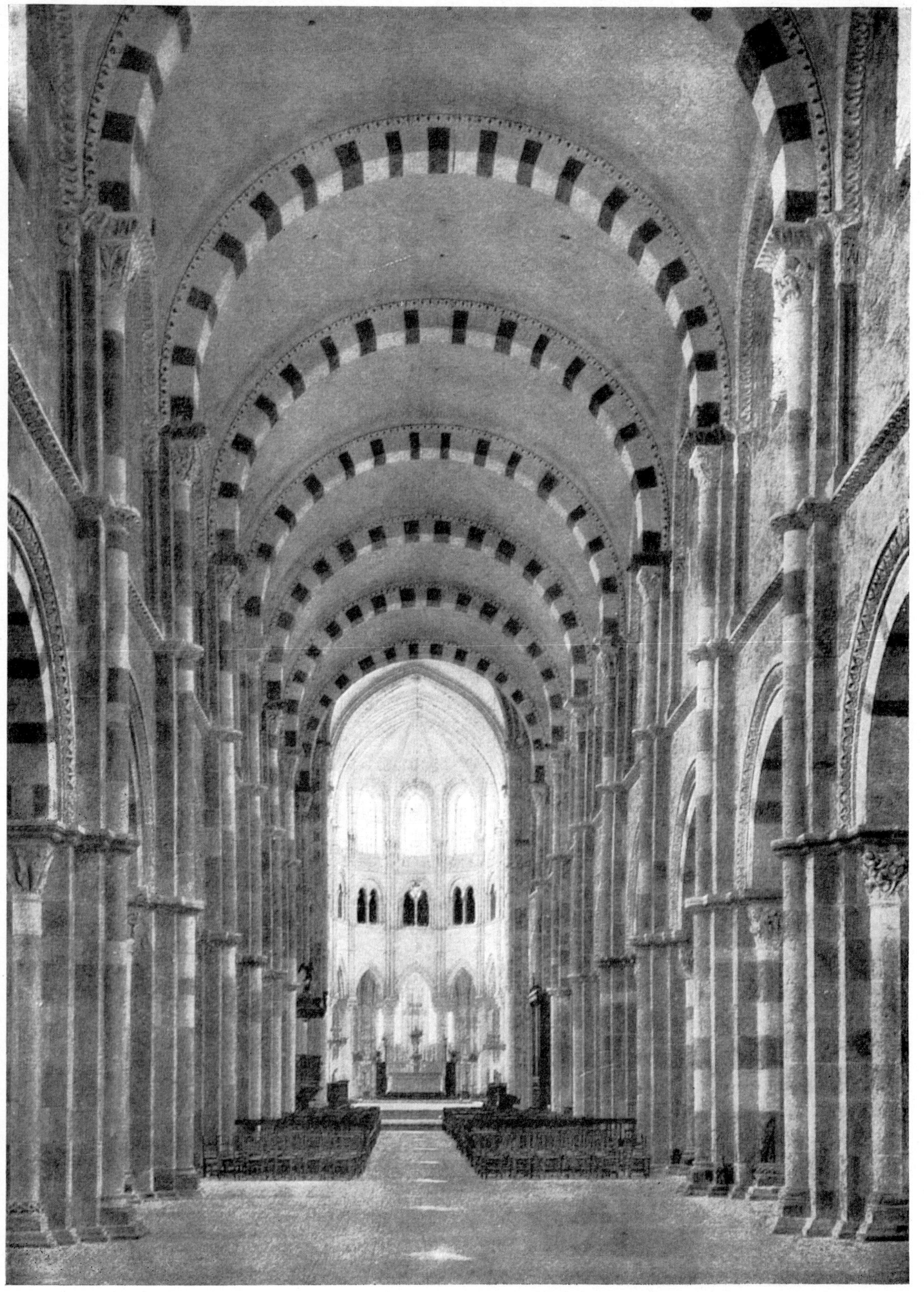

71. Interior of the basilica of Sainte-Madeleine, Vézelay. 1104 – 20.

a

b

c

72. (A) Part of a golden altar table from Basel Minster. About 1220. (Cluny Museum, Paris.)
(B) Figure of an Apostle from the screen of St George's choir, Bamberg Cathedral. About 1230.
(C) The Last Judgment. Table of the arch above the main entrance of the cathedral of Saint-Lazare, Autun.

a

b

73. (A) Two figures from the western doorway of the cathedral of Chartres. Second quarter of twelfth century.
(B) The Emperor Henry II and the Empress Cunigunde, on the left jamb of the Adam doorway of Bamberg Cathedral. About 1238.

a

b

c

74. (A) Worms Cathedral from the north-east. About 1200.
(B) Romanesque cloister in the monastic church of Königslutter. End of twelfth century.
(C) Twofold chapel in the castle, Nuremberg. About 1180.

Chapter XVIII

ROMANESQUE ART

*

THE term *Romanesque,* first applied by Caumont to the Post-Carolingian art of western Europe between the beginning of the tenth century and the middle of the thirteenth century, is more appropriate than the names of many other styles.

Between Romanesque and antique art there is an interval of many centuries, during which the Northern tribes made their entry into history. This period of folk-migration is one of prehistoric arts and crafts such as are already familiar to the reader.

Various discoveries of golden ornaments and coins show the long route followed by the Germanic tribes in their journey from the East into France and Spain. The careless and simple beauty of the jewellery of the Merovingian king, Childeric, who died in 481 (below), betrays the influence of classical traditions, which were not, however, just feebly accepted, but adapted in a masterful way, often without full understanding, much as one picks a flower where one happens to find it. The Merovingian period was not a bridge between antiquity and the Middle Ages; it produced no late flowering of the ancient culture and literature, such as Gothic-Roman culture did in the writings of a Cassiodorus or a Boëtius. After Theodoric the Great had secured a leading position by alliances with all the Germanic states, it seemed at first as though Rome, under Gothic rule, would peacefully combine the old and the new; but the Merovingians, under Clovis, made this impossible. In the East, Byzantium was able to hold out for some centuries only because she could draw upon the hardy highland peoples of the Balkans and Asia Minor. In western Europe the centre of evolution moved northwards, for there were its new sources of energy.

Golden Signet Ring of King Childeric I. From his tomb at Tournai

The old Norse decorative art is often discussed and described, but is usually misunderstood: emphasis is always laid on the interlacing straps or ribbons, the knots and loops, and unconvincing attempts are made to relate these to the technique of weaving. But more important than their ultimate origin is their autocratic disdain of symmetry, their avoidance of geometrical forms, and their restless, undisciplined energy. If one wanted to invent a new art to express an age of restless transition, one could imagine nothing more appropriate than this, which never derives its motives from geometry, but always creates a living and organic pattern.

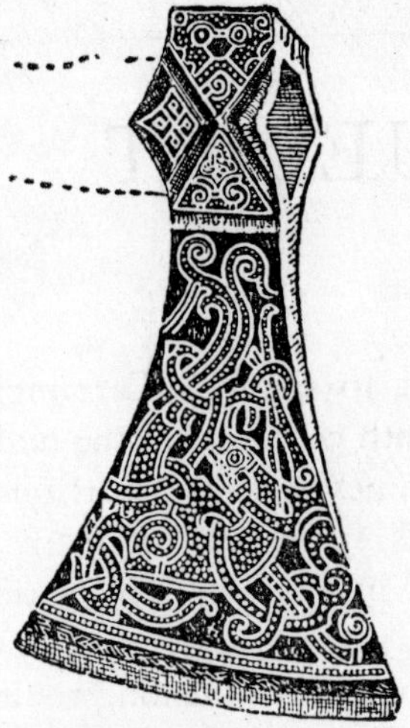

Iron axe-head from Jutland, with ornamentation of the Viking period

Irish decoration in a manuscript from the monastery of St Gall

In the illuminated manuscripts of the early Christian period, in particular those of the Irish and the Anglo-Saxons—peoples who as early as the fifth century had their Christian churches and monasteries—the spiritual character of this new art is clear. Thanks to the far-reaching missionary activities of the Irish monks, we have not only such priceless seventh-century illuminated manuscripts as the Book of Durrow and the Book of Kells, but also manuscripts with richly illuminated initials from such Continental centres as St Gall (above), Paris, Toulouse, and Laon (right). The art of Northern and Eastern Europe (above) is comprised in its lively trellis-work and in its animal motives, whether in the miniatures of its manuscripts, or the ornamental metal-work of tools and weapons, or the brooches of which so many have been discovered—the so-called *fibulae*. Only the West (right) is still faithful to the style of the Byzantine and Armenian miniatures, but without succumbing to hieratic stylization, indulging rather in the unruly, vital fantasies of the Age of Migration.

Merovingian-Frankish Miniature with stylized heads of the Evangelists in the form of their animal symbols. Title-page of a manuscript of Orosius. Laon: Public Library

In their architecture, on the other hand,

they were more influenced by Roman forms; indeed, this architecture was at first a synthesis of antique prototypes, rather than a new creation.

Carolingian Gatehouse at Lorsch

The tomb of Theodoric the Great in Ravenna; Charlemagne's chapel in Aix, built on the model of the church of San Vitale, and consecrated in the year 805; or the Carolingian gatehouse at Lorsch (above), are various stages in the acceptance of these traditional forms, which the new rulers adopted with delight, as they might have put on fine but unfamiliar garments. Thus the whole of the Carolingian period, from 700 to 900, must be regarded as pre-Romanesque, and in a certain sense as a survival of antiquity.

Spiritual Foundations

About A.D. 1000 the influence of Christianity had spread to all parts of Europe. Although the course of history, during this process, was not untroubled, and although the Middle Ages were disturbed by violent conflicts between Emperor and Pope, and by the Crusades, yet one cannot fail to realize the power and the unity of the feelings quietly at work behind the turmoil.

Followers of a faith which taught them to worship the Sun as the life-giving Power and personified the forces of Nature as gods, yet fearing life in spite of all their magic, the heathens encountered the Christian philosophy. It seemed to them that there was great magic in the Christian scriptures, and they painted the letters as living creatures. Knowledge of Latin taught them the values of a high and ancient civilization, to which they dedicated their unspoiled energies. For these peoples

Christianity was not a refuge for the weary, but a new assurance of life, an ordering of the universe such as they had not found in the old doctrine. Since there was a Judge in heaven, who looked into the hearts of mankind, and since the new faith told them, even to the least particulars, what was right and wrong, the young Christian could really look up to God as to a loving father in heaven. Only the general piety can explain the fact that the influence of authority was often incredibly disproportionate to its power.

While one cannot find a common denominator for the infinitely rich and varied life of many centuries, yet the Romanesque world does seem to be one vast community, united by Christianity. The Middle Ages have been called a night lasting almost a thousand years; but the night was bright with stars. In spite of the universal religious control, Romanesque, and much later, Gothic man, was able to realize his individual personality. Art needed powerful stimuli; at first there were churches and monasteries, then universities and religious orders, and finally states, cities, and individual patrons.

The result of all these various forms was that little remained of the antique forms, apart from the ornamental motives. The unifying sense of Romanesque art appears in the intimate union of poetry and music; metrical accentuations, and, above all, the rhymes, indicate the revival and independence of the sense of rhythm, to which the Latin quantitative metre had become unintelligible.

The founders of the monastery of Cluny, at the beginning of the tenth century, reformed the rules of the Benedictine Order in accordance with the spirit of the times, threw off the last traces of Byzantine stiffness, and established a spiritual order, above political confusion and threatening social dissolution, which made war upon ignorance and immorality and provided a refuge for scholars. This combination of religious idealism with organizing ability gave life a purpose; what remained after the disintegration of the Carolingian empire, which had been too closely wedded to antiquity, had now to find its place in the new religious community, which laid down the future conditions of European civilization. For everyone a spiritual attitude was prescribed, to which the individual was subordinated, and which was maintained in the peasant's hut as well as the king's court, in the monastic cell no less than in the bishop's palace.Only thus could such a personality as Bernard of Clairvaux, a simple abbot, not only govern the Cistercian Order for a whole generation, but rule the destinies of the entire Western world.

The finest expression of this monastic piety was the Romanesque style.

The Churches

In Romanesque architecture practical considerations were gradually superseded by aesthetic; from the outwardly simple meeting-house of the Christian basilica, the church, even in its external aspect, became a majestic monument.

The individual parts of the early Christian basilica survived the longest; but the whole aspect of the structure very quickly changed. The ratio of height to width, which in early Christian art were approximately equal, increased until the nave was sometimes twice as high as the building was wide. The bell-tower, the campanile,

Reconstructed view of the Benedictine church of Cluny in Burgundy.
(Dehio and von Bezold)

which had hitherto stood by itself, now moved up against the body of the church, which often had two such towers. At first the twin towers were built on either side of the façade, while the ground-plan assumed the form of the Latin cross, with a transept coming between the chancel and the nave. The crossing of nave and transept was crowned by a dome or a tower. In the apse, where the choir stood, there was too little room for the clergy, always very numerous in the great monastery churches; so the nave was continued beyond the crossing, providing a chancel for the choir. As a rule this was shut off from the nave and the transepts by stone barriers or screens, and the screen facing the nave often contained a sort of platform, the lectorium or lectern, from which the Gospels were read.

When wooden roofs, still very usual in the Romanesque churches, were abandoned —often for practical reasons, and on account of the danger of fire—in favour of vaulted roofs, the crossing of nave and transepts determined the whole ground-plan of the Romanesque basilica (page 221). On account of the strong lateral thrust the semi-cylindrical barrel vaulting was seldom adopted, but preferably the cross-vaulting which had already been used by the Romans for covering wide spans. This cross-vaulting is produced when two barrel-vaults intersect each other at right angles above a square ground-plan (Fig. 74b). The load is then carried by the four corner-posts or piers. But since the nave is twice as high as the aisles, the so-called engaged Romanesque system becomes a necessity. In this the square intersection or crossing determines the span of the rest of the nave, which is intersected at intervals by two bays from the aisles.

The columns of the nave which carried the heaviest load were gradually replaced by piers, until Romanesque architects came to use only the latter. As vertical components of the walls they belonged to the body of the building, while the columns were parts of the articulated structure; it was only in the late antique that they were inharmoniously burdened with masses of rising masonry. This substitution of the pier for the column in Romanesque architecture is a simplification comparable to the inclusion of the forecourt of the basilica (page 180) between the towers (page 221), whereby the ancient atrium became the so-called parvis, and the ancient font shrank to the proportions of a holy-water stoup.

Reliquary from the Guelph treasury, Vienna. The work of Cologne goldsmiths, about 1175

On the other hand, the old Roman colonnade or peristyle, was revived in the form of the cloister connecting the church and the monastery. The Romanesque church was almost always connected with a monastic foundation, in which all sorts of rooms were required for the community life of the monks —such as the chapter-hall for assemblies, the refectory for meals, and the dormitory for sleeping. The whole abbey was often surrounded with fortified walls and towers, and constituted a little self-contained city. As a rule, the only departure from the plan of the basilica was the baptistery, which was usually a transeptal building, such as is represented in miniature by the domed reliquary from the Guelph treasury (above).

In the North, however, larger churches, tending toward the cruciform or transeptal plan, were sometimes built over Roman foundations. Such was the church of St Gereon in Cologne. In the case of castle or fortress chapels the form of the double church was adopted in order to save space; here two chapels were built with the same plan, one above the other, the lower of the two often being used as a sepulchral chapel. Examples of this kind are to be seen, above all, in Nuremberg (Fig. 74c), Eger, and Goslar. The ordinary Romanesque church, where the whole of the chancel, the *presbyterium* was raised several steps above the nave, while under it was the *krypta*, a vaulted crypt, the burial-place of the founders of the church and other notable people, is a variation of this arrangement.

From these basic forms, the Romanesque architecture of Europe evolved ever richer, more beautiful and refined methods of construction. The various ways of applying and carrying out these methods in the individual portions of the fabric gave the Romanesque building its special character.

Architectural Monuments

In the foregoing chapters the term Romanesque is applied only to the art in which the Nordic peoples, after adopting Roman civilization, succeeded in impressing upon it a new and individual stamp, and Italy therefore is excluded; but the chief features of their Romanesque architecture will be mentioned in the chapter on Italian Renaissance architecture. To elucidate the main lines of development it seems better, for the moment, to say that the influence of antiquity (which one may describe as the proto-Renaissance) radiating from the South of France, was felt as far northwards as Cluny in Burgundy, the province on the frontier of the Celtic-French and Germanic populations.

In the great Benedictine church (page 213), begun in 1089, the Southern French barrel-vault was adapted to a cruciform basilica, of the type which had evolved in the North. Only from a reconstruction is it possible to realize the magnificence of this Romanesque building, which rose from the ground-plan of a two-armed cross, with its various towers, crossings and apses, and which, with its five naves and its two transepts, was regarded at the time as the most important church in Christendom. What cannot be seen from the few existing remains may be inferred from the details of the monastic church at Vezelay (Fig. 71), the Cathedral of Autun (Fig. 72c), and other French buildings. Compactness, and a tendency toward systematic sub-division were characteristic of Burgundian Romanesque; this may be seen also in the neighbouring churches of western Switzerland, in the porch of Romainmôtier, or the great collegiate church of Payerne.

Contemporary Norman buildings are far more primitive-looking. Where southern influences had not penetrated, even after the introduction of stone, the old system of timber construction dictated the form of the structure, and it was not until after the conquest of England in 1066, when the Normans ruled over wide areas of Europe, that their increased self-consciousness found expression in architecture. The conventual churches of Sainte-Trinité and Saint-Etienne at Caen, founded by William the Conqueror and his wife, and erected about this time, concentrate all their strength in the piers and buttresses, the walls being little more than connecting screens. A new chivalric order of architecture had made its appearance, from which the Gothic would presently develop in all parts of Europe.

It was in Germany, however, that the Romanesque architecture lingered longer than elsewhere, and produced some of its finest masterpieces. If we regard it as a style of a period of suspicion, then the buildings of the end of the close of the 'Staufisch' era must be included in it: the magnificent churches of Limburg, Bamberg and Naumburg, which, with other buildings of the period, are often attributed to a so-called transitional style, or to a separate 'German Gothic' style. These terms have little justification when we reflect that those buildings represent the completion and perfection of the Romanesque rather than a step towards a new style.

To describe the developments in chronological order: In the German-speaking East, as in Normandy, the ceilings of the basilicas—apart from the crypts and the apses—were for a long time always flat. The collegiate church at Gernrode, founded in 961, like the churches built on the model of the conventional church of St Michael, in Hildesheim, and the great basilica at Hersfeld, are of this type. So are the churches of St Emmeram and St Jacob in Regensburg, and the church of St Peter in Salzburg, which was restored after a fire in 1127; and the cathedral of Gurk in Carinthia.

In the Rhineland, in the course of the eleventh century, a series of cathedrals was built with vaulted ceilings. In 1016, the old cathedral of Trier was rebuilt; and from the same century date the three magnificent cathedrals of Speyer, Mainz and Worms (Fig. 74a). As well as the Romanesque ground-plan, imposed by the vault, they had the double chancel characteristic of German churches. This plan was introduced in the famous church of St Gall at the beginning of the ninth century, but is rarely seen south of the Alps, though one example is to be seen at Valpolicella, near Verona. One of the principles of the Romanesque style was to lay the individual stones of ecclesiastical buildings in closely-set courses; but in Worms we see a tendency - which came to fruition in Bamburg and Naumburg—to soften and enrich the rigid construction by ornamental forms of masonry.

The abbey church of Laach, in the Middle Rhine, discarded the conventional system, and to make more space the span of the vaulting was as great in the aisle as in the nave, with the result that the transverse arches of the bays were of different heights. It would take too long to describe these developments in detail.

A simplification of the prevailing style was effected in the monastery at Hirsau. The monks, who were trained in the Benedictine traditions of Cluny, always built uniform, flat-ceilinged, triple-naved basilicas, with the arches supported by columns, and without crypts, like the Minster at Schaffhausen. A typical building of the end of the Romanesque period is the Minster at Basle, with a polygonal chancel, a gallery, and a triforium above the arcades of the nave. In the Gothic period it was made wider, with five naves or aisles.

Of secular buildings the most important, apart from the first urban dwelling-houses, are castles and palaces. A fortified tower, the donjon, rectangular or circular in form, constituted the citadel, the place of refuge. As long as its defensive function dictated its form, aesthetic had to give way to utilitarian considerations. Only after the eleventh century were separate dwelling-houses built inside the larger fortresses, and then they were often decorated outside. Especially where the dwelling-house, as a prince's palace, was detached from the fortress and built in the open, as at Gelnhausen (page 217), the way was open for artistic developments. In the existing remains at Gelnhausen we see a trefoil arch above the entrance, beside groups of late Romanesque windows, and there is also a Romanesque gate-house, in the upper floor of which Romanesque rose-windows were probably inserted. The ornamental forms applied to secular buildings were those of ecclesiastical architecture. The walls

a

b

c

75. (A) The Minnesinger Walter von Hohenklingen (right) at the tourney. Page from the Manesse codex of songs. Early fourteenth century (Heidelberg).
(B) The Cathedral of Notre Dame, Laon. View of West front. The prominent counter-pillars before the portals were originally perforated. Façade between 1190 and 1210.
(C) Central portion of a late Gothic tapestry, representing card-players. Height, 42 in. Produced in Basle, about 1490. (Historical Museum, Basle).

76. (A) Notre-Dame, Paris. View from the south.
(B) South-eastern aspect of Wells Cathedral.

b

77. South-western view of the Cathedral of Amiens. Begun 1218; the lower part of the façade built before the middle of the thirteenth century, the upper part, in the fourteenth and fifteenth centuries.

78. (A) The group of the Visitation on the right side of the western mid-portal of Rheims Cathedral. On the left, Mary; on the right, Elizabeth. About 1230. (B) Two Prophets of the Old Testament from the right-hand side of the central door of the West front of Strassburg Minster. About 1310. (C) The 'Krumau Beauty', the Mother of God. Portion of a limestone statue with traces of an older setting. Height in all, 3 ft. 7 in. About 1400. (Kunsthistorisches Museum, Vienna). (D) Part of statue of a Prophet on the left wall of the main portal of Strassburg Minster.

were divided by pilasters, and by the round corbels characteristic of Romanesque art. Dwarf-arched galleries, like those built inside the churches, in the triforium, are often seen on the outside of Romanesque buildings (Fig. 74a). In these, as in the pillars of the naves, or cloisters (Figs. 74b and 74c) we constantly find the Romanesque cushion or cuboid capital. The transition from the round shaft of the column to the square spring of the arch is effected fairly neatly by the interpenetration of cube and

Reconstruction of the Imperial Palace at Gelnhausen.
Built about 1220

sphere. After the middle of the twelfth century, but not before, it was always ornamented. Other artistic features of Romanesque buildings will be considered under the headings of sculpture, painting, carving, etc.

Sculpture, Painting and the Minor Arts

Long after the ornamental animal motives of the period of migrations had been forgotten, sculptured animal forms of all kinds played an important part in the details of Romanesque buildings. In spite of their fantastic character, one can trace a definite development, an approach to greater realism. Nordic fantasies are mingled with the dragons, lions, basilisks and vipers mentioned in the Bible and in ancient fables, as we see them represented in the mediaeval bestiaries. The carvings so often found on windows, capitals, pedestals, friezes, corbels, tables of arches, and elsewhere, are the prelude, and accompaniment, of the sculpture of the human figure with which Romanesque art enriched the Christian world.

The invasion of the cultural area of the Mediterranean by the spiritual power of Islam in the eighth century had finally separated Europe from the Oriental world. While the influence of Islam aroused the first opposition to the veneration of images in Byzantium, Italy refused to take part in the great iconoclastic revolt. Many Byzantine artists, workers in mosaic and carpet-weavers above all, made their way into Italy, bringing with them such images of the saints as they could rescue. At this time Italy severed the political bond with Byzantium and elected the Frankish king as the protector of the Italian church.

Since the wall-paintings and sculptures of the Carolingian period have almost completely disappeared we know only from written records that the churches of the North were decorated with paintings like those of the South. There were two Northern additions to the iconography of the Italian church: the crucifixion of Christ and the Last Judgement, the latter being a theme which later Romanesque art never tired of representing. Still in rather low relief at first, the figures in the tympana of arches in the early cathedrals (Fig. 73c) are crowded together in confusion. Byzantine taste enclosed the figure of Christ in a *mandorla* (an elliptical aureole surrounding the whole figure; the word means, in Italian, an almond); the representation is more conventional but at the same time more plastic than was possible within the ancient nimbus. A century later the figures had become less conventional and national differences had modified the details.

The figures on the west front of the cathedral of Chartres (Fig. 73a), which were the work of one of the greatest of the mediaeval masters, still seem to be fastened to the pillars, but in the altar-front of the time of Henry II (Fig. 72a) the figures begin to step out of the flat surface. Their movement is still spasmodic and uncertain in the chancel screen of the Bamberg cathedral (Fig. 72b), but only a few years later, in the Adam doorway (Fig. 73b), they have the free and noble bearing of the figures of Naumburg, with their perfect individuality. These date from the beginning of the Gothic period.

It is difficult to form any comprehensive idea of Romanesque painting, and even harder in the case of the minor arts. At the beginning of the thirteenth century the West was flooded with examples of the minor Byzantine arts; but even before this, ecclesiastical respect for tradition had imposed the early Christian and Byzantine idiom. This idiom was very evident in Italy and the south of France; in Germany, the north of France and England it was gradually superseded. It is often very difficult to decide what was due to Byzantine influence and what to the individual, Nordic sense of form. For example, the coronation mantle of Henry II (page 220) is believed to be the product of a Bavarian convent. It was probably women's hands that gave the figures their naïvely natural attitudes, in spite of the respect for tradition shown by the symmetry of the design.

We must not imagine Romanesque churches as bare, empty buildings. Even the floors and the flat wooden ceilings were not without decoration. In the cathedral of Hildesheim, as in the crypt of St Gereon, in Cologne, there are brightly coloured mosaic floors. We have an excellent example of the paintings on the oldest ceilings in Poeschel's work in the church of Zillis, in the Grisons. Embroidered carpets and tapestries adorned the floors and walls, the altars and stalls. The long, frieze-like tapestry of Bayeux, worked in coloured wools on white linen, which described the conquest of England by the Normans, is one of the best-known examples. The cloisters on the Island of Reichenau, in Lake Constance, as early as the tenth century an active artistic centre, enable us to form some notion, from the wall-paintings which are still preserved in the church of St George, at Oberzell, of the permanent wall-decorations to be found in almost all the larger churches of the time. The paintings run along the walls between wide borders of scrollwork, and on the mitres of the arches in the arcades the busts of saints, or of superiors of the Order, are set in medallions. Where the pictures are not easily comprehensible they are elucidated by metrical inscriptions, *tituli*.

Stained-glass windows soon began to replace the tapestries: as early as 1000 the Abbot of Tegernsee boasted of their beauty. In Zürich, at Werden, on the Ruhr, and in many other monasteries, there were stained-glass windows even earlier. It is less easy to say when they were first introduced into France and England, but in the Early Gothic cathedral of Chartres are various medallions rescued from the old Romanesque cathedral, which in their strictly linear designs, have retained a wonderfully luminous colouring. According to written records, Saint-Remy, in Reims, had stained-glass windows in the second half of the tenth century. After 1100 their use became general.

The Flight into Egypt. Medallion from a Romanesque stained-glass window in the cathedral of Chartres. (Gélis-Didot)

As well as sculpture and stone-carving, the art of ivory carving was practised with enthusiasm in the Romanesque period. Ecclesiastical accessories of all kinds, in particular, reliquaries, which could be set up in the house like little altars—or even carried by the owner when travelling—and fine book-covers, and many other treasures, have been preserved.

No less important, and no less assiduously practised since the time of the Saxon emperors, was the art of metal-working. In Hildesheim, under Bishop Bernward, was a school of bronze-casting, whose masterpieces, the Bernward pillars, the bronze doors of the cathedral, and the font, show how greatly this art, originally of the Age of Migrations, had been refined in the Romanesque period. At first the antique forms and Byzantine attitudes were adopted, but later on there was a new refinement. By the end of the eleventh century the peoples of the West had chosen to go their own way, even in the minor arts. From the twelfth century onwards the Crusades, with their flocks of pilgrims, the merchants, the craftsmen who wandered to and fro across the face of Europe, and the troops of stonemasons and goldsmiths who travelled from place to place, were preparing the West for that secularization of art which finally wrested it from the exclusive possession of the monks.

Romanesque embroidery in gold on Byzantine silk.
The so-called coronation mantle in Bamberg Cathedral

First of all, in the minor arts urban industries appeared which rid themselves of the last traces of Byzantine influence, so that even where the church was still the employer, the popular taste had more scope. Gold was replaced by copper and bronze; the process of enamelling on copper made possible a more independent and fluid treatment of the metal base and the enamel than was possible with the more costly Byzantine technique. One can see, even in the minor arts, the same sort of liberation that occured in monumental architecture in the thirteenth century; nothing more or less than the expression of a new spirit, a new taste: the Gothic.

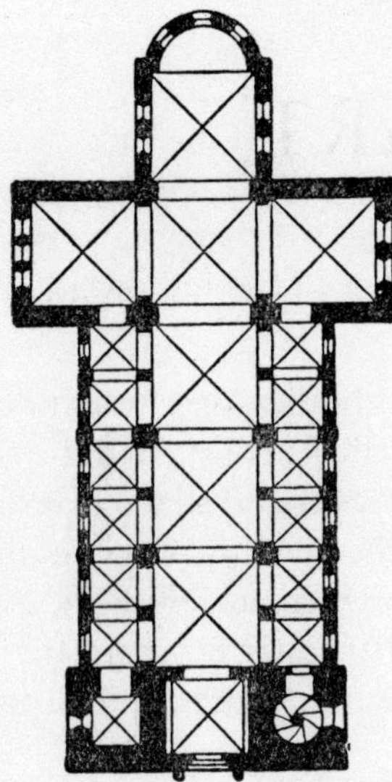

Ground plan of a Romanesque church. Engaged system. Text page 213

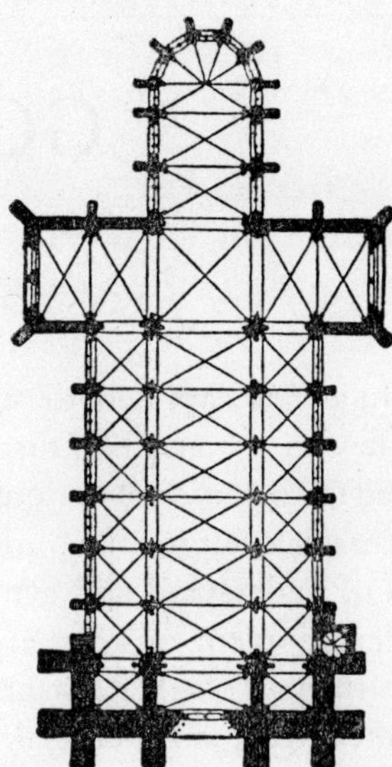

Transformation of the Romanesque system by the Gothic. Text page 226

Chapter XIX

GOTHIC ART

*

THE term *Gothic,* applied to the style of the late Middle Ages, was first used by Vasari, half in jest and half disdainfully, since the Italians considered the Goths had destroyed the beauties of antiquity. In this word was expressed all the aversion which the Renaissance felt for the Middle Ages, as well as the inability of the southern sense of form to understand and sympathize with the northern achievement. For Gothic was a development of northern Romanesque, and there is no sharp dividing line between them. To call Romanesque the style of the round arch, and Gothic that of the pointed arch, is superficial.

To understand the nature of Gothic art we must remember the gradual stratification of mediaeval culture. It began in the cloister, and Latin became the language of the educated classes in the West. For a long while the clergy hesitated to defile their parchment with the speech of the common people, although they wrote down the Strassburg oath of Ludwig of Germany in 842, and after 1000, the first Italian and Spanish clauses appear in title-deeds.

Romanesque art had represented unity in multiplicity, but it could impose this unity on a heterogenous culture only while it was supported by the two powers which were intimately related to it; namely,the secular power of the Empire, with its spiritual consecration, and the spiritual Papacy, always striving for secular power. In time, the Church became increasingly divided between the monastic orders and the clergy, who had very different aims, while the secular power came into violent conflict with its vassals. While their faith, with its conception of a future life, urged men to fear God and flee the world, in practise they often behaved with the most savage cruelty and unbridled sensuality. In a later century Dante deplored this divergence, which had long been realized by those who renounced the world to enter the cloister, or took refuge in the dream-world of poetry. Heroes, beautiful women, benevolent saints--these were the noble and consoling figures, human in spite of their fantastic trappings, to whom people looked up in admiration. As the world of monkish imaginings became replaced by one of chivalric fancy, the cult of the Virgin Mary, which was constantly increasing, changed too: the homage of courtiers raised the Mother of God to a new position as an adored mistress; she now became Domina, Madonna.

The transformation of form which occurred in Gothic art reflected a change in the whole of Western culture; the isolated Romanesque monasteries and castle were succeeded by cities, in which evolved a society different from that which had gone before, but which was still held together by the international conception of Christendom. In crowded towns the Gothic cathedrals arose, built by secular hands. Chronicles and charters tell of the religious impulse that inspired both nobles and common people in the time of the Crusades.

The fact that the whole people participated in it, explains the secular temper of Gothic art. A cheerful and human realism took the place of the old hieratically stylized forms. Instead of the antique acanthus-leaf, thistles, oaks and vines appear as decorative motives; this is part of the same naturalistic tendency to be found in mediaeval literature, which presented the legends of the Virgin, and the miracle and mystery plays, in a robust and realistic idiom.

While the greatest achievements of Romanesque art expressed an absolute subjection to authority, Gothic art, at its height, was the synthesis of late mediaeval thought, the accommodation between spirit and matter, God and the world. When the men of the Age of Enlightenment declared that the scholastic philosophy was nothing but an attempt to drive the camel of faith through the needle's eye of reason, they forgot that the scholastic philosophy flourished, not after mysticism, but at the same time.

The flat-roofed Greek temple, standing serenely content in this world, and the Gothic cathedral, restlessly aspiring to heaven, express two fundamental attitudes of mind, which have always affected art. The difference between High Renaissance and Baroque has the same foundation. For this reason a final survey of these influences may be left to the chapter on Classicism and Romanticism.

The Origin in France

The Gothic style, as a pattern for the whole Western world, first originated in France, and only by starting there can we understand it, trace its development, and follow its changes in other countries. In France, the system of chivalry evolved more rapidly and brilliantly than elsewhere; language blossomed in poetry, and scholasticism was taught everywhere, not only in Paris; France stood on the summit of Western culture. Art was no longer confined to the courts and the old, aristocratic monastic orders, but became the common possession of the lesser nobility and the merchant class, and also of the new Orders of Franciscan and Dominican friars, who mixed with the people.

In this beginning of a new age the new Gothic style was born, though no one realized this at the time. When Abbot Suger of Saint-Denis, in 1140, began the chancel of his Abbey, consecrated on the 11 June, 1144, before a select congregation of secular and spiritual princes, he did not suspect that he was present at the birth of a new style. In a very thorough and detailed account he recorded everything from the quarrying of the stone to the inscriptions on the superb stained-glass windows. Yet there is no reference to the new style. For the men of that age Gothic was the natural expression of their essential selves.

When the Gothic style, after long oblivion, was at last rediscovered, it was some time before its development was thoroughly understood. The statement of Lefèvre-Pontalis, at the end of the nineteenth century, that 'Gothic art in its entirety has its origin in the ribbed vault, which, like a grain of corn, contains the germ of a rich harvest', expressed the general opinion of scientific positivism, and was repeated as late as 1922. If this is correct, then a technicality was the origin of a style which was to last for centuries and influence sculpture and painting no less than architecture.

One might go further, and mention the Islamic pointed arch which the Crusaders saw in the East; to say nothing of the influence which Arabic literature and the Arabic humanities had in France about this time. That, in the matter of decoration, Gothic art owes much to the East cannot be denied; but no one who looks at a Gothic cathedral without prejudice will be able to explain it by the ribbed vault, or by the model of Islamic art, which is not functional, but decorative in its intention.

It was not until the psychological studies of the present century that a correct approach to the problem of the origin of Gothic architecture became possible. During the last century an enormous wealth of detail was collected, and now, after further research, we have a definite idea of the order of succession of the individual buildings and can to some extent explain the origin of the Gothic style.

There are many churches of the transitional period with groined vaulting or pointed arches, which remain essentially Romanesque in conception; while on the other hand there are Gothic churches which incorporate ancient forms. If we are to draw the dividing line between Romanesque and Gothic, knowledge of the individual parts is less important than an understanding of the architectural conception as a whole.

On page 215 we mentioned the churches of Caen, one of which, Saint-Etienne, was consecrated in 1077. Although only parts of it have preserved, and although the chancel has been restored, it shows, in purely Romanesque terms, an intention that would in itself have been enough to start a new style. The huge west front, built about 1080, rises above an inconsiderable base, and the upward-pointing tendency is unmistakable; but only in places does the building break away from the cubic mass and begin to *move*. More interesting than the cathedral of Angers and the Cistercian church of Pontigny, which in Anjou and Burgundy embody the early Gothic, is the cathedral of Laon, begun about 1165. Its façade (Fig. 75b) shows clearly that the transition to Gothic could be carried out quite independently of the pointed arch. Here the architectural tendency of the twelfth century, the period of the French Early Gothic, is expressed with wonderful completeness. No line, no surface, exists any longer for its own sake, as in the Romanesque building (Fig. 74a). If one imagines the towers of Laon bearing tall octagonal steeples, each storey loses its

III. Rogier van der Weyden (c. 1399–1464): Portrait of a Lady.
(National Gallery, London)

79. Interior of Cologne Cathedral, looking eastwards. Text p. 229.

a

b

c

d

80. (A) Part of the south front of the Doge's Palace, Venice. Fourteenth and fifteenth centuries. In front, the colun with the Lion of St Mark; beginning of thirteenth century.
(B) Eastern wing of the Council House, Tangermünde. Märkish brickwork. First half of fifteenth century.
(C) Cloister of Gloucester Cathedral. 1351 – 77.
(D) The great refectory in the Marienburg, West Prussia. The former banqueting-hall of the castle, built under the Grar Master Dietrich von Altenburg (1335 – 41).

a

b

c

31. (A) West Front of Florence Cathedral, begun in 1296. At the right a part of the Campanile, constructed by Giotto, 334 – 36. The dome was completed by Brunelleschi in 1434. The façade was finished in the nineteenth century. In the left oreground, the Baptistry, an early Christian creation, restored about 1200.

B) The Palazzo Vecchio in Florence. Begun in 1298 by di Cambio.

C) Façade of the Ospedale degli Innocenti, the Foundling Hospital in Florence. Begun by Brunelleschi in 1419.

a

b

c

82. (A) Donatello: Marble statue of St Mark the Evangelist 1412 (San Michele, Florence.)
(B) Botticelli: The Annunciation (Uffizi Galery, Florence).
(C) Giotto: The Massacre of the Innocents. 1303 – 5. (Capella Scrovegni, Padua).

obvious delimitation, and seems to grow on to the next. By means of connecting links a sense of lively movement is instilled into the fabric, which thrusts itself vigorously upwards, not in a single rush, but with repeated efforts, while the diagonal corner-pieces give oblique views that catch the eye from every point of view.

By the twelfth century, in the cathedral of Chartres, and in Notre-Dame in Paris. (Fig. 76a), the next stage of this logical development was reached. The cathedral of Reims, begun in the year 1212, is even freer and bolder in form. Finally, all the earlier tendencies were brought together in Amiens cathedral, built in 1218—88 (Fig. 77), and the purest embodiment of the Gothic style, which gave an example of the 'High Gothic' from which the whole of Western Europe had much to learn.

Such pure forms are of great importance to the modern observer, who only too easily forgets that whole generations worked at the building of the mediaeval churches, most of which are Romanesque churches restored or enlarged by Gothic builders. Thus, at Amiens (Fig. 77), we see four-centred window-openings high up in the left-hand tower, and the great rose-window in the centre bears the characteristic fish-bladder pattern of the *flamboyant style,* as late Gothic was called in France from the beginning of the fifteenth century. A fine example of the high Gothic form of the rose-window is in the transept of Notre-Dame (Fig. 76a). The classic age of 'High Gothic' in France coincides approximately with the reign of St Louis (1226—70). In a very short time the country was covered with new cathedrals, built of shining white sandstone. In the volatilization of architectural masses this art reached the limits of the possible. For example, the Sainte-Chapelle, in Paris, begun under Louis IX in 1243, is a church with a single nave superimposed on a church with three aisles; in its superstructure the wide quadripartiete windows have almost entirely replaced the wall.

By comparison with the magnificent new churches in Normandy and the centre of France, those in the southern part of the country, as a result of the proto-Renaissance there, were rather cold and unimpressive. Only in Burgundy did a small group of churches adopt the Gothic style, and pass it on to Geneva, and to Lausanne, where there is the finest Gothic cathedral in Switzerland.

After the Gothic had reached its height in France, and had come to its logical climax, there was a natural pause. In Normandy, the old lucid, but rather sober spirit of the country made itself felt again; less in the construction of the great cathedrals, like that at Rouen, than in the new buildings at Coutance and Bayeux. The Bourges cathedral followed the model of Notre-Dame of Paris; it goes back to the year 1179, but was finished, after many delays, only in the fourteenth century. It has five aisles, and the two inner aisles, as in the chancel of Le Mans cathedral, are higher than the outer ones. This tends, of course, to break up the spatial unity of the interior, but it does not fully express the essential spirit of the Gothic system. This system must now be briefly described, so that it may be seen how the Gothic style, evolved in France, was adopted in the rest of Europe.

The System of Construction

Something of the old Romanesque plan (page 221, left), survives in the plan of a simple Gothic church (right); in the classical cathedral (left) it is elaborated and refined to the last degree. Constructional needs brought about the change. The Romanesque round arch required very massive piers to support the weight of the walls, but even so the thrust of the heavy cross-vaulting constantly threatened to push the walls out of plumb. The attempt to relieve them of their load led inevitably to the pointed arch, which made the lines of pressure more nearly vertical. More important was the possibility, given by the pointed arch, of covering spans of unequal size by arches of the same height. This restored the freedom which was lost in the Romanesque 'engaged' system. Now the tyrannical quadrate of the central nave could be divided into two rectangles, each of which harmonized with a square bay of the transept. The difference between the pillars of the arcades and the pillar of the bays was abolished; the rhythm was less insistent, but the orchestration was far richer. The heavy vaulting, which dictated the whole structural system of the Romanesque church, was replaced by light fillings which were spread as panels between the intersecting ribs (Fig. 79). The ribs alone, instead of the whole of the heavy vault, carried the load.

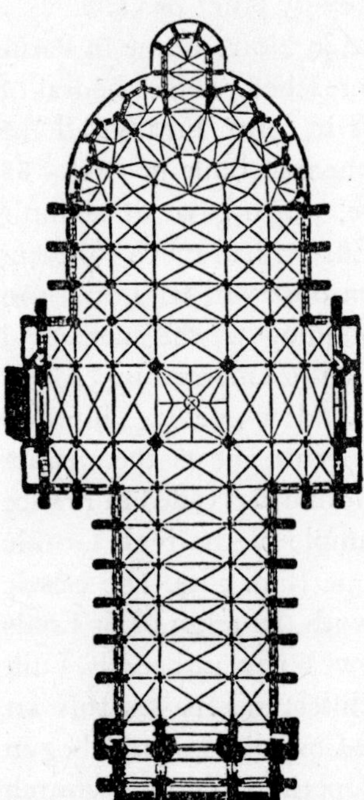

Ground-plan of the Gothic cathedral of Amiens. (High Gothic)

In order to prevent the walls from being thrust out of plumb, the Gothic building had strong counter-pillars on its outer walls, from which flying buttresses, like supporting arms, reached over the side aisles (Fig. 76a, right). The structure was put on the outside of the building, so that the nave could rise freely upwards. In Romanesque churches the ratio of height to width was 2 : 1, it now became 3 : 1 and even more, so that the eye could no longer take it in. The nave had three or five aisles, while the transept usually had three. The side-aisles continued round the polygonal chancel, the elaborate plan of which now offered no difficulty, since the most complicated areas could be covered with vaulting. Pillars take the form of clusters of half- and three-quarter-columns (the so-called vaulting-shafts), so that the cylindrical nucleus almost disappears. The ascending portions of this cluster, which support the longitudinal and traversal ribs, are stronger than the others, while the slighter shafts join the diagonal ribs.

From these clustering stems the stone seems to stretch upwards, like a plant so that one is never conscious of the downward-impending load. The capital loses its original significance as a support; now, sparingly employed, it becomes an accent in the rhythmic scheme.

To avoid any look of weight on the outside of the Gothic cathedral, small pinnacles are placed on the flying buttresses. Above the quadrilateral body of the pillar rises the pyramidal spire (right). On the corners of the masonry little crockets creep upwards, joining, at the summit of the spire, in a finial. Sometimes the ornaments are shaped like living beings, as when the gargoyles take the form of animals. The greatest concentration of ornament is on the façade. Above the doors, which repeat the motive of the roofs, rise pointed gables with their hood-mouldings, the triangular space being filled with Gothic tracery of the kind that fills and frames the pointed windows. It was on the 'royal galleries' which in French Gothic often appear above the doors, and especially on their jambs-stones or casings, that the Gothic sculptors lavished their greatest skill.

Counter-pillar flying buttress and pinnacle on Strassburg Minster, with typical ornaments, such as gargoyles, crockets, etc.

Sculpture and Painting

To understand Gothic sculpture we must first consider it in France. At that time the South of France was still rich in antique sculpture, which the sculptors of Saint-Trophîme, in Arles, Saint-Pierre, in Moissac, and the abbey Church of Saint-Gilles, took as models. The Roman practice of making the porch a decorative feature was far better adapted to the Gothic than to the Romanesque, where the self-contained, cubical fabric was entered only by doors with shallow frames. In Gothic architecture it was for the first time possible for the inexhaustible wealth of forms, which the imagination of a whole people had gradually created, to display itself on the wide doors.

The group of the Visitation at Reims (Fig. 78a), in which Mary seems to move with the light step of youth, while Elizabeth has the austerer bearing of an elderly woman, shows, precisely because these figures are represented in classical costume, what the North had made of antique art. Here the Gothic ideal of the human figure is clearly revealed. Throughout Europe, in France, as in Germany, a wise moderation had become the standard of aristocratic life. In spite of differences of style and costume, the prophets of the Strassburg Minster (Fig. 78b and 78d) and the Krumau Virgin (Fig. 78c), with calm nobility, make the same restrained and solemn gestures. The human body, for the Greeks the expression of the soul, had now to surrender to the idiom of raiment. The body, which Francis of Assisi had called Brother Ass, was for the Gothic artists a nonentity. Even as it vanished for the mystic, so for the sculptor it disappeared within the muffling garments; but the head still rose from it, the eternal expression of the spirit.

From 1250 in France, and from 1300 in Germany, these churches were built almost entirely by secular architects and stonemasons. The old corporations of masons were replaced by permanent guilds. Individual masters and pupils sometimes distinguished their work by their private marks, but they were all inspired by the same ideal, and Gothic sculpture can be regarded as a homogenous creation. Though the figures on Notre-Dame, in Paris, suffered during the French Revolution, and in the nineteenth century were restored by Viollet-le-Duc, we can study the comparatively early and austere style, related to the style of these figures, in the statues around the door of Amiens Cathedral, which were made about 1240. The figure of Christ at the main entrance, 'le beau Dieu d'Amiens', bears a suggestive resemblance to the two thousand figures and reliefs, large and small, of Chartres (Fig. 73a), in most of which the Romanesque stiffness still survives. But it is in the main façade of Reims cathedral, built at the end of the thirteenth century, that French Gothic sculpture reaches its highest level.

For wall-paintings the cathedrals, with their skeleton structure, and their lack of wall-space, had far less room. For effects of colour they had to rely on stained-glass windows, which had now become very much bigger than in the Romanesque period. Eventually, as the wealth of the cities increased, embroidered and woven fabrics appeared, with ornamental designs and representations of the human figure, in which the Gothic style exhausted its ingenuity (Fig. 75c).

In all other arts the new style was triumphant. Altars and sepulchral tablets (page 229, as well as secular buildings, were decorated in the Gothic style. The illumination of manuscripts took on a fresh impetus, the simple pen-drawing being emphasized by a more generous application of colour.The artist was no longer content with lightly brushing in the roughly sketched outlines, but carefully filled them with body-colour. An example of this is the manuscript of songs known as the Manesse codex —Manesse being the name of a Zürich family—which contains 140 pictures by three different artists. (Fig. 75a).

In the second half of the fourteenth century, towards the end of the true Gothic period, especially in Germany, and above all in 'Golden Cologne', which was then, thanks to its trade and industry, richer than ever, various schools of painting were instituted. Inspired, if not by the spirit of mysticism, at any rate by an emotional enthusiasm, they produced altar-pictures and panels in which—as in the charming idyll of the 'Madonna in the Rose-Garden'—a new sense of natural beauty appeared. Art was gradually ceasing to be anonymous. Such names of painters as we know, like Stephan Lochner, are more than mere names. Besides the painting in Cologne cathedral which was the masterpiece of this artist, who was working between 1442 and 1452, there are a number of compositions, such as the 'Madonna with the Violet', the 'Madonna in the Rose-garden', in which the Middle Ages seem to bid us a smiling farewell.

Angel playing on rebeck. Engraved on a bronze sepulchral tablet, Schwerin

The Diffusion of Gothic Art

'High' Gothic, as it evolved in France, was always an alien form in Germany; there the most magnificent monument of Gothic art, the cathedral of Cologne, whose foundation-stone was laid in the year 1248, came to a standstill after the completion of the chancel. The building dragged on into the sixteenth century, but by 1560 both the will and the means to do any more seemed to be exhausted. Work was begun again in 1862 and by 1880 it was finished. Its ground plan was designed in the Middle Ages on the lines of Amiens (page 226) and Beauvais. The interior, with the light pouring into it (Fig. 79), gives a perfect impression of the classical Gothic cathedral.

In 1208, before Cologne cathedral was begun, the chancel of Magdeburg cathedral had been built after the French pattern, and between 1227 and 1243 the Liebfrauenkirche at Trier was built in the form of a circle intersected by a cross, in contrast to the usual French plan. On the Rhine, at Strassburg or Freiburg, the western influence was still at its strongest, but this was no longer the case farther east, though even there, as the chronicles often record, churches were built by *opere francigebo*—stonemasons brought from France.

Cologne, Monstrance

By its brick buildings, a material which demanded a simpler form of ornamentation and a different arrangement of the walls, north Germany enriched the Gothic style. The inexpensive material made it possible to plan large buildings, of which the most brilliant example is the Marienburg, which displays in its great banqueting hall (Fig. 80d) the consummate skill of the late Gothic.

With these, and with such buildings as the Hallenkirchen, or the church of St George, at Dinkelsbühl, one comes to a point beyond which new architectural forms were created, which will be dealt with in a later chapter.

In the house-fronts of German mediaeval cities, in the course of time, the Gothic assurgency gradually—though not without recurrences—settled down into the tranquil rhythm of the Renaissance, while obstinately adhering to Gothic forms. Things were much the same in the Netherlands, where, towards the end of the

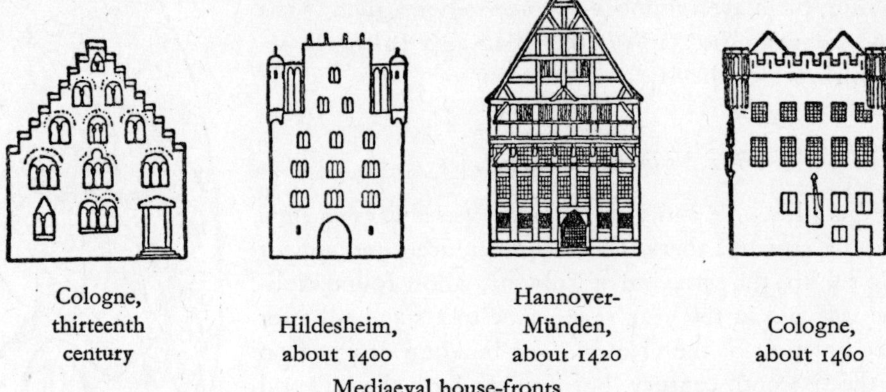

Cologne, thirteenth century — Hildesheim, about 1400 — Hannover-Münden, about 1420 — Cologne, about 1460

Mediaeval house-fronts

Gothic period, in the many wealthy commercial centres, richly ornamented town halls and guild halls were erected: long buildings with oriel-windows and high gables. A tall, strongly-built tower, the belfry, rose defiantly above the roofs of Brussels, Bruges, and other cities. The Gothic style had conquered the whole North; in Sweden, in 1287, the cathedral of Upsala had been built by a French architect; while in Norway the cathedrals of Stavanger and Trondheim were derived from the English Early Gothic. To England the new style of architecture came, by way of Normandy, earlier then to Germany; nevertheless, it was in England that the late Gothic style found its widest sphere of expansion.

In their comfortable blending of the ecclesiastical buildings with the dwelling-houses of the clergy, in their quiet retirement behind protecting walls and gate-houses, the English cathedral closes are a charming picture of the Middle Ages. They are not always set down in the middle of the city, like those on the Continent; often the green churchyard surrounds the cathedral and leads sometimes to the open country beyond. Following the old Norman fashion, the body of the cathedral, with its various divisions, is of great length, and in order to receive the processions of pilgrims the choir was often expanded at the eastern extremity (Fig. 76b, right).

The Chain Gate, Gatehouse on the Bath Road, at Wells, Somerset. Late mediaeval

The complete Gothic system was brought to Canterbury in 1175 by William of Sens, who rebuilt the cathedral. In the Early English style (1175—1250) the pointed arch was victorious, but only where the French influence was completely predominant was the English trend toward horizontal lines suppressed. Salisbury cathedral, built and completed in the years 1220—58, must be regarded as the finest example of this style. In Wells cathedral (Fig. 76b) the transept and nave, and the façade, with its unusual wealth of decorative figures, are still Early Gothic, while the choir was not added until the fifteenth century.

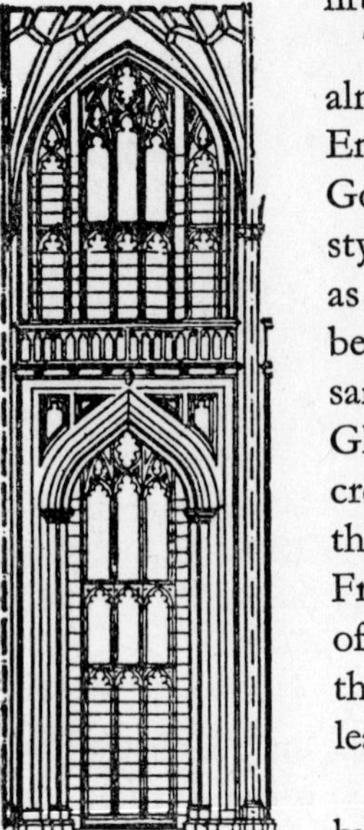

Inner face of late Gothic window in Winchester Cathedral

The 'High Gothic' or Decorated style, 1250—1375, appeared almost fifty years later than in France. It is rightly regarded as an English style, for it had not the logical character of French Gothic; it gave full scope to decorative details, and was the first style to make extensive use of flowing lines in its tracery, as well as the graceful fan-vaulting which was so favoured, from the beginning of the fourteenth century, by the English, Renaissance-like, Late Gothic, or Perpendicular style. The cloister of Gloucester Cathedral (Fig. 80c) is one of the most perfect creations of this kind, in which English art seems to anticipate the course of evolution, and provide a starting-point for the French flamboyant style, which, apart from the isolated example of the star-vaulting of Amiens, did not appear until 1375. France, the original home of the Gothic style, had something to learn from the innovations of the English.

While Exeter Cathedral, of which the principal parts were built in the same style, is the purest example of the English High Gothic of 1327—69, the nave of Winchester Cathedral rebuilt after 1393, with its magnificent vaulting, the effective articulation of its piers, and the blind galleries in the place of the Gothic triforium, represents the transition to a new style. The four-centred arch, which was introduced in England after 1290, and was still the predominant form in Winchester Cathedral, was flattened a little at the point from about 1450, becoming the 'Tudor arch' of the following period, of which the finest and most artistic examples are to be seen in Westminster Abbey. We shall return to this later.

Where sculpture is concerned, while England was closely connected with France, English sculpture did not differ very greatly from Continental. The smaller doors of the English cathedrals made it necessary to place the larger decorative features on the façades. At Wells more than six hundred figures escaped the iconoclastic fury of the Puritans, and these give one a fair notion of the English sculpture of the period.

In its love of decorative effects it applied itself especially to the production of tombs, in which the feudal magnates of the country are immortalized with a characteristic realism.

The tomb of the poet Gower is a fine example of the purely formal spirit of the

Tomb of John Gower. Southwark Cathedral

later period. The baldachino consists of three pointed arches, in which the two middle pillars are lacking. Here the spirit of Gothic architecture is transformed into its antithesis: the old constructuve form of the triforium, originally intended to support a load, hangs downwards as a curtain, and has become a mere decoration. The upward tendency is checked by the static horizontals. In order to understand what lies behind this transformation we must now leave the North and enquire what had been happening in the South, and particularly in Italy, during the centuries which had seen the growth of Romanesque and Gothic art to the north of the Alps.

83. Leone Battista Alberti: S. Francesco, Rimini, begun 1446.

84. Donato Bramante: The Tempietto, S. Pietro in Montorio, Rome. 1502.

a

b

85. (A) Antonio da San Gallo: Palazzo Farnese, Rome. 1530–46. Top storey by Michelangelo.
(B) Baldassare Peruzzi: Palazzo Massini alle Colonne, Rome. Begun 1535.

a

86. (A) Andrea Palladio: Villa Rotunda, Vicenza. Begun *c.* 1567.
(B) Michelangelo: Anteroom to the Laurenziana Library, Florence. Begun in 1526.

b

Chapter XX

THE RENAISSANCE IN ITALY

*

FROM the standpoint of artistic evolution, Italy's experience of the Middle Ages was very superficial; indeed, one might almost say that Italy escaped the Middle Ages. In the North of Italy, if we examine such a building as St Mark's in Venice (Fig. 62a), we see that the lower portions are Romanesque and the upper portions Gothic, but in view of the Byzantine masonry, the many-coloured marbles, and the magnificence of the exterior, we must describe its style as on the whole Byzantine. Here the surviving art of Byzantium outlived even the Middle Ages.

The final liberation of the individual from mediaeval constraint, a liberation which was the essential significance of the real Renaissance, was of necessity perceptible in its art; for all great spiritual and intellectual changes are accompanied by great stylistic changes. As the citizen of the late Middle Ages was embedded in the community, so the individual parts of the late Gothic buildings were, so to speak, anchylosed into the whole. But as men began to give greater attention to individual personalities they began also to regard architectural components as independent objects. Yet this comparison does not tell the whole truth. The South had an innately different sense of form.

In this connection, nothing is more instructive than a survey of the Gothic architecture of Italy—or better still, of such Italian architecture as was tending toward the Gothic. Though Italy may never have known a period of 'High' or complete Gothic, yet the cathedrals of Siena, Orvieto and Milan, like the Doge's Palace in Venice (Fig. 80a), were all built in the late Gothic period, and are fundamentally Renaissance buildings in a Gothic disguise. They do not follow an irresistible upward impulse; with all their towers and pinnacles, they rest serenely on the earth. The constructive ideas of Gothic art were hardly understood in Italy, and its forms were adopted merely as fashionable trimmings.

Even in its structural organization the architecture of the South obeys other than the Gothic laws. In a purely Gothic cathedral no component part exists for its own sake. If one were to remove it one would inflict an injury upon the whole, and the part removed would be a meaningless fragment. We do not find this organic cohesion in Italian architecture; there we can see that a statue, a column, even a gable could be removed without serious aesthetic damage to the whole. Moreover, the

[1] The façade of Siena Cathedral was projected about 1282; that of Orvieto about 1310; Milan Cathedral was begun in 1386, and the main portions were completed in 1418.

component part, regarded in isolation, remains a well-designed work of art, capable of independent existence.

This difference is still perceptible if at a first glance we compare the façade of Florence Cathedral (Fig. 81a), designed after the pattern of Siena and Orvieto, with the Rathaus of Tangermünde (Fig. 80b). Here, through the transposition of masonry into brickwork, it was possible to create a façade which to some extent resembles that of the Italian buildings; it is a frontal mask, divided into three portions, and the quiet lustre of variously coloured glazes is a substitute for the sheen of marble. Yet the essential difference is unmistakable. What an upward rush, what a picturesque and lively coherence is expressed in the Tangermünde façade, as against the calm serenity and self-sufficiency of the individual parts of the Italian building! Compared with the effortless upward movement of the cathedrals of the North (Figs. 76 and 77), how heavily the brickwork of the Doge's Palace seems to weigh, like a Roman *attica*, on the outwardly Gothic foundation!

Painting: The Fifteenth Century and Earlier

Giotto (1266—1337) may be called the first painter of the Renaissance. Giotto's own master, Cimabue, seems to have painted in a style derived from Byzantine examples. That is to say a linear style, essentially flat and two-dimensional. Giotto, though he sprang from these origins, was the first to create real figures, instead of conventions standing for them, and the first to set these figures solidly in a three-dimensional space. The emphasis which Giotto laid upon *form,* and in particular, the form of the human body, was to remain the particular interest and preoccupation of the Florentine school. Giotto was such a revolutionary genius that, for a hundred years after his death, his significance was still not fully understood: his immediate followers, the so-called 'Giotteschi', could not absorb him, and it was not until Masaccio (1401—*c.* 1428), that the next great step forward was taken in the history of Italian painting. Massaccio's frescoes in the Brancacci Chapel in the Church of the Carmine in Florence, were the school at which all the Florentine painters learnt for a century and more. His figures have the monumental grandeur and solidity of Giotto's, with an even greater mastery in dealing with anatomical and spatial problems. He, and the Florentines of the next generation, were interested above all in two things: the human figure, and the application of the recently formulated rules of perspective, to produce an illusion of depth in space. This serious and highly intellectual art, characteristic of the intelligent and self-sufficient citizens of a city state—as Florence then was—came, in the early fifteenth century, into conflict with the so-called International Gothic, which originated in Burgundy and spread down through north Italy, in particular Verona and the Marches. It is essentially an aristocratic court art, having affinities to illuminated MSS. and embroideries, and with a fresh and childlike pleasure in the decorative adjuncts of life, flowers, birds, animals, rich clothes and jewels. It lasted only a short time in Florence, but even so it managed to produce one masterpiece, Gentile di Fabriano's (*c.* 1360—1427) 'Adoration of the Kings', now in the Uffizi.

Of Pisanello (*c.* 1395—1455), the greatest medallist of the Veronese school, only about seven paintings are known, one of which, St Hubert, is in the National Gallery. The separate details of this picture are exquisite, but as a whole it lacks entirely the architectonic unity of the works which were being produced at the same time in Florence: it remains a mediaeval, rather than a Renaissance work, and is far closer to Northern miniature painting. The other important school affected by International Gothic is Siena: Duccio (*c.* 1255—1319), whose place in Sienese painting corresponds to that of Giotto in Florence, remains more influenced by Byzantine art. The later Sienese, Simone Martini (*c.* 1284—1344), the brothers Pietro (active 1305—48) and Ambrogio (active 1319—48) Lorenzetti, Giovanni di Paolo (*c.* 1403—82), and Sassetta (1392—1450), had a more linear, calligraphic and decorative conception of form than their Florentine contemporaries. In the delicacy and purity of its colour and the expressive subtlety of its line, Sienese fourteenth and fifteen-century painting approaches more nearly than any other European school to the art of the Far East. Florentine art was never, like Sienese, transcendental; it was always firmly in contact with reality. The one exception to this is perhaps Fra Angelico (1387—1455), whose frescoes in S. Marco, and whose altar-pieces, have an exquisite freshness and purity of sentiment, which makes them in some sense akin to Sienese art. His great altar-piece of the Last Judgement (*c.* 1440) is an example of the quality of this mind: the damned and the devils in Hell, on one side of the picture. are painted with complete lack of conviction, while Paradise on the other side, is represented with all the joy and gaiety of a profound and serene faith. But figures are modelled with an entirely Florentine solidity, and often, particularly in the single figures, with a massive grandeur comparable to Masaccio himself.

The other important names in this period are Uccello (1397—1475), Castagno (1390—1457), Domenico Veneziano (*d.* 1461), and Filippo Lippi (*c.* 1406—69). Uccello was preoccupied—obsessed would perhaps be a better word—with problems of perspective. The 'Rout of San Romano' combines a certain Gothic feeling with elaborate attempts to render fore-shortening and three-dimensional depth in space. Castagno's few surviving works have an almost brutal force and realism; while Filippo Lippi's Madonnas have the gentle tenderness and humanity which recur in the work of his great pupil Botticelli (1444—1510) (Fig. 82b). These three embody all the tendencies typical of the Florentine in the fifteenth century.

The next generation in Florence included Alessio Baldovinetti (1427—99), to whom the profile portrait of a lady in the National Gallery, London, has been attributed, and himself a pupil of Veneziano, who was the master of the brothers Domenico (1449—94) and Davide Ghirlandajo (1452—1525); Antonio Pollaiuolo (1429—98) was Castagno's pupil, and both in his sculptures, and his masterly paintings and drawings of nude figures in violent action, inherited much of his master's harsh realism. All these artists were realists, interested above all in the truthful representation of facts; but side by side with them, others, of which the greatest was Sandro Botticelli, inspired by the Neo-Platonic humanism of the Medici court, blended Christian and Pagan sentiment in a style which appeals to the emotions rather than to the intellect. In 1490 he became a convert to the preachings of the fanatically puritanical monk, Savonarola, and his later pictures contain an extraordinary intensity of religious emotion. Another painter who must be mentioned with Botticelli is Piero di Cosimo (1462—1521), who in such works as 'The Death of Procris' (Fig. 90b), suggests a subtle, and somewhat un-Florentine, tenderness.

The greatest Florentine of the end of the fifteenth century is undoubtedly Leonardo da Vinci (1452—1519) (Figs. 88a and 88d), the most remarkable example of the many-sided man of the Renaissance. He was a pupil of the sculptor and painter Andrea Verrocchio (1435—1488), but did not confine himself to sculpture and painting: science—geology, botany, anatomy—architecture, engineering, occasional sculpture (though nothing survives which can be with certainty attributed to him, except drawings for the Sforza monument at Milan), and occasional painting, were among his interests. His notebooks and drawings (the largest collection of which is in the Royal Library at Windsor) reveal a mind of incredible profundity and width. Of his paintings the best known are the frescoes of the Last Supper at Milan, the 'Virgin of the Rocks' in the National Gallery, and the 'Gioconda' in the Louvre. He settled in Milan in 1482, and his strongly marked style exerted a powerful influence on the local school on such men as Luini (*c.* 1475—1532), Boltraffio (1467—1516), and Ambrogio da Predis (active 1472—1506), who could copy his mannerisms, but were deprived of all originality and initiative by the master's overpowering genius. Though Leonardo, considering his supreme gifts, left surprisingly little mark, except indirectly, upon the development of Italian painting, his importance as an individual, as the most perfect example of the Renaissance 'Complete Man', and as the culmination of the Florentine Quattrocento, is enormous.

Of the other schools of painting, outside Florence, we have already touched on Verona and Siena in connection with the International Gothic style. The school of Umbria, the mountainous district to the south of Tuscany, was closely allied to that of Florence. Pietro Perugino (1445—1523), a painter whose work is often charming and sometimes beautiful, is important as being the master of Raphael. Among his other pupils were Bernardino Pinturicchio (1454—1513) and Lo Spagna (*c.* 1450—1528). Excluding Raphael, who hardly counts as an Umbrian except in his very earliest, and immature works, the greatest figure in the Umbrian school is Piero della Francesca (1416—92), whose stature is indeed as great as that of Raphael himself. Like Raphael, Piero was Umbrian only by birth, for he was trained in Florence under Domenico Veneziano. His important works are the frescoes of the Legend of the True Cross in the Cathedral at Arezzo, the fresco of the Resurrection at Borgo

San Sepolcro, and a few panel-paintings, of which three are in the National Gallery. He ranks with Giotto, Masaccio, and Raphael, as one of the supreme classical painters, placing his figures of monumental stature and gravity in settings of ideally conceived architectonic form. His importance as a painter cannot be exaggerated.

His two pupils, Luca Signorelli (*c.* 1450—1523) and Melozzo da Forli (1438—94), are worthy of their master: in particular Signorelli, whose paintings of nude figures in violent action, especially those at Orvieto Cathedral, are reminiscent of Antonio Pollaiuolo rather than of Piero, whose figures stand and move in an almost sculptural serenity. It is significant of the change which had come over the art of Florence at the end of the century that Piero was never once asked to carry out any commission in Florence itself, but that his chief work was carried out in Arezzo, and Urbino, where the Duke was his patron; this was the case, in spite of the fact that Piero was the direct heir of the artistic ideals of Masaccio, Uccello, and their contemporaries.

The important centres of Northern Italian painting in the Quattrocento were Ferrara, Verona, Padua and Venice. Veronese painting reached its height, as has been said, with Pisanello. Padua is dominated, during the whole of the latter half of the century, by Andrea Mantegna (1431—1506) (Fig. 91b), whose first training was under an ill-defined master, Squarcione, to whom no surviving pictures can be attributed, but who has given his name to the style, derived largely from antique motives, which is characteristic of Mantegna and his followers. Donatello was working in Padua from 1443 to 1453, and it is he who must be considered Mantegna's real master: Mantegna's heroic figures which seem to be not so much flesh and blood, as cast in bronze, suggest that his inspiration was sculpture rather than painting. But it was not only by Donatello (Fig. 82a), but also by the antique, that Mantegna was influenced. The Renaissance is often spoken of as being the revival of antiquity, and in architecture and sculpture, the fact of there being imitable models at hand led to a close copying of antique prototypes. In painting there is (not unnaturally, in view of the scarcity of antique paintings) no direct imitation, but rather inspiration of one art by another; in Florentine painting the majestic proportions and dignity of the remains of antiquity are reflected; but Mantegna's passion for ancient Rome led him to fill his pictures with fragments of Roman ruins, to choose, as far as possible, subjects from Roman history, and even, as in the case of the 'Triumph of Scipio', in the National Gallery, which is painted in *grisaille,* to try and imitate a Roman frieze carved in bas-relief.

Venice was very different from Florence or Padua. In place of an austere, highly intellectual, and essentially linear art, we find a school preoccupied not so much with *line* as with *colour*, not so much with *forms* as with *light.* The Quattrocento Venetian painters, among whom were the brothers Giovanni (1430?—1516) and Gentile Bellini (1429—1507), Vittore Carpaccio (*c.* 1455—1526), Bartolommeo Montagna-(1450—*c.* 1523), and Cima da Conegliano (*c.* 1459—*c.* 1517), were content on the whole to execute elegant and graceful variations on familiar themes, which often approach *genre*. Mantegna was the Bellinis' brother-in-law, but his influence was not enduring in Venice except in the case of Carlo Crivelli (*c.* 1430—95) who painted in a dry, elaborate, bejewelled style, close to that of the so-called 'Squarcioneschi'.

The climate of Venice made fresco painting difficult. This fact, combined with its geographical position as one of the main gateways to Italy from the north, and with the nature of Venetian painting itself, caused oil painting as practised in the Netherlands to be used also in Venice during the fifteenth century. The oil medium, if properly used, is impervious to damp, and, with its possibilities in the way of transparent glazes of colour, is better able to express tone values and atmospheric gradations than the opaque 'tempera' which was the medium of Florentine artists.

Ferrara, like all the lesser schools of north Italy, was dominated by Padua. Cosimo Tura (c. 1430—95) with his twisted metallic forms, clearly owes much to the sculptural influences at work in Padua, but there is a feeling for the grotesque which is entirely his own, and which makes him one of the most individual stylists in Italian painting. His contemporary Francesco Cossa (*c.* 1435—77) worked in much the same style. The third Ferrarese painter of importance, though less so than the other two, is Ercole Roberti (1450—96).

The Sixteenth Century: High Renaissance and Mannerism

Raphael (1483—1520) (Fig. 88) is the High Renaissance painter *par excellence*. Born in Umbria, he was a pupil of Perugino, and his early works are entirely Peruginesque and *quattrocento* in character. In 1504 he came to Florence, where his style was affected by Michelangelo (Fig. 89) anb Leonardo (Figs. 88a and 88), whose works were then the most developed and sophisticated examples of the Florentine tradition. Raphael's chief Florentine works were his Madonnas; our very familiarity with these many variations on a simple theme may lead us to forget their amazingly subtle and expressive linear quality, which, though combined with something of the plasticity of Michelangelo and Leonardo, still remains essentially *quattrocento*. In 1508 Raphael went to Rome, which, under Julius II, was beginning to supersede Florence as a centre of artistic activity. He entered the service of the Pope, and was employed in the decoration of the Vatican; here, working on a grand scale and inspired by the colossal relics of antiquity all around him, he achieved his masterpieces. The *stanze*, which he and his associates decorated, are a series of small rooms in the Vatican; the *stanza della signatura* contains the two great frescoes, opposite one another, the *School of Athens* and the *Disputa*, and on the side-wall, the *Parnassus*. In these, the ideals of the High Renaissance, lucidity, balance, order, and a logical and architectonic system of space-construction, find their highest expression. Serene, untroubled, and (as far as anything can be) perfect, these frescoes, from the time they were painted, have been the inspiration and the ideal of classic European art. Raphael was kept so busy by the Pope, who appointed him architect of St Peter's in 1514, on the death of

Bramante, that he had little time for commissions from other people, though he did take a share in the decoration of the Villa Farnesina, built *c.* 1510 by the Sienese banker Agostino Chigi. Like Rubens a hundred years later, this made it necessary for him to employ numerous helpers, by whom the work was in many cases executed on lines laid down by Raphael in a drawing or cartoon.

One of the constant features of artistic style is that it must be continually developing. With Raphael, the High Renaissance reached a point of perfection from which no development was possible in the same direction, and the period of 'Mannerism', which succeeded the High Renaissance, was a reaction against it. The concept of Mannerism has only comparatively recently been analysed by art-historians; previously, the art of the last two-thirds of the sixteenth-century, between the High Renaissance and the Baroque, was either dismissed as decadent or regarded as a kind of 'proto-Baroque'. In fact, as is now realized, Mannerism is an independent and sophisticated style with rules of its own. Its greatest exponent was Michelangelo (1475—1564), whose genius could not be bound by the restraint of the High Renaissance style, but developed individual and strange means of expression; so individual, that his contemporaries and followers were able only to reproduce the shell, the outward form in which it expressed itself; so that, in spite of his many imitators, he stands very much alone.

We are concerned with him here only as a painter, and with the exception of a very few easel pictures, his only paintings are the frescoed decorations in the Sistine Chapel (Fig. 89b) and in the Cappella Paolina, both in the Vatican. Michelangelo was a Florentine, a pupil of Ghirlandajo, and in the true Florentine tradition, the nude was the base of his art. But he carried further than anyone, before or since, the treatment of the nude as a means of expression. The ceiling of the Sistine Chapel, with its elaborately simulated architectural framework, on and round which are grouped, gigantic and majestically beautiful, the figures of Sibyls, Prophets and others, and the *Last Judgment* on the east wall, which seems to be a cascade of writhing and inextricable limbs, are, together, one of the most splendid creations of the human intelligence. This expressionism was not without its dangers, even for Michelangelo himself, in spite of his anatomical knowledge and superb draughtsmanship; but his followers and imitators, exaggerating his forms, distorted the human figure out of all recognition. This is not to say that Mannerism was entirely due to Michelangelo; but simptly that, as one of the earliest, and certainly the greatest, exponents of the tendency, he was bound to exercise a considerable influence on its development.

Like every other style, mannerism was a reflection of contemporary conditions. The style of the High Renaissance was the product of an age of serene and confident Humanism; mannerism reflected a more troubled period of social and intellectual insecurity. The secular tendency towards absolute princely rule, and that in the Church towards the dogmatic arbitrariness of the Counter-Reformation, which disliked any suggestion of human perfectibility, produced a sophisticated, mystical, transcendental kind of Court art. Classical art was still studied and used as an example and as a source of motives, but in a narrower spirit of antiquarianism; representative of the 'learned' tendency in Mannerism is the Sienese, Baldassare Peruzzi (1481—1537), a painter and architect who worked mostly in Rome, and whose importance, both for his own works and for the influence he exerted on the Roman school, and particularly on Raphael, is only now beginning to be recognized. Generally speaking, Mannerism bore rather the same relation to the High Renaissance as a photographic negative has to a photograph; where one is serene and lucid, the other is agitated, obscure and neurotic (a favourite mannerist trick is to let the action of a picture be carried out by small background figures, while the foreground is filled with large figures who contribute nothing to, and often actually seem to ignore, the actions of the main participants); where human proportions, in one, are normal, sometimes to the point of insipidity, in the other there are fantastic distortions; where one is based on an entirely logical system of spatial relations, in the other there is a curious sense of 'false space', rather like what one finds in a later Hellenistic bas-relief. Two works, of rather the same kind by Michelangelo and Raphael, illustrate these points: when Raphael first came to Florence, Michelangelo's cartoon of the *Bathers* (destroyed, and known only from a copy in the collection of the Earl of Leicester) was one of the chief sights of the city; we know that Raphael made copies of some of the figures, and it is very probable that his knowledge of it is reflected in his composition of the *Massacre of the Innocents,* dating from *c.* 1508 (known only from Marcantonio's engraving). The *Bathers* illustrates an incident in the war against Pisa, when the Florentine soldiers, bathing in a river, were surprised by the sudden approach of the enemy. Michelangelo, it must be remembered, was primarily a sculptor, and this composition is, indeed, like an enormous bas-relief, in which each figure seems to be modelled separately and to have no connection with those round it; though their attitudes suggest violent action, they seem to be in a state of slow motion, and there is no general movement animating the whole composition. In Raphael's composition, on the other hand, there is a free, flowing, symmetrical movement, both parallel and at right angles to the picture-plane; the figures are in a marked rhythmic relation of one another, and the figure of the woman, running straight forward in the exact centre of the composition, gives an immediate sensation of spatial depth. Raphael borrowed this motive from the *Bathers,* but it is significant that there the old man, who is in a similar pose, plays no such part; he is pushed to the side of the composition and partly obscured by a figure in front. The *Bathers* is in essence mannerist, while the other is entirely High Renaissance, though Raphael himself, towards the end of his life, submitted to the current tendencies and developed in the direction of mannerism; his *Transfiguration* (1517—20), and the paintings which were executed by his assistants, under his instructions, on the ceiling of the *loggie* (the so-called 'Raphael's Bible') are far removed, in feeling and style, from *The School of Athens;* while his pupils, Giulio

a

b

87. (A) Michelangelo: The Bathers (The Battle of Cascina). *Grisaille* copy of the lost cartoon, 1504–5, in the collection of the Earl of Leicester.
(B) Raphael: The Massacre of the Innocents (from an engraving by Marcantonio) *c.* 1509.

a

b

88. (A) Leonardo da Vinci: Virgin and Child with St Anne and the Infant St John *c.* 1506 – 10. (Louvre).
(B) Raphael: The Nuptials of the Holy Virgin (*Lo Sposalizio*), 1504. (Brera, Milan).
(C) Raphael: Pope Julius II. Study for the portrait of the Pope in Santa Maria del Popolo, or the fresco 'The Delivering of the Decretals'. Red chalk *c.* 1510. (Chatsworth Collection).
(D) Leonardo da Vinci: Study for the angel's head in the Virgin of the Rocks. Silverpoint, heightened with white. *c.* 1484. (Royal Library, Turin).

c

d

). (A) Michelangelo: Pietà. [arble. 1498 – 1500. (St Peter's, ome).
3) Michelangelo: The Creation of dam. Part of the fresco in the stine Chapel. Text. p. 239. 1509 –). (Vatican).

a

b

90. (A) Raphael: St. Catherine. (National Gallery, London).
(B) Piero di Cosimo: The Death of Procris. (National Gallery, London).

a

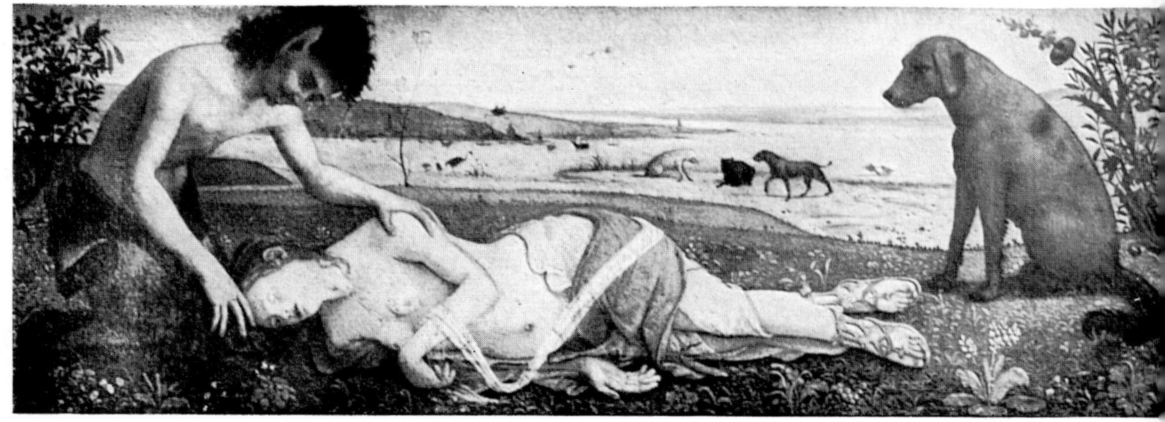

Romano (*c.* 1491—1546), Polidoro da Caravaggio (*c.* 1500—43) and Perino del Vaga (1500—47), in the decorations which they executed after his death in the Vatican, in the Sala di Constantino and elsewhere, reveal themselves as fully developed mannerists. After the sack of Rome in 1527, which did away with the last traces of the High Renaissance, Raphael's pupils developed this Roman mannerism in various ways, in other parts of Italy: Giulio in Mantua, Polidoro in Naples, and Perino in Genoa.

Florence and Rome were the two main centres of Mannerism. Pontormo (1494—1556), Bronzino (1503—72) and Rosso (1494—1540), the latter also known for his work at Fontainebleau, are the chief mannerists of the first generation, greatly influenced by Michelangelo; the second generation is represented by Vasari (1511—71), better known as the biographer of the Italian artists, and Francesco Salviati (1510—63); while late Mannerism, when the style had become a popular and universal convention, is represented by the brothers Taddeo (1529—66) and Federigo Zuccaro (1542-3—1609). Outside Florence, Correggio (1485—1534) (Fig. 91a), of Parma, who stands rather apart from the course of artistic development in the sixteenth century; he seems to anticipate the Baroque in his great decorative schemes, full of light and depth and movement, while his sensuous handling of paint, and his delight in its quality almost reminds one of the French eighteenth century. Parmigianino (1504—40) of Parma, his follower, and Tibaldi (1527—96) of Bologna, produced an Emilian, or central Italian, Mannerism, with which the style of Primaticcio (1504—70) a Bolognese pupil of Giulio Romano who worked at Fontainebleau, and Niccolo dall'Abbate (1512—71) of Modena (who also worked at Fontainebleau), has affinities, while Mannerism in Venice is represented by Tintoretto.

The nature of Venetian life, and the isolation of Venice, both politically and geographically, from the rest of Italy, caused Venetian art to develop certain particular characteristics. It is by far the most *worldly* (in the best sense of the word) of all the Italian schools, appealing as it does to the sense of luxury, civic pride, and private ownership.

Giorgione (1478—1510) (Fig. 92a) originated many of the commonplaces of Venetian sixteenth-century painting; it was he who invented the idyllic picture, groups of figures, sitting under trees, listening to music, and making love; pictures with no intellectually conceived iconographic meaning, but expressing, in much the same way as music, an emotion hitherto not expressed by the medium of painting. Giorgione died young, and his works are few in number; among those which recent criticism most readily admits to be his work are the Altar of the *Madonna and two Saints* at Castelfranco, the *Tempest* at Venice, and the *Fete Champetre* in the Louvre. He carried even further the luminism and colour of Bellini, Carpaccio, and the earlier Venetian school. There are several painters who copied Giorgione's manner, of which the most important was Titian (c. 1480—1576), whose work, until about 1540, was fully Giorgionesque (Fig. 92b); also Palma Vecchio (1480—1528), Paris Bordone

(1500—71) and Cariani (1480—1544). Titian eventually outgrew a specifically Giorgionesque manner, and the works of his maturity and old age (for he lived to be nearly a hundred, and painted right up to the end of his life) have a mature and sumptuous magnificence (in particular this is true of his numerous portraits), and delight in what Machiavelli called 'the truth of outward things', a phrase which seems to sum up the Renaissance in general, and Venice in particular.

Besides Titian, the other two predominant masters of the Venetian sixteenth century were Paolo Veronese (1528—88) and Jacopo Tintoretto (1518—94). Veronese carried on the Venetian tradition of luxurious splendour and display, filling his great canvases with figures in gorgeous clothes, bathed in that clear golden light which seems the especial property of the Venetian school. Tintoretto was the chief exponent of Mannerism in Venice. He adopted Michalangelesque forms; but his genius was so powerful that he was able to transmute the idiom of Mannerism into an intensely personal style. He seems to foreshadow the 'tenebrist' painters of the next century in his use of violent *chiaroscuro* effects. He is also remarkable for his influence upon El Greco, who in his earliest period must be regarded not as a highly individual Spanish master, but as a late Venetian mannerist.

Architecture

The centre of the early Renaissance was Florence, a young and progressive city-state, controlled by rich and independent merchants. In 1332 Giotto was chosen to design and superintend the building of the Campanile (Fig. 81a); the fact that one who was not an architect, but the greatest living painter, should have been chosen for this most important task is significant of the beginning of the Renaissance with its conception of the 'universal man'. In the cathedral itself, the fourth largest church in Europe, unprecedented means were taken to create a spacious interior. Four groined vaults span the nave, which is nearly sixty-five feet wide, and the arcades cover the 234 feet between the west front and the crossing in four gigantic arches. In 1423 Brunelleschi (1377—1446), the first great Renaissance architect, created the dome, almost as wide as that of the Pantheon but twice as high, and so impressive in its majestic lightness that it almost dwarfs the campanile itself.

Two years before, in 1421, Brunelleschi had begun the first properly Renaissance building, the Innocenti, or Foundling Hospital. This consists of a colonnade on the ground floor, with arches supported by Corinthian columns, supporting a first floor with widely spaced windows (Fig. 81c). The source of this, entirely classic though it is in its harmonious proportions, is not so much the antique Roman as the Tuscan Romanesque style. The same is true of S. Spirito (begun in 1435), the old Sacristy in S. Lorenzo (built 1421—28), and the Pazzi Chapel in S. Croce (about 1430).

Though the motives are taken from Romanesque rather than Roman originals, the conscious perfection of the proportion of these buildings marks them as Renaissance. The key to understanding the architecture, and much of the painting, of the early and high Renaissance, is their conception of a building, not as something carved out, and free-standing in space, but rather as a matrix enclosing, or moulding, an ideal, perfectly-proportioned and finite space. This idea of space as something with a positive existence is the centre of Renaissance aesthetics. But Brunelleschi still retained something of the sculptural conception of architecture, and it was an architect of the next generation, Leon Battista Alberti (1404—72) who was the first, consciously and completely, to carry out the new ideals. In his *De re aedificatoria* (published 1485) he defined what seemed to him to be the essential of architecture: 'The harmonious unity of every part, combined in such a way that nothing can be added, subtracted, or altered, that is not for the worse.' The façade of the Palazzo Rucellai in Florence (1446—51), with its perfect harmony and proportion, exemplifies this maxim; so do his churches, S. Andrea and S. Sebastiano at Mantua, S. Francesco at Rimini (usually known as the Tempio Malatestiana—see Fig. 83), and S. Maria Novella at Florence.

In the churches built by Alberti and other architects in the late fifteenth and very early sixteenth centuries, there is a frequent use of the Greek cross plan that is to say, a cross with equal arms, as opposed to a Latin cross in which one arm, the nave, is longer than the other three. This is another instance of the early Renaissance conception of space, with its ideals of clarity, lucidity and order, and its idea of a building as something as unified and harmoniously proportioned as a crystal.

Florence was the centre of the early Renaissance, but about the turn of the century the centre moved to Rome, where all the great architects of the High Renaissance, Bramante (1444—1514), Raphael (1483—1520), Michelangelo (1475—1564) and Peruzzi, none of them Roman by birth, gravitated.

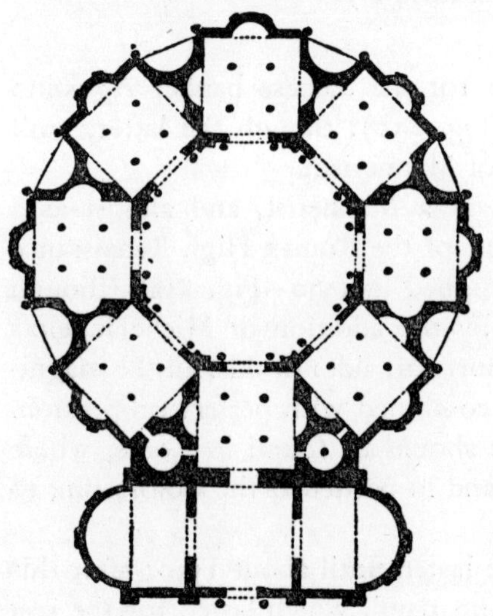

Leonardo da Vinci: Design for a church

Bramante was a Milanese, and must have been affected by Leonardo's architectural ideas; Leonardo's notebooks are full of imaginary designs for buildings, almost all of them ingenious and elaborate variations on the central plan. Bramante's first building in Rome is the so-called 'Tempietto' in the courtyard of S. Pietro, in Montorio, built in 1502 on the spot where St Peter is traditionally supposed to have been executed. This is a small circular building with a dome, surrounded by a colonnade: its exquisite proportions make it perhaps the most perfect example of High Renaissance architecture (Fig. 84). The Pallazzo della Cancelleria (1486–98) was at one time attributed to Bramante. Though there are reasons for doubting this, the palace façade, with its subtle rhythm of pilasters and windows, might well be his work. By Raphael are the Palazzo Caraffa and the Chigi Chapel in S. Maria del Popolo, and by

Palazzo Strozzi in Florence.
Begun in 1489 after a plan by Benedetto da Maiano
and completed by Simone Cronaca in 1536

Peruzzi, the Villa Farnesina (built in 1509–11 for the Sienese banker Agostino Chigi) and the Palazzo Massini alle Colonne (Fig. 85b); though the latter, built in 1535, already hints at the later development of Mannerism.

Apart from St Peter's, which really counts as a Mannerist, and almost as a Baroque, structure, perhaps the grandest example of the Roman High Renaissance is Antonio da San Gallo's Palazzo Farnese (designed in 1530—Fig. 85a)—though the effect of this at the present day is spoilt by the addition of Michelangelo's cornice on the exterior and top storey on the courtyard side. In this, all the magnificence and solidity of Roman architecture are combined with perfect proportion. It is not surprising that this hugeness of scale should be found in Rome, where architects had all the monuments of antiquity, and in particular the Colosseum, to inspire them.

This High Renaissance period of architecture lasted until about 1530; after this another developed, the so-called period of 'Mannerism', which lasted for the rest of the century. It is only recently that Mannerism has been distinguished from Baroque. It is true that one led to the other, but they are entirely different.

Mannerism in architecture is a reaction against the serenity, logic and gravity of the High Renaissance. Each unit of the building is finite and separate, as in classical architecture, and there is no attempt to impose a plastic unity on the whole building, which is the distinguishing mark of the Baroque. Unlike Baroque, it makes use of the classical framework; but inside it there is deliberate discord and illogicality.

In the Cancelleria, or the Palazzo Cafarelli, the façade is logical, echoing the structure of the interior; in the Palazzo Massini alle Colonne (Fig. 85b) the *piano nobile* is only suggested by the greater height of the windows, the whole of the upper part of the façade is unarticulated and covered with rustication, the voluted surrounds of the upper windows are purely decorative with apparently no structural function. Apart from Michelangelo, the principal mannerist architects were Guilio Romano (1494—1546), Sanmichele (1484—1558) and Serlio. The latter's treatise on architecture became a standard pattern book, particularly in France where he worked, and influenced the architects of the School of Fontainebleau; but his reputation and influence are disproportionate to his merits as an architect. Giulio Romano's chief architectural work is at Mantua, where he designed the Ducal Palace and the Palazzo del Té for the ruling family, the Gonzagas; Sanmichele's is at Verona.

Palazzo della Cancelleria, Rome, 1486 - 98

At first sight these may seem to be ordinary classical buildings, but in reality they are the opposite; classical motives are used, but in such a way as to give an impression of disproportion and insubstantiality, to create almost a sense of *malaise* in the mind of the spectator. Perhaps the best example of this is Michelangelo's vestibule of the Biblioteca Laurenziana in Florence, begun in 1526 (Fig. 86b). Here one is conscious of definite discomfort: the columns, instead of carrying, or seeming to carry, the weight of the cornices, are recessed in niches, and seem to be supported on small consoles; every detail of the interior, the tabernacles between the pairs of pilasters, and the square panels over them, are designed with an exquisitely logical illogicality. In Michelangelo's hands architecture becomes an art almost as abstract, and as far reaching in its possibilities, as music. But none of his followers had the genius to continue his developments, and Mannerism in its turn became a convention.

Various causes have been suggested for Mannerism: it is a symptom of an over-civilized, sophisticated, and neurotic society, what we should call today *fin de siècle*. It is possible as well, to trace some connection with the Counter-Reformation: the lucidity and logic of classical architecture had stood for Humanism and the doctrine of human perfectibility, doctrines out of keeping with the Counter-Reformation's revival of sacredotalism and spiritual absolutism. This tendency of religion to affect art is exemplified by the history of St Peter's. In 1506 Julius II commissioned Bramante to rebuilt the old cathedral. Bramante's plan, if carried out, would have made the church the most splendid monument of Renaissance architecture: it was a Greek cross, perfectly symmetrical in plan (so that it is impossible to tell even which arm of the cross was intended to contain the high altar), with a central dome over

Donato Bramante: Original plan for St Peter's, Rome, 1506

the crossing and four smaller domes round it, and apsidal ends to the arms of the cross. After Bramante's death in 1514, Raphael produced the first Latin cross plan, Peruzzi a Greek cross, Antonio da San Gallo the Younger a Latin cross, and finally, in 1546, Michelangelo again proposed a Greek cross. His plan was a simplified version of Bramante's, keeping the ambulatory but without the small chapels or the corner sacristies: though he kept the central plan, he altered the details, in particular the proportions of the orders, to give an impression of colossal, almost monstrous size. Bramante's St Peter's would have been a building, huge, but of human proportions: Michelangelo's is inhuman, having the proportions of a much smaller building magnified. But to that the Mannerist answer would have been that a church should not be human, but divine.

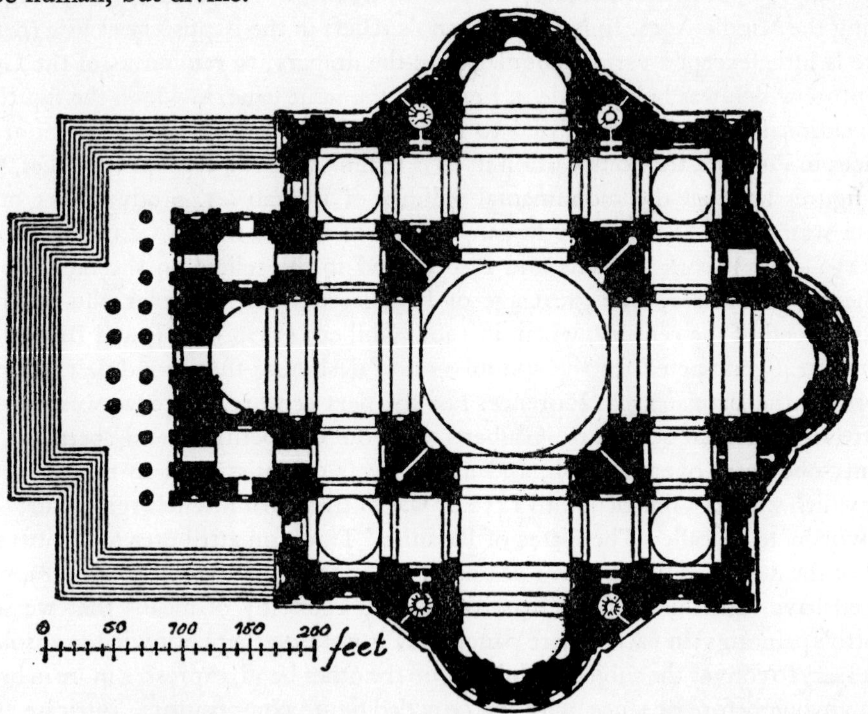

Michelangelo: Plan for the completion of St Peter's, Rome, 1546

Bramante had proposed a semi-spherical dome, but Michelangelo's is an elongated form, apparently based on Brunelleschi's Gothic dome at Florence, treated in a way which comes close to the Baroque. The final state of the building, with its arcaded forecourt by Bernini, its dome, and its Latin cross plan (the nave and west front are the work of Carlo Maderna, and were only completed in 1614) seems to be a high Baroque building. It is, in fact, a kind of palimpsest of the history of Italian Renaissance architecture (Fig. 95a).

Another architect must be mentioned, Andrea Palladio (1518—80), a native of Vicenza, in north Italy, who is important, not only for himself, but for the influence his *Architettura* had on Inigo Jones and on the English architects of the eighteenth century. Palladio based his style on Roman examples, and on Vitruvius, and though a certain amount of Mannerist licence can be detected in some of the palaces at Vicenza, as a rule his buildings, chiefly palaces and villas, have a classical simplicity and elegance, and an almost exaggerated symmetry, which extends even to the disposition of the rooms (Fig. 86a).

Sculpture

In sculpture, as in architecture, the Roman tradition was never entirely forgotten during the Middle Ages. In Niccolo Pisano's reliefs in the Baptistery at Pisa (*c.* 1260) there is little, except a certain angularity in the drapery, to remind us of the Gothic sculpture which was being made in France at the same time, in which the figures are conventionalized and spiritualized to a point where they are almost without substance; in Pisano's, the composition itself is reminiscent of a Roman bas-relief, while the figures have all the monumental solidity of Roman art. Study of the human figure was always the basis of Italian sculpture; we see this in Giovanni Pisano's (*c.* 1250—1317) work at Siena and Pistoia, and in the reliefs on the façade of the Cathedral at Orvieto. The great age of Italian sculpture, however, did not begin until the end of the century, when, in 1401, Ghiberti (1378—1455) and Brunelleschi (1377—1446) competed for the commission of designing the second pair of bronze doors for the Baptistery at Florence. For the next century, Florence was to be the centre of all Italian sculpture. Ghiberti won the competition, and spent the next twenty-one years over the task, and in 1425 was commissioned to make a second pair which were not finished until 1452. It was of these that Michelangelo said; 'They are worthy to be called The Gates of Paradise.' Tradition attributes to Giotto some part of the design of the first pair of doors, by Andrea Pisano (*c.* 1270—1348), which indeed have something of the massiveness and economy of means that we see in Giotto's paintings; in each square panel there is nothing there but what is absolutely necessary to convey the subject. Ghiberti, on the other hand, expresses more in bronze than anyone before or since, with his crowded figure compositions, intricate effects of perspective, and elaborate architectural and landscape backgrounds. The influence of Ghiberti extended, not only into sculpture, but into painting as well, for Masaccio, Pollaiuolo and Uccello were his assistants at various times, and the tendency towards an expressive naturalism which characterized Florentine painting in that period owes much to the ever-visible example of Ghiberti's doors. Donatello (1386—1466) was also Ghiberti's pupil. Inspired by antique examples, he gave his works a realism, a profundity, and a tenderness, which the antique had never known. His sojourn in Padua in the 1450's was to have an overwhelming effect on Mantegna, and through him, on much of North Italian painting. It was there he executed the great statue

a

91. (A) Correggio: Madonna with the Basket. (National Gallery, London).
(B) Mantegna: The Agony in the Garden. (National Gallery, London).

b

a

92. (A) Giorgione: Venus. *c.* 1509. (Art Gallery, Dresden).
(B) Titian: The Venus of Urbino. *c.* 1538. (Uffizi Gallery, Florence).

b

a

b

93. (A) Konrad Witz: Catharine and the Magdalen. *c.* 1445. (Art Gallery, Strassburg).
(B) Dürer: Lucas Paumgärtner as St Eustachius. Altarpiece. *c.* 1500. (Alte Pinakothek, Munich).
(C) Hans Holbein the Younger: Portrait of Jean de Dinteville. 1533.
(D) Dürer: Portrait of Jacob Muffel. 1526. (Staatliches Museum, Berlin).

c

d

a

94. (A) Matthias Grünewald: The Crucifixion from the Altar at Isenheim. Completed in 1515. (Colmar Museum). (B) Hans Memling: Virgin and Child. 1487. (Hospital, Bruges). (C) Roger van der Weyden: Philippe de Croy. *c.* 1459. (Art Gallery, Antwerp).

b

c

of Gattamelata, which disputes with Verrocchio's Colleoni statue at Venice the title of the greatest equestrian statue in the world. Donatello was the most versatile of sculptors: he could produce large-scale single statues, small figures, and reliefs with equal ease in marble and bronze. Contemporary with Donatello was the Sienese, Jacopo della Quercia (1367—1438), whose chief works are the Fonte Gaia at Siena, the Tomb of Ilaria at Lucca, and the reliefs on the façade of S. Petronio at Bologna. Of the stone sculptors of the next generation, the most important are: Desiderio da Settignano (1428—64), Mino de Fiesole (1431—84), Benedetto da Maiano (1442—97), and the two brothers Bernardo (1409—64) and Antonio Rossellini (1427—78), and, above all, Luca della Robbia (1399—1482), who worked also in glazed clay, and whose reputation has suffered from the modern manufacture of replicas of his clay reliefs; but in such works as the *Cantoria,* or singing Gallery, in Florence Cathedral, or the bronze doors of the New Sacristy, in the same building, he is the equal of all but the greatest. Agostino di Duccio (1418—after 1480) should also be mentioned; exiled from Florence his chief work was in the Tempio Malatestiana at Rimini, which he decorated with low reliefs in a very personal style, which undoubtedly increased in individuality owing to his absence from Florentine influences.

Verrocchio (1435—88) and Antonio Pollaiuolo (*c.* 1432—98 are, the leading Florentine bronze sculptors. In bronze, even more than in marble, the Florentine genius, for expressing the nude in violent action, showed itself. Verrocchio's most distinguished pupil was Leonardo da Vinci. He is known to have done sculpture, but nothing survives which can certainly be attributed to him; his masterpiece, the equestrian Sforza monument at Milan, was never cast in bronze, and the full-size model was destroyed a few years after its completion. Towards the end of the century, the impulse given by Ghiberti and Donatello to sculpture seemed to have spent itself, and there was an ever-increasing tendency towards sentimentality and prettiness. Michelangelo resuscitated sculpture, though in this field, as in architecture and painting, his genius was so overpowering and individual as to overwhelm those who followed him. His early works, the *St John* at Berlin, the *David* at Florence, the *Pietà* in St Peter's, (Fig. 89a) and the reliefs like the *Battle of Centaurs and Lapiths* at Florence, and the circular *Madonna and Child* at Burlington House, are in the Florentine *quattrocento* tradition. His style became increasingly personal: the *Slaves* and other figures on the unfinished tomb of Julius II, occupy a position midway between the early works, and the very late, and extraordinarily expressionistic, *Pietà*. In the Mannerist period, sculpture became more subordinated to the other art. Among mannerist sculptors are Benvenuto Cellini (1500—71), whose fame rests more on his Autobiography, Jacopo Sansovino (1486—1578), and Giovanni Bologna (1529—1608), a Northerner working in Florence. Their tendency was to produce small, exquisitely worked, *objects de vertu* (Cellini's gold salt cellar is an example), though they often did work on a larger scale.

Chapter XXI

THE RENAISSANCE ERA IN THE NORTH

*

WHERE the *forms* of art were concerned, the North knew as little about the true Renaissance as Italy did of the genuine Gothic style: but the intellectual movement by which Western Europe emerged from the Middle Ages was as strong in the North as in the South. If we date the beginning of the new age from about 1500—or from 1492, the year in which the New Woıld was discovered—this is only the turning-point of the revolution. The movement that led to it had begun at least a hundred years before, since when Europe had experienced a complete reconstruction of its culture.

In the Netherlands an energetic bourgeoisie looked out towards the outer world, away from its restricted homeland; their change of attitude was more phlegmatic than in Italy. As in the South, the Northern quattrocento looked back into its own past, and used what it found there, to produce new ideals. This explains the difference in external forms. In Italy the model was antiquity; but in the North the Gothie style lent its ancient idiom to the new art. This explains the curious fact that the northern Gothic seems to go on for centuries: but the Gothic shell was animated by very different forces. If we compare Fig. 78 with Fig. 93a, we see the same Gothic drapery though in the latter it is more vigorously rumpled; but this art has at the same time acquired a naturalism in which Konrad Witz's St Catherine and St Mary Magdalene (Fig. 93a), are comparable with the creations of the southern artists. Yet these northern creations are distinguished from the marmoreal smoothness of the South by their resistent use of Gothic forms. Nevertheless, the Western art of the fifteenth century was everywhere the product of a new urban civilization, and the liberal outlook of a free and awakened bourgeoisie.

The Beginnings of Graphic Art

Long before Gutenberg, about the middle of the fifteenth century, had begun to print books from founts of moveable type, small *briefs,* printed from wood blocks, had a wide circulation. Rather later, *block-books* made their appearance: bound series of woodcuts with a few lines of text.

In the woodcut the white portions of the drawings are cut down in the wood block until the drawing stands out in relief, when it can be inked. In etching and engraving, on the other hand, the artist engraves or etches ('bites' with acid) the lines

Christophorus. Woodcut with prayer for indulgence and the date 1423. From a manuscript of 1417, emanating from the Buxheim monastery. Rylands Library, Manchester

on a metal plate. The ink, retained only by the incised lines, is absorbed under pressure by a sheet of paper. Thus the copperplate-engraving can work with fine, intersecting lines and much more freely, than the wood-engraver, who at first (above, and page 252 top) carefully avoided all cross-hatching. It was some time before they reached a degree of perfection which made it possible to obtain half-tones (page 254).

While the illustration reproduced on this page is often described as the earliest dated woodcut, we cannot absolutely rely on the printed date, since we see from the legend that this may relate not to the woodcut itself, but to the indulgence: but in any case, this is one of the oldest existing woodcuts.

In the next illustration, ascribed to Konrad Witz, which represents St Dorothy in a rose-garden, the sense of natural beauty, which in the North was hesitating between Gothic and Renaissance, produces a charming unity of figure and ornament. The formal progress made since the woodcut of St Christopher is unmistakable.

St Dorothy with the child Jesus. A woodcut of the middle of the fifteenth century, widely distributed as a New Year's greeting. State Library, Munich

Rather later than the woodcut, the copper-engraving attained an even wider distribution. Copper engravings were the work of goldsmiths, who were experienced draughtsmen. The new technique of metal-engraving was not merely for reproducing ephemeral drawings; a more flexible art, and one more capable of development, it took over the task of book illustration from the miniature-painters.

Beside the master known only by his initials, 'E.S.', Martin Schongauer (post 1445—91) deserves particular mention. One hundred and thirteen of his engravings are known, all bearing his monogram. The

Martin Schongauer: The Miller and the Ass. Copperplate engraving. About 1482

example here reproduced illustrates not only the technical difference between the woodcut and the copperplate engraving, which allows of much greater delicacy, but also the transition from constraint to freedom, and from stylization to naturalism, which took place in the North in the fifteenth century. In the free idiom of line many things could be expressed which the more elaborate use of colour would have inhibited. For this reason even the great masters of the sixteenth century resorted to line-drawings to express their deepest feelings.

The German Masters

The two greatest masters of the Renaissance era in Germany were Albrecht Dürer, of Nuremberg (1471—1528), and Matthias Grünewald (*c.* 1460—1528). Dürer visited Italy twice, in 1494 and 1505, and, not unnaturally, was influenced by Italian, and particularly Venetian, painting. This influence was only on the surface; a certain magnificence of colour, greater broadness of handling, together with something of the Venetian treatment of light, are apparent in his work of about this time. But,

Dürer: Madonna and Crescent. Copperplate engraving. About 1500

unable to absorb the real significance of Italian classicism, he remained essentially a Northern artist, a draughtsman, thinking always in terms of line. He might have been able to absorb more of the lesson of Italy in Florence; Venetian painting was too remote from his own vision for him to understand it properly. Even in his paintings he remains a linear artist, and the larger part of this *oeuvre* consists of drawings and engravings, both on wood (such as *The Apocalypse* series, 1448, the two sets of *The Passion,* and the *Life of the Virgin*), and on metal (which include the famous single plates, the *St Jerome, The Knight, Death and the Devil,* and the *Melancholia*). His paintings include religious subjects and portraits (Figs.93b and 93d), modified to some extent by Italian conceptions of form, but always quintessentially German in feeling. Dürer is among the great draughtsmen of the world. The minute intensity of his observation and his power of setting down exactly what he saw, as in the famous drawings of animals, and grass, and hands, at Vienna, has never been surpassed. The same objectivity, almost impersonality of vision, is apparent in his landscape drawings; the watercolours which he made on his various journeys have an amazing freshness and exactitude of observation altogether unlike the romantic fairy-tale landscapes of Altdorfer.

Grünewald has only lately emerged from anonymity and obscurity. His paintings did not have the same influence on his contemporaries as the easily reproduced woodcuts and engravings of Dürer. His colouring, a hundred years in advance of his time, was hardly understood, and there is no evidence to show whether, or how, he influenced Hans Baldung-Grien, or the young Holbein, or the work of the sculptors

Dürer: The Last Supper, 1523. Woodcut

from the Main to the Upper Rhine. So solitary, enigmatical and mysterious was Grünewald, even in his lifetime, that in 1598 the German Emperor was unable to ascertain the name of the painter of the Isenheim altarpiece.

In the monastery of Isenheim, in the Vosges, he produced the greatest work of his career, the high altar in the choir of St Anthony's chapel, which in a later age was admired as the most wonderful pictorial expression of German Gothic (Fig. 94a).

Grünewald stands alone, in solitary grandeur, while Dürer had many disciples: among them were Hans Springinklee and Albrecht's brother Hans Dürer, who was afterwards influenced by Altdorfer. Other artists of Dürer's circle were Wolf Traut, Leonhard Schäufelin, and the brothers Beham.

In the wealthy imperial city of Regensburg the Danubian school was developed. In his cruder, more careless, and often very romantic idiom, Albrecht Altdorfer (*c.* 1480—1538) stands out as its greatest master. As an original creative painter and engraver (page 256) he is, in his landscape drawings and woodcuts, one of the most attractive of the lesser artists of the period.

Hans Holbein the Younger (1497—1543) was a member of a family of artists living in Augsburg, where besides his father, Hans Holbein the Elder, were the Burgkmair family and many other artists, all working in the tradition which, ever since Dürer, had become the common property of German artists. The younger Holbein, with the originality of genius, opened new possibilities. In his nineteenth year he removed to Basel, on the frontier between the German and French cultures, a city filled with the spirit of humanism, where he found a more enlightened atmosphere. Here, he made the final break with the Middle Ages. Dürer and Grünewald had belonged above all to Germany; Holbein belonged to the world.

Since Erasmus, of Rotterdam, had come there in August, 1514, Basel had become the home of international humanism. The humanistic ideal demanded a man of universal culture, distinguished not only for knowledge, but for self-control, courtesy, and good taste. How greatly this age depended on visual observation we may judge from the statement of Paracelsus, who appeared in Basel about this time. 'Experience never deceives', he declared. 'It is the greatest teacher; the eyes, which delight in experience, are the true professors.'

Dance of Death from a prayer-book. F rom Bourges. 1512—30

Holbein's portraits of Erasmus produced at this time, like the other Basel portraits—for example, the Burgomaster Meyer and the Bonifazius Amerbach—are the confident achievements of a youth of twenty who was to become one of the world's greatest portrait-painters.

Not only the scholars, however, but the great Basel printers also have their place

Albrecht Altdorfer: Lovers in the Forest.
Woodcut. 1511

in the history of art; for their productions were often the doors through which humanism made its way into the world, and for them Holbein made, between 1516 and 1532, over 1,200 drawings for woodcuts. The 'Dance of Death', printed from wood blocks after Holbein's designs (page 257), bear witness to the technical and artistic perfection of the Northern art of wood-engraving, just as the woodcuts in Luther's translation of the Bible (page 257) did much to help the introduction of Italian forms. Holbein, above all, may be said to have rounded off the Renaissance movement in the North. When, at the instigation of Erasmus, he finally left Basel in 1532, to become court painter to Henry VIII of England, he cut himself off from the advantages of a wealthy and artistic community, within which Urs Graf (page 259) and many others continued to work on safely established lines.

Whether we consider the works he produced in Switzerland, or the portraits, which he painted in England, of Henry VIII and his queens, and the French

95. (A) St Peter's Rome. Cupola by Michelangelo. 1547. Fountains and façade by Maderna, 1610 and 1606 – 26 respectively. Colonnades by Bernini, 1656 – 63.
(B) Villa Aldobrandini, Frascati, nar Rome. Great Cascade, by Giacomo della Porta and Giovanni Fontana.

b

a

b

96. (A) Façade of Pilgrim's Church, Vierzehnheiligen, near Bamberg. Begun 1743 by Balthasar Neumann. (B) Wall pavilion, in the Zwinger, Dresden. 1711 – 22, built by Matthäus Daniel Pöppelmann. (C) The Princes Hall in Schloss Bruchsal. Begun 1731. Stucco-work by J. M. Feichtmayr. Ceiling painted by J. Zich, 1751.

c

97. Church of St Johann-Nepomuk, Munich. Begun by the brothers Asam, 1733.

98. (A) Great staircase in the castle of Bruhl. 1743–8, by Balthasar Neumann.
(B) View of the garden front of the Palace of Versailles. Begun 1668 by Louis le Vau, modified 1678–89 by Jules Hardouin-Mansart.

a

b

Hans Holbein the Younger.
St. Paul. Woodcut. About 1521

Hans Holbein the Younger.
'The Old Man'.
Woodcut from the 'Dance of Death',
published in 1538

ambassador to the English court (Fig. 93c), or, above all, the magnificent series of portrait drawings of Henry VIII's courtiers, we find a cool, impartial, and profound search for truth, united with a consummate mastery of linear technique.

The Netherlands

The masterpieces of a nation's painting are usually the climax of long years of development; but in the Netherlands the opposite is the case. The Van Eycks, who were the founders of the early Netherlandish school, were also its greatest masters, and for the two hundred years after them, until the emergence of Rubens, the history of the school is almost one of anti-climax.

Such art as there was in the Netherlands before the Van Eycks, belongs to the so called 'International Gothic' style, which originated in France and spread south into Italy, and north into the Rhineland cities and the Netherlands; but it is not from this that they spring, but rather from the tradition of the illuminators—among whom the Limbourg brothers are most conspicuous—who were working about the turn of the fourteenth century for the Duc de Berry. Hubert Van Eyck (*c.* 1365—1425) was himself an illuminator, for parts of the Milan-Turin Hours, made for John of Bavaria in 1417, are now unanimously ascribed to him. The whole Eyckian technique is that of illumination on a large scale, but, thanks to the scale and the oil-medium, of a hitherto undreamed-of perfection and brilliance. Their masterpiece is the great polyptych of the *Adoration of the Lamb,* at Ghent. This, with its multiplicity of small panels, is obviously the work of men trained as miniature painters and unable to cope with the problem of filling large spaces. It is a joint work of the two brothers. By Hubert alone, who is a more nebulous figure than Jan (*c.* 1385—1441) there are, beside the Milan-Turin miniatures, two wings of an altarpiece at Leningrad, and the *Three Marys at the Sepulchre,* until recently in the Cook Collection, Richmond, and now in the van Beuningen Collection in Holland. By Jan there is an impressive list of signed and dated works, of which the most important is probably the London portrait of Arnolfini and his wife, but even so it is impossible to find out anything about the artist himself, except that he was one of the world's great realistic painters. In his religious paintings, such as the so-called 'Rollin *Madonna*' in the Louvre, there is little religious feeling; the subject is used only to give a pretext for a realistic study of an interior. In this he is the opposite of his younger contemporary, Robert Campin (1375—1444), who has now been identified with the Master of Flémalle. The Van Eycks were Dutch, and were court-painters patronized by the nobility; Campin was Flemish, from Tournay, and a painter working for middle-class patrons. His religious paintings, and to an even greater extent those of his pupil Roger van der Weyden (1398—1464), (Fig. 94c), are charged with emotion and passionate religious feeling. This cleavage was to persist throughout the history of Netherlandish painting, right up to the time of the great Dutchman, Rembrandt, and the great Fleming, Rubens. The painters working under Roger's influence were Dirck Bouts (1410—75), Simon Marmion (1401—65), Hans Memling (*c.* 1430—94) (Fig. 94b) of Bruges, and, most individual of all, Hugo van der Goes (1440—82), who even managed to transcend Roger's influence. The famous 'Portinari' altarpiece at Florence is perhaps the most magnificent and intensely passionate work of this period of Flemish painting, and its influence on Florentine painting was far-reaching.

Dutch painting, or, as one should say at this period, the painting of the northern Netherlands, was more old-fashioned, clumsier, and more naïve; yet if it lacks the suavity of the Flemish, it gains in force and in feeling. Hieronymus Bosch is the one great fifteenth-century Dutchman, but mention should also be made of Albert van Ouwater, Geertgen tot sint Jans (*c.* 1465—93) the Master of the Virgo inter Virgines (working *c.* 1480—1510), and Petrus Christus (*c.* 1400—73), the closest follower of the Van Eycks.

Bosch (*c.* 1450—1516) was a strongly individual figure, with his grotesque fantasies, which were to have so strong an effect on the elder Brueghel. But he could in such religious subjects as the National Gallery 'Crowning with Thorns', achieve an effect fully as intense as any of the Flemings.

About the turn of the century the Italian Renaissance began to make itself felt in the Netherlands. Up to then, it had been the Italians who were affected by the North, particularly the Venetians, who, in their oil technique and the problems of representing light, had more in common with the Flemish. Justus of Ghent worked at Urbino about 14—, but his style, though influenced by Italian largeness of scale, and subject matter, remained recognizably Flemish; while it would be impossible to deduce from Roger van der Weyden's pictures that he, too, made a journey to Italy about 1450. The first Fleming to show any Italian influence in Flanders was Jan Gossaert de Mabuse (*c.* 1480—1533); but he remains fundamentally entirely Flemish, with only a veneer of Italian subject-matter and style. Mabuse had considerable influence on the so-called 'Antwerp Mannerists', such as Jan de Beer (*c.* 1475—1536), and also on Bernard van Orley (1493—1542) of Brussels, known particularly for his tapestry designs, and his pupil, Pieter Coecke (1502—50), the master of the elder Brueghel.

The effects of the Renaissance were much the same in Holland as in Flanders. Lucas van Leyden (1494—1533) is more famous as an engraver and draughtsman than as a painter, and his delicate and sensitive draughtsmanship shows the influence of Dürer and of Raphael. Jan Scorel of Utrecht (1495—1562) was the most sucessful of any Netherlandish painter in assimilating the example of Raphael. Martin van Heemskerch (1498—1574) and his successors of the so-called 'Haarlem Academy', Henrik Goltzins (1558—1617), Abraham Bloemart (1564—1651) and Jan Saenredaem (1565—1607), derive, unlike Scorel, from Michelangelo, and display an exaggerated mannerism.

There was also a flourishing school of landscape in the Netherlands at about the same time. Pieter Brueghel the elder (*c.* 1530—69) cannot be considered as a landscape painter pure and simple, for much of his work consists of large figure compositions in the grotesque and essentially native, as opposed to Italianate, manner of Bosch; but such pictures as the 'Winter Landscape' or the 'Fall of Icarus', are really as much 'landscapes with figures' as anything by Claude, while there also survive numerous pen and ink drawings of landscape, many of them executed for the engraver. Joachim Patinir (*c.* 1490—1524) is another landscape painter; his pictures are smaller, and less original in conception, since they seem to derive more from the fanciful landscape backgrounds in earlier works. Paulus Brill (1554—1626), an Antwerp artist, settled early in Rome, where he came under the influence of the German Elsheimer, and occupies an important place in the history of landscape painting, bridging the gap between Elsheimer and Claude.

Urs Graf: The Standard Bearer. Woodcut, 1521

Chapter XXII

THE AGE OF THE BAROQUE AND ROCOCO

*

THE FRENCH word *baroque* (odd, curious) was adopted by later generations to express their somewhat astonished appreciation of a bygone period. But originally the word expressed also a certain aversion; there was something slightly contemptuous about it, whether one went back through the French to the Latin *verruca* (wart, bump, protuberance, hump), or thought of a Greek word for 'crazy'. The word 'rococo' is derived from the French *rocaille* (shell-work), and the very name is suggestive of the sweeping, shell-like, half-abstract and half-vegetable curves of scroll ornamentation (Fig. 99d), betraying the fact that it refers to a kind of decoration rather than to a great and significant style. For this reason Baroque and Rococo are considered together in the following chapter; moreover, the term Rococo is applied also to the last phase of the Baroque movement.

Broadly speaking, the age of Baroque may be described as the reimposition of new restrictions, in place of the old ones from which western Europe had broken away in the Renaissance. The 'freedom of a Christian man', as understood by Luther, did not last long. In the North a period of religious wars and social conflicts was approaching, and in the South the Church was preparing for the Counter-Reformation. Royal power increased and courtly etiquette became stricter than ever; and authority grew from strength to strength. Louis XIV, with his motto: 'L'état, c'est moi', was typical of the period of late Baroque. But the new restrictions, compared with those of the Middle Ages, were more worldly. Europe had not experienced the Renaissance for nothing. Individuality was not suppressed; and indeed it often found ruthless expression in the despotic ruler. Art suffered the same transformation. In some ways a new Gothic, a new subordination of details to the whole, might have been expected, but in art, as in the world, history never repeats itself exactly. Art had also experienced the Renaissance, and for this reason it is often difficult, at first, to distinguish Baroque from the Renaissance; architecture, for example, continued to make use of Renaissance forms, and it is only on close examination that the fundamental difference of manner is perceived.

The difference between the art of the sixteenth and seventeenth centuries, between high Renaissance and Baroque, can be defined as that between the clearly delimited linear or plastic art compared with a less defined and often quite indistinct picturesqueness, as closed tectonic form compared with open atectonic form, as a multifarious unity compared with a homogeneous unity, as absolute lucidity compared with relative lucidity. That these formal differences subsist to a very great

The Piazza di San Pietro, Rome, with the third wing projected by Bernini in the right foreground

extent will be seen from individual comparisons in the illustrations, while some further discussion of the historical development of form, and the whole problem of formal expression, may be left for Chapter XXIV, which concludes our discussion of stylistic evolution.

Italy

The stupendous creative energy of Michelangelo, as expressed in his later works, had burst through the rigid laws of classic form. The age which followed sought a more emotional expression in painting, an art less inhibited by refractory material or external necessities. Indeed, the seventeenth century was so pictorial that even its architecture was subordinated in every way to the standpoint of the picturesque. Churches and palaces lose their firmly-based tranquility and seem to move in the landscape like living creatures. Sharp contours assure the supremacy of light and shade, and no technical means are rejected that may lead to final vitality and urgent expressiveness.

Lorenzo Bernini (1598—1680) was the most famous and influential representative of this new mode of architecture. Through his efforts the countenance of Rome was essentially modified. The history of St Peter's (Fig. 95a) is in itself a history of the transition from Renaissance to Baroque. We have already spoken of Michelangelo's dome (page 247). Soon after his death Carlo Maderna (1556—1629) built a nave which is not altogether a happy feature of the plan, considered as a whole, for every attempt to expand one arm of the central space, as planned by Michelangelo, into a nave, was bound to degrade the miraculous achievement to a mere intersection of nave and transepts. Behind the façade, over 320 feet in width and 150 feet in height, the dome was concealed up to half the height of the drum. It is true that the eight columns of the entrance, the giant order of pilasters, the massive entablature, and the attic, are as Michelangelo intended. High Renaissance forms are combined with the exuberance of the Baroque, in a premonition of the coming style. In 1667 Alexander VII set Bernini the great and difficult task of giving the Church of St Peter its urban setting. He added a tower to Maderna's façade, but it fell and lay about in a waste of fragments. No one dared again to subject the foundations to the weight of fresh building. The stumps of the towers were left, rising to the level of the cornice of the attics, unduly widening the façade and destroying the balance of the structure. But now, as before, the church was to be given a portico. Bernini, in the most ingenious manner, took the opportunity of transforming the disadvantageous widening of Maderna's façade into an improvement. To increase the actual height of the façade was technically impossible, but Bernini, in the true spirit of the Baroque, produced an impression of height by ingeniously misleading the eye. The open space before the church rose in a slight gradient, and this was crossed by pathways which approached it obliquely, not meeting the façade at right angles, but enclosing an acute angle. This obliquity escapes the casual glance, which unconsciously transfers the smaller distance between the ends of the pathways to their starting-point, so that the façade seems narrower and, owing to the upward slope, also higher than it is in reality. In front of this forecourt, by which the eye is doubly deceived, Bernini now levelled an open space which he enclosed with open colonnades, thereby enhancing the effect of Michelangelo's dome, which had been diminished by the addition of the nave. Bernini completed his Baroque illusion by enclosing, with his arcades, an oval courtyard, which appears larger than it is in reality. The eye, expecting to see a circle, transfers the obvious width of the oval to the depth, which is not so great. The colonnades, in their simplicity, play their part by directing the attention to the façade.

But even as this façade was begun under an unlucky star, so Bernini's plan has not been fully realized. He wanted to place a third portico, as a terminal structure between the two semicircles (page 261). Owing to its omission—probably on account of the death of Alexander VII—the gap which now exists between the colonnades forms part of a typical Italian *rondo* (Fig. 95b), still further enhancing the overwhelming majesty of the whole, and especially the effect of the dome.

A characteristic example of Italian Baroque is the little church of S. Carlo alle Quattro Fontane by Borromini (1599—1667). Significantly, the plan of this tiny church is built up of oval forms. We have seen how the centrally planned church, either circular or Greek cross, was used by early and High Renaissance architects to express, their ideal of perfect lucidity and order. The oval, producing a precisely opposite effect, that of confusion and uncertainty, and above all, of *movement,* was in the same way a favourite motive with Baroque architects. The effect of the interior is one of complete plastic unity; the building might have been carved out of one block of stone, for there is no sense of its having been constructed out of separate elements. The same applies to the façade, built up of an elaborate and subtle combination of convex and concave forms, which again have no constructive purpose.

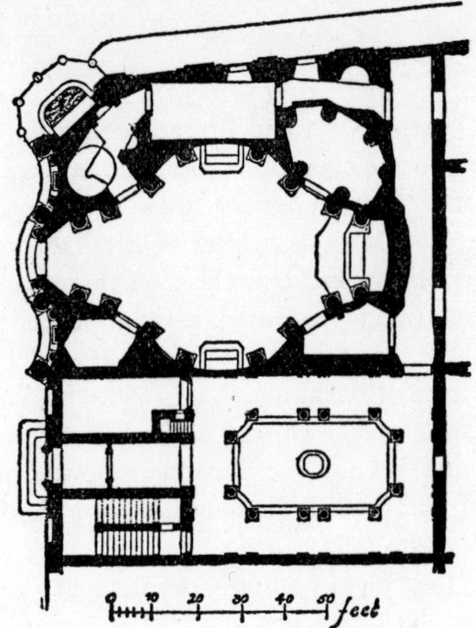

Borromini:
S. Carlo alle Quattro Fontane, begun 1633

The Baroque is essentially an art of illusion, in which all the tricks of scene-painting, false perspective and *trompe-l'oeil,* are employed without scruple to achieve a total effect. It was also the first step back towards a conception which the Middle Ages knew, but which the High Renaissance abandoned, that of the subordination of painting and sculpture to the plastic unity of the building they were to decorate. A Renaissance altar-piece or statue was conceived as an isolated thing by itself, without very much relation to its surroundings; Baroque painting or carving is an integral part of its setting, and if removed from it, loses nearly all its effect.

By the seventeenth century the golden age of Italian painting was over: this is not to say that much delightful and accomplished work was not done during the seventeenth century, but Italy did not produce any artist to rank with the great names of the fifteenth and sixteenth centuries. The great seventeenth-century painters were from the north, Rubens and Rembrandt in the Netherlands, and Claude and Poussin from France. The Italian seventeenth century was dominated by three things: the academic eclecticism of the Carracci and their school, with its centre in Bologna, the Naturalism of Caravaggio and his followers, with its centre in Naples, and the Baroque, with its centre in Rome.

The Carracci, Agostino (1557—1602), Ludovico (1555—1613) and Annibale (1560—1609), though they belong chronologically to the sixteenth, come more appropriately into the section dealing with the seventeenth century. They aimed to combine the various excellencies of the earlier masters, the drawing of Michelangelo and Raphael, the colouring of Titian, and the grace of Correggio; but these qualities, instead of enhancing each other, cancelled each other, and the result was a cold and rather insipid academicism. Annibale was the greatest of the three; he shows remarkable powers as a draughtsman and his frescoed decorations in the Pallazzo Farnese in Rome, done in 1604, anticipate the Baroque.

Of their followers the best known are Guido Reni (1575—1642), Guercino (1591—1666), and Domenichino (1581—1641). The latter is perhaps the best; his elaborate classical compositions were to influence Nicolas Poussin, and he was one of the forerunners of landscape painting.

The Baroque painters specialized in covering enormous areas of ceilings and walls in palaces and churches. Of these the eldest was Giovanni Lanfranco (1582—1647), by birth a Parmesan, and influenced by the frescoes of Correggio in the cathedral there. He worked at first in Rome, but in 1633 left it for Naples, leaving the field clear for Bernini (1598—1680) and Pietro da Cortona (1596—1669). Bernini is more famous as architect and sculptor, and typifies the energy and swaggering self-confidence of the Baroque mood. A more classical tendency in the Roman painting of the period is exemplified by Andrea Sacchi (1599—1661) and his pupil Carlo Maratta (1625—1713).

Caravaggio (1569—1609) spent most of his life in the sixteenth century; but his revolutionary and individual genius belongs, in its tendency and results, to the seventeenth century. He is an early instance of the outlawed artist, cut off from society, refusing to accept any restrictions or laws, a lonely and embittered exile. Instead of the ideal forms and classical rules of composition, which painting had hitherto followed (mannerism, it is true, diverged from these ideals, but so deliberately that it admits the validity of the classical rules by the very divergence), Caravaggio introduced a harsh and brutal realism, choosing rough peasant models, and achieving striking effects by means of extreme contrasts of light and shade and elaborate foreshortening. His temperament seems to have had closer affinities with the Spanish rather than the Italian character, and Naples, which had close connections with Spain at this period, was the centre of the Caravaggiesque influence; the early paintings of Velasquez show it, as do those of other seventeenth-century Spanish masters such as Ribera (1588—1656) and Zurbaran (1598—1664). But his influence extended much farther than Spain, though it is there that the master's manner was most closely followed. In Holland, Gerard van Honthorst (1590—1656) seems to have transmitted something of Caravaggio's dramatic use of *chiaroscuro* to his great countryman, Rembrandt; while in France the still somewhat mysterious, and only recently discovered master, Georges de la Tour (1593—1652), was a skilful, but apparently isolated, exponent of 'Tenebrism', as this use of deep shadows cast from a single source of light, to give unity to a composition, is called. Elsheimer (1578—1610) was another influential representative of this tendency; while it is perhaps just worth mentioning in this connection the name of the one English tenebrist, Joseph Wright 'of Derby' (1734—97).

Of Caravaggio's Italian followers, the most prominent were Mattia Preti (1613—1669) and Domenico Fetti (*c.* 1589—1624); while Salvator Rosa (1615—1673), also a Neapolitan, has affinities with him in his taste for savagery and low-life scenes, of bandits fighting and carousing among wild and rocky scenery. Salvator is particularly of interest for his importance in the development of romantic landscape; the

Tiepolo: One of the twenty-four etchings, 'Scherzi di fantasia'. 1718—20

eighteenth-century Genoese, Magnasco (*c.* 1667—1749) has something in common with him.

In the eighteenth century there was a final burst of flame from the gradually expiring fire of Italian painting: Venice, where there has been no painting of interest during the previous century, suddenly produced Giovanni Battista Tiepolo (1696—1770), his son, Giandomenico (1727—1802), Antonio Canaletto (1697—1768), Francesco Guardi (1712—93) and Giovanni Battista Piranesi (1720—78). All of these, except the last, spent their working lives in Venice although Canaletto visited England in 1746. The elder Tiepolo, a brilliant and facile artist, specializing in decorative schemes for walls and ceilings, inherited the luminous splendour of Veronese, but without his solidity and sense of form. Longhi, and to a lesser extent, the younger Tiepolo, portrayed the daily life of Venice, the former in small canvases, the latter in drawings; while Canaletto and Guardi painted outdoor scenes on the canals and *piazze*. Piranesi, though born in Venice, came to Rome in 1738. No paintings by him are known, and his fame rests entirely on his etchings of architecture and ruins. Others, notably Pannini and Sebastiano Ricci, both of the previous generation, had painted ruined buildings, and there is no doubt that they influenced Piranesi; but their ruin-pieces, painted quite without feeling, are little better than superior furniture pictures. Piranesi's vision, of gigantic, decaying Roman ruins, and fantastic prison interiors, has a powerful, almost sinister, and sometimes almost mad, intensity. His publications of designs for furniture and fireplaces had considerable influence on Robert Adam and the rest of the classical revival in England, while there can be little doubt that the architecture of Soane and Dance (in particular the latter's masterpiece, the design for Newgate Prison) were strongly affected by him.

Germany

The Baroque style in architecture was one of propaganda: in palaces, it impressed on the onlooker the importance of the absolute monarch; in churches, it was at the service of the Counter-Reformation. We may therefore expect to find it outside Italy, in Catholic and absolutist countries. The Catholic states of South Germany, such as Bavaria and Austria, produced a Baroque architecture as magnificent as such as anything in Italy. The greatest of the South German Baroque architects was Balthasar Neumann (1687—1753) who produced a miracle of palace architecture in the Würzburg *Residenz;* this went hand in hand with the building of monasteries and churches; for bishops and abbots, no less than princes, pretended to wordly importance. Neumann found himself confronted, in the case of the ingeniously designed wing of the Banz monastery at Brühl, by the necessity of inserting a well-staircase (Fig. 98a) in a building erected by Schlaum in 1725—28. Here we see at its highest his unique ability for producing an effect of unlimited space by optical illusion, the inclusion of picturesque vistas, and by tricks of lighting. In the well-staircase

Central portion of Schloss Sans Souci, Potsdam. Built 1745—47 by Georg Wenzeslaus von Knobelsdorff

and the banqueting halls of Schloss Bruchsal (Fig. 96c) he produced what is, in consistency, design, magnificence, and lighting, one of the greatest masterpieces of German architecture. In church architecture his most impressive creation was the *Vierzehnheiligen* (the Fourteen Saints) near Bamberg (Fig. 96a). On entering the building one is overwhelmed by a flood of light. Everything is moving; the interior seems to be enclosed by circling, undulating forms: even in the ground plan it appears to be completely disintegrated. Even when no special circumstances are operative, as in the church of the 'Fourteen Saints', we see that the customary ground-plan of a Baroque church has almost completely abolished the straight line, and even the façades are curved. Unlike the façades of Italian Baroque churches, German churches have usually kept their towers. It was in the decoration of these churches that this whirling combination of forms reached its height. In the churches in which the brothers Asam co-operated, as, for example, the monastery church at Einsiedeln, and the Carmelite church at Regensburg, and, above all, the church of St John Nepomuk, in Munich (Fig. 97), they reached the limits of the possible in the combination of reality and illusion. Effects of hidden lighting, the inclusion of fresco painting in stucco decorations, and every other possible illusionist trick, make these churches seem now like a pompous Baroque opera-house, now like a Rococo stage improvised for a festival, entirely without the quiet solemnity and the piety which are bound up with the conception of Romanesque or Gothic art.

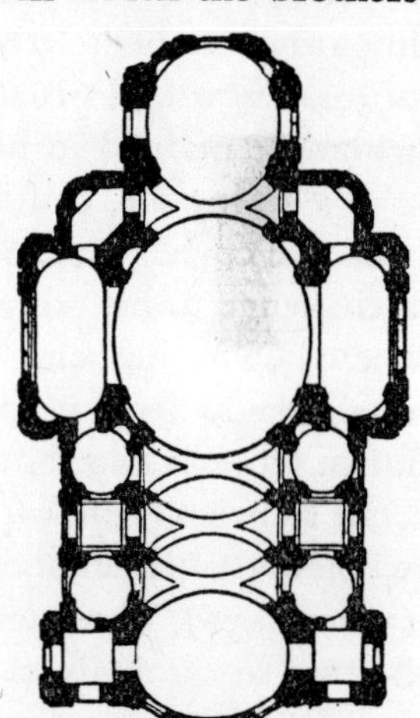

Ground plan of a German Baroque church with towers flanking the façade

The Netherlands

Netherlandish painting in the sixteenth century had been in transition between Northern and Italian influences; it was Peter Paul Rubens (1577—1640) who first digested, absorbed and fused the two, creating a new style, which was to have a powerful and lasting effect on all painting north of the Alps. Ruben's first master was Otto van Veen, an uninspiring Antwerp mannerist; but in 1600 he visited Italy, where he remained for the next eight years, broken by a visit to Spain, on a mission on behalf of Vincenzo Gonzaga—the first of his diplomatic employments. All that the art of the past could tell him in Italy and Spain he eagerly absorbed; not in a spirit of tame imitation, but with a high-spirited exuberance. It was characteristic of him that his first attempts, at the age of twenty-five, should represent scenes of violent activity, like the *Hercules and Omphale*. Probably, too, the great *Judith* dates from the Italian period. Here four angels, in childish simplicity, report the scene of sensual cruelty that is being enacted below them, where the vengeful woman is decapitating Holofernes with her sword. His *Tarquin and Lucretia* (Fig. 101a), in which the deed of violence is committed, not by a woman, but by a man, is greatly superior to the 'Judith'. The whole picture is wonderfully composed, and it shows, in the intricate modelling of the flesh, that the Baroque had already found its way to the Netherlands.

Shortly after his return from Italy the young Rubens painted the archducal pair of Austria in almost strident tones of red, yellow and green. The restlessness of youth, the hesitation between Antwerp and Italy, of which Rubens spoke in a letter of the 10 April, 1609, was brought to an end by his marriage.

Towards the end of 1611, no longer affected by what he had seen last, but as a free, independent artist, Rubens set foot on the first steps of the 'High Baroque', to become its chief representative in northern Europe. He now achieved a consistency and comprehensiveness which have made his pictures known to all the world. A period of incomparable fertility followed: with his delight in portrait-painting, he immortalized his relatives, his brother, his children, and four years after the death of his first wife, in 1626, he was painting the young and lovely Helène Fourmont, whom he married in his fifty-third year. Her grace and youth endowed him with a new springtide, and he was never weary of recording her beauty. The time came when he could not, unaided, carry out all the commissions he received. They were a challenge to his powers of organization, for with all his overflowing vitality, he knew how to husband his energies and to exploit them to the full, and he had soon established a large workshop in which selected pupils and assistants carried out his ideas. At least two thousand pictures were produced in this way.

In Rubens, Flemish painting found its natural centre and his style conquered the whole of the Netherlands. Its influence was most enduring, perhaps, on Jacob Jordaens (1593—1678), whose temperament was similar to that of his master, in whose studio he was working about 1617. But of all his pupils, none became so famous or so independent as Sir Anthony van Dyck (1599—1641). In Ántwerp, after Rubens, in 1623, had begun his diplomatic career, Van Dyck was the undisputed master, but the many religious paintings of this period are not among his best; they are obviously influenced by Rubens, and also by Titian and the Bolognese school, boldly painted compositions in which the unbridled energy of Rubens is tempered by a fastidious elegance, which never deserted Van Dyck, and is best of all displayed in his portraits (Fig. 101b), even though these were produced with mechanical regularity. Many of them are fluently painted, with a skilful and easy technique, in which white, black and

IV. Rembrandt van Rijn (1606–69): Saskia as Flora (National Gallery, London)

grey are predominant, as though the master were fastidiously avoiding the garishness of colour. His sense of harmony led him toward a solution in which grey united all colours in itself. With Flemish thoroughness he painted lace collars, ruffs, chains and jewels, without the pedantic uniformity shown by so many of his contemporaries. The majority of his subjects were aristocrats, who, in their sumptuous garments and their dignified, and indeed often arrogant bearing, could only gain by the grace and refinement of Van Dyck's treatment. With fastidious refinement he shrinks from all that is not ornamental, or elegant, or beautiful, and in his Biblical scenes his shepherds and malefactors are dressed like gentlefolk and bear themselves accordingly. In 1630 Van Dyck was appointed court painter to the Princess of Orange, and also to the King of England, by whom in 1632 he was knighted; he had now reached the zenith of fame and prosperity. Everyone wanted to be painted by Van Dyck, who was one of the first fashionable portrait-painters, able to give an appearance of refined elegance to subjects who lacked those qualities: the courtly, handsome, and noble figure of Charles I, as he exists today in our imaginations, owes a great deal to Van Dyck; as portrayed by other painters, with more honesty and less skill, he is a very different, and less appealing, figure.

Unlike the aristocratic Van Dyck, the Flemings, Adriaen Brouwer (1606—38) and the two Teniers, portrayed the life of the people with realism. In their scenes of tavern life, fairs, dances, and village junketings they, like the great animal painter, Frans Snyders (1579—1657), expressed their delight in reality. But in painting such subjects they were leaving the Baroque, which was still a link between the Catholic Flemish Netherlands and the courtly art of Spain and Italy, for the art of Holland, in which the family, and domestic life, were preferred before public spectacles.

Frans Hals (*c.* 1580—1666) was the first great Dutch master of this period. He has been called a joyous pessimist, as Rembrandt might be described as a melancholy optimist. Hals, in his brimming vitality, for all his poverty and debt, could always console himself by painting the portrait of a jolly toper or a fool; he saw that the swaggering strength of the Jongheer van Heythuysen (Fig. 102b) should be portrayed, not in the brilliance of a finished portrait, such as Rubens had taught people to expect, but by a new picturesque improvisation, owing its charm to its easy, loose, brushwork. One of Hals's pupils was Adriaen van Ostade (1610—85). From depicting scenes of everyday life, the painters of this school began to produce the great Baroque landscapes (Fig. 100b), of which the finest examples were created by Jacob van Ruisdael (*c.* 1628—82), Philips Koninck (1619—1688), Meindert Hobbema (1638—1703), and, above all, by Rubens himself, particularly towards the end of his life.

An intermediate position between the genre painters, with their technical skill, and the elegance of Van Dyck, was that of Vermeer of Delft (1632—75). The artist who in his only self-portrait (Fig. 102c), if it is really anything of the kind, deliberately, and as though symbolically, turns his back on the observer, has remained completely concealed behind his works. Only from his portraits of elegant women do we realize how little is known of him, who, the always poverty-stricken father of eleven children, had hardly ever left his native city, where he ate his heart out in longing for the aristocratic life.

Rembrandt. Self-portrait. Etching

It was Rembrandt Harmensz van Ryn (1606—69) who gave a new spirituality to the realistic art of Holland. He kept the methods of realism, but gave them a hitherto unknown, translucent luminosity. His chiaroscuro is not the result of placing the subject in a shadowy room, as, for example, in Dürer's engraving of St Jerome, nor of the darkness of the skies of Holland (in which case a complete climatic revolution must have occurred before he began to paint). Rembrandt, while keeping to its laws, developed the art of his period to its ultimate pictorial possibilities. The picturesque is by no means dependent upon colour; this is proved by the three hundred odd etchings of the master, which may be compared with his seven hundred paintings. Already, in the self-portrait of 1631 (above), the strictly linear outlining of the face is broken; a year later, in his 'Vendor of Rat-poison', (page 271) after various preliminary sketches, he produced his first finished composition, significantly a scene of plebeian life. A late work, such as his 'Philosopher', shows how he progressed in his exploitation of picturesque possibilities. If we compare his pen-drawing (Fig. 100a) with Renaissance work (Figs. 88c, and 88d) we see the entirely different uses to which line is put; it ceases to be elegant or calligraphic, as when, for example, on the right it marks the inner surface of the wall, but on the left only indicates the curtain, or, in the shadow of the 'Philosopher', hints at the backs of the books rather than depicts them. The superficial effect of plasticity is replaced by depth. Instead of the absolute clarity of classic art we have the relative clarity of the Baroque, a unity achieved, less by attention to every part, than by concentration on the essential.

At about the same time as the above-mentioned etchings—in 1632—Rembrandt produced his first great painting, the *Anatomy Lesson of Dr Tulp,* which all Amsterdam applauded. His fortune was in the ascendant—not only in art, but also in life—for in 1634 he married the charming and wealthy Saskia van Uylenburgh, a patrician's daughter.

In this period, the happiest of his life, he produced many portraits, in warm, golden tones, historical scenes, and landscapes steeped in light and colour, like the *Stormy Landscape* in the Brunswick gallery. In 1642 his wife died, and the work into

Rembrandt: The Vendor of Rat-poison. Etching. 1632.

which he had put his whole self, the so-called *Night Watch,* was misunderstood and repudiated. Under such blows Rembrandt withdrew more and more into himself, and it was now that he produced his wonderful scenes from the Old Testament.

What the Rembrandt of 1654 could achieve in the way of objective representation is shown by the portrait of Burgomaster Six (Fig. 102a), one of the painter's greatest triumphs. No reproduction could do justice to the splendid red of the cloak, or the harmonious contrast of the delicate grey of the coat. Only in front of the original can one detect the recurrence of the red in the hair, and its echoes in the background; but it can show the naturalness of the gestures, the inherent dignity and humanity, not only of the model but of the painter also.

In 1656 Rembrandt lost all his property; a calamity from which he was rescued solely by the energy of Hendrikje Stoffels. Misfortune could not shatter the giant. He painted in darker colours, and it seemed as though the song of his glowing red and golden tones was silenced for ever. But in the last few years before his death the colours of his prime appeared once more, as though in farewell, in the glorious picture, now at The Hague, of *David playing before Saul.*

Spain

Up to the end of the sixteenth century Spanish art was almost entirely under foreign influences. El Greco, Domenico Theotocopoulos (1541—1614), was born in Crete, then a Venetian possession, and began as a Venetian mannerist, under the influence of Tintoretto. Nevertheless, it is customary to describe him as a Spanish master; though for Spain he has always been El Greco, 'the Greek'. Titian had ceased to paint reclining women and dreamy landscapes. In accordance with the spirit of the age, his colours had grown darker. The Turkish armies were threatening Europe in the East; in the North there was the Reformation. The painters of the South began to place their figures in rooms as gloomy as the closets of the Inquisition. The young Greco took his subjects from Titian's paintings, but did not paint them in the Venetian manner, on canvas, but on small wooden panels, like the Triptych at Modena, on which he set his signature, 'Domenikos', in Greek letters.

El Greco did not stay in Italy after 1576, for Rome was no longer the centre of the world. The Italians were wearing Spanish costumes, and the heart of the Counter-Reformation was in Spain. The Escorial (Fig. 103c) was being built as the new citadel of the Faith, and the palaces of Toledo were being turned into monasteries and convents. Beauty had to give way to holiness. In the Catholic empire which Charles V had created there was no demand for a national Spanish art, since it included both Italy and the Netherlands. Fernando de Llanos and Ferrando Yañez were pupils of Leonardo's; El Mudo emulated Titian, and Sanchez Coello, or Pantoja de la Cruz, painted the Spanish nobles very much in the manner of Anthonis Mor, the Dutch court painter of Philip II. Tintoretto's paintings, like those of other Italian, and even those of Northern painters, found their way into the Escorial.

In the spring of 1577 El Greco found in Toledo the familiar shapes of his Cretan home, the buildings of the Mohammedan East, all in the urgent and emphatic Spanish form. He spent two years in painting his first great work, the altarpiece for San Domingo el Antiguo. The passionate and often extravagant spirit of the Baroque had now possessed him. His wooden panels and modest canvases were forgotten; he now painted pictures of enormous dimensions.

Among the important paintings of the following period was the representation of the miracle which was said to have occured during the burial of Count Orgaz, when St Augustine and St Stephen appeared and discharged the duties of the clergy. In grey and yellow, black and white, the colours of the stormy sky, El Greco has

a

b

c

103. (A) El Greco: Portrait of Julian Romero with tutelary Saint, 81 in. by 51 in. About 1586 – 94. (Prado, Madrid). (B) El Greco: Descent of the Holy Ghost. *c.* 1604 – 12. (Prado, Madrid). (C) The Escorial, near Madrid. Begun under Philip II in 1563, in accordance with the plans of Juan Batista of Toledo, and completed in 1585 by Juan de Herrera.

a b

c

104. (A) Murillo: The Madonna of the Rosary. Canvas, 65 in. by 43 in. About 1650 – 60. (Prado, Madrid).
(B) Velasquez: Aesopus. Formerly in the hunting-lodge of Philip IV, probably together with Rubens' representatio of Heraclitus and Democritus. Canvas, 76 in. by 37 in. After 1636. (Prado, Madrid).
(C) Velasquez: Venus and Cupid (the 'Rokeby Venus'). Canvas, 48 in. by 69 in. About 1642. (National Gallery, Londo

a

b

c

105. (A) Gainsborough: The Blue Boy. *c.* 1771. (Formerly in London, now in a private collection in America).
(B) Watteau: Detail from the painting 'L'Amour au Théâtre Français'. 1718 – 20. (Kaiser-Friedrich Museum, Berlin).
(C) Hogarth: The Toilet, from 'Marriage à la Mode'. 1745. (National Gallery, London).

106. (A) Turner: Crossing the Brook (National Gallery, London).
(B) Claude: Aeneas at Delos. (National Gallery, London).

b

painted the miracle in an unearthly light, not as a supernatural, but rather as a supremely natural event, to which the whole Spanish people, its priests, its nobles, and its faithful, bear witness by their presence on the solid floor of the church. Some have called El Greco's pictures ascetic, ecstatic, cruel, nerveless and colourless. Nevertheless, a portrait like that of the Grand Inquisitor is painted with the strongest colouring; it is only in El Greco's saints that we find deliberate distortion and an unearthly radiance. When he paints ordinary human beings, like his daughter, it is as though they were reflected in a mirror. In the altarpiece of the chapel of St Joseph, in Toledo, there are angels painted in warm colours and with plastic modelling.

The final development of El Greco's art places him, in spite of his peculiarities, in the heart of the Baroque period, as one who had overcome the world, and, indeed, had almost entirely renounced sensual perception. Thus, his paintings (Figs. 103a and 103b), from ordinary worldly events to heavenly ecstasies, abandoned Renaissance laws of composition and colour and move towards the international art of the Baroque period. He is no longer a Greek, and it is not the spirit of Spanish art that inspires him. With Matthias Grünewald, he is one of the world's greatest religious painters.

Diego de Silva y Velasquez (1599—1660), a Spaniard by birth, was the greatest Spanish artist. A friend and fellow pupil of Francisco Zurbaran, he left the school of art in Seville for Madrid, where he outstripped all his teachers and rivals. Painters knew how to paint light; but Velasquez added to light the magic of space and atmosphere. His colours and colour values seemed to come from his brush without effort; with his bold, free touch he seemed to pour life into his realistic and exactly observed figures.

When we consider Velasquez's paintings, the question arises whether the supreme style of the period was the Baroque, or the Naturalism which had been developing ever since the fifteenth century. But if we compare one of the ripest works of the master, the 'Rokeby Venus' (Fig. 104c), with similar paintings of the High Renaissance, we see how much the artistic perception of reality had changed in the course of a century. Renaissance artists were constantly representing the nude, and Giorgione's 'Venus' (Fig. 92a) is still presented in classic, clearly delineated forms. This serene clarity was obscured, at the end of the century, by mannerism.

Velasquez had at his disposal all the methods of the Baroque; no creatures of the every-day world intrude into the picture, in which Beauty nonchalantly turns her back upon the observer, while Cupid holds up a mirror before her. The mirror was already a familiar trick, often used in Roman Baroque villas and palaces to give an impression of spaciousness. Its ambiguous lighting and refraction increase the picturesque effect of the device. Instead of the marble calm of Giorgione's classic Venus the Baroque presents us with a charming, but entirely human and un-divine, study of the nude.

To this extent Velasquez was the child of his period, the Baroque; but we should fail in our appreciation of this great personality if we looked for nothing more than the style of the period in him. As a Spaniard, Velasquez was far more in sympathy than El Greco with the Spanish sense of realism. In 1623, Philip IV summoned him to the Court, and from the first his portraits pleased everybody by their verisimilitude and their serene dignity. Apart from two visits to Italy, in 1629—31 and 1649—51, Velasquez never again left Madrid and the Court, where he was promoted to the dignity of a chamberlain. Though he was a court painter he did more than paint the king, his retainers, his ministers, and even his jesters; he immortalized the whole Spanish people, in its many types, and its history in such pictures as the *Surrender of Breda.* At an early stage of his career, in his *Topers* and his *Vulcan's Forge,* Velasquez had already treated mythological scenes; but it was their composition, not their subject, which gave them, like his later masterspiece of the *Tapestry-weavers,* the reality of life. It may be an exaggeration to describe Velasquez as the father of *plein air* painting, but the lighting of his pictures seemed unrefracted by time. In the buoyancy with which the little Prince Balthasar dashes across country, and also in the picture of *Las Meniñas,* a close observer may detect a certain Baroque theatricality. But under the stiff garments, and behind the courtly etiquette, a mysterious inner life seems to dwell. Velasquez put his heart into painting of Æsop (Fig. 104b), overlooking the fabulist's hump; in his portrait of Queen Maria Anna of Austria, a childish, insignificant person, he depicted her with due respects, faithfully portraying her blond tresses and her blue eyes, but without omitting the obstinate expression of the Habsburg mouth. But this man of the world, in the best sense of the word, was never one to wear his heart on his sleeve. This explains why one learns so little, despite all the dates and historical details, of the essential, human Velasquez.

Bartolomé Esteban Murillo (1618—82) (Fig. 104a) was a painter of very different quality. A native of Seville, like Velasquez, he belonged to a younger generation, and from 1660, when he founded an art-school there, he was active as a teacher. He did not need to play the pioneer, for art had reached its height in the Spanish empire. In the nineteenth century both Romantics and Naturalists looked at Murillo with equal enthusiasm, but today one would not speak of him in the same breath with Velasquez If his 'Melon-eater', and similar genre subjects, are still popular, it should be realized that the pleasure which they give is that which would be derived from a well-posed 'period' photograph, without considering its artistic virtuosity.

Chapter XXIII

THE CLASSICAL TRADITION

*

In the foregoing chapter the reader has learnt to regard the forms of Mannerism as the external expression of the period of ecclesiastical schism, and the forms of Baroque art as the expression of a reinforced ecclesiastical authority, as manifested in the predominantly Catholic countries of Italy and Spain, and the Catholic portions of the Netherlands and Southern Germany, during the seventeenth and eighteenth centuries.

In Protestant England, on the other hand, and in France, the native soil of the Enlightenment, evolution followed a different course. In these countries the classical tradition of the Renaissance had become a mighty pillar of the native art, which the surging waves of Baroque and Rococo could never quite overthrow. Supported by her insular situation, England, faithful to tradition, preserved for centuries her heritage of the Gothic style, and again for centuries preserved the classical forms of the Renaissance. In France, on the other hand, it was the influential idea of the organizing omnipotence of the State, soon to become more powerful even than the Church, which fostered *le grand style* in art. It is typical of the attitude of *le grand siècle* that it regarded art as a universal realm, subject only to its own laws. According to the opinion of this period, the various orders of columns, like the composition of a painting, must obey laws of universal validity. Hence the great seriousness, the passionate earnestness with which the artists of this period dealt with problems of proportion and construction, and the logic with which they occasionally tolerated a freer style, *una maniera licenziosa*. Thus, the severity of the classical style in the West, which in France became the truly national style, is in manifest opposition to the unrestraint, the bold improvisation and the national flavour of the Baroque in eastern countries. For this reason the classical style in France and England, although it was its contemporary, must be clearly distinguished from the Baroque of Italy, Southern Germany and Spain. England consciously rejected this Baroque as Catholic, just as France deliberately eschewed it after she had made the acquaintance of the Italian masters. The entire dispute between the disciples of Rubens and those of Poussin centred on the contrast between the classical and the Baroque conceptions of art, and when in 1665 Bernini was summoned to Paris to design the façade of the Louvre, but was presently replaced by Claude Perrault, France decided in favour of a new classical style, which was not, however, immune to the influence of Baroque and Rococo.

English Architecture

Henry VIII, like his contemporary François I of France, made an attempt to Italianize English architecture, with rather the same results; that is to say, English builders continued to build in the late Gothic manner, and Italians were employed to apply decoration to the result. There was nothing in England, at this period, of the scale and importance of the Loire *chateaux* except perhaps Hampton Court, entirely late Gothic with very little Italian ornament, and Nonesuch Palace (begun in 1537, now destroyed), which seems to have been richly decorated with Italian plaster-work. The most important Italian artist to work in England was Torrigiano, a Florentine sculptor, whose chief work is Henry VII's tomb at Westminster. The Reformation caused English relations with Italy to diminish, while those with the Netherlands and Protestant Germany became correspondingly closer. Under Elizabeth there was an influx of Dutch and German craftsmen, and Elizabethan houses, while still mediaeval in plan and general design, were decorated both inside and out, with debased classical motives usually taken from German or Dutch pattern-books. English architecture in the sixteenth century, and in the first quarter of the seventeenth century, was still in transition: the Renaissance idea of the architect as an artist, as the responsible designer of the building as a whole, had not yet ousted the mediaeval idea of the master-mason, building by rule-of-thumb, along traditional lines.

The man responsible for the change was Inigo Jones (1573—1652). Until after his second visit to Italy, in 1614, Jones had been less an architect than an engineer, and designer of scenery and mechanical devices of the masques which were then such a feature of court life: but he came back from Italy having thoroughly absorbed the lessons of Italian architecture. It is interesting, in view of later developments in English architecture, that Jones, though he was in Italy at the height of the Baroque revival, shows no signs of it in his work, which is based mostly on Palladio. In 1616 he designed the Queen's House at Greenwich, a work entirely mature, elegant, restrained and simple, and displaying a complete mastery of material. The Queen's House is a combination of two Italian villas, Scamozzi's Villa Molini, near Padua, and the elder San Gallo's at Poggio a Caiano, near Florence, made with such tact as to seem entirely in place in England, unlike some of the eighteenth-century versions of Palladian villas. In 1619 he began his designs for Whitehall Palace; if this enormous building, with a façade 1,280 feet long, had been carried out, London would have had one of the largest and most magnificent palaces in Europe. The fact that Jones could make such a monumental plan, at a time when England as a whole had not thrown off the architectural ideals of the Middle Ages, is a measure of his genius. The plans show the Palladian desire for rooms, carefully related to each other in size, disposed symmetrically round a central axis; while the façades are composed of Palladian elements. The only part to be built, the

Banqueting House, is a very close adaptation of a Palladian palace. Among Jones's other works are parts of Greenwich Hospital, parts of old Somerset House (now pulled down), and Wilton House, near Salisbury, with its magnificent interiors. He also planned the piazza at Covent Garden, with its arcaded sides and the church, a daringly simple elevation, with a Tuscan portico supporting a heavy pediment. Jones is one of the greatest of classical architects. He said himself: 'The outward ornaments should be solid, proportionable according to the rules, masculine, and unaffected', and no English architect, not even Wren himself, has so consistently lived up to those principles.

The period of the Commonwealth is of little interest architecturally, the one architect of distinction before Wren being Jones's pupil, John Webb (1611—74). His chief houses are Thorpe Hall, near Peterborough, and Ashdown house, in Berkshire. Webb has none of Jones's taste or instinctive feeling for proportion, and his buildings are clumsy by comparison, but with a solid strength.

Christopher Wren (1632—1723) was not an architect by training, but a scientist and astronomer, a man with an extraordinarily practical and inquisitive mind. He did not begin to practise architecture until he was nearly thirty; his first important work, the Sheldonian Theatre at Oxford, is clumsy and coarse both inside and out, but, characteristically, is remarkable chiefly for the mechanical ingenuity by which the architect made a flat ceiling sixty-eight feet across. In 1665 he went to Paris for six months, and he is known to have seen Bernini's designs for the Louvre and to have met the French architects of the time. This was the only training he had, if it can be called training: otherwise, with a basis of excellent mechanical knowledge, he was content to learn by experience. The great fire of London in 1666 gave him his opportunity: what he saw in Paris must have affected the plan he drew up for the rebuilding of the City, with its clearly laid out wide streets, intersecting at circular

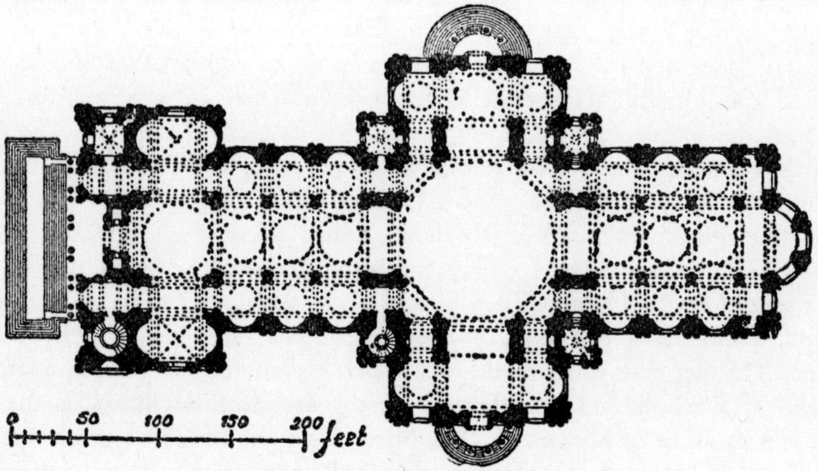

Wren: St Paul's Cathedral, London, 1675—1710

rond points: this plan was never carried out, but Wren did rebuild St Paul's, and fifty-three of the City churches. In the latter he solved, with great ingenuity, the problems arising out of awkward and irregularly shaped sites, combined with the main requirement of a Protestant church, that the pulpit should be everywhere visible. The spires are the most remarkable features of the churches; in them, classical motives are combined with an elegant ease, free from any touch of pedantry. Analysis of St Paul's Cathedral (1675—1710) reveals the number of different influences which Wren drew on. His first plan, and design for the dome, was based on Bramante's St Peter's. Wren, a true classic artist, planned a Greek cross, and it is interesting that, as in the case of St Peter's, religious considerations (not the Counter-Reformation, but the Catholic tendencies of the Restoration Court) obliged him to change to a Latin cross. The effect of the interior suffers from this change of plan. His second plan for the dome is based on Michelangelo's St Peter's and Mansart's Invalides. The final design is a combination of the two previous plans. Various Roman baroque motives can be detected in the West tower, the fenestration, and the semi-circular porticos on the North and South fronts. But St Paul's is a unified and homogenous masterpiece; and in spite of the baroque motives, the building remains classical and static, with none of the movement of the true baroque.

Hampton Court is another of Wren's masterpieces. The Garden front is unmistakably a palace, and at the same time it is a gentleman's house, unlike the cold, vulgar, magnificence of Versailles. Wren's triumph is the greater when one remembers that this effect of stateliness is obtained with red-brick, with stone only used in the facings. Hampton Court is an outstanding example of Wren's ability to combine grandeur with intimacy.

At Greenwich, Wren was faced with the problem of combining in his plan the Queen's House and a block of buildings to the west. Though Vanbrugh, Hawksmoor, Campbell and Ripley all had some part in the palace as it now stands, the main scheme is Wren's. He solved the problem by embodying the western block in an enormous composition of two main blocks of buildings, parallel, and at right angles to the river, with the Queen's House as their axis. Greenwich and Hampton Court are the two finest English palaces. With Wren, English architecture reaches its maturity; its characteristics are reason, originality and urbanity, with neither the crudity of his predecessors (Jones always excepted), nor the academic formality of his successors.

Of the architects who came immediately after Wren, Vanbrugh and Hawksmoor are the most important. John Vanbrugh (1666—1726) is a unique figure in English architecture; like Wren he did not turn to architecture until fairly late in life, but he spent his earlier life not as an inventor or engineer, but as a playwright. His chief works were Castle Howard (1702—14), Blenheim Palace (1705—22) and Seaton Delaval (1720—21). These are the nearest England ever got to the Baroque, for Vanbrugh, possibly because of his early association with the theatre, always regarded architecture as a question of disposing masses of masonry to obtain a general effect, regardless of interior convenience or suitability. Castle Howard is an attempt at a Baroque palace in the Continental manner: the effect of the huge domed house, the fountains, and the outbuildings. the Temple, and Hawksmoor's Mausoleum, is very splendid; the same is true of Blenheim, which is in a more distinctive and characteristic style. Vanbrugh is in no sense of the word a 'classic' architect, for his emphasis on total effect, his fondness for broken skyline with towers and pinnacles and his deliberate return to the 'castle-style', make him the first, and perhaps the greatest, of English romantic architects. This in a way explains his failure: for to talk of architecture an art which depends for its effect on the classic virtues of restraint, proportion and order, as 'romantic' is a contradiction in terms.

Vanbrugh's style, which appealed only to a sophisticated taste, never became popular. One or two architects, however, were inspired by him. Chief among them was Nicholas Hawksmoor (1661—1736), who worked under Wren for thirty years, and then for Vanbrugh. His work shows these two irreconcilable elements, blended not altogether successfully. From Vanbrugh came his feeling for size, and the freedom with which he uses classical motives: from Wren, his technical mastery, far greater than Vanbrugh's. His chief works are the Gothic Quadrangle at All Souls', and the front Quadrangle at Queen's College, both at Oxford, and some London churches, chief of which are Christ Church, Spitalfields, and St George's, Bloomsbury. Another pupil of Vanbrugh's whose work also approaches the Baroque is James Archer, who designed the churches of St Philip, Birmingham , and St John's, Smith Square in London, a church almost square in plan with its façades curiously composed of broken pediments flanked by towers at each corner, like an overturned footstool. But this tendency towards the Baroque, and any tendency to continue the tradition of Wren and make a specifically English classical style, was stopped by the Palladian revival. This was largely due to the influence of Lord Burlington (1695—1753), a noble patron of the arts, who has himself been credited with the design of several buildings. Here we meet for the first time the eighteenth-century conception of 'correct taste', and the dictatorship of the cultivated amateur, the 'man of taste', over the professional. The chief Palladian architects were Colin Campbell (b. 1729, whose works include the excellent, and surprisingly, un-Palladian Houghton Hall; Wanstead House, now destroyed; and Mereworth Castle, an absurd adaptation, entirely unsuited to the English climate, of Palladio's Villa Rotonda); Giacomo Leoni an Italian (1686—1746, who built Moor Park, Herts, and Lyme Hall, Cheshire);Thomas Ripley (d. 1758, who built the rather unsuccessful Admiralty in London); and William Kent (1684—1748, the best-known, who built Holkham Hall, plain and ill-proportioned outside, but magnificent inside; Chiswick House, another and more suitable adaptation of the Villa Rotonda; Lord Powys's house in Berkeley Square; and the Horse Guards, an axcellent example of Palladian composition: Kent was equally successful as a designer of interiors and furniture). Others were Isaac Ware

(d. 1766), John Vardy (d. 1765), James Flitcroft (1697—1769), the Woods of Bath (*c.* 1705—54), who produced at Bath one of the best pieces of eighteenth-century town-planning, and Sir William Chambers (1726—96), best known today as the architect of Somerset House, who was responsible for introducing the taste for *chinoiserie* into England, and who continued, in spite of the Adams's Classical Revival in the 1760's, to design in the Palladian manner.

There is one architect who differs from his Palladian contemporaries, and deserves separate mention: this is James Gibbs (1682—1754), who had worked in Rome under the Baroque architect Fontana. He is really the only eighteenth-century architect who can be said in any way to have continued in the tradition of Wren. The first of his London churches, St Mary-le-Strand, with its crowded composition and decorative use of pediments and swags, shows that Gibbs had seen the Roman Baroque; St Martin's-in-the-Fields is more in the English tradition: the composition of the spire is worthy of Wren, but, as Gibbs's Palladian critics were quick to point out, it should not have been allowed to seem to balance on the roof, behind the portico: Wren always took care to support his spires on towers standing directly on the ground. But Gibbs's attempt to combine the temple form (that is to say an oblong, and essentially horizontal building, with a portico), with the vertical spire, influenced all subsequent classical church building, Gibbs's other principal work is at Oxford and Cambridge: at Cambridge he designed the Library and Senate House, and a block of buildings at King's College; at Oxford he produced one of his finest works, the Radcliffe Camera, a vast circular domed building, which may well have been inspired by Wren's design for the Mausoleum of Charles I. Gibbs is not always strictly correct; but his work at its best has a richness, a solidity, and an individual quality, which distinguishes him from the orthodox Palladians. Gibbs and Hawksmoor are perhaps the two best architects of the early eighteenth century.

Palladian architecture has the virtues of decency, sobriety, and order; the minor architecture of the eighteenth century, the middling-sized houses and churches built in what is loosely called the 'Georgian' style, with their agreeable, unpretentious, good taste, owe much to the dissemination of Palladianism by means of architectural pattern-books, which established a tradition of excellent building rules which could be put into practice by any competent country builder. A Georgian town like Bath, or parts of eighteenth-century London like Bloomsbury, or the Adams's New Town at Edinburgh, illustrate this; the general effect, founded as it is upon a tradition of good order and proportion, is one of great architecture, though this may not be true of the component parts. Palladianism produced no work of overwhelming genius; but, what is almost as good, it gave England a sound building tradition.

English Painting

England's geographical position has always tended to isolate her from continental movements, and as far art is concerned, the effect of the Renaissance was delayed for many years. In the sixteenth century, Henry VIII employed the younger Holbein as his court painter; the numerous English portraits called 'Holbein Style', which exist, were presumably the work of English pupils of the master, but little is known of them. The one art which did flourish in Tudor and early Stuart England was that of the portrait-miniature, of which the two chief exponents were Nicholas Hilliard (1547—1619) and Isaac Oliver (*c.* 1566-1617).

Charles I was a connoisseur of real taste and ability, and it was thanks to him that Rubens and Van Dyck came to this country; but painting was still in the hands of foreign masters, and Dobson (1610—46) and Walker (died 1658), the two principal native painters of the period, though not without ability, confined themselves to portraits in the popular Van Dyck manner. The foreign leadership continued right through the seventeenth and some way into eighteenth century; the demand for painting was confined to portraits, of which the principal painters were Sir Peter Lely (1618—80), a Dutchman, and Sir Gottfried Kneller (1648—1723), a German, and large-scale decorative paintings on walls and ceilings supplied by the Italian Verrio (1639—1707) and the Frenchman Laguerre (1663—1721). In this latter branch an Englishmen did compete, very successfully, with his continental rivals—this was Sir James Thornhill (1676—1734); but though he was able to beat foreigners at their own game, it was a foreign, not an English, game, and it was only with his son-in-law William Hogarth (1697—1764) that the English school, as such, can be said to have begun. Hogarth's pictures, in particular his series, *The Rake's Progress* and *Marriage à la Mode* (Fig. 105c), contain two things which, in spite of all fashions, remain dear to the English: a story and a decided moral judgment. His declared aim was to be a 'moralist' in paint.

Hogarth owes less to foreign influences than almost any other English artist, and he may be regarded as the founder of the English school. His work was consolidated and carried on by Sir Joshua Reynolds (1723—92), the first President of the Royal Academy, who placed painting as a liberal profession beside literature, and whose *Discourses* contain the most complete exposition of the academic and eclectic theory of art. But Reynold's pictures painted in accordance with this theory are few, and less successful than the portraits of which the larger part of his *oeuvre* consists.

The portrait predominates in English eighteenth-century painting. There was no demand for religious pictures, as there would have been in a Catholic country, and the nobility, who were then the patron-class, demanded above all portraits of themselves and their families. Reynolds, Gainsborough (1727—1788) (Fig. 105a), Romney, Hoppner, Beechey, Raeburn, Lawrence, all the chief painters of the period, were first and foremost painters of portraits. Gainsborough (Fig. 107a) did paint landscape, beginning in a style modelled on Dutch seventeenth-century masters like Hobbema and Ruysdael, and developing into a broader and more personal manner; but though he preferred to paint landscape, he could not make a living except by portrait painting. Richard Wilson (1714—82) is the one exception. When in

William Hogarth, 1734

Italy, he had studied the work of Claude, Dughet and the other seventeenth century masters, and in his landscapes, Italian and English, the classical tradition of composition and arrangement is combined with English solidity; but it is significant that Wilson had no success at all with his landscapes during his lifetime (Fig. 108a). The popular medium for landscape in the eighteenth century was watercolour. At first this was a tinted pen and ink or pencil drawing, with the tones put in first in grey monochrome: later, direct painting, body colour, and other technical expedients improved the process so that it became almost as expressive, and as varied in its possibilities, as oil. The chief names in the history of the eighteenth-century English watercolour school are: Paul Sandby (1725—1809); Gainsborough, who, though not strictly speaking a watercolour painter (his landscape drawings are almost always in black chalk with occasional touches of colour), had a great influence on the development of English landscape art; Francis Towne (1740—1816); Alexander Cozens (*c.* 1717—97), and his son John Robert Cozens (*c.* 1752—97).

The climax of the English Watercolour School is reached in the work of Thomas Girtin (1775—1802), John Sell Cotman (1782—1824), and J. M. W. Turner (1775—1851); but the work of these artists, and Turner especially, will be considered in the chapter dealing with the nineteenth century.

There were, of course, other forms of painting besides portrait and landscape: Thomas Rowlandson (1756—1827), an amazingly prolific draughtsman, in his countless humorous or satirical figure-compositions carried on, to some extent, the tradition of Hogarth; George Morland (1763—1804) and Thomas Wheatley were responsible for a very popular school of sentimental rustic genre; while George Stubbs (1724—1806), the great animal painter, particularly of horses, was the first of the English sporting artists, though he himself was much more than a mere 'sporting artist'.

French Painting

Painting in France was, like architecture, subject at first to Italian influences. Francis I had brought Leonardo to France, where he died in 1519; and in 1527 a Florentine and a Bolognese mannerist, Rosso and Primaticcio, were sent for to Fontainebleau, to superintend the decoration of the château. These two, and Niccolo dell'Abbate, laid the foundations of the so-called 'School of Fontainebleau', of which the principal French followers were Caron, Jean Cousin and Dorigny, who continued with an even greater elaboration and artificiality the traditions of Italian mannerism, a tradition which persists with considerable vivacity, in the etchings of Jacques Callot (who was born in Nancy, but who may almost be considered a Florentine by adoption), and the works of Jacques Bellange (1594—1638), also from Nancy. Mention should also be made of the school of portrait-painters and draughtsmen

Jacques Callot (1592—1635).
Etching from the *Balli di Sfessania,* 1622—27

known by the name of its chief members, Jean Clouet (1475—1540) and François Clouet (1505—72); these worked in a Flemish rather than an Italian tradition, a tradition carried on into the next century by the brothers Le Nain, Antoine (1588—1648), Louis (1593—1648), and Mathieu (1607—77), who came from the north of France, and painted *genre* and still-life with a realism which makes them stand rather alone in the French seventeenth century, dominated as it was by Claude and Poussin.

Both Claude Gellée (1600—82), usually known as Claude Lorrain, and Nicolas Poussin (1594—1665), spent most of their working lives in Rome. Claude (Fig. 106b) was one of the first painters to paint nothing but landscapes, elaborately, and sometimes rather artificially, composed scenes whose chief beauty lies in the artist's apparently instinctive ability to render effects of light and atmosphere. His landscape studies of which there is a large collection in the British Museum, have an extraordinarily fresh spontaneity, and their technical skill is the more surprising when they are put beside his rather incompetent figure drawings; he is said to have said 'I sell my landscapes, but I give away the figures in them.' He owes nothing to French and little to Italian traditions; the roots of his art may be found in the work of the northern landscape painters working in Rome in the early seventeenth century, the brothers Bril, and especially the German, Adam Elsheimer. Claude was a born painter, who painted as it were by instinct; Poussin (Fig. 107b), equally a born painter, developed his style by assiduous and devoted study of the Italian masters. He is one of the supreme classical painters, constructing compositions of an ideal lucidity and grandeur. His landscapes have nothing, except very superficially, in common with Claude's dreamy idylls: they are constructed with a subtle and austerely intellectual architectonic sense, a feeling for spatial relations which looks on to Cézanne. Poussin is a painter in whom, above all, one is conscious of pure intellectual power. This sets him apart from the Baroque period, which in France itself was represented by a series of competent, but uninspired, official artists, of whom the most important were Charles Lebrun (1619—90) and Simon Vouet (1590—1649). Of the other painters of the time Eustache Le Sueur (1616—55), whose works, with their charm and unpretentious beauty, seem to anticipate much of later French painting, and Philippe de Champaigne (1602—74) whose portraits, carried out in subtle shades of grey and white, belong to the Northern tradition of French painting, are the most important.

At the end of the century a reaction started against the cold pomposity of the grand style. Under the Regency the elaborate public display of life at Versailles gave place to a highly civilized society living in the intimacy of small rooms. This required a new style of painting, in opposition to the official academic style. Antoine Watteau (1684—1721), who was the originator of this new style, was one of the greatest of European painters. Born at Valenciennes, and by birth more Flemish than French, his technique owes much to Rubens. Yet his pictures are the quintessence of all that one thinks of a typical of the French eighteenth century; by the side of their exquisite,

François Boucher (1703—70). Sleeping Child. Etching

aristocratic melancholy, Rubens' brilliant vitality seems almost vulgar. The popularity of his *Fêtes galantes* produced a number of imitators, of which the most conspicuous were Lancret (1690—1743), Pater (1695—1736), Lemoyne (1688—1737), and Mercier (1689—1760), who is known to have worked in England.

Watteau may perhaps be said to typify the Soul of eighteenth-century France, François Boucher (1703—70), with his great decorative sense, and his frankly sensual delight in the texture of satins and silk and flesh, equally well typifies the Body, the luxury and refined sensuality of the period. Honoré Fragonard (1732—1806) continued the tradition, though often influenced by Italian examples; so did the other eighteenth-century *petits maitres,* St Aubin (1724—80, Moreau le Jeune (1741—1814), Charles Eisen (1720—78), and Lavreince (1737—1807).

J.-B. S. Chardin (1699—1779) is the only other great painter produced by eighteenth-century France; but he is unlike Watteau in being entirely un-aristocratic, content to paint a still-life of objects on a *bourgeois* kitchen-table, or intimate interiors of middle-class family life, reminiscent of the Dutch masters of the previous century. Hardly ever has such perfect technique been combined with such accurate and subtle vision; Chardin can stand beside the very greatest French masters.

Of the later eighteenth century the typical painter is Greuze (1725—1805), whose pictures have the insincere sentimentality of the period.

Architecture in France

The course of architecture in France is not unlike that of painting; there is first a deliberate introduction of Italian architecture, which, having been gradually assimilated, produces a kind of classicism unmistakably and essentially French in character. During the first half of the sixteenth century, Charles VIII and François I imported Italian painters, sculptors and architects into France; but the mediaeval tradition of building died hard, and there was constant enmity between the Italians and the native French master-masons. The latter continued to build in the old way, and the Italians covered their buildings with fussy and unnecessary decoration. The result is to be seen in châteaux like Azay-le-Rideau (1516—24), Chambord (1519), or Amboise (1496), all on the Loire, which are really mediaeval buildings with a superficial Italianate veneer. By the middle of the century, the French themselves had begun to assimilate the Italian tradition. The principal architects of the latter part of the century were Philibert de l'Orme (*c.* 1515—70) and Jean Bullant (*c.* 1515—78). De l'Orme built, among others, the château at Anet for Henry II's mistress, Diane de Poitiers, the Gallery at Chenonceaux, and the Tuileries (destroyed in 1871): Bullant added to the Tuileries, and built the Châtelet at Chantilly, and the Chapel at Anet. When these buildings are compared with those of the latter part of the century, it is clear that there has been a great advance: there is an evident striving towards symmetry, balance, and proportion, while the former mediaeval rule-of-thumb methods of the master-masons are abandoned in favour of the modern conception of the plan, designed and carried out by the architect himself. But these architects had not fully digested the lesson of Italian architecture; they were still pedantic in their use of classic detail, over-fond of such motives as the superimposed orders, and had not yet learnt that classic architecture means restraint, rather than the application of classicistic details to buildings.

During the first sixty years of the seventeenth century, under Henry IV and Louis XIII, French architecture was allowed to develop naturally, without the centralized control which the totalitarian policy of Louis XIV and his minister Colbert imposed upon it during the latter part of the century. Henry IV, unlike his predecessors, did not regard architecture as a means of personal self-glorification, but was concerned to make art of service to the state as a whole. Under him there was a recrudescence of a vernacular style, a simple, elegant, and unpretentious use of brick with stone facings, such as one finds in the Cour Henri IV at Fontainebleau or the Place des Vosges, in Paris (1604). This was frequent during the first half of the century, though after Henry's death in 1610 the influence of the Queen Mother, Marie de Medici, tended to cause a return to Italian methods. The Luxembourg Palace, begun for her in 1615 by Salomon de Brosse, is reminiscent of such Florentine buildings as the Pitti Palace.

Among the other architects of this period were Jacques Lemercier (d. 1654) and François Mansart (1598—1666). Lemercier's chief surviving work is the Sorbonne, at Paris (begun 1635), and he also designed the Château (now mostly destroyed) and town of Richelieu, as well as the Palais Richelieu (later the Palais Royal and now much altered) and considerable and important additions to the Louvre. Mansart is the greatest French architect of this, and perhaps of any, period. The Château de Balleroy, in Normandy (1626), built in the vernacular brick and stone idiom, with two small pavilions flanking the entrance court, and high-pitched roofs, is a characteristic early work. The north wing of Blois (begun 1635), with its coupled pilasters between the windows on each storey, and elegant ground floor colonnade, and the Château des Maisons, near Paris (begun 1642), which repeats many of the same motives, to name only two of his later works, are among the masterpieces of neo-classic architecture, combining restraint, proportion, and scholarship which, while accurate, is never pedantic, with individuality and character. He built many *hotels* (or town houses of the nobility) in Paris, of which the best known is perhaps the Hôtel d'Argonge, now the Musée Carnavalet; as well as churches like the Visitation de Ste Marie, in Paris, with its circular plan.

Though the period from 1600 to 1661 (the date of Mazarin's fall from power) is perhaps the period when French architecture was at its height, political circumstances prevented any great building activity; but from 1661 to about 1690 an enormous programme of building was carried out. Mazarin had allowed the royal architects to build more or less as they liked, but under Colbert, who succeeded him, artistic activity of every kind was rigidly centralized and controlled, being regarded purely as a means of glorifying the King and the totalitarian state which he represented. (This difference between the political structures of England and France, that Louis XIV broke the power of the nobility, degrading them as far as possible to little more than personal attendants of his own, while in England, from 1688 onwards, active political power was in the hands of the great patrician families, had this effect on the architecture of the two countries, that there is very much less private, as distinct from royal, patronage in France, and consequently French architecture is, while more magnificent, at the same time more standardized, leaving less room for the display of individual genius). In 1671 Colbert founded the Academy of Architecture, which, while it encouraged standardization, also laid the foundation of the admirable and unsurpassed tradition of technique and craftsmanship in French architecture.

The two great undertakings of the period were the completion of the Louvre, and the building of Versailles. For the former project, Bernini had been invited to Paris and produced a design which, however, presupposed the destruction of all the existing buildings, and the commission was in the end given to Claude Perrault, who produced the magnificent east front, with its colossal peristyle of coupled Corinthian columns on a high basement, which must surely owe something to Bernini's design, for it has a grandeur and hugeness of scale rarely found outside Rome, as well as being characteristically Baroque in that it is purely decorative, designed regardless of convenience and with no consideration of the already-existing structure. Versailles is largely the work of two men, André le Nôtre and Jules Hardouin Mansart, (Fig. 98b), the great-nephew of François Mansart: Mansart was responsible for the palace, enormous in size and petty in detail, which Voltaire called 'a masterpiece of magnificent bad taste'. It is, indeed, a waste of a unique opportunity: the main façade is nearly 1,900 feet long, with a central block 330 feet wide projecting 280 feet in front of the side wings, so that the gigantic bulk of the palace appears to be split into three, and the details of this façade, though correct, are too small in proportion to the whole, and too monotonous. The magnificence of the palace is mostly due to Le Nôtre's formal lay-out of the gardens, with their combination of fountains, statuary, trees and water, which were to influence the whole of eighteenth-century garden design until the appearance of the romantic, informal, *jardin anglais*. Le Nôtre also laid out the gardens at Vaux-le-Vicomte, the most perfectly preserved example of a château and garden of this period, built by Louis le Vau (1612—97), whose other well-known work is the Institut de France, in Paris. Mansart was, from a worldly point of view, extremely successful; he seems to have had in his hands all the official architecture of France. His other works include the Church of the Invalides, in Paris, the Place Vendôme, and the College of St Cyr. No one man could have produced such a mass of work, and much of it must have been really by assistants; but this monopoly of taste had a disastrous effect on the architecture of the succeeding century.

After Mansart's death, his tradition was carried on by the various architects trained under him: Desgodetz (1653—1728, who was probably responsible for the Orangery at Versailles), Robert de Cotte (1656—1735), and Germain Boffrand (1667—1754, who built the Hôtel de Soubise in Paris, and the Archives Nationales), and Jean Aubert (d. 1741, who was responsible for the magnificent stables at Chantilly). Louis XIV's extravagance, and the consequent impoverishment of the country, caused a slackening in the intense architectural activity which continued through the late seventeenth century: many French architects in the eighteenth century worked for foreign patrons. Of these, François Cuvillès deserves especial mention, for it was he who designed that masterpiece of baroque-rococo decoration, the Nymphenburg Palace at Munich. Of those who worked in France, Emmanuel Héré de Corny (1705—63), and the two Gabriels, Jacques Jules (1667—1742), and his son, Ange Jacques (1698—1782), are the most important. Héré is known for his work at Nancy, which he remodelled for his patron, Stanislas, Titular King of Poland. Begun in 1745, this is one of the most magnificent pieces of eighteenth-century town-planning to survive, and can be compared to John Wood's work at Bath. It is not alone, for several other French provincial towns produced something of the same kind. The elder Gabriel produced several excellent buildings, in particular the Place de la Bourse at Bordeaux, the Cathedral at La Rochelle, and the Hôtel de Ville at Rennes. His son, who succeeded him in 1742 as 'premier architecte du Roi', had greater opportunities; he designed the Place de la Concorde in Paris (1748), one of the finest squares in the world, the École Militaire in Paris (1751—73), and the Petit Trianon at Versailles (1763). These are the masterpieces of neo-classic architecture, unsurpassed in restraint, proportion and taste; beside them even the most accomplished English Palladian work appears somewhat clumsy and provincial. Claude-Nicolas Ledoux (1736—1806) worked also in the classical tradition; but while Gabriel's architecture seems to be the culminating point of the architectural tradition of the French Renaissance, Ledoux anticipates, in a curious way, the functionalism of modern industrial civilization. He uses the classical idiom of his time, but with such restraint that his works are often only saved from bleakness by the excellence of their proportions. His later buildings, and even more his unexecuted—and unexecutable—designs for vast town-planning and engineering projects, become increasingly abstract and austere, depending for their effect more and more upon combinations of such fundamental forms as the sphere, the cube, and the cylinder. He had great influence on later architects, particularly in France and Germany (e. g. Schinkel, see page 291), and much of what is called 'Empire' architecture is due ultimately to him, though it lacks the particular vigour and austerity of his idiom.

V. Paul Cézanne (1839–1906): Old Woman with Rosary.
(National Gallery, London)

107. (A) Gainsborough: Landscape. (British Museum. London).
(B) Nicolas Poussin: The Golden Calf. (National Gallery, London).

b

a

108. (A) Wilson: Cader Idris. (National Gallery, London).
(B) Constable: Near Stoke-by-Nayland. (National Gallery, London).

b

a

b

109. (A) The Capitol, Washington. Foundation stone laid 1793. The dome, 300 ft. in height, was completed in 1862. (B) The interior of the Pantheon, in Paris. Begun in 1764 by Jacques-Germain Soufflot (1709 – 80) and completed after his death by his nephew François and other architects. (C) The Propylaea. Munich. Built in 1848 – 60 by Leo von Klenze. (1784 – 1864).

c

a

b

c

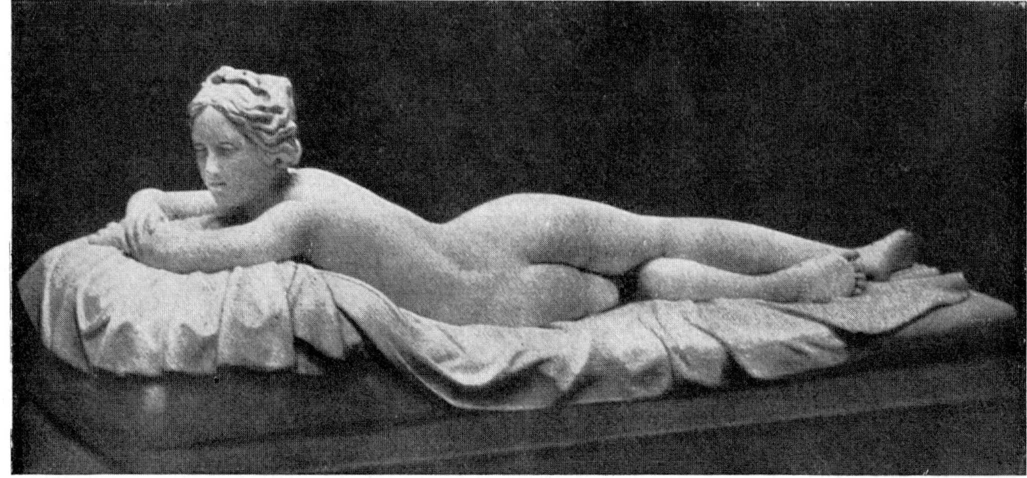

110. (A) Antonio Canova (1757 – 1822): Hebe. Marble. Height, 63 in. 1796. (National Gallery, Berlin). (B) Jean-Auguste Ingres (1780 – 1867): Venus Anadyomene. 1848. (Musée de Chantilly). (C) Gottfried Schadow (1764 – 1850): Resting. Marble. Length $37\frac{1}{2}$ in. 1826. (National Gallery, Berlin).

Chapter XXIV

FROM CLASSICISM TO IMPRESSIONISM

*

THE ROCOCO period merged into the period of *Sturm und Drang* ('Storm and Stress'). These words fit not only the literature, but also the art of the period.

All Europe, except for England, was at first under the spell of the French Revolution, but the result of revolution, in France, was not liberty, but Napoleon. Before long he laid claim to despotic power, declaring that he loved power as an artist loves his violin. Of this music Europe heard only a monotonously shouting and commanding voice. Its expression in art was the Empire style; a cold, heavy, severe, soldier's style, which helped the seed of Classicism to germinate: its derivation from the antique Roman style was based on the admiration felt by the Revolution for ancient Roman virtue; later, at the time of Napoleon's Egyptian campaign, Egyptian motives were fused into it.

After Napoleon's fall the nineteenth century acquired its familiar aspect. But before this happened wide areas of France, Germany and Russia were laid waste, while victorious England was bankrupt. An intellectual escape into a dream-world seemed only natural.

While the process of intellectual and economic reintegration which ushered in the nineteenth century cannot be fully described here, the social decadence of the period must not be overlooked, since it had the greatest influence on the development of the arts. We must not be misled by the purely political explanation, that the French Revolution added, to the upper Estates, a Third—namely, the bourgeoisie—and finally, as a Fourth Estate, the working class. Intellectually, the society of the nineteenth century was confused and uncertain as never before. It had lost all the basic ideals which had held it together in the past.

Before the French Revolution art had spoken in a common language, which could usually be called the style of the period; but after the Revolution, the idea of style, in the profounder sense, was no longer valid; there were only artistic movements. The further evolution of art was now a matter of frequent changes, of opposing and collaborating theories.

To understand this development, we must ask ourselves what means of approach to the world are possible. There are two above all which constantly reapear and, in effect, repeat themselves. Even in antiquity the linear and the picturesque styles of art could be described, in philosophy, by such terms as Aristotelean and Platonic; now the terms used, in literature as in art, are Classical and Romantic. The difference between the two ways of looking at the world can be expressed by the symbol of the circle: the classical artist contains the centre in himself. This is the typical attitude of the Greek, who, self-centred, his own master, and indeed, his own god, crosses the circle of life with vigorous steps, observing the world, with open eyes and ears, from the central point of his own person. Here is no struggling spirit, wrestling with problems; of him, rather, it is true, that he experiences what Goethe called the greatest happiness of the thoughtful man, in having investigated what could be investigated, and in quietly worshipping what could not. Here the word 'quietly' should be emphasized. From this quiet veneration comes much of the noble simplicity and silent majesty which can be seen in the art of antiquity.

Library of Columbia University, New York

If this symbol is to be applied to the romantic artist, he is best compared to a parabola. In the case of the egocentric classic, the circle surrounds the central point, producing quietude, equilibrium and self-confidence; in the case of the romantic parabola, the focus is infinitely remote. Its open curve disappears into infinity, as though seeking there its polar complement. The mediaeval mystics, like the modern Romantics, called this longing for God, and reaching into the other world; the philosopher regards it as irrational.

Why this opposition of the circle and the parabola? Because it shows us most clearly that in every pair of contrasting aesthetic concepts, we are dealing with two names for the same thing. The really great works of art are often both classic and romantic: Goethe's *Faust* is not only a great classic creation, but it is also full of the romantic spirit; while Michelangelo combines elements of Renaissance and Baroque.

Classicism and Romanticism are not two entirely different ways of looking at the world; both were born in a new, historically conscious age, and in reaching back into the past they met.

Architecture and Sculpture

The 'Classicists' (as they are called, to distinguish them from the genuine Classics), were not naïve; they had turned back to antiquity, inspired by a profound longing, and their preference for linear forms was bound to lead them toward architecture. Classical, antique, architecture had always been known in Europe, and from about the middle of the eighteenth century its study received a fresh impetus (the excavations were begun in Pompeii in 1748, and Winkelmann arrived in Rome in 1755).

It was natural enough, in a progressive age, that the antique should be studied and held up as an academic model, and indeed, as the highest ideal.

In the nineteenth century the whole world began to cover itself with classicistic buildings, making use of Greek and Roman forms; and a more romantic generation presently revived the Gothic style.

Buildings of Yale University, New Haven, U.S.A.

In America, where there was no old and thoroughly mature monumental architecture, the new buildings, which used old forms (above, page 290, and Fig. 109a) like mementos of an honourable inheritance, often have a pleasant effect in a country burdened with few traditions.

Classicism was most original in the hands of a gifted architect like Karl Friedrich Schinkel (1781—1841). He kept to the classic moderation, but without pedantry. In Berlin he built the Neue Wache (the New Guard-house) as a cross between a Doric temple and a castle, and in the Schauspielhaus he solved the ticklish problem of combining classical forms with the practical requirements of the modern stage. It is characteristic of Schinkel that by way of an interlude he planned a 'Gothic' cathedral

Karl Friedrich Schinkel.
Design for country house. About 1830

Friedrich Weinbrenner (1766—1828):
Project for a Napoleonic Monument

to be erected on the Leipziger Platz. As for Schinkel's villas, they would need a chapter to themselves. Whether we take the plan of a country house for the Russian Tsarina on the steep, forest-clad coast of the Crimea, or the design on the previous page, we always find the same aristocratic grace, and a delightful sense of animation.

The best work of this period expressed a kind of romantic classicism—which, as was explained at the beginning of this chapter, is only an apparent contradiction. The Romantic love of Nature animated the otherwise austere classicistic forms, with results often far superior to the productions of a dismal and historically minded art in the so-called neo-Classicistic or neo-Renaissance style.

In France, Jacques-Germain Soufflot, inspired by the Roman Pantheon, built his Pantheon in Paris (Fig. 109b), providing a classicistic model for St Issac's Cathedral in Leningrad, and the Church of St Nicholas in Helsinki. Eugène Emmanuel Viollet-le-Duc (1814—79), on the other hand, was typical of the Gothic-Romantic movement. Devoting himself to the care of the historical buildings of France, he restored Notre-Dame. A zealous restorer, his work is spoilt by a rather over-pedantic aridity. In Germany, Friedrich Gärtner (1792—1847) restored the cathedrals of Speyer, Bamberg and Regensburg. Charles Garnier (1825—98), in the great Opera House in Paris, created a sort of neo-Baroque, a typical example of the fashionable striving for effect which towards the close of the nineteenth century filled half the world with examples of the most impossible admixture of Romanesque, Spanish and Chinese styles.

During this period of decadence the only country to retain a certain dignity was England, the land of tradition.

As we have seen, Palladian classicism was dominant all through the first half of the eighteenth century; but about 1760 Robert Adam (1728—92) and his brothers marked the beginning of the classical revival in England. Adam published, in 1763, an account of the ruins of Diocletian's palace at Split; and in 1762 Stuart and Revett had published their'Antiquities of Athens'. The Adams's influence was profound, but it had more effect on the interior planning and decoration of buildings than the exterior elevations: his elevations were designed more or less according to Palladian rules, though in his desire to achieve the greatest possible 'movement' he tended to sacrifice coherence and unity by splitting the elevation into separate elements. Indoors, however, the change was far-reaching: instead of the heavy, and sometimes even clumsy, plasterwork and carving of the earlier style, the Adams' introduced a style of decoration in delicate low relief, with conventional patterns and motives, such as figures, urns and sphinxes, borrowed from the antique, against coloured backgrounds. In interior planning they revolutionized the existing conception of space: instead of the definite space of Palladian rooms, proportioned to exact mathematical rules, they made space indefinite, by using and combining the circle, the oval, the semi-circle and the polygon, and by such devices as giving a room a curved end, with a half dome, separated from the rest of the room by a screen of pillars, supporting an entablature, thus deliberately making the spatial content of the room uncertain.

About the turn of the century the Greek revival—the so-called Regency style—began to dominate. The greatest architects of this style were Sir John Soane (1753—1837) and John Nash (1752—1835). Soane is by far the greater; he had a truly original and inventive mind, and his architecture, though it is possible to find similarities between it and the work of the slightly older Frenchman, Claude-Nicolas Ledoux (1736—1806), was the last genuinely original contribution to the art to appear in England. Soane used Greek motives, notably the unfluted Doric order, but combined them in a way without antique precedent, and his austere, unadorned, monumental style, massive in a way which suggests Vanbrugh (of whom Soane thought highly, calling him 'the Shakespeare of Architects' and mentioning his 'power of making small things interesting', a power in which Soane himself excelled) suggests the approaching factory age. But it was a lesson which the nineteenth century was to forget. Nash, largely because of the fact that he was patronized by George IV, is better known than Soane; there is also the fact that his greatest work, the layout of Regent's Park, is one of the most conspicuous surviving fragments of Georgian London. This is not to underestimate Nash. He had a real grasp of planning, and an ability to think, and even more important, to execute, on a large scale. Regent's Park and Regent Street, before the latter was wantonly pulled down, were among the greatest pieces of English town-planning, comparable with the earlier Bath and New Town at Edinburgh, and the contemporary Cheltenham. But when his architecture is looked at more closely, it is clear that he lacked originality of mind and refinement of detail. He did not, as Soane did, evolve a new and personal style; in fact, he had no objection to designing in any style required of him: the Regent's Park terraces are classical, East Cowes Castle is an example of his work in the revived

Gothic style, the Brighton Pavilion (for which, as it stands today, he is largely responsible) is in a mixture of *chinoiserie* and so-called Hindoo, while he built *cottages ornés* in a sophisticated pseudo-rustic manner, and country houses in the 'Italian Villa' style which was to become so popular in the middle of the century. This diversity of styles marks the beginning of the complete collapse of architectural tradition which took place in the nineteenth century, and from which we have not yet recovered. Most of them are not important enough to be discussed in so general a survey as this, but the Gothic Revival should be mentioned: it began in the eighteenth century, as one of the products of the new Romantic sensibility. At first it was an aristocratic diversion, when Horace Walpole was carrying out his Twickenham villa, Strawberry Hill; but the decoration there shocked the Gothic purists of a later generation, since it is really closer to the rococo than to the Gothic proper. Later in the century the Gothic style became vulgarized and popular, though it was rarely used for any really important building: an occasional country house, such as Ashridge or Fonthill (both by James Wyatt, 1748—1813, who began, incidentally, as one of the most successful imitators of the Adams), was built in the Gothic style, but for the most part it was used for parish churches, chapels, summerhouses, pavilions and lodges.

The year 1839 marks the decisive victory of the Gothic Revival, for it was then that the first stone was laid of the new Houses of Parliament at Westminster, designed by Sir Charles Barry (with the assistance of Pugin) in the so-called 'Tudor-Gothic' style. About the same time the High Church 'Tractarian' revival, in its reaction against the ultra-Protestant Anglicanism of the eighteenth century, proclaimed Gothic as the only suitable ecclesiastical architecture. The revival had a powerful champion in John Ruskin, who, characteristically confusing ethics and aesthetics, denounced classical architecture as pagan and immoral, and declared Gothic to be the only true architecture. Thus the Gothic-Revival, which began as an ultra-precious aristocratic whim, came to be believed in almost as passionately as an article of faith. The neo-classical style did not die without a struggle, and several very distinguished public buildings were built, such as Smirke's British Museum (1824—47), Cockerell's Ashmolean Museum, Oxford (1840—42), or St George's Hall at Liverpool (designed by Harvey Lonsdale Elmes and completed after his death, in 1847, by C. R. Cockerell in 1854).

In Italy, ever since Piranesi, Classicism, as a natural heritage of the native art, had been latent rather than active; but there it was always outshone by the genuine original. Sculpture, on the other hand, whose model was always the living human being, was less oppressed by tradition. In Antonio Canova (Fig. 110a) the South produced the great artist who guided Italian sculpture from the Baroque into Classicism.

His work, in its easy and unconstrained style, and its graceful animation, qualities which it retained in spite of the rigid austerity of Classicism, was reminiscent of the architecture of Schinkel. One may take exception to many of his statues, as being either too pretty or too pretentious, but in this sepulchral monuments he made an end of the Baroque productions, then the fashion, which had more of the carnival than the funeral about them, and by returning to the ancient form of the stele restored the monumental memorial to the dead.

The other great neo-Classic sculptor was the Dane, Bertel Thorwaldsen (1770—1844). No other artist so perfectly expressed the spirit of his period. In his works the features of Classicism and Romanticism were combined, in spite of all theories. His lions, in Lucerne, are inseparable from the environing landscape. In England, John Flaxman (1755—1826) and Francis Chantrey (1781—1841) were both distinguished neo-Classical sculptors.

Painting and Illustration

One of the most vigorous pioneers of modern painting, Francisco Goya y Lucientes (1746—1828), the greatest Spanish painter since Velasquez, was a child of the period of *Sturm und Drang*. The wars of the French Revolution inspired the eighty etchings in which he recorded his impressions—the *Caprichos* (Fig. 111b) and the *Desastros de la Guerra*. His portraits of Charles IV, who made Goya his court painter, and those of the rest of the Royal family, were painted with a truthfulness that defied all etiquette. Goya had learnt much of his mastery of light and colour from Velasquez, and much of the technique of etching from Tiepolo. But whatever he may have learned from the past, he was a man of the future.

In Germany, to begin with, Classicism had things all its own way. Asmus Jacob Carstens took the final step towards a strict Classicism, resolutely dispensing with colour and relying on 'noble contours'. With his theoretical extremism, he exerted a fertilizing influence on German art; not so much through his disciples, as through the opposition which he aroused in such painters as Gottlieb Schick and Philipp Otto Runge.

Whether we call the first a Classicist, and the second a Romantic, is of no great importance; what is important is the fact that talented artists like Josef Anton Koch (1768—1859) or Caspar David Friedrich (1774—1840), by their quiet, unpretentious treatment, produced pictures informed by a warmer and more genuine vitality than the works of the romantic and enthusiastic group of the 'Nazarenes', who 'with palpitating hearts and religious awe' proceeded to Rome, where they founded a 'religious community of artists' in the deserted premises of a former monastery (1810—18). Friedrich Overbeck (1789—1869) and Peter Cornelius were the most significant members of this circle, which is only of historical interest; and is in some ways a parallel to the English Pre-Raphaelite Brotherhood. Other German artists of this time were Alfred Rethel (1816—89), Ludwig Richter (1803—84), Moritz von Schwind (1804—71) and Karl Spitzweg (1808—85).

French Painting

In France, the only painter of importance—and perhaps important less for what he painted than for the extent of his influence—who can properly be called Classicistic, is Jacques Louis David (1748—1825). David was an enthusiastic supporter of the French Revolution, and consequently, in revolt against the French eighteenth-century tradition of painting, which to him symbolized the *ancien régime*. His pictures show the effect of the taste for antique Roman severity and virtue, fashionable among the leaders of the Revolution: in them subjects from classical history are rendered in a dryly austere style, with hard outlines and the minimum of colour, to approximate as closely as possible to sculpture. So strong was the reaction against beauty of handling and surface texture, that David's pupils, to show their contempt, used to throw their dirty brushes at Watteau's *Embarquement pour Cythère*. Of these pupils the only important one was Jean-Auguste-Dominique Ingres (1781—1867), a painter who entirely transcended his master. Ingres was not Classicistic, he was Classical, in the sense that Raphael or Poussin or Cézanne were classical; it is between the two latter masters that Ingres, their equal in stature, stands in the development of French painting. Ingres sacrificed some of the beauty of surface texture to the creation of ideal form, with a line as expressive, as subtle, as refined, and as alive as that of Raphael himself. But while a romantic artist stimulates, a classic artist tends to circumscribe the imagination of his followers; and for this reason Ingres stands rather by himself. Of his pupils, Chassériau (1819—56) is the most important, and even he was almost as much influenced by Delacroix as by Ingres. Indeed, it is the attempt to reconcile the two that gives his work its quality, the quality which caused Gautier to say of him that he was an 'Indian who had studied in Greece'.

The two masters of what must, rather unsatisfactorily, be called the Romantic movement in painting are Eugène Delacroix (1798—1863), (Fig. 111c) and Jean-Louis-André-Théodore Géricault (1791—1824). Both were powerfully influenced by English painting, in Delacroix's case by Constable in particular. Instead of the classicism of perfect form—so fine in the case of Ingres, so insipid in the case of most of his and David's followers—the Romantic artists returned to the tradition, if not exactly of Watteau, at any rate of Rubens: harmonies of sumptuous colour, wild and exotic subjects, and a free and expressive handling of paint. Géricault was probably as great a painter as Delacroix, but he died too young for his influence to be properly felt.

Jean Baptiste-Camille Corot (1796—1875), their contemporary, is too often known only for the hazy woodland landscapes of his later years, painted to suit the taste of his patrons; but the landscapes painted during and after his visits to Italy in 1827 and 1835 have a quality reminiscent of Claude. It is not that Corot consciously imitated Claude; but both reacted in somewhat the same way to the same scenes. Corot's landscape has not the enchanted other-worldliness of Claude's, but they were

a

b

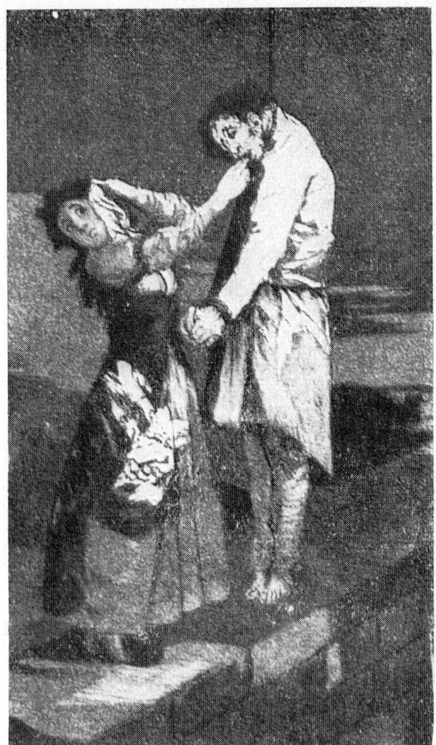

c

111. (A) Henry Fuseli: Hüon frees the Babekan attacked by lions. Illustration for Wieland's 'Oberon'. *c.* 1797. (Private Collection, Au am Zürichsee). (B) Francisco Goya: Etching from 'Caprichos'. 1797. (C) Eugène Delacroix: 28 July, 1830. Freedom leads the People to the Barricades. 1831. (Louvre).

a

112. (A) Ford Madox Brown: Work. (Manchester Art Gallery).
(B) Edgar Degas (1834 – 97): Absinthe. *c.* 1876. (Louvre).
(C) Edouard Manet (1853 – 83): Le Printemps. 1881.

b

c

a

b

113. (A) Paul Cézanne (1839 – 1906): Still life. Between 1883 and 1887. (Laroche Collection, Paris).
(B) Vincent Van Gogh (1853 – 90): Sunflowers. 1888. (New State Gallery, Munich).
(C) Ferdinand Hodler: The Cabinet-maker. 1875. (Kunsthaus, Zürich).
(D) Paul Gauguin (1848 – 1903): Two Girls, Tahiti. (Osborn Collection, New York).

c

d

a

b

c

114. (A) Auguste Renoir (1841 – 1919): Les liseuses. *c.* 1890.
(B) Auguste Rodin: A Burgher of Calais, 1884 – 88. (Musée Rodin, Paris).
(C) Pablo Picasso: l'Arlésienne. 1912.

the painters who perhaps most of all were able to express the particular quality of Italian light.

Corot and Constable between them may be said to be largely responsible for the so-called Barbizon School of landscape painters, Rousseau (1812—67), Millet (1814—75), Daubigny (1817—78) and Diaz; but it is Corot's later, rather than his earlier manner, that affected these artists, while Constable's brilliant impressionism was conventionalized into a formula of rather uninspired realism. Millet was the most considerable of this school; but his more ambitious pictures, such as the famous 'Angelus', though superior to the trivially realistic landscapes of the rest of the school, fall perhaps into something of the same error as certain of the works of the English Pre-Raphaelite School, that is, of trying to express more than can properly be expressed in paint.

Gustave Courbet (1819—77) was the great realist of the French nineteenth century; but his realism was anything but trivial, founded as it was on a thorough study of the great sixteenth and seventeenth-century masters, in particular Caravaggio, Velasquez, Hals and Rembrandt. The mistake he made was in confusing artistic with political doctrines, thinking that realism was in some way connected with social democracy, and consequently on occasion wasting his powers in painting pictures inspired by some motive of political or anti-clerical propaganda. But at his best his work is powerful and uncompromising; and his doctrine, that the artist may paint whatever he likes, provided it interests him, and that no subject is too low or commonplace, though taken for granted today, had a great effect in clearing the air, and preparing the way for the culmination of French nineteenth-century painting, the Impressionist Movement.

Some mention should be made of the black-and-white illustrators and draughtsmen. The introduction of lithography made possible cheap and almost unlimited duplication of an actual drawing, not, as previously, of a drawing interpreted by an engraver. Of the many who took advantage of this, the greatest was Honoré Daumier (1808—79), whose enormous output, while achieving, at its best, a vivacious and brilliant facility, was too often betrayed into insincerity or bombast. Of the many other lithographers Gavarni (1804—66), Devéria (1800—57) and Monnier (1805—77) are perhaps the best known. Constantin Guys (1805—95) was not a lithographer, but a draughtsman, preoccupied always by the problem of setting down some ephemeral, evanescent moment in the life around him: in this he was, in one

Honoré Daumier: The Poetaster. Woodcut, 1842

sense, a true impressionist, and the impressionist draughtsmen: Forain, Degas and Toulouse-Lautrec owed much to him.

The 'Impressionist School' suggests a number of artists with a definite programme, all painting in very much the same way like, for example, the English Pre-Raphaelites. This is not the case; but the artists who are called Impressionists, Edouard Manet (1832—83), Edgar Degas (1834—1917), Claude Monet (1840—1926), Auguste Renoir (1841—1919), Camille Pissarro (1830—1903) and Alfred Sisley (1840—94) had several things in common. One of these is realism, which took various forms. Manet derived strongly from Courbet, and, like him, was a student of the seventeenth-century Spanish and Netherlandish masters. There is no doubt that many of his compositions were inspired by earlier works; for example, the celebrated *Déjeuner sur l' Herbe* is an obvious reminiscence of Giorgione and of Raphael, as the *Olympia* is of Titian. Degas, on the other hand, was inspired by the newly discovered science of photography to paint, not so much compositions, in the traditional sense, as snapshots. We may here recall Constable's way of painting the fleeting and evanescent, rather than the static, effects of Nature; he can truly be called the ancestor of Impressionism, through the intermediate Barbizon School. Another manifestation of realism was the application of the new scientific discoveries concerning the spectrum and the nature of light to painting. The spectrum breaks light up into the primary colours; therefore the painter should not mix his colours on the palette, but, by laying tiny strokes of pure colour close together, let them combine in the eye of the spectator. 'The Light', it was said, 'is the principal person in a picture.' (Turner, above all in his later pictures, some of which seem to consist of nothing but light, also affected the Impressionists, in particular Monet and Pissarro). Monet, Pissarro and Sisley remained more or less faithful to this rather doctrinaire theory of *plein-air* luminism, of painting the light playing round things rather than the forms of the things. Some of the others, notably Renoir, passed through a phase of it. Renoir was a sensuous painter, delighting in prettiness and in the texture of his paint; he is thus entirely in the French tradition. His beautiful texture he owed partly to the fact that as a youth he was employed in a china factory, painting designs on the unbaked porcelain, which, since it was porous and instantly absorbent of the colour, would not admit of any re-working or second touches: this gave his painting a particular directness and beauty of touch. Renoir was an instinctive artist, a born painter. Degas was an intellectual, and above all, a draughtsman in the tradition of Ingres. He exploited to the full the 'snapshot' idea of Impressionism; it may be so called more accurately in his case than in that of most of the other Impressionists, since not only his vision, but his whole conception of composition and treatment of light, was powerfully affected by the newly-discovered invention of photography. Japanese woodcuts, which have now become so commonplace, but which were not known in Europe until the 1850's, showed Degas how things seen at odd angles and with no attempt at composition could be combined into patterns. From the Japanese artist Utamaro he also derived his fondness for depicting women bathing or at some moment of their toilet—seen, as he said, through the keyhole (Figs. 112b and 112c; 114a).

Seurat (1859—91) called himself a neo-Impressionist, and *pointillisme* certainly owes something to the Impressionist technique of 'petites touches'; but he was a more classical artist, using this particular technique, of juxtaposing small dots of pure colour to build up forms, to construct compositions of classical weight and solidity.

English Painting

In England official, Academic painting kept to the rules laid down by Reynolds. Benjamin West (1738—1820), who succeeded Reynolds as President of the Royal Academy, is an example of the deplorable results of the application of these rules by a painstaking man with little talent. The popularity of Dutch seventeenth-century cabinet pictures among English collectors was reflected in the demand for sentimental or facetious genre pieces, supplied by Morland, Wheatley, and above all Wilkie.

But, surreptitiously, as it were, behind the official art of the late eighteenth and early nineteenth centuries, the beginnings of romantic art can be seen. William Blake (1757—1827) is the most conspicuous and striking of English romantic artists; he is the final flowering of certain tendencies which can be seen, before him, in a modified form, in the work of Henry Fuseli (1741—1825), James Barry (1741—1806) and John Mortimer (*c.* 1741—79). Of these Fuseli, a Swiss by birth, is the most important; his work may be compared with the so-called 'Gothic' novels of the late eighteenth century, with emphasis of the supernatural, grotesque, and fantastic. Fuseli, and Blake as well, make use of a typical 'storm and stress' *terribilità* (Fig. 111a).

Blake was trained as an engraver, and knew Michelangelo's work entirely through engravings. This gives his work a clear-cut clarity of outline characteristic of a draughtsman rather than of a painter. He had no sympathy with Reynolds's theory of aesthetics, and absolutely no idea of the manipulation of oil paint, which he very rarely used. Most of his work is in watercolour, though he was fond of experimenting with new media, few of which have stood the test of time. His work was mystical and intense; sometimes magnificent, and sometimes, when inspiration was lacking, as absurd and bombastic as that of any of Michelangelo's Italian followers. He cannot be said to have had a school, but two artists, Samuel Palmer (1805—81) and Edward Calvert (1803—83), owed much to his inspiration; the former in the paintings dating from the late 1820's, in which landscape is rendered with a feverish and visionary intensity; the latter in the dozen or so tiny engravings, and the one drawing, which are all that survive of his from the same period.

The highly personal, intense and visionary quality of the work of these artists, recurs frequently in English painting; its next appearance is some twenty years later, in the Pre-Raphaelite movement.

But before that is discussed, the other artists of the early nineteenth century must be dealt with. The two greatest names among these are those of Constable and

Turner. Constable (1776—1837) is the originator of modern landscape. Previously (if we exclude some of the water-colourists), painting of landscape lacked the freshness and spontaneity born of direct contact with nature, being for the most part either artificially composed (like those of Gainsborough, who used pieces of broken glass and lumps of coal, arranged on the table in roughly the form of a landscape, as the basis of his compositions), or worked up in the studio from sketches made out of doors. Constable was the pioneer of *plein-air* painting; his aim was not to impose form on nature, but to render nature exactly as she was, with all her brilliance, and, if necessary, all her formlessness. There is a well-known story of Sir George Beaumont, a connoisseur, dilettante and amateur artist, who declared, in Constable's presence, that the colour of a landscape should be that of an old violin; Constable, without saying anything, took a violin and placed it on the green grass of the lawn. This shows what Constable thought of the classical landscape school. As well as his great, finished pictures, he made innumerable small oil sketches. From studying these, one can see that his main preoccupation was an attempt to catch, and fix, some transient and momentary appearance of the scene before him; to paint, as it were, in snapshots. He is thus a forerunner of the French Impressionist School, and it is a fact that the exhibition of his 'Hay Wain', in Paris, in 1824, had a profound and lasting effect on the development of French painting (Fig. 108b).

Turner started by painting watercolours in the orthodox eighteenth-century tradition, but soon grew dissatisfied with its narrow limits. Like Constable, Turner (1775—1851) was preoccupied with rendering the exact truth of nature; but while Constable restricted himself to rendering the intimacy of the English countryside, Turner, with the widest and most all-embracing vision of any landscape painter, rendered nature in her vastest and most elemental aspects; his later work shows the sea in every mood (he is the greatest of all marine painters), and the vast heights and distances of mountain landscape. Towards the end of his life, his pictures and drawings often reach the extreme limit of representation, consisting merely of some intensely observed and exquisitely rendered effect of light or atmosphere. In this Turner, no less than Constable, was a forerunner of the Impressionists, yet his work was less often seen, and less well known, on the Continent (Fig. 106a).

An English painter who did have a great influence in France was Richard Parkes Bonington (1802—28). His family settled in Calais, and he was a pupil of Baron Gros; his romantic watercolours influenced Delacroix and Corot, and through them much of the French painting of the middle of the century.

The English landscape school is overshadowed by Turner and Constable, but there are several others, chiefly watercolour painters, who should be mentioned: John Sell Cotman (1782—1842), Thomas Girtin (1775—1802), an exact contemporary and friend of Turner, who died before his brilliant promise could be fulfilled, Peter de Wint (1784—1849), John Varley (1778—1842) and David Cox (1783—1859) are the most important.

Apart from landscapes and portraits, English painting in the early nineteenth century consisted, broadly speaking, of the heroic or 'historical' school, best exemplified in the tragicomic career of B. R. Haydon (1786—1846), and the sentimental or anecdotal genre school, of which Wilkie is the most conspicuous.

In 1848 the formation of the Pre-Raphaelite Brotherhood, which may perhaps be compared with the German romantic and 'Nazarene' painters of the previous generation, gave a new direction to English painting. The principal Pre-Raphaelites were Dante Gabriel Rossetti (1828—82), John Millais (1829—96), William Holman Hunt (1827—1910), Arthur Hughes (1830—1915) and Ford Madox Brown (1821—93). They believed in choosing a significant subject and rendering it with the maximum of intensity and detail. They take their place in the lyrical, literary tradition of English art: yet the very intensity with which they felt and worked could not be maintained for more than a few years, and by about 1860 the force of the movement had spent itself. Rossetti's later work, and that of his pupil, Edward Burne-Jones (1833—98), was responsible for much of the 'aesthetic' movement in painting during the last half of the century, an art inspired neither by life, nor corrected by direct observation of nature, but reflecting an essentially literary, and imaginative dream of ideal beauty. Pre-Raphaelitism proper was encouraged and fostered by the writings of John Ruskin (1819—1900), perhaps the most influential aesthetic philosopher who has ever lived, and who deserves, on that account, a place in the history of art. A passionate love for Gothic architecture, and for the work of Turner, caused him to denounce the whole achievement of the Renaissance as pagan, and founded on false principles, and to declare that absolute truth to nature was the only criterion by which a work of art should be judged. His theories, based as they are on instinct and emotion rather than on reason, are often contradictory; yet such was the passion with which he expressed them that they influenced profoundly the whole of English nineteenth-century art (Fig. 112a).

One other painter of the middle nineteenth-century should be mentioned: George Frederick Watts (1817—1904). As a young man Watts spent several years in Italy, but unlike the majority of English artists at the time, it was not Florentine so much as Venetian paintings which fascinated him: of all English artists he perhaps came closest to finding the 'Venetian Secret' which so fascinated the painters of the late eighteenth and early nineteenth centuries. The work of his early and middle periods has much of the transparently luminous richness of paint of the great Venetians. Whatever his fault, Watts was a *painter*, and, not like the Pre-Raphaelites, a draughtsman who happened to be using oil-paint. Towards the end of his life he fell into the characteristic English fault of excessive moralizing, and in such pictures as *Hope* or *Love and Death*, the morality appears as something external to, and not fully assimilated with, the painting. Yet, at his best, Watts is by no means one of the least in the tradition of English painting.

Chapter XXV

FROM IMPRESSIONISM TO EXPRESSIONISM

*

CLASSICISM and Romanticism had reached into the past, but Impressionism had made itself the interpreter of the life of the period. Even today it strikes us as the most vital expression of the century which was to see the greatest changes ever recorded in history.

This new, unprecedented, vividly colourful art was revolutionary in its effect, and all Europe was up in arms about it. In 1893 the rebels against the old methods of painting foregathered in Munich as the 'Secession'. In 1899 Max Liebermann (1847—1935), who in his formative years had been subject to the influence of the art of Menzel, placed himself at the head of a North German secession, while the Müncheners found an intellectual leader in Fritz von Uhde (1848—1911). From Munich, which presently struck off in a different direction, Lovis Corinth (1858—1925) and Max Slevogt removed to Berlin. Corinth did not stipple his pictures with dots of colour, but slapped great blots of paint on his canvases, while Slevogt's flying pen illustrated his prolific fancies.

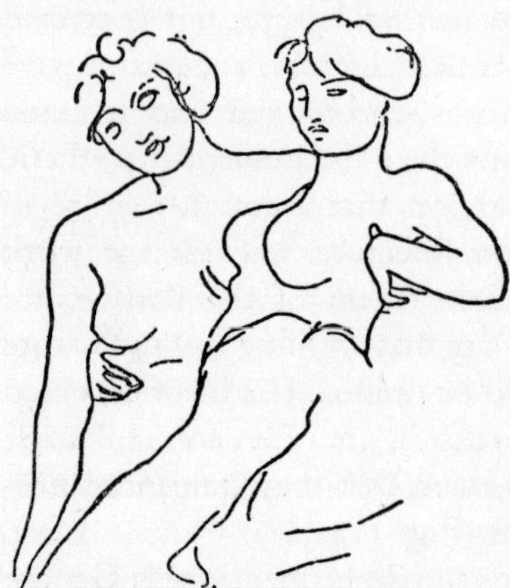

Auguste Rodin (1840—1917). Original litograph. 1902

All these brilliant artists regarded themselves as revolutionaries. For them, light, atmosphere, and colour were everything; the subject hardly mattered. It was all one to them—they would have said—whether they painted the head of a minister of State or a potato. In the exaggeration of *L'art pour l'art*—an art intended only for artists—Impressionism finally worked itself to death.

Later Developments

The historical significance of Impressionism went far beyond the creations of its original adherents, for it instilled new life into the art of Western Europe. Its influence on those artists who held themselves somewhat aloof, seeking to realize their own ideals, was unmistakable. Of these one of the most important was James McNeill Whistler (1834—1903), an American, who studied in Paris, and then settled in London. Spanish painting (especially that of Velasquez), the new enthusiasm in France for the art of the Far East, the beginnings of Impressionism, and perhaps also something of the romantic inspiration of Pre-Raphaelitism, combined to produce an eclectic and intensely tasteful art. Whistler's fault was perhaps that his taste was too perfect; a cosmopolitan expatriate, he was denied the deep-stretching roots which give strength to artists brought up in a native tradition. Yet in spite of its obvious echoes of Velasquez, one cannot deny that *Miss Cicely Alexander* is a masterpiece; nor that *The White Girl,* or the *Nocturnes,* with their exquisitely matched and subtle tones, are equal to almost anything being produced in France at the same time.

Whistler, in spite of his fashionable vogue, stood alone in English painting; it was not until 1886, when the New English Art Club was founded, that the full effect of French impressionism was felt in England. English painting, from 1860, had been, to an unparalleled degree, incoherent and untraditional; but the example of France, and the study of the earlier English masters, in particular Constable, provided the group, including P. W. Steer (1860—1934), and Sickert (1860—1942), with a tradition and a coherence to which younger artists could attach themselves.

In the clear, luminous atmosphere of the Engadine, Giovanni Segantini (1858—99) painted his pictures of the high Alps, welding the *pointille* of the Impressionists into regular, clearly defined streaks of colour, with a marvellously luminous effect.

But first of all Paul Cézanne (Fig. 113a) replaced Segantini's little spots of colour by broad, compact surfaces. He wanted to transform the Impressionism of his youth into *quelque chose de solide et de durable,* and before long he filled his canvases with compositions of increasing beauty and austerity. This gives his paintings their unprecedented power and certainty of construction, and it is this that has made this master the Columbus of modern painting. If Cézanne, in the heyday of Impressionism, was already revealing himself as a forerunner of Cubism, another great solitary and individualist, Vincent van Gogh (Fig. 113b) could with equal justice be called the forerunner of Expressionism. It is true that this artist was still practising the technique of Impressionism in its *pointilliste* form; but, not contented with the mere reflection of life, he sought once more to imbue art with the aristocracy of the intellect and made it the expression of his profanely religious spirit. Simplicity of heart, not the search for a visual stimulus inspired the paintings of Henri Rousseau (1844—1910) the Parisian revenue officer, and the 'Father of the Sunday painters'. Full of a mystical closeness to Nature, this *peintre naif* produced paintings of 'still life', landscape, and visionary scenes which in their graphic integrity, their rhythms, and their unrealistic coloration are far in advance of their age. Subsequently, quite a number of 'Sunday painters' cleared the way for a fuller appreciation of Rousseau's art, and Maurice Utrillo (1883—1955) has continued it until the present day.

In another way, Symbolism hand in hand with the so-called *style des jeunes,* or *Jugendstil,* sought to break away from the impressionistic consideration of surfaces and to probe the depths of psychic experiences. While the *Jugendstil,* together with the Japanese woodcut, were the chief formal inspiration of such artists as Félix Valloton (1865—1925) or Aubrey Beardsley (1872—98), the antimaterialistic tendencies of this period were concentrated in the mystical art of Odilon Redon (1840—1916), Gustave Moreau (1826—98), and others. Before long art was declared a substitute for religion, and all sorts of esoteric groups devoted themselves to its cult. Thus, one of the most gifted of the fathers of the Symbolist movement in art, Paul Gauguin (Fig. 113d), founded the group of the 'Nabis', the Prophets. Maurice Denis is another typical representative of the Symbolism that was born of Impressionism.

The influence of impressionism was not confined only to painting. Even the modern art of caricature learnt something from it; a way of jotting down rapidly perceived, superficial observations, without the tedious thoroughness of the Romantics (page 297) or the impersonal, stereotyped grotesques of the seventeenth century (page 283). The rapid outlines of such caricature cannot be mistaken for the genuine contours of classic art. Even in its drawings, Impressionism aims at a picturesque appearance. Like the impressionist painters, Rodin (1840—1917), the greatest Impressionist sculptor, was obsessed by the fear of depriving his work of its vitality by giving it a definite roundness. If we consider his *Thinker,* or a figure from the group of the *Burghers of Calais* (Fig. 114b), we see that the classical laws of composition are treated with disdain, and only the surface appearance is regarded. The latter work also demonstrates emphatically the essential drawback of this way of seeing things: magnificent though the single figures are, Rodin is incapable of combining them into a group. In his great and entirely picturesque sculpture, as in the works of the Impressionists, nothing is stated that is not confirmed by the literature and philosophy of the nineteenth century. Classicism had been by far its weaker component; but Romanticism had conquered, and in Impressionism it turned its attention, not to the past, but to the present, seeking to grasp it as one might seek to grasp a beautiful mirage.

The Rise of Expressionism

About the turn of the century Expressionism made its appearance, at once the result and the antithesis of Impressionism. Whether the term was coined by Henri Matisse or another, it is highly suggestive. By 1901 it was already in general use. It meant that art was no longer content to concern itself with the surface of things; that the impression received from the surface no longer seemed as essential as the psychic experience to which the artist gives external expression.

In France, Expressionism evolved in the most organic manner, without diverging from the straight path. It is true that what seems today a logical development was

(A) The Rockefeller Centre, New
k. Designed by Reinhard and
'meister; Corbett, Harrison and
Murray; Hood and Fouilloux. 1931 – 39.
The tobacco factory of Erven de
l. J. van Nelle, Rotterdam, Designed
Brinkman and van der Vlugt, 1929.

a

b

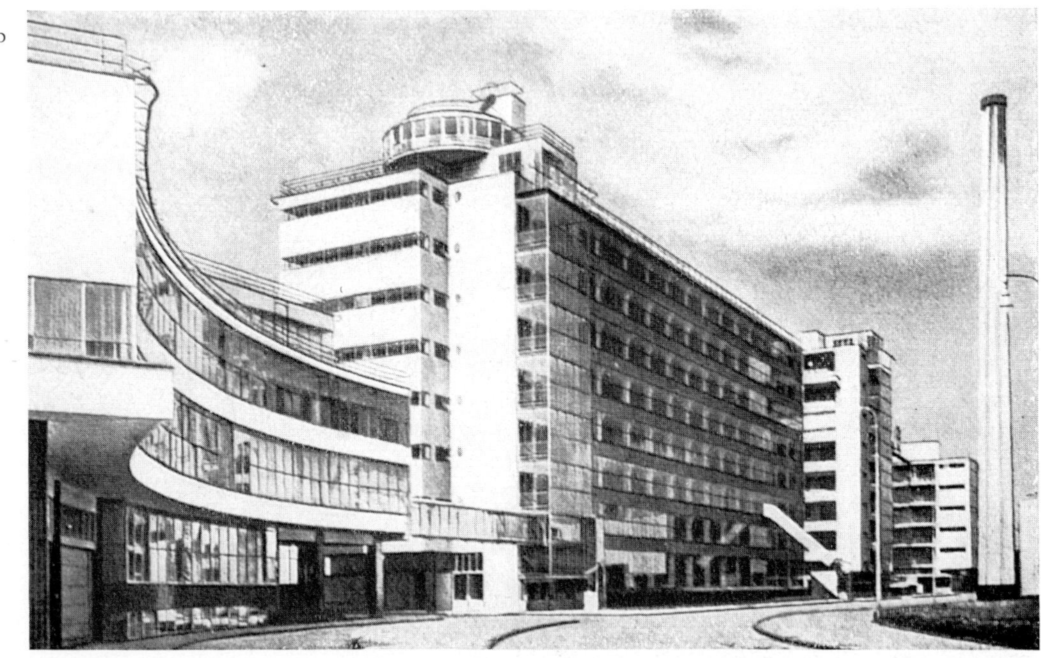

a

b

116. (A) Model hotel at the Swiss National Exhibition, Zürich, 1939. Dreyer, architect.
(B) Kollegienhaus, University of Basel; view in the Gardens. Completed 1939. Rohn, architect.

then regarded as a startling rebellion. The seed which the great solitaries had sown had germinated. While Van Gogh had succeeded in selling only one picture in his lifetime, and while people were hardly aware of his existence, the merits of the new movement were now warmly debated by the general public. In 1905, in the autumn exhibition at the Grand Palais, there was a press of visitors in the room from whose walls the pictures of reckless youth seemed to cry aloud. The exasperated critics spoke of *cage de fauves*, 'a cage of wild beasts', and the name of *Les Fauves* had once for all attached itself to the early French Expressionists. The programme of *Les Fauves,* which was followed by the sculptor Aristide Maillot, and the painters Henri Matisse. Georges Rouault, Dunoyer de Ségonzac, Albert Marguet, André Derain, Raoul Dufy, Georges Braque, and Othon Friesz, the Fleming Maurice de Vlaminck, and the Dutchmann Kees van Dongen, called for *peinture pure.* Henri Matisse (1869—1954) is the most consistent representative of the movement. In his pictures the natural scene or model is actually as Cézanne once demanded that it should be, 'merely a pretext for a game with lines and colours'. With ever more frugal means, this artist, setting all problems aside, has finally developed colour into a cultivated art of surfaces.

While the French followed the ancient Latin ideal of moderation and lucidity, the artists of Central and Eastern Europe plunged headlong into the problematic spirit of the period, and in this theatre Expressionism became the typical utterance of the spiritual indigence of the two world-wars, an utterance in which the psychic content was more important than any mere formal qualities or laws of composition. This tendency of Central European art began with the great Norwegian artist Edvard Munch (1863—1944) (page 306), who in his early work still displays the long, curving lines characteristic of the *Jugendstil.* Often enough the revolution occurred in one and the same artist. For example: Emil Nolde (right) went from St Gallen to the Munich Academy, where under Corinth he became an Impressionist. However, the moment he had mastered the technique of his art, he turned away from the past and flung himself passionately into the new movement.

Emil Nolde. Head of a Prophet. Woodcut. About 1915

Grünewald and El Greco were now regarded with enthusiastic admiration, and even more passionately than Gauguin the new generation sought to learn from the Primitives, perceiving their profoundly religious intention. But the movement was impelled, not by childlike simplicity, but by a highly intellectual austerity, and felt obliged to insist on the configuration of space on a plane surface.

Edvard Munch (1863—1944).
Death-chamber. Litograph. 16 in. by 21 1/2 in., 1896

'*Absolute*' *Art*

Wassily Kandinsky is the typical representative of 'absolute painting'. With him, Adolf Hölzel in Stuttgart and August Giacometti in Zürich. resolved to abandon all imitation; only forms and colours must be allowed to 'speak', while 'inner resonances' would be heard by the observer. It was characteristic of this movement that Kandinsky gave his colleagues his book *On the Spiritual in Art;* a doctrine of chromatic harmony, in which it is asserted, for example, that eccentrically moving yellow, flowing toward the spectator, being material, readily unites with the aggressive plane figure, the pointed triangle. Blue, on the other hand, fleeing into the distance, is at home, as a concentrically moving spiritual entity, in the self-contained circle. The simple colours red, yellow and blue, with their mixtures green, orange and violet, have their place between white, which is mere possibility, and black, the negation of life.

But as soon as such explanations became necessary, the art of the period, so fond of appealing to the primitives, forgot that the power of religion, from which the primitives drew their strength, has no need of these crutches. In the South Seas, or in Africa, if one asks the natives the meaning of this or that shape or colour, they are never in any doubt. If they are sufficiently acquainted with their European questioner they will readily tell him what the magic signs mean. But the modern artist sees that the public, looking at his pictures in the picture-galleries, laughs, and asks whether by any chance they have been hung upside down. Their laughter is of little importance in itself; for the great revolutionary movements in art have often had to wait for the appreciation of a generation unborn. 'Absolute painting', since eventually it must logically renounce intelligible symbols, had reached its limit as a means of expression. Then came the first World War, and other artists, like Oscar Kokoschka, Paul Klee and Lionel Feininger, to name only a few of many talented workers, were shut off from the world. From the confusion of the war, beside the already existing 'Futurism', which was noisy rather than effective, there emerged the witches' sabbath of an inflationary art. From the carnival antics of 'Dadaism', which amidst its concoctions of nails, cotton wool, splinters of glass, wheels, feathers, and bits of waste paper, could only stammer its 'da, da' with mounting hysteria, there grinned the image of a world that had left its orbit.

The New Tendencies

Despite all resistance, with the resolution of *les Fauves* and the temporary supremacy of Expressionism, the eruption into the field of modern art was effective and irrevocable. Of the artists who were responsible for it many are still living and working. In a continual struggle, a general melée in which the majority often changed sides and embarked on the most contradictory experiments, six main tendencies or movements finally emerged which are fairly distinguishable one from another. While it cannot be the task of a historical survey to pass final judgments on a process which is still continuing, one may at least endeavour to insert a few elucidatory accents and to give the reader a few useful hints.

The Spanish painter Pablo Picasso (Fig. 114c) invented Cubism. He began as a pupil of Cézanne, but after 1906 he left *les Fauves* and with his friend Georges Braque he evolved a new method of representing masses or volumes. Reverting to the Gallic lucidity and order, since 1910 the influential group of Cubists, which had been joined, among others, by Delaunay, Gleizes, Léger, and Picasso's compatriot Juan Gris, sought to represent spatial elements not by the rigid abstractions of the Egyptians, but by alternating points of view. Only when this is properly understood do the changing contours, the displaced eyes, etc., of the Cubist paintings, in which the layman often sees only distoded frontal aspects, become intelligible, for in reality he is observing different profiles, whose purpose is to achieve a timelessly valid aspect instead of the fortuitous quality of a single view. Some remnant of the natural model nearly always persists in the creations of such Cubist innovators, even if only as a text for a free composition. Instead of relying on the old central perspective, stronger and softer, colder and warmer harmonies of colour are achieved by superficial arrangements, and the illusion of space is evoked by geometrical sections.

Related to Cubism in its early stages, and not merely an Italian version of Expressionism, for which it is apt to be mistaken, *Futurism* was founded, in its literary form, in 1910, and in 1912 was for the first time the sensation of various exhibitions. Like Cubism, it sought for changes in the visual field, but these were obtained not by the adoption of different points of view, but by a change of scene. By this pseudo-cinematographic technique absolutely novel subject-matters were introduced in modern painting; for example, the intrusion into a house of the noise of the street, or the representation of the consecutive movements of a dance by the juxtaposition of changing images on a flat surface. But since the ranks of the Futurists contained no such pre-eminently gifted artist as Picasso, and since such painters and sculptors as Umberto Boccioni and Carlo Carra were the victims of their literary and political ambitions, Futurism has not exerted any great influence outside Italy.

A certain reaction against the efforts of 'absolute art' found utterance in the expressionistic 'Verism', which after the first World War engaged in a vigorous criticism of the age. Inspired at its birth by the will to a 'new objectivity', and compelled to return to the reproduction of natural forms, it also produced such masters as George Grosz and Otto Dix, who portrayed the epoch in their countless satirical paintings and drawings. For caricature, if it is to be recognizable and effective, urgently requires that a glimmer of the natural forms shall show through the veil of grinning distortion, which in turn may well be borrowed from the expressionistic arsenal. Such pictures as Gino Severini has recently been painting very often amount to a caricature and a derision of the reality. In these examples of the 'new objectivity' a surreptitious tendenciousness portrays absolutely irrelevant natural objects, in often completely nonsensical associations, with an exaggerated emphasis which sets the beholder conjecturing what can possibly be concealed behind this external semblance.

Like Verism, and with aims not dissimilar from those of the 'new objectivity', Surrealism or 'Magism' returns to recognizable natural forms, although it often distorts them into demonic and often merely monstrous and repulsive ugliness, in order by the methods of bathypsychology to drag the most secret strata and impulses of the soul from their darkest hiding-places into the light of day. Of these 'magical' pictures André Breton says in his 'Surrealist Manifesto', that they are like 'the images of the opium-eater', and denies that they exhibit 'the slightest degree of previous consideration'. If the Surrealists are constantly referring to the great masters of the past, and above all to Hieronymus Bosch, we should remember that his pictorial representations, contrary to all that has been said hitherto, were rooted in social realities. He did not seek to lift reason, logic and morality from their bearings; he only wanted to serve them, while this religious earnestness is wholly lacking in the best creations of the Surrealists. Many of the works of Giorgio di Chirico, Juan Miró, Salvador Dali, Frederico Castellon, Max Ernst, Walter Stümpfig, etc., do not impress one, as is constantly asserted, as 'metaphysical statements', but often enough as rather self-conscious fables, and even more frequently they are unintentionally comical.

While the four movements known as Cubism, Futurism, Verism and Surrealism had not yet entirely dispensed with a more or less diminished natural model, the exponents of *abstract art*, in obedience to the peremptory requirements of 'absolute painting', bade farewell to the last trace of objectivity. Such artists as Willi Baumeister, William Baziotes, Jackson Pollock and Otto Ritschl declared that natural forms were entirely irrelevant and were not worth representing. For this reason 'Abstract Art' described itself also, through a comical misunderstanding, as 'Concrete Art', considering that it has evaded the unreality of the natural model and penetrated to the real, unobjective object of art. Apart from this peculiar logic, Abstract Art can base its works only on the general laws of musical composition, and being debarred any other possible experiences it has to take refuge in the mere enjoyment of forms and colours. At the same time, it forgets that while the ethereal activity of music has the advantage of the dimension of time, abstract painting is transfixed in lifeless rigidity. If after twenty thousand years of history nothing was left of art than the forms and colours of the abstract painters—however beautiful they may sometimes be—we should have to take a pessimistic view of the history of art. Fortunately, however, even in this movement only one of many possibilities has to be considered. From pure form, to which the exponents of Abstract Art are so fond of referring, the path to the future leads onward by way of *Constructivism*.

Constructivism

The accompanying illustrations, and a few brief comments, will help the reader to understand what is meant by Constructivism. As soon as the demand for 'absolute

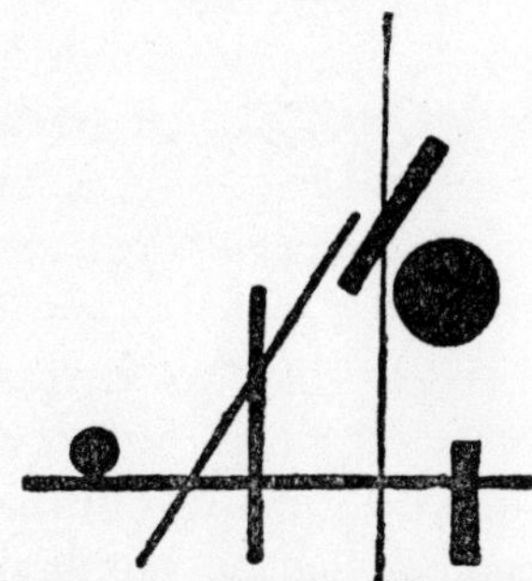

Composition of vertical, horizontal and inclined straight lines in conjunction with circles

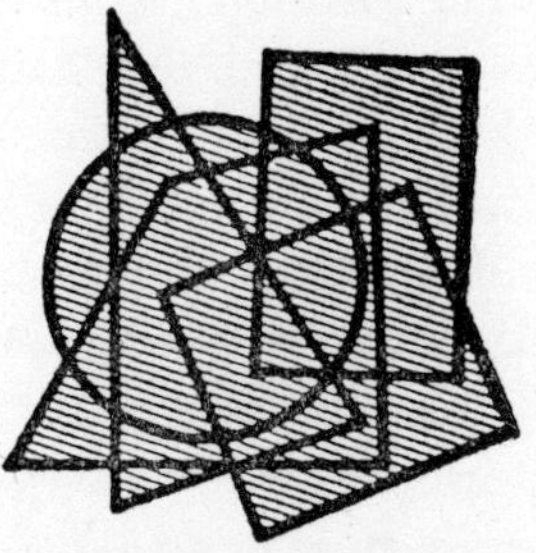

Play of figures on a plane surface

Erection of plane surfaces in space. Expressive and impressive effect

painting' had been made, the problem arose of the intrinsic value of the formal elements. The Machine Age revealed in Constructivism its faith in progress, founded on technique. It is typical of technical thought that it seeks to reduce everything to a formula, and in Constructivism human beings themselves become schemata. Before its achievements we ask ourselves whether they are more at home on canvas, as works of art, or whether they should not be relegated to the engineer's study or the office. However, in the tasteful combination of lines, coloured surfaces, and drawing geometrical figures, the Constructivist movement has produced many attractive wallpapers and designs for carpets.

Seen in perspective, Constructivism, during the ten years after the first World War, did some really constructive work. But it was by no means as revolutionary as it claimed to be. In the ornamental art of all periods and peoples the sound elements of Constructivism have played a vital part.

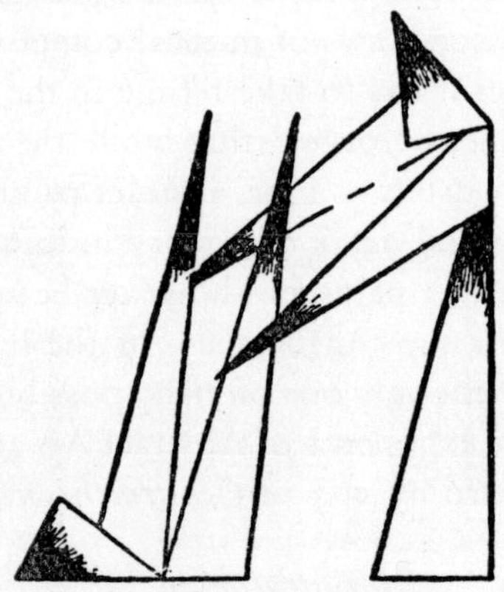

William Wauer: Help!

Chapter XXVI

ART TODAY

*

IN the same way as we can see a mosaic only from a suitable distance, so we can understand the history of art only when we look back on it from some distance of time. About the art of the immediate past no historical judgment can be formed; for any historical survey must conclude with a question mark; but we can try to give the reader some idea of the tendencies of modern art.

Whether we like it or not, the fact is that the twentieth century has become a machine age; but the machine, instead of a blessing, has become a curse; instead of a servant, a tyrant.

Imaginary view of a modern factory as a harmoniously self-contained unity

As soon as 'absolute painting' sought to interpret a definite mental content, instead of confining itself to formal harmonies, it inevitably came to grief on the fact of sensuous perception. Cubism had already tried to represent the third dimension; and the best Constructivist artists promptly abandoned painting for a kind of sculpture which resembled the art of the pattern-maker. But the supreme realization was still that of genuine architecture, which is what it seems.

Spatial expression of the graphic and technical features of a Printing Works

Architecture

At the end of the twenties, when the world seemed to be recovering from the consequences of the first war, a new architectural ideal appeared, inspired by serious artistic intentions, which was no longer content to be merely functional, nor to be any kind of archaistic revival.

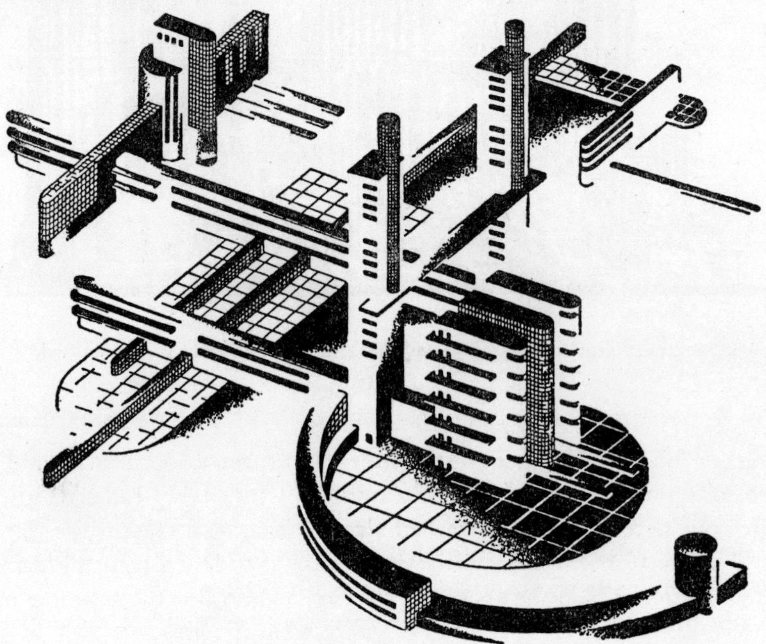

Project for a Metallurgical Research Institute in open country

In the illustrations published by Chernikov, and reproduced on pages 311—12, it is clear that something more than functionalism is aimed at. We can well imagine how in the city of the future the inner life of its buildings will be far more visibly and variously expressed in their external forms, and also in the total picture, than of old, in the Middle Ages, when the houses of the citizens all crouched low beneath the heavenward-pointing cathedrals. To the objection that these pictures are merely fantasies one must reply that without fantasies no new art has ever come into existence. But it is perhaps better to study buildings which have actually been carried out, in which the ideals of modern architecture have been realized. The Tobacco

Frans Masereel. Sketch. About 1920

Factory in Rotterdam (Fig. 115) still hesitates between mere objectivity and a novel expression. The Rockefeller Centre in New York (Fig. 115), however, is something entiıely different from the old skyscrapers that surround it. Unlike them, its fourteen buildings rise skywards as spatially isolated towers. In well-considered degrees of altitude, they are related by virtue of their proportions, and are sited so skilfully that none of them casts its shadow on any of the others.

It was not only because of the requirements of traffic inside these giants which had risen from the ground that ideas ormerly fcarried out only in a horizontal direction were now applied in the vertical direction also. Their lateral disposition relates them, for the general observer, to the largest structure, the seventy-storeyed Radio Building, 920 feet in height. The aerial photograph gives only a very inadequate notion of the coherence of this group of buildings, to which the general aspect of the city owes far more than to the arrogant Empire State Building with its one hundred and two storeys.

However, the modern architect seeks to express his ideas, not only in business premises and factories, which express the essential character of the busy capital more truly than the monumentality of its governmental or departmental buildings, but also in public assembly rooms, where people foregather for recreation or study. In Switzerland, for example, where in 1939 the peoples of Europe were able to meet in peace for the last time in many years, one could see, in the Zürich Exhibition (Landesausstellung: Fig. 116a) and elsewhere (Fig. 116b), the tendency of modern architecture to set its buildings in pleasant natural surroundings. It is not to the detriment of such efforts if one sees, in this, a feature of the Japanese dwelling-house. The Impressionists also—Degas, for example—showed the influence of East Asiatic art in their paintings, and yet created something quite new and original, which reinvigorated the entire field of European art. Architecture, in designing the settlement—assuredly the finest and most urgent of its future tasks—may adapt suggestions from many parts of the world, but need not therefore decline into plagiarism.

Sculpture and Painting

If the reader wishes to understand the art of the present day he must not judge everything by ready-made standards. Every period has to solve its problems in its own way. That is why most people seem to learn so little from history; they should open their eyes to the wealth of artistic possibilities, which alone should silence all debates about the end of art! Even if humanity, in the twentieth century of the Christian era, threatens to lapse into a civilized barbarism, yet it cannot rid itself of its knowledge of its eternal possessions, and of its longing for them. Art is immortal.

But today, as always, art remains the unmistakable finger-print of the age. That many people do not understand its language is due, on the one hand, to their artistic education, in which the emphasis is always on historical elements or the contents of the museums, and on the other hand to the complicated and indecipherable aspect of the modern world. Not art alone, but also physics or chemistry is far more difficult to understand than it used to be, and yet no one reproaches the natural sciences on this account, as art is constantly reproached. No purchaser of a motor-car would be filled with enthusiasm for a model that was built after the pattern of the old post chaises. Yet many people expect the artist to paint as our grandfathers did.

This is obviously unfair, and it is as obviously to the credit of the modern artists that in spite of many rebuffs on the part of the public they should have held fast to their point of view, whereas it would have been much easier, by a facile compromise, to paint as they were expected to do.

One of the chief reasons why modern art is so difficult to understand is the fact that since the rococo period there has been no fundamental style, generally understood and accepted. All the more, then, are we eager to seek for such a style, to discover how the spirit of the present day expresses itself in art. If the complaint is made that modern painting—in the art of portraiture, for example—no longer has any respect for the individual countenance, or that it mercilessly exposes the most secret recesses of the human soul to the general gaze, one should realize that this *demontage* of the personality, this disregard of the individual, is to be seen in many directions, elsewhere than in art, as a typical feature of the modern State. If, on the contrary, the multiplicity of movements and opinions in the art of today is extolled as an expression of modern individualism, there is something to be said for this attitude also. But one must not forget that the urgent tendency to stylization which is manifested everywhere has quite a different connotation. If a historian of art, born on a remote planet, had studied the development of style on our earth only as far as Rococo, and had then arrived here without further preparation, he would have had to judge merely from the formal and to some extent graphological expressions of our modern art what manner of men inhabited the earth. For hitherto emphatic stylization has always appeared as a concomitant phenomenon of extreme spiritual and social subjection. So it was in the remote ages when the hunter was transformed into the husbandman; so it was in Byzantium when a millennial culture became congealed, and so it is again today, in the age of the machine, when the individual sees himself threatened by the danger of complete submergence in the mass, of mechanization by means of ideologies and slogans which seem to harness one and all to new communities and new allegiances. Who would seek to stand aside from such problems of the future, from the historical choice between compulsion and freedom? Who can believe in the purpose of art when the earth is writhing in the birth-pangs of futurity? Here indeed is a gigantic spectacle, a vast drama of the spirit, which expresses itself in a thousand ways in the plastic arts.

As in sculpture, Rodin was succeeded by Maillol, whose indefatigable creative energy expressed itself also in drawings (page 316), so new talents are always appearing. In graphic art, as in painting, there are countless schools, movements and theories. Some come to terms with modern life, as the Expressionists did before them (page 312); others, while retaining the Expressionist motive, portray naturalistic forms, and others again revert to the eternal human form, or to pure landscape.

Judgments of the lasting value of individual efforts must be left to history. Those who complain that there are too many mediocrities must remember that this has always been the case. To form a just estimate of the present situation, even as it existed in the comparatively favourable period before the war, one must not forget what an enormous amount of artistic energy is absorbed, in modern life, by industry, poster art, black-and-white art, and—on an ever-increasing scale—by engineering.

Is this to be regretted? What Toulouse-Lautrec (1864—1901) was able to do in the later days of Impressionism is easy for his successors. Toulouse-Lautrec, by long practice in the art of the poster, first acquired the assured touch that marks the ripe artist; for it is not the soft or pointed brush that leads the artist to the mastery of his art, but the way in which the brush is used. Not every modern painter can become a Rembrandt or a Michelangelo. But the perception of triviality in art, and the true valuation of quality, are today far more general than they were a few years ago.

The clash of contrary opinions and the criticisms of the daily Press are not without their uses. While their standards may be ephemeral they prevent stagnation. Life, however, is stronger than derivative theories of art, which in the end confront the work of art as philosophy confronts the enigma of the universe. Those who take art seriously should learn that they must not be too quick to condemn, but must try to understand it in its historical and racial setting. Here the history of art is of inestimable assistance. Programmes and schools of art are of less importance. We need not always pay much attention to what the artists themselves declare as to their intention, for their intention is the resultant of very different forces. Vocation, however, is no empty word. Because of this, the artist works on indefatigably—because he must. That is the answer which the artists must give to the question; why they create their works of art.

Aristide Maillol (1861—1944)
Woodcut. 1926

List of Colour Plates

I. Katsukawa Shunsho (1726–92): Scene from a Play. Japanese colour woodcut. (British Museum, London) *Frontispiece*

II. Greek Black Figure Vase. 5th Century B.C. *facing page* 154

III. Rogier van der Weyden (c. 1399–1464): Portrait of a Lady. (National Gallery, London) *facing page* 224

IV. Rembrandt van Rijn (1606–69): Saskia as Flora. (National Gallery, London) *facing page* 268

V. Paul Cézanne (1839–1906): Old Woman with Rosary. (National Gallery, London) *facing page* 288

List of Monochrome Plates

		between pages
1 A, B	Polychrome Wall-paintings of the Ice-Age in the Caves of Altamira	16–17
2 A	Ivory torso from the Pope's Cave, Brassempouy	16–17
B	Carved bone implements from Southern France	16–17
C	Wild Horse. Wall-painting in the Cave of Niaux	16–17
3 A	Stonehenge	24–25
B	Rock-drawings of the Bronze Age, near Riksö, Sweden	24–25
C	Incised images on a stone kist at Kivik, Sweden	24–25
4 A–D	Vessels and cultic objects from the New Stone Age to the Iron Age	24–25
5 A	Ceremonial model of chariot, from the older Nordic Bronze Age; Trundholm	24–25
B	Bronze chariot of the early Iron Age; Strettweg	24–25
6 A	A Female Idol from Boeotia	24–25
B	Earthenware statuette of pre-Hellenic age	24–25
C	Reclining Stag from the Kuban	24–25
7 A	Earthenware figure from a grave of the Bronze Age; Yugoslavia	32–33
B	Sword-hilts of Bronze Age	32–33
C	Husbanmdan ploughing, from Boeotia	32–33
8 A–C	Works of art from the Palace of Knossos, Crete	32–33
9	Female bust, found at Elche	32–33
10 A	Woman's head, the work of the Joruba	32–33
B	Wooden figure of Man on horseback; Joruba	32–33
C	Massa village to the south-east of Lake Tchad	32–33
11 A	Bust of a Brass figure from Dahomey	40–41
B	Stylized Antelope from Senegal	40–41
C	Lion, of sheet silver; Dahomey	40–41
12 A	Girl's head. Bronze cast from Benin	40–41
B	Three children. Bronze plaque from Benin	40–41
C	Bronze head from Benin	40–41
13 A	Large colour-box in carved wood from New Zealand	40–41
B	Wooden mask from New Caledonia	40–41
C	Shield with ancestral image; New Guinea	40–41
D	Wooden Club; Polynesia	40–41
14 A–E	Art of Easter Island	40–41
15	'Tiki'. Ancestral figure enthroned	48–49
16 A	Polychrome carving from New Mecklenburg, Melanesia	48–49
B	Wooden figure from New Guinea, Melanesia	48–49
C	Dance of Bats. Bark-cloth Painting, from Dutch New Guinea	48–49
17 A	Leather cuirass of Haida workmanship	48–49
B	Objects made from walrus tusk; Alaskan Eskimo	48–49
18 A	Stone figure of late Huaxtec culture, found at Vera Cruz, Mexico	48–49
B	Mayan Calendar	48–49
C	Inner courtyard of palace and doorway at Mitla	48–49
19	'Temple of the Warrior', Chichen-Itza, Yucatan	64–65
20 A	Funerary urn from Zaachila, Mexico	64–65
B	Earthenware vessel from Azcapotzalko, Mexico	64–65
C	Earthenware bowl of the Cholula culture	64–65

		between pages
21 A, B	Earthenware vessels, Chimu	64–65
22 A	Head of a stone statue, from Tiahuanaco	64–65
B	Blackish-grey amphora in pure Inca style	64–65
C	View of the Inca fortress of Machu Picchu	64–65
23	Five-footed bull from the palace of Sargon II at Khorsabad, near Nineveh	80–81
24 A	Achaemenian capital from the palace of Darius at Susa	80–81
B	Winged Ibex from the end of the Persian era	80–81
C	Assurbanipal hunting the lion; alabaster relief from Nineveh	80–81
25	Four-winged Assyrian god; alabaster relief	80–81
26 A	Part of a Sumerian mosaic	80–81
B, C	Impressions of ancient seals from the valley of the Indus	80–81
D	Seated figure of the princely priest, Gudea	80–81
E, F	A Babylonian cylindrical seal	80–81
27 A	Northern gate of the great Stupa at Sanci	88–89
B	Lion capital of a memorial column at Sarnath, Northern India	88–89
C	Interior of the Cave Temple of Karli	88–89
28 A	Marble temple of Somnathpur, near Mysore	88–89
B	Naga with his wife and serving-women; relief from Ajanta	88–89
C	Pair of royal founders; from the rock-temple of Karli	88–89
29 A	Apsaras and servant; from the frescoes of Sigiriya, Ceylon	88–89
B	Avalokiteshvara; from Binar or Bengal	88–89
C	Yakshi; relief from the Surya Deul Temple, Orissa	88–89
30 A	The eleven-storeyed Gate-town of the Vishnu Temple at Kumbakonam	88–89
B	Part of the Ramayana frieze on the Shiva Temple, Prambanan, Java	88–89
31	Shiva dancing, from the Great Temple of Madura	96–97
32 A	Pagoda amidst the ruins of Pagan	96–97
B	Small pagoda at Ava, near Mandalay	96–97
C	Head of a giant Buddha, near Polonnaruva, Ceylon	96–97
33 A	Saddled horse; painted earthenware of the Tang Dynasty	96–97
B	Bronze cauldron of the Chou Dynasty	96–97
C	Bronze vase in the form of a bird	96–97
34 A	Mandarin from the tombs of the Ming Emperors	96–97
B	Bust of a Bodhisatva of the Wei period	96–97
C	Brick pagoda of the Temple of Sung-yueh-sse, Honan	96–97
D	Colossal figure of Buddha; Wei period	96–97
35 A	View of the 'Hall of Annual Prayer', Temple of Heaven, Peking	112–113
B	Typical Chinese use of wood in the Temple of Confucius, Wanhien	112–113
36 A	Porcelain beaker; Kang Hsi period of the Ching Dynasty	112–113
B	Porcelain vase of the 'Black Family', Kang Hsi period	112–113
C	Colour print from the Manual of Painting of the Grain-of-Mustard-Seed-Garden	112–113
37 A	Chinese Landscape by the Master Wang Chien-chang	112–113
B	Han-shan and Shih-te. Monochrome painting ascribed to Shubun	112–113
38 A	Head of a Heavenly Commander in the Shinyakushigi Temple, Nara	112–113
B	Part of the gigantic figure of a divine gatekeeper, 'Temple of the Azure Clouds', Peking	112–113

		between pages
38 C	Polychrome ceramics on the 'Nine Dragon Shrine', Forbidden City of Peking	112–113
39 A	Landscape with Bridge. Coloured woodcut by Hokusai	120–121
B	Coloured woodcut of the Hishi-Kawa Moronobu school	120–121
40 A	Head of Búddha, by Kuratsukurino Obito Tori	120–121
B	Portrait of a Priest. Black lacquered wood. Ashikagu period	120–121
C	'No' mask, 'Deigan'. Work of the wood-carver Echi Yoshifune	120–121
D	Lohan. Life-sized figure of glazed terra-cotta	120–121
41	Sethos and the Sun-god; relief in the sanctuary of Abydos, Egypt	120–121
42 A	Prince Rahotep; statue from Medum	120–121
B	Nofret, wife of Rahotep. Seated figure of painted limestone	120–121
C	The Sphinx, Gizeh	120–121
D	The pyramid of Chephren, Gizeh	120–121
43 A	Chephren. Part of a statue from the Valley Temple of the Chephren Pyramid	128–129
B	Limestone bust of Fourth Dynasty	128–129
C	Fishing scene on the mastaba of Akhuthotep	128–129
44 A	Clustered sandstone columns in the temple of Luxor	128–129
B	Colossal Columns at Karnak	128–129
C	Façade of the Rock-temple of Abu-Simbel	128–129
45 A	Model bust of Queen Nofretete	128–129
B	The lunar deity Chons; granite statue from Karnak	128–129
C	Part of the relief decoration of a limestone column	128–129
D	Limestone relief from the colonnaded hall at Karnak	128–129
46 A	Geese. Part of a painting in a tomb, Medum	128–129
B	The anubis, Wall-painting in the tomb of Sennudjem, Karnak	128–129
C	Reapers in the Kingdom of the Dead; from a wall-painting in the tomb of Sennudjem, Karnak	128–129
47 A	Late archaic female head in the temple of Aegina	136–137
B	Herakles; from the Aphaia Temple, Aegina	136–137
C	Korê. Found to the west of the Erechtheum in 1886	136–137
D	Attic Vase in mixed style, with red and black figures	136–137
48 A	Head of a charioteer, at Delphi	136–137
B	Head of the statue of a Greek athlete; Benevento, Italy	136–137
C	The Orpheus relief; reproduced from the best Roman copy of the lost original	136–137
D	Part of the front of the so-called 'throne' found in the Villa Ludovisi	136–137
49 A	The Hermes of Praxiteles	136–137
B	The Venus of Milo	136–137
50 A	North view of the Temple of Poseidon	136–137
B	Part of the Assembly of the Gods, from the Parthenon frieze	136–137
C	Panel from the Parthenon frieze	136–137
D	South-eastern aspect, Temple of Nike, Athens	136–137
51	Part of the southern side of the Porch of the Maidens; Erechtheum, Athens	144–145
52 A	Figures on a black-figured vase	144–145
B	Drawing on a white lecythus	144–145
C	Galloping quadriga, with Hermes; relief from Phaleron	114-145

		between pages
53 A	Wounded Galatian	144–145
B, C	Relief on the sides of the 'Borghesian Vase'	144–145
54 A	Rustic idyll. Marble relief	144–145
B	Dionysos, with Ikarios. Reproduction of a Hellenistic work	144–145
55 A	Head of Caesar	160–161
B	Marble bust of Roman lady of the time of Trajan	160–161
C	Marble bust of the Emperor Caracalla	160–161
56 A	Interior of the Pantheon	160–161
B	Exterior of the Colosseum, Rome	160–161
57 A	The Arch of Constantine, Rome	160–161
B	The socket of the column of Antoinus Pius	160–161
58 A	Flagellation and Dionysiac dance; fresco in the 'Villa of the Mysteries' at Pompeii	160–161
59 A	Portrait of boy. Painting from second century, A.D.	176–177
B	Portrait of unknown man, found at Ephesus	176–177
C	Assembly-room in the catacomb of Petrus and Marallinus, Rome	176–177
60 A	Interior of San Paolo Fuori le Mura, Rome	176–177
B	Basilica of Sant' Apollinare in Classe, Ravenna	176–177
61 A	Mausoleum of Galla Placidia, Ravenna	176–177
B	Part of the mosaic decoration of the great Mosque, Damascus	176–177
62 A	St Mark's, Venice	176–177
B	Interior of the Hagia Sophia, Constantinople	176–177
63	Baptistry of St Mark's, Venice	184–185
64 A	Story of the Fall; Jakobus codex in the Vatican	184–185
B	Panel with symbols of Christ, vines and peacocks. Basilica Sant' Apollinare Nuovo, Ravenna	184–185
65 A	The monastery of St Joseph, Wolokolamski	184–185
B	The church of Peter and Paul, Iaroslavl	184–185
66 A	Saint George, icon from Novgorod	184–185
B	The Mother of God; icon by Simon Ushakow	184–185
C	A panel from the bronze doors of the cathedral of St. Sophia, Novgorod	184–185
67 A	The second room in the bath-house of the Imperial Palace, Delhi	192–193
B	Persian jug in the Minai technique; Rhages	192–193
C	Large hanging lamp, for use in a mosque	192–193
68 A	Court of the Virgins; Alcazar, Seville	192–193
B	Interior of the mosque of Cordova	192–193
C	The Court of the Lions; Alhambra, Granada	192–193
69 A	The Taj Mahal, Agra	192–193
B	Mosque of Sultan Selim II, Adrianople	192–193
70 A	Horseman fighting. Page for a bound Persian volume	192–193
B	Iskender's fight with the dragon. Part of a Persian brocade	192–193
C	Portrait of a Persian prince	192–193
71	Interior of the basilica of Sainte-Madeleine, Vézelay	208–209
72 A	Part of a golden altar table from Basel Minster	208–209
B	Figure of an Apostle from the screen of St George's choir, Bamberg Cathedral	208–209
C	The Last Judgment. From the cathedral of Saint-Lazare, Autun	208–209
73 A	Two figures from the western doorway of the cathedral of Chartres	208–209

		between pages
73 B	Henry II and Cunigunde, from the Adam doorway, Bamberg Cathedral	208–209
74 A	Worms Cathedral from the north-east	208–209
B	Romanesque cloister in the monastic church of Königslutter	208–209
C	Twofold chapel in the castle, Nuremberg	208–209
75 A	The Minnesinger Walter von Hohenklingen; Manesse codex	216–217
B	The Cathedral of Notre Dame, Laon	216–217
C	Central portion of a late Gothic tapestry	216–217
76 A	Notre-Dame, Paris	216–217
B	South-eastern aspect of Wells Cathedral	216–217
77	South-western view of the Cathedral of Amiens	216–217
78 A	The group of the Visitation; western mid-portal, Reims Cathedral	216–217
B	Two Prophets of the Old Testament; Strassburg Minster	216–217
C	The 'Krumau Beauty', the mother of God	216–217
D	Part of statue of a Prophet; Strassburg Minster	216–217
79	Interior of Cologne Cathedral	224–225
80 A	Part of the south front of the Doge's Palace, Venice	224–225
B	Eastern wing of the Council House, Tangermünde	224–225
C	Cloister of Gloucester Cathedral	224–225
D	The great refectory in the Marienburg, West Prussia	224–225
81 A	West Front of Florence Cathedral	224–225
B	The Palazzo Vecchio in Florence	224–225
C	Façade of the Foundling Hospital in Florence	224–225
82 A	Donatello: Marble statue of St Mark the Evangelist	224–225
B	Botticelli: The Annunciation	224–225
C	Giotto: The Massacre of the Innocents. 1303–5	224–225
83	Alberti: S. Francesco, Rimini	232–233
84	Bramante: The Tempietto, S. Pietro in Montorio, Rome	232–233
85 A	San Gallo: Palazzo Farnese, Rome	232–233
B	Peruzzi: Palazzo Massini alle Colonne, Rome	232–233
86 A	Palladio: Villa Rotunda, Vicenza	232–233
B	Michelangelo: Anteroom to the Laurenziana Library, Florence	232–233
87 A	Michelangelo: 'The Bathers' (The Battle of Cascina)	240–241
B	Raphael: The Massacre of the Innocents	240–241
88 A	Leonardo da Vinci: Virgin and Child with St Anne and the Infant St John	240–241
B	Raphael: The Nuptials of the Holy Virgin	240–241
C	Raphael: Pope Julius II	240–241
D	Leonardo da Vinci: The angel's head in the Virgin of the Rocks	240–241
89 A	Michelangelo: Pietà	240–241
B	Michelangelo: The Creation of Adam	240–241
90 A	Raphael: St. Catherine	240–241
B	Piero di Cosimo: The Death of Procris	240–241
91 A	Correggio: Madonna with the Basket	248–249
B	Mantegna: The Agony in the Garden	248–249
92 A	Giorgione: Venus	248–249
B	Titian: The Venus of Urbino	248–249
93 A	Konrad Witz: Catharine and the Magdalen	248–249
B	Dürer: Lucas Paumgürtner as St Eustachius	248–249

		between pages
93 C	Holbein the Younger: Portrait of Jean de Dinteville	248–249
D	Dürer: Portrait of Jacob Muffel	248–249
94 A	Matthias Grünewald: The Crucifixion	248–249
B	Hans Memling: Virgin and Child	248–249
C	Roger van der Weyden: Philippe de Croy	248–249
95 A	St Peter's, Rome	256–257
B	Villa Aldobrandini, Frascati	256–257
96 A	Façade of Pilgrim's Church, Vierzehnheiligen, Bamberg	256–257
B	Wall pavilion, in the Zwinger, Dresden	256–257
C	The Princess Hall in Schloss Bruchsal	256–257
97	Church of St Johann-Nepomuk, Munich	256–257
98 A	Great staircase in the castle of Bruhl	256–257
B	View of the garden front of the Palace of Versailles	256–257
99 A	Part of Bernini's altar, Santa Maria della Vittoria, Rome	264–265
B	Tiepolo: Madonna with Saints	264–265
C	Georges Raffael Donner: St Martin	264–265
D	J. M. Feichtmayr: Group of children	264–265
100 A	Rembrandt: The Philosopher	264–265
B	Jacob van Ruisdael: Landscape	264–265
101 A	Rubens: Tarquin and Lucretia	264–265
B	Van Dyck: Prince Charles Stuart	264–265
C	Rubens: Isabella Brant	264–265
102 A	Rembrandt: Portrait of Jan Six	264–265
B	Frans Hals: Willem ven Heythuysen	264–265
C	Vermeer van Delft: The painter in his studio	264–265
103 A	El Greco: Portrait of Julian Romero	272–273
B	El Greco: Descent of the Holy Ghost	272–273
C	The Escorial	272–273
104 A	Murillo: The Madonna of the Rosary	272–273
B	Velasquez: Aesop	272–273
C	Velasquez: Venus and Cupid	272–273
105 A	Gainsborough: The Blue Boy	272–273
B	Watteau: Detail from the painting 'L'Amour au Théatre Français'	272–273
C	Hogarth: The Toilet, from 'Mariage à la Mode'	272–273
106 A	Turner: Crossing the Brook	272–273
B	Claude: Aeneas at Delos	272–273
107 A	Gainsborough: Landscape	288–289
B	Nicolas Poussin: The Golden Calf	288–289
108 A	Wilson: Cader Idris	288–289
B	Constable: Near Stoke-by-Nayland	288–289
109 A	The Capitol, Washington	288–289
B	The interior of the Pantheon, Paris	288–289
C	The Propylaea, Munich	288–289
110 A	Canova: Hebe	288–289
B	Ingres: Venus Anadyomene	288–289
C	Schadow: Resting	288–289
111 A	Fuseli: Hüon frees the Babekan	296–297
B	Goya: Etching from 'Caprichos'	296–297

		between pages
111 C	Delacroix: 28 July, 1830	296–297
112 A	Ford Madox Brown: Work	296–297
B	Degas: Absinthe	296–297
C	Manet: Le Printemps	296–297
113 A	Cézanne: Still life	296–297
B	Van Gogh: Sunflowers	296–297
C	Hodler: The Cabinet-maker	296–297
D	Gauguin: Two Girls	296–297
114 A	Renoir: Les liseuses	296–297
B	Rodin: A Burgher of Calais	296–297
C	Picasso: l'Arlésienne	296–297
115 A	The Rockfeller Centre, New York	304–305
B	The tobacco factory of Erven de Wed. J. van Nelle, Rotterdam	304–305
116 A	Model hotel at the Swiss National Exhibition	304–305
B	Kollegienhaus, University of Basel	304–305

List of Illustrations in the Text

Cave-drawings from Font-de-Gaume and Les Combarelles	*page* 8
Cave-drawings from the Trois-Frères Cavern	11
Drawings in the cave of Font-de-Gaume	13
Incised drawing on slate, Saint-Marcel	13
Ice Age articles of bone and antler, Arudy	14
The Venus of Willendorf	15
Capsian wall-paintings from Eastern Spain	17–20
Neolithic stylized female figure from the Petit-Morin cave	24
Sketch of a further slab of the kist at Kivik	27
Bronze figure from Kiev	28
Warrior's tombstone of the first Iron Age	29
Part of a bronze bucket of the Hallstatt epoch	29
Urns in the form of Bronze Age Houses	30
Gold Ornament from Hallstatt	30
The Lion Gate, Mycenae	31
Cretan Seal	32
Rock paintings and drawings from the Western Sahara	35
Rock-painting by Bushmen	37
Outline drawing on a rock wall, Algeria	38
Cattle-raider, scratched in sandstone; Sahara	38
Section of vaulted building at Mokwa, Western Sudan	39
Typical West African chieftain's throne	41
Drawing engraved on an ivory beaker from Benin	43
Drawing on an elephant tusk from Benin	44
Rock-painting from North-West Australia	49
Painting on the roof of a cave on the Upper Glenelg	50
Section of a soot-drawing by Australian Blackfellows	51
The Ship of the Dead; rock-picture, New Guinea	54
Signatures of two Maori chiefs	54
Script of a 'Speaking Board', Easter Island	54
Rock-painting of Algonquin Indians	58
Totem-pole of Haida Indians	60
Page from the Aztec hieroglyphic manuscript	61
Aztec picture-writing	62
Indian figure from the State of Tabasco	63
Male Mayan figure	64
Maya hieroglyphs	65
Kneeling figure of Mayan woman	66
From the frescoes in the Temple of the Jaguars, Yucatan	66
Pillars of Mayan architecture	67
Old Peruvian earthenware figure from Pachacamac	68
Jug shaped like a stepped Pyramid	69
The Pyramid of Etén	69
Various forms of ancient Peruvian ceramics	70
South Peruvian vases	71
The Echenique Disc	72
Golden head-ornament from Chongoyape, Peru	73

Prehistoric vases from Susa *page* 75
Relief from the palace of Sanherib, Nineveh 78
Assyrian Relief, Nimrud 79
The God Assur, the disc of the Sun, and the Tree of Life 80
The Palace of Sargon II 81
Alabaster plaque; Phoenician 83
Palace guards; frieze at the Palace of Susa 85
The God Indra on the three-headed Elephant 88
Ground plan of the Cave-Temple of Karli 90
Part of a wall-painting, Ajanta 92
Interior of the Indra-Sabha Temple, Elura 94
Plan of the Dravidian Temple, Tiruvannamalai 95
Stylus drawings on a slip of bleached and polished palm-leaf 97
Portraits of Founders, Ming Oei, Turkestan 97
Funerary Boat, Indonesia 100
Wayang figure from a Javanese shadow-play 101
Rubbing of a flat stone relief of the Han period 106
Principal forms of Chinese script 109
Three of the Ten styles of Drawing in East Asiatic art 110
Painting by Yiu-Rien-Tsien-Tun 111
Landscape of the Ming period 114
Plan of the temple of Kibitsu-jinja 122
Gold-plated handle of flint knife. Predynastic Egypt 125
Back of an ancient Egyptian rouge-palette 126
Egyptian Mastabas at Gizeh 127
She-ass and Foal, from the interior of a Mastaba 128
Reconstruction of the Pyramids at Gizeh 128
The evolution of the Egyptian column 131
Loading the ships of Queen Hatshepsut, on the walls at Karnak 132
Sketch in the sepulchral chamber of Sethos I 133
Reconstruction of a temple at Karnak 134
The Goddess of Heaven, Nut 135
Fragment of a painted vase from Tiryns 138
Golden jewel from Ægina 139
Early Greek painting on a Rhodian earthenware plate 140
Attic Lekythos 141
Plane representation of an early-figured Amphora 142
Development of the Greek Temple 145
Front of a Doric treasury 146
The Doric, Ionian and Corinthian styles in the Greek Temple 147
Reconstruction of the Acropolis of Athens 151
Evolution of bodily attitude in Greek vase-painting 152
Reconstruction of the Mausoleum of Halicarnassus 157
Part of a Mosaic floor discovered in Pompeii 158
The small round temple at Baalbek 159
Upper portion of the Laocoon group in Overbeck's restoration 160
The Roman She-Wolf; Etruscan bronze 163
Etruscan sepulchral painting, Veji 163
Plan of an Etruscan Temple 164

Sarcophagus of Cornelius Lucius Scipio *page* 166
External elevation of the Pantheon 168
Section through the Pantheon 169
Composite Capital on the Arch of Titus, Rome 170
The Pont du Gard, Nîmes 171
Typical arrangement of the Peristyle in a Pompeiian house 173
Section of the relief on Trajan's Column 175
Ancient Christian lamps found in the catacombs 178
An early Christian basilica 180
Ground plan of San Stefano Rotondo, Rome 182
Longitudinal section of Hagia Sophia, Constantinople 184
The Archangel Michael. Mosaic in the church of Daphni, near Athens 187
The Emperor of Byzantium at the Circus 189
The Emperor and Empress of Byzantium; fresco in St Sophia, Kiev 190
Carving on the throne of Ivan the Terrible 191
The Pokrovsky (Vasili) Cathedral, Moscow 192
Miniature from the Slavonic manuscript of Silvestrovskiy Sbornik 193
Baroque Gatehouse to the Russian convent of St Laura 195
Bird's-eye view of Mecca 197
Stalactite vaulting from La Cuba, near Palermo 198
Arabesque with Kufic script 199
The Persian poet, Sadi, after a later miniature 201
Golden Signet Ring of Childeric I 209
Iron axe-head from Jutland 210
Irish decoration in a manuscript; monastery of St Gall 210
Merovingian-Frankish Miniature 210
Carolingian Gatehouse at Lorsch 211
Reconstructed view of the Benedictine church of Cluny 213
Reliquary from the Guelph treasury, Vienna 214
Reconstruction of the Imperial Palace, Gelnhausen 217
Medallion from a window in the cathedral of Chartres 219
Romanesque embroidery in gold on Byzantine silk 220
Ground plan of a Romanesque church 221
Transformation of the Romanesque system by the Gothic 221
Ground-plan of the Gothic cathedral of Amiens 226
Counter-pillar, flying buttress and pinnacle on Strassburg Minster 227
Cologne Monstrance 229
Engraving on a bronze sepulchral tablet. Schwerin 229
Mediaeval House-fronts 230
The Chain Gate at Wells, Somerset 230
Inner face of late Gothic window in Winchester Cathedral 231
Tomb of John Gower: Southwark Cathedral 232
da Vinci: Design for a church 243
Palazzo Strozzi in Florence 244
Palazzo de la Cancelleria, Rome 245
Bramante: Original plan for St Peter's, Rome 246
Michelangelo: Plan for the completion of St Peter's, Rome 247
Woodcut from a manuscript of 1417 251
A woodcut of the middle fifteenth century 252

Schongauer: The Miller and the Ass *page* 252
Dürer: Madonna and Crescent 253
Dürer: The Last Supper 254
Dance of Death from a prayer-book 255
Altdorfer: Lovers in the Forest 256
Holbein the Younger: St Paul 257
Holbein the Younger: The Old Man 257
Urs Graf: The Standard Bearer 259
The Piazza di San Pietro, Rome 261
Borromini: S. Carlo alle Quattro Fontane 263
Tiepolo: One of the twenty-four 'Scherzi di fantasia' 265
Central portion of Sans Souci, Potsdam 267
Ground plan of a German Baroque church 267
Rembrandt: Self-portrait 270
Rembrandt: The Vendor of Rat-poison 271
Wren: St Paul's Cathedral, London 277
William Hogarth: etching 282
Callot: Etching from the Balli di Sfessania 283
Boucher: Sleeping Child 284
Library of Columbia University, New York 290
Buildings of Yale University 291
Schinkel: Design for country house 291
Weinbrenner: Project for a Napoleonic monument 292
Daumier: The Poetaster 297
Rodin: Original lithograph 302
Nolde: Head of a Prophet 305
Edvard Munch: Death-chamber 306
Composition of vertical, horizontal and inclined straight lines 310
Play of figures on a plane surface 310
Erection of plane surfaces in space 310
Wauer: Help! 310
Imaginary view of a modern factory 311
Spatial expression of the graphic and technical features of a Printing Works 312
Project for a Metallurgical Research Institute 312
Masereel: Sketch 313
Maillol: Woodcut 316

Index

ABBASID DYNASTY, 201
Abder-rahman I, 206
'Absolute Art', 308
'Abstract Art', 309
Abusir, 129
Abu-Simbel, 134
Abydos, graves near, 125
Acheulian age, 10
Acropolis, 144, 151
Adam brothers, 292–3
Adrianople, 207
Ægean art, 31–3, 137
Ægina, school of, 144
Æolians, 137
Africa, art of, 34–47
Agriculture, beginnings of, 21
Ajanta, cave paintings of, 91–2
Akbar, 205
Akhnaton, 133
Akkad, 75
Alberti, 243
Alcazar, 206
Alexander, 158–9
Alexander VII, 262
'Alexander's Victory', mosaic, 158
Alexandrian art, 159
Algerian rock-drawings, 37
Algonquin rock-paintings, 58
Alhambra, 207
Almohad dynasty, 206
Altamira, cavern of, 11–12
Altdorfer, 255
Amasis, 31
Amerindian art, 55–74
Amiens Cathedral, 225–6, 228
Amphora, 142
Ancestor worship, 40, 42
Andaman islanders, 49
Angkor Thom, 100
Angkor Vat, 99–100
Angelico, Fra, 235
Antinous, 172
Apollinare in Classe, Sant', 181
Apollo Belvedere, 157
Apollodorus 153
Arch, in Islamic architecture, 202, 205, 22
Architecture, 31; English, 276–80; French, 285–8
Archivolt, 167
Arctic peoples, 56; rock-paintings, 24
Aristides, 156
Art of the age, 7–20
Arudy, bone carvings from, 14
Ashikaga period, 122–3
Asiatic sources of Amerindian art, 55
Asia Minor, art of, 82–6
Asoka, 88, 204
Assouan, 129
Assur, 75
Assurnasirpal 79–81
Assyrian art, 78–82
Athens, 144; fall of, 154
Australia, art of, 48–50
Australian aborigines, 48
Autun cathedral, 215
Aztecs, art of, 61; picture writing, 62; masks of, 63

BAALBEK, 159
Babel, Tower of, 82
Babylon, conquest of, 82
Babylonian Empire, 78
Babylonian art, ancient, 77–8; new, 81–2
Baghdad, 201
Bakuba art, 45
Baldovinetti, 235
Barbizon school, 297
Baptistery, Florence, 248
Baroque, in Russia, 188; in Italy, 245
Baroque, age of the (260–74); in Germany, 266–7; in the Netherlands, 267–9
Barrows, 21
Barry, Sir Charles, 294
Basilica, 179–81
Basel, 255
'Bathers, The', Michelangelo, 240
Batik, 100
Beardsley, 304
Beaumont, Sir George, 300
Beaver motive, 59
Bechuanas, 40
Beehive huts, 39
Bel, 78, 82, 83
Bell-flower pottery, 25
Bellini, 237
Benin, art of, 42–5
Benedictine Order, 184
Bernini, 262, 264, 287
Beni-Hasan, 131
Bet-el-Wali, rock temple, 134
Black-and-White artists, 297
Black-figure vases, 142
Blake, 299
Boddhisatvas, 120
Boghaskoi, 83

Bonington, 300
Borromini, 263
Bosch, Hieronymus, 258
Botticelli, 235
Boucher, 285
Bouts, Dirck, 258
Bourges Cathedral, 225
Bow, introduction of, 17
Brahma, 94
Bramante, 243–4, 246–7
Braque, 307
Breughel, 258–9
Bril, 259
Bronze Age, 25–30; trade routes of, 26–7
Bronzes, Chinese, 103, 117; mediaeval, 219
Bronzino, 241
Brouwer, 269
Brown, Ford Madox, 301
Brunelleschi, 242–3, 247
Buddha, 88; types of, 91
Buddhism in China 107; in Japan, 119
Buddhist art, 88–97
Bullant, 285
Burlington, Lord, 278
Burne-Jones, 301
Burton, Sir Richard, 42
Bushmen, African, 36–7
Byzantine art, 184–7
Byzantine churches in Russia, 188
Byzantium, 188

CAEN, CHURCHES OF, 224
Cairns, 21
Cairo, 205
Callot, Jacques, 283
Calvert, 299
Campanile, 180
Campbell, Colin, 279
Campignian culture, 19
Canaletto, 266
Canova, 294
Canterbury cathedral, 230
Capsian art and culture, 16, 20, 22, 34
Carolingian period, 211, 218
Caravaggio, 214–15, 241, 264–5
Carpaccio, 237
Carpets, Oriental, 203
Carracci brothers, 363–4
Carstens, 295
Carthaginians, 150
Catacombs, 178–9
Catherine I, 195
Castles, 216
Cave monasteries, Indian, 89
Cave paintings, 7, 11
Cave temples, Indian, 90, 95
Cellini, 249
Celts, 28
Cézanne, 303
Chambers, Sir Wm., 280
Chamisso, 53
Charles I, 281
Chardin, 285
Charlemagne, chapel of, 211
Chatti, Hittite capital, 83
Chartres cathedral, 218–20
Chavin style, 72
Cheops, pyramid of, 128
Chephren, King, 129
Chien-lung, Emperor, 117
Chichen-Itza, 65–6
Chillat blankets, 59
Childeric, 209
Chimu Indians, 67
Chin dynasty, 104
China, 102–18; method of writing, 102; history, 103; mediaeval, 104 ff
Chinese Bronzes, 118; glass and porcelain, 116
Chinese Buddhist art, 119
Chinese painting, 109–11
Chirico, 309
Chiton, 159
Choroteg Indians, 67
Christ in Roman art, 176–7
Christian art, early, 176–83
Christianity in Japan, 183
Classic art of Greece, 149–50
Classical tradition, the, 275–88
Classicism, 289ff; in Germany, 295; in France, 296
Classicists, the, 290–2
Cloisters, 214
Clouet brothers, 283
Claude Lorraine, 283–4
Cluny, church and monastery, 212–13, 216
Cockerell, 294
Colbert, 286
Cologne cathedral, 228–9
Colosseum, 166–7
Columbus, 55
Colour-prints, Chinese, 114–15
Comb pottery, 24
Combarelles, caves of, 8, 11, 12
Composite capital, 170
Conegliano, 237
Confucius, 104
Constable, 297, 300
Constantine, Arch of, 177
Constantinople, 184

Constructivism, 209—10
Cook, Captain, 59
Copper-plate engraving, 251—2
Cordova, 206
Corinth, fall of, 165, 302
Corinth, L., 302
Corinthian style, 140, 149, 158—9
Cornelius, 295
Corot, 296—7
Correggio, 264
Cossa, 238
Cotman, 282, 300
Courbet, 297
Cox, David, 300
Cozens, A., and J. R., 282
Cretan influences, 140
Cretan-Mycenaean art, 138
Cretan 'palace style', 32
Crete, devastation of, 25, 130
Cro-Magnon, caves of, 15
Crypt, 214
Cubism, 303, 307—8
Cuneiform script, 77
Cuvillès, 288
Cuzco, 72—3
Cyprus, 27, 84

DAGOBAS, 93
Dali, 309
Damascus, 206
'Dance of Death', 256
Darius III, 159
Daphni, mosaics at, 187
Dark Continent, the real, 36
Daubigny, 297
Daumier, 247
David, J. L., 296
Decorated style, 231
Degas, 298
Delhi, 204—5
Delacroix, 296
Denis, M., 304
De l'Orme, 285
Diadochian cities, 155
Diaz, 292
Dinkelsbühl, 229
Dobson, 281
Dogs, 18
Dolmens, 21
Dome, appearance of the, 159
Domenichino, 264
Domenico, 253
Domitilla, catacomb of, 176
Donatello, 237, 248
Dongen, van, 305
Dordogne, caves of, 15
Dorians, migrations of the, 25, 137, 151
Doric style, 147—8
Dravidians, 87
'Drawing, Ten Styles of', 110
Duccio, 235
Dur-Sarrukin, 80—1
Dürer, 253—5
Dwelling-houses, 230

EARTHEN SEPULCHRES, 21
Earthenware figures, 27
Easter Island, 48; stone figures on, 53—4
Ecbatana, 85
Egypt, 22 (125—36); burial of mummies in, 125; hieroglyphs, 126; Old Kingdom of, 127; Middle Kingdom, 130; New Kingdom, 131—6
Egyptian art, 205
Egyptian-Arabian art, 206
Elam, 75
Elephant tusks, carved, 46
Elephanta, 95
Elgin Marbles, 153
Elura, rock temple of, 4, 96
English architecture, 276—80
English painting, 280—2
Erasmus, 255—6
'E. S.', 252
Etruscan art, 162—5
Etruscan, the, 25, 160, 162
Eumenes II, 160
Euphranor, 156
Euafrica, 34
European civilization, ascent toward, 21—33
Exekias, vase-painter, 143
Exeter cathedral, 231
Expressionism, 304—9
Eyck, van, 257—8

FAMILLE NOIRE, ROSE, VERTE, PORCELAIN, 117
Farnese Bull, the, 160
Fatimids, 205
Fauves, Les, 305
Feather ornaments, 71
Feininger, 307
Fetishes, 45—6
Fetti, Domenico, 265
Five-colour Printing, 117
Five Dynasties, in China, 107
Flavian, 108
Flitcroft, Jas., 280

Florence cathedral, 234
Flying buttresses, 226
Fo, Foism, 107
Fontainebleau, School of, 283
Font-de-Gaume, cavern of, 8, 11, 13
Forbidden City, the, 113
Fragonard, 285
Franco-Cantabrian culture, 10, 12
French Painting (282-85); during and after Classicist revival, 246—7
French Revolution, the 289
Frobenius, 44
Fujiwara period, 120
Fuseli, 209
Futurism, 308

GABRIEL, J, J., AND A. J., 288
Gainsborough, 281
Galla Placidia, mausoleum of, 186
Gandharan art, 90, 97
Gautama, 88, 91
Gauguin, 305
Gavarni, 297
Gelnhausen, 216—7
Genghis Khan, 190, 201
Gericault, 296
Ghiberti, 248
Ghirlandajo, 235
Giacometti, 306
Gibbs, Jas., 280
Gilgamesh, 77
Giorgione, 241
Giotto, 234, 242
Girgenti, 147
Girtin, 282, 300
Giulio Romano, 241
Gizeh, pyramids of, 128
Glass, Chinese, 116
Glass, stained, 219
Gleizes, 307
Gloucester cathedral, 231
Golden Gate (of Theodosius), 184
Gothic art (222—32), origin of, 223; in Italy, 233
Gothic church, plan of, 226—7
Gothic, German, 215
Gothic Revival, 294
Gothic sculpture, 227—8
Gower, tomb of, 232
Goya, 295
Graecia Magna, 137
Granada, 207
Graphic art, 250—3
Graves, Egyptian, 125
Great Wall of China, 104
Greco, El, 272—3
Greece (137—54); settlement of, 137; art of, 237; Oriental influences in, 139; adapts alphabet, 139; archaic art in, 140
Greek vase-painting, 142; sculpture, 144; temples, 145—52; painting and sculpture, 152—4
Gris, 307
Grünewald, 253—5, 273, 305
Guardi, 266
Gudea, age of, 76
Guercino, 264
Gupta empire, 91
Gutenberg, 250
Guys, C. 297

HADRIAN, 168
Hagia Sophia, Constantinople, 184, 208
Haida Indians, 59
Hakuho Period (Japan), 120
Halicarnassus, mausoleum of, 157—8
Hallstatt epoch, 28—30, 163
Hals, Frans, 269
Hammurabi, 78
Han dynasty, 105
Harappa, 75, 87
Harun al Rashid, 201
Hatshepsut, Queen, 132
Hawksmoor, 278—9
Hegira, 109
Heidelberg Man, 8
Heike Period (Japan), 121
Heliopolis, 129
Hellenistic art (155—61), 165
Henri IV, 286
Henry VIII, 256
Hermodorus, 165
Herodotus, 82
High Gothic, 231
Hilliard, 281
Hinayana, 91
Hiroshige, 124
Hittites, 78, 83
Hobbema, 281
Hogarth, 281
Hokusai, 124
Holbein the Elder, 255—7
Holbein the Younger, 255—7
Hölzel, A., 306
Homeric poems, 137
Homo sapiens, 9, 10
Honey, 18
Honthorst, G. van, 264
Hopi Indians, 60
Hoppner, 281

Hu Chang Yen, 114
Huaxtec Indians, 63
Hughes, Arthur, 301
Hung Wu, 112
Hunt, Holman, 301
Hyksos, the, 38, 131–2

IBERIANS, 25
Ice Age, 7, 9; end of, 21; art of,
Icons, Russian, 193–4
Idols, 40
Ikat, woven fabric, 100
Illyrians, 28
Imhotep, 127
Impressionism, 302–4
Incas, art of, 72–4
India, art of, 87–98
Indo-China, art of, 98–100
Indonesia, art of, 100
Indra, 87–8
Ingres, 296
Interglacial period, 9
Ionic style, 198–9
Irish MSS., 210
Iron Age, 28–30
Islam, art of (197–208): origin of, 199; in India, 204–5; in Mediterranean basin, 205–8
Italian architecture in Russia, 192
Ivan I, 191
Ivan III, 191
Ivan IV, 191

JACOPO DELLA QUERCIA, 249
Jains, 96
Japan, art of (119–24); architecture, 112–2; modern period, 133–4
Jones, Inigo, 226
Julius II, 246

KAABA, THE, 199
Kaffirs, 40
Kamakura period of Japanese art, 121
Kandinsky, 306
Kang-hsi porcelain, 117
Kangra schools of art, 98
Karli, cave temples, 90
Karnak, 133–4
Kells, Book of, 210
Kent, William, 279
Khmer art, 99
Khorsabad, 81
Kibitsujinja temple, 122
Kiev, 188–90
Klee, 307
Klitias, 143
Kneller, Sir Gottfried, 281
Knossos, 33
Kojiki, the, 119
Kokoschka, 307
Kremlin, the, 190, 192
Krishna, 93
Kublai Khan, 113
Kufic script, 199
Kuo Hsi, on painting, 110
Kuratsukuri Tori, 119
Kwannon, 120–1

LAACH, ABBEY, 216
Lacustrine culture, 25
La Mouthe, grotto of, 11, 12
Laocoon, 160
Laon, cathedral of, 224
Lanfranco, 264
La Pileta, caves of, 19
Late Stone Age, 9, 10
La Tène epoch, 30
Lawrence, 281
Le Brun, 284
Le Cog, 94
Ledoux, 288
Leger, 387
Lekythos, 142
Lemercier, 286
Le Nain, 283
Le Notre, 287
Leonardo da Vinci, 236, 238, 243, 282
Le Vau, 287
Liebermann, Max, 302
Liebfrauenkirche, Trier, 229
Lion Gate, Mycenae, 31
Lippi, Filippo, Fra, 233
Lithography, 296–7
Los Casares, cave of, 19
Louis XIV, 286
Louvre, 287
Lucas van Leyden, 259
Lung-men, rock temples of, 106
Lustre ware, 201
Luxor, 134

MACARTNEY, LORD, 111
Machu Picchu, Inca city, 73
Madagascar, 48
Maderna, 247, 262
Magdalenian epoch, 16; art of, 18
Maghreb, the, 205
Magical power of objects, belief in, 40
'Magism', 308

Mahavira, Jain founder, 96
Mahayana, 91
Mahommed II, 191
Maillol, 315
Maillot, 305
Makimono, scroll paintings, 121
Mammoth, 13
Manesse codex, 228
Manet, 297
Mannerism, 239—41, 244—5
Mansart, 286—7
Mantegna, 237
Maoris, art of, 52; script, 54
Marcellus, Theatre of, 167
Marco Polo, 113
Marduk, 78
Marsoulas, caves of, 11
Masaccio, 234
Masks, African, 40
Massa, villages of, 39
Mastaba, 127
Matisse, 305
Mayan manuscript, 65
Mayas, art of, 61; calendar of, 63—4; art, 65, 67; Old and New Empires of, 63; architecture and sculpture of, 65—6
Mazarin, 286
Mecca, 199
Medici, Marie de, 286
Medina, 200
Megalithic culture, 25
Melanesian art, 50—2
Melozzo da Forli, 237
Memling, 258
Memphis, 129
Menes, founder of ist Dynasty, 126—7
Menhirs, 21
Menzel, 302
Merovingians, 209
Mesolithic epoch, 18—20, 24
Mesopotamia, 24
Mexico, 55; ancient art of, 60—3
Mexico City, 61
Miao people, 102
Michelangelo, 238—41, 246—7, 249, 261
Michelsberger ceramics, 25
Micronesia, 50, 52
Middle Kingdom, Egyptian, 130
Migrations, Age of, 30
Mikado, 119
Milan, 182
Millais, 301
Millet, 297
Milo, Venus of, 154, 161
Minai Vases, 201
Ming Emperors, tombs of, 114
Miniatures, English, 281
Minoan culture, 32
Mixtec Indians, 62
Mohammed, 199—200
Mohammed II, 207
Mohenjo Daro, 75, 87
Monet, 298
Mongols invade Russia, 190
Monte Cassino, 184
Morland, 282
Mosaic, 185—7
Moscow, 191—3
Mosque of Omar, 200
Mosques, Islamic, 199—200
Mousterian epoch, 10
Mudejar style, 206
Mummies, Peruvian, 70, 71
Munch, Edvard, 305
Munich Secession, 302
Murillo, 274
Muscovite Art, 191—3
Muscovite Czars, 188
'Mustard-seed-Garden, the', 115
Mycenae, 31
Mycenaean art, 137—8
Mysteries, Villa of the, 174

NANDI, 93—7
Napoleon, 289
Naram-Sin stele, 77
Nash, John, 293
Naturalism, 21, 23
'Nazarenes, the', 295, 301
Nazca, art of, 70—1
Neanderthal Man, 8
Near East, ancient art of, 75—86
Nebuchadnezzar II, 81
Negro art, 40, 41; modern, 45—7; negro architecture, 389
Neo-Brahmanic art, 93
Neolithic age, 9, 21—5
Nepal, art of, 98
Netherlands, art of, 250, 257—9
Neumann, Balthasar, 266
New Caledonia, 50
New Kingdom, Egyptian, 131—6
Niaux, caves of, 11, 13
Nihongi, Japanese chronicle, 119
Nile valley, 126
Nimes, aqueduct, 170—1
Nineveh, 75, 79
Nofretete, 135

Normans in Sicily, 207
Norman architecture, 215
Norse decorative art, 209
Northern Border, art of, 97
Notre Dame, Paris, 225
Novgorod, 189, 190
Nut, 135

OCEANIA, 48, 50–4
Old Palaeolithic Age, 10
Old Stone Age, 9–10, 18, 23
Oliver, Isaac, 281
Olympic Games, 137
Olympus, 152
Omnayyad period, 200, 206
Orange, Roman theatre at, 167
Ornament, prehistoric, 23
Ostade, A. van, 209
Ostrich eggs, drawings on, 34
Ottoman Turks, 191, 207
Overbeck, 295

PAESTUM, 147
Pair-non-pair, caves of, 11, 12
Palace style of Crete, 32
Palaeolithic art, 9, 16
Palettes, Egyptian, 126
Palladio, 248
Palladian architecture, 250
Palma Vecchio, 241
Palmer, 299
Pantheon, 168–9, 292; of Paris, 292
Parliament, Houses of, 294
Parthenon, 152–3
Parvati, 93
Patinir, Joachim, 259
Pekin, 112
Pekin Man, 8
Peloponnesian War, 154
Pergamos, 159–60
Periclean Age, 150
Perpendicular Style, 231
Persepolis, 84
Persian art, 84–6; new, 200–2
Peru, 55
Peruvian ceramics, 70, 71
Peter the Great, 188, 194
Pharaohs, the, 129, 130
Pharos of Alexandria, 159
Phidias, 153, 157
Philip of Macedonia, 156
Phoenician influences, 83; alphabet, 139
Picasso, 306–7
Piero della Francesca, 236–7
Pipe of Peace, 57
Piranesi, 266
Pisanello, 235
Pisano, Andrea, 248
Pisano, Niccolo, 248
Pissarro, 298
Pitfalls, 13
Pointilisme, 299
Pokrovsky cathedral, 192
Pollaiuolo, 237, 249
Polonnaruva sculpture of, 93
Polyclete, 156
Polychromatic painting, 12
Polygnotas, 153
Polynesian art, 50, 52
Pompeii, 172–5
Pont du Gard, 171
Porcelain, Chinese, 116–18
Portraiture, art of, 97
Potter's wheel, 24
Poussin, 283–4
Portraits, English, 281
Portraits, Roman, 171, 177
Praxiteles, 154, 156–7
Pre-Raphaelites, 295, 299–301
Priam, treasury of, 82
Primitive art, 41–2, 74
Printing, early Chinese, 116
Prome, ruins of, 99
Protolithic age, 10
Protoman of Java, 8
Pueblo Indians, 60
Pugin, 294
Punt, 130
Pygmies, 37
Pyramids, stepped, 62; American-Indian, 69
Egyptian, 127–8

QUIMBAYA INDIANS, 67

RA, SUN-GOD, 129
Raeburn, 281
Rahotep, 129
Rameses II, 133
Rameses III, 134
Raphael, 236–41
Ravenna, churches of, 81–3, 211
Realism, 297
Recuay style, 72
Red Square, Moscow, 192
Redon, O., 304
Regency style, 293
Rembrandt, 270–2
Remus, 163

Renaissance, in Italy (233—49); in the North, 250—9; Gothic idiom in, 250
Reni, Guido, 264
Renoir, 298
Reynolds, Sir Joshua, 281, 299
Rhages, 201
Rhineland, cathedrals of, 216
Rhodes, 160
Ribbon pottery, 25
Ribera, 264
Rig-Veda, 87
Ripley, Thos., 279
Robbia, della, 249
Rock paintings, prehistoric, 17, 19, 27, 35; Australian, 49
Rock temples, Chinese, 105—6; Egyptian, 154
Rockefeller Centre, 313
Rococo, age of, 260—74
Rodin, 304
Roman Empire, 25 (162—75)
Roman wall-paintings, 172—5
Romanesque Art (209—21), churches, 212—14
Romans in Greece, 155
Romantic movement in French art, 296
Romney, 281
Romulus, 163
Rosa Salvator, 265
Rossetti, 301
Rotunda, the Christian, 181—3
Roualt, 305
Rousseau, 297
Rousseau, Henri, 303
Rowlandson, 282
Rubens, 265—9, 271
Rudra, 94
Rufo, Marco, 192
Runge, 295
Ruskin, John, 294, 301
Ruysdael, 281

SAFARVID DYNASTY, 202
Sahara, art of, 35; pottery, 75
Saint-Denis, Reims, 223
Saint-Mark's, Venice, 253
Saint Pater's Rome, 180, 246—7
Saint Sophia, Kiev, 188
Salmanassar II, 80
Samagupta, 91
Sandby, 282
San Stefano, Rome, 182
San Vitale, Ravenna, 183
Sargon II, 80
Sargonides, 80
Scandinavian culture, early, 24
Schaffhausen, 236
Schick, 295
Schinkel, K. F., 291—2
Schliemann, 82
Schöngauer, 252
Scipio family, tombs of, 166
Script, Chinese, 109
Sculpture, prehistoric, 16; Chinese, 105; archaic, 143; Greek, 151; Roman, 171
Seals, 77
Segantini, 303
Selim II, Mosque of, 207
Seljuk Turks, 201, 207
Semitic forms of art, 77
Sesshu, 123
Sethos I, 135
Seurat, 299
Shah Nameh, the, 202
Shiva, 93
Shubun, 123
Shun, Emperor, 103
Sicily, Moorish art in, 207
Sickert, 303
Sicyon, school of, 156
Siennese school, 235
Signorelli, 237
Sioux Indians, 57
Sisley, 298
Six, Burgomaster (Rembrandt), 271
Skopas, 156—7
Slavonic influences in Byzantine art, 189
Slevogt, 302
Smirke, 294
Snofru, King, 128
Soane, Sir John, 293
Solutré, ancient camping ground, 9
Solutrean epoch, 10, 12
Solon, 141
Soufflot, J. G., 292
Southwark Cathedral, 232
Spain, art of, 272—4
Sphinx, 128—9
Spitzweg, 295
Squarcione, 237
Stained glass, 219
Stalactite vaulting, 199
Steer, 303
Steppe country, 8
Stoffels, Hendrikje, 271
Stone monuments, 21, 34
Strassburg Minster, 227
Strettweg, bronze car of, 28
String pottery, 25
String writing, 102

Stubbs, George, 282
Stupas, 88
Stylization, 21—3
Sudan, architecture of, 38—9
Sudanese negroes, 38
Suger, Abbot, 223
Sumer, 75
Sumerian art, 76—7
Sun-Deer, the, 28
Sun, eclipse of, 103
Sun worship, 28
Sung dynasty, 106, 112
Sung pottery, 116
Surrealism, 308
Susa, 75
Syrian art, 83

TAJ MAHAL, 205
Taiping rebellion, 117
Tamerlane, 202, 204
Tangermünde, Rathaus of, 234
Tang dynasty, 106—7, 120
Taoism, 107—8
Tapestry, 219
Tardenoisian culture, 19
Tarquin, 165
Tea ceremony, 123
Temple, the Greek, 145—9; Roman, 168
'Ten Bamboo Hall', 114—15
Tenebrism, 264
Teniers, 269
Tenno, title of Mikado, 119
Tertiary period, 7
Textile arts of Persia, etc., 203
Thayngen, epoch of, 10
Theatre introduced into Italy, 165
Thebes, 131, 133
Theodoric, tomb of, 211
Theodosius, 183
Thornhill, Sir James, 281
Thorwaldsen, 295
Tien-lung-shan, grottoes of, 106
Tiepolo, 265—6
Tiahuanaco, periods I and II, 72
Tiruvannamalai, temple of, 95
Tiles, glazed, 85, 101
Tintoretto, 242
Titian, 241—2
Titicaca, Lake, 71
Titus, Baths of, 167; Arch of, 312—16
Tivoli, 170
Tlinkit Indians, 59
Today, art of, 312—16
Tokugawa period, 124
Tomb paintings, 173
Torrigiano, 276
Totonac Indians, 63
Toulouse-Lautrec, 316
Tour, G. de la, 264
Toyotomi period, 123
Tractarian Revival, 294
Trade, prehistoric, 26
Trajan, Column and Forum of, 167—8, 175
Trinil, protoman of, 8
Trois-frères cavern, 11
Troy, conquest of, 25; excavation of, 82
Tudor arch, 231
Tung dynasty, 107
Tura, 218
Turkestan, various influences in, 97—8
Turks, in Europe, 207
Turks, Seljuk, 201, 207
Turner, J. M. W., 282, 298, 300
Tutankhamen, 133
Tutmosis, 123
Tyrants, age of, 143—4

UCCELLO, 235
Uhde, von, 302
Umbrella, in rock temples, 89
Umbrian School, 236
Utrillo, 235
Ur, 76

VAHANAS, 89
Valley of the Kings, 132
Vanbrugh, 278—9
Vancouver, George, 59
Van Dyck, 268—9, 281
Van der Goes, 258
Van Eyck, 257—8
Van Gogh, 203, 305
Vases, forms, of Greek, 142
Vaulted roofs, 213
Vedas, 88
Vedic gods, 93
Veen, O. van, 267
Velasquez, 264, 273—4
Venetian art, 241—2
Venice, Doge's Palace, 233
Venice, St Mark, 233
Venus of Milo, 154, 191
Venus of Willendorf, 15
Verism, 308
Vermeer, 269—70
Veronese, 242
Verrochio, 249
Versailles, 287

Vesuvius, 173
Vihara, Buddhist, 89
Vine motive, 177
Viollet-le-Duc, 228
Virgin of Vladimir, 194
Vishnu, 33—4, 91, 99
Visitation, Reims, 227
Vitruvius, 165
Vladimir, 188
Vlaminck, M. de, 305
Von Luschan, 44

WALL-PAINTINGS:
prehistoric, 11, 12
Roman, 172
Pompeian, 173—5
'Water-halls', Byzantine, 184
Watteau, 283—5
Watts, Frederick, 301
Wayang or shadow-play, 101
Webb, John, 277
Wells Cathedral, 231
West African art, 41
West, Benjamin, 299
Weyden, van der, 258
Wheatley, 282
Whistler, 303
Wilkie, 299
William the Conqueror, 215
Wilson, Richard, 281—2
Winchester Cathedral, 231
Witz, Konrad, 250
Wolf, She-, the Roman, 163
Woodcuts, 251—2
Woods of Bath, 280
Wren, Sir Christopher, 277—8
Writing, invention of, 102
Wu-tan-tzu, 107
Wyatt, James, 294

XAVIER, ST FRANCIS, 123
Xerxes, 84

YAKSHI, 96
Yakushi (Kwannon), 120
Yale University, 291
Yuan dynasty, 112
Yucatan, 55

ZAPOTEC INDIANS, 62
Zarathustra, 84
Zen sect, the, 121, 123
Ziggurat, 80, 81
Zoset, King, 127
Zurbaran, 273
Zurich Exhibition, 314